Thomas S. Cronce.

Saginaw City

Mich.

THE FIRST LANDING OF COLUMBUS ON THE ISLAND OF SAN SALVADOR.

A SCHOOL HISTORY OF THE UNITED STATES,

FROM THE DISCOVERY OF AMERICA TO THE YEAR 1870.

By DAVID B. SCOTT.

ILLUSTRATED WITH MAPS AND ENGRAVINGS.

NEW YORK:
HARPER & BROTHERS, PUBLISHERS,
FRANKLIN SQUARE.
1874.

PREFACE.

THERE are certain points in the School History of the United States now submitted to the public to which it is proper to ask the attention of teachers.

The work is profusely embellished with ENGRAVINGS. These serve not only to illustrate the text, but will be of assistance in fixing on the memory many of the important occurrences mentioned.

Numerous MAPS are inserted at suitable places.

At the close of various marked periods in the narrative will be found GENERAL REFLECTIONS, which, it is hoped, will prove interesting and instructive to both teachers and pupils. In these sketches an attempt has been made, within the small limits that can be spared in a school-book, to outline, in the form of generalizations, the habits, industries, and character of the people, the growth of the country, and the causes as well as effects of the more prominent events in its history.

In the account of those wars where simultaneous operations were carried on at widely-separated points, particularly in the Civil War, the movements of the different campaigns are, with trifling exceptions, kept together. It is believed that in this way a clearer idea of the progress of military events can be given to a young student than by a purely chronological order. The table at the end of the book, if carefully studied, will supply whatever knowledge of this sort may be deemed desirable.

Questions for review will be found interspersed.

With this brief statement, the history is introduced to the notice of teachers.

NEW YORK, June, 1870.

TABLE OF CONTENTS.

CHAPTER I.

EARLY DISCOVERIES AND EXPLORATIONS.

Section		Page
I.	Discovery of America by Columbus.—The Cabots	1
II.	The Aborigines east of the Mississippi	8
III.	Spanish Discovery and Explorations after the Year 1500	15
IV.	French Discovery and Exploration to the Year 1608	19
V.	English Discovery and Exploration previous to the year 1607	22
VI.	Early Dutch Discovery and Exploration	27
VII.	GENERAL REFLECTIONS ON CHAPTER I	28

CHAPTER II.

COLONIAL HISTORY TO THE BEGINNING OF THE WAR OF THE REVOLUTION.

I.	Early Southern Colonies.—Virginia and Maryland	33
	GENERAL REFLECTIONS	49
II.	New England Colonies—Massachusetts	55
	Connecticut	72
	Rhode Island	78
	New Hampshire	80
	GENERAL REFLECTIONS	82
III.	Middle Colonies—New York	90
	New Jersey	99
	Delaware and Pennsylvania	101
	GENERAL REFLECTIONS	106
IV.	Later Southern Colonies.—North Carolina	113
	South Carolina	115
	Georgia	116
V.	French Explorations in the West and Southwest	119
VI.	French and Indian War	125
	GENERAL REFLECTIONS	144
VII.	Causes of the Revolutionary War	148

CHAPTER III.

THE WAR OF THE REVOLUTION.

I.	Events of 1775	159
II.	Events of 1776	167
III.	Events of 1777	179
IV.	Events of 1778	189

Section Page
V. Events of 1779........ 196
VI. Events of 1780........ 201
VII. Events of 1781........ 209
VIII. Events of 1782–83—Close of the War........ 217
IX. From the Treaty of Peace to the adoption of the Federal Constitution........ 219
GENERAL REFLECTIONS........ 223

CHAPTER IV.

FROM THE COMMENCEMENT OF WASHINGTON'S ADMINISTRATION, 1789, TO THE CLOSE OF JEFFERSON'S IN 1809.

I. Washington's Administration........ 232
II. John Adams's Administration........ 237
III. Jefferson's Administration........ 240

CHAPTER V.

MADISON'S ADMINISTRATION.—WAR OF 1812.

I. Events previous to the Second War with England........ 247
II. Events of 1812........ 249
III. Events of 1813........ 254
IV. Events of 1814–15, and to the Close of the Administration........ 261

CHAPTER VI.

FROM THE YEAR 1817 TO THE BEGINNING OF THE MEXICAN WAR.

I. Monroe's Administration........ 274
II. John Quincy Adams's Administration........ 279
III. Jackson's Administration........ 280
IV. Van Buren's Administration........ 284
V. Administrations of Harrison and Tyler........ 286

CHAPTER VII.

POLK'S ADMINISTRATION.—WAR WITH MEXICO.

I. Commencement of Hostilities with Mexico........ 292
II. Events of 1847–48........ 297

CHAPTER VIII.

FROM THE END OF POLK'S ADMINISTRATION TO THE BEGINNING OF LINCOLN'S.

I. Taylor's Administration........ 306
II. Fillmore's Administration........ 307
III. Pierce's Administration........ 309
IV. Buchanan's Administration........ 311
V. GENERAL REFLECTIONS ON THE CAUSES OF THE CIVIL WAR.. 320

CHAPTER IX.

FROM THE COMMENCEMENT OF THE CIVIL WAR TO THE YEAR 1870.

Section Page
I. Lincoln's Administration—Events of 1861 321
II. Events of 1862 332
III. Events of 1863 353
IV. Events of 1864 363
V. Events of 1865 382
VI. Johnson's Administration, April 15th, to March 4th, 1869 385
VII. Grant's Administration 390

CHAPTER X.

SETTLEMENT AND GROWTH OF THE PACIFIC STATES.

California 391
Oregon 394

Declaration of Independence 399
Constitution of the United States 402
Chronological Table 415

MAPS AND ILLUSTRATIONS.

Landing of Columbus. Frontispiece.
Map of the World as known to Europe in 1418 .... Page 2
The World as known in our own Day ... 2
Columbus before Ferdinand and Isabella ... 4
Vessels of Columbus ... 5
Columbus in Chains ... 7
Indian Wigwam ... 8
Indian Shield and Weapons ... 9
Indian Picture-writing ... 10
Warrior and Squaw ... 11
Indians in Council ... 11
Indian Ruins, Central America ... 12
Map of early Discoveries and Explorations ... 14
De Soto discovering the Mississippi ... 18
Queen Elizabeth knighting Raleigh ... 24
One of Raleigh's Ships ... 25
Hudson ascends the River in the Half Moon ... 27
Map—Early Voyages of the Spaniards. 28
Arrival at Jamestown, 1607 ... 33
Portrait of Captain John Smith ... 35
Map—Early Settlements in Virginia and Maryland ... 37
Marriage of Pocahontas ... 39
Cultivation of Tobacco at Jamestown, 1615 ... 40
Indian Massacre, 1622 ... 43
Ruins of Jamestown, 1676 ... 45
Exploration of Plymouth Bay, 1620 ... 55
Signing of the Compact on board the Mayflower ... 58
Map—New England Colonies ... 63
The great Swamp Fight in R. Island. 65
Death of King Philip ... 67
Indians attacking the Settlers ... 74
The Discussion over the Connecticut Charter ... 76
Final Landing-place of Roger Williams ... 78
Wampum Belt and Currency ... 84
Pine-tree Shilling and other Currency. 84
Tail-piece—Charter Oak ... 89
Block building a Vessel on Manhattan Island ... 90
Landing of the Walloons ... 92
The Wrath of Peter Stuyvesant. Page 95
Sloughter signing the Death-warrant. 97
Map—Middle Colonies ... 99
Penn's arrival at New Castle ... 103
Portrait of Benjamin Franklin ... 105
Dutch Family Scene ... 106
Portrait of Oglethorpe ... 116
Portrait of La Salle ... 120
Map—English, French, and Spanish Occupation, 1750 ... 124
Washington on his homeward Journey ... 126
Map—Chief Scene of Operations, French and Indian War ... 128
Map—Acadia, Cape Breton Island, and Nova Scotia ... 130
Washington warning Braddock in his Tent ... 132
Capture of Fort Du Quesne, 1758 ... 139
Map—Quebec and vicinity, 1759 ... 141
Monument to Wolfe and Montcalm .. 141
Battle of the Heights of Abraham ... 142
Portrait of Patrick Henry ... 152
Portrait of Samuel Adams ... 156
Portrait of John Hancock ... 159
The firing at Lexington ... 160
Map—Boston and Vicinity, 1775–6 ... 162
Portrait of Joseph Warren ... 163
View of Boston from Dorchester Heights, 1774 ... 167
Attack on Fort Moultrie ... 169
Map—Battle of Long Island ... 170
Surprise of the Hessians at Trenton .. 174
Map—Seat of War in New Jersey ... 179
Map—Philadelphia and Vicinity ... 183
Map—Burgoyne's Campaign ... 185
Surrender of Burgoyne ... 188
Portrait of General Lee ... 192
Map—Scene of Operations in the South ... 196
Map—The Hudson. Newburg to New York ... 198
Map—Charleston and Vicinity ... 202
Portrait of Lafayette ... 205
Portrait of Benedict Arnold ... 206
Capture of Major André ... 207
Medal given to Morgan after the Battle of the Cowpens ... 211

Portrait of General Greene.....Page 213
Map—Siege of Yorktown............ 216
Washington bidding farewell to his Officers............................ 219
Map—The Southwest Territory...... 222
Franklin at the Court of France..... 225
State-house, Philadelphia........... 230
Mount Vernon....................... 231
Portrait of President Washington... 232
Federal Hall, New York............. 233
Portrait of Alexander Hamilton..... 234
Portrait of John Jay................ 236
Portrait of President Adams........ 238
Portrait of President Jefferson...... 240
Duel between Burr and Hamilton... 243
Fulton's Steam-boat................ 244
Portrait of President Madison....... 247
Map—United States in 1812......... 250
Map — Niagara Frontier. Western Part of Lake Erie................. 251
Destruction of the Guerriere by the Constitution...................... 253
Perry changing his Ship during the Battle of Lake Erie................ 256
Map—Seat of the Creek War........ 259
Map—Battle of Plattsburg........... 263
British attempting to cross the Saranac................................ 263
Map—Vicinity of Washington, 1814.. 264
Remains of the Capitol after the Fire.............................. 265
Map—Vicinity of Baltimore, 1814.... 265
Battle of New Orleans............... 268
Portrait of President Monroe........ 274
Whitney's Cotton Gin, 1793.......... 276
Portrait of President J. Q. Adams.... 279
Portrait of Daniel Webster.......... 280
Map—Scene of the Seminole War.... 281
Portrait of President Jackson....... 281
Portrait of John C. Calhoun......... 282
Portrait of President Van Buren 285
Portrait of President Harrison...... 287
Portrait of President Tyler.......... 287
Professor Morse explaining his Telegraphic Machine................. 290
Portrait of President Polk........... 292
Map—Campaigns in Mexico......... 294
Capture of Monterey................ 295
Map—Scott's Campaign in Mexico... 298
Bombardment of Vera Cruz......... 299
The Army in sight of the Valley of Mexico........................... 301
The American Army in the City of Mexico........................... 303
Portrait of Lieut. General Scott...... 305
Portrait of President Taylor......... 306
Portrait of Henry Clay.............. 307
Portrait of President Fillmore....... 308
Portrait of President Pierce..........310
Portrait of President Buchanan.Page 312
Portrait of Jefferson Davis........... 314
Fort Sumter.......................... 315
Portrait of President Lincoln........ 321
Destruction of the Navy Yard at Norfolk.............................. 323
Map—Vicinity of Fortress Monroe... 324
Map—Campaign in Western Virginia. 325
Map—The Battle of Bull Run....... 326
Harper's Ferry....................... 327
Map—Missouri and Arkansas....... 328
Map—Kentucky and West Tennessee................................ 334
Map — The War in the West and Southwest........................... 339
Map—From New Orleans to the Gulf. 340
Map—Forts Jackson and St. Philip... 341
Passage of Forts Jackson and St. Philip............................ 341
The Monitor and the Merrimac...... 344
Map—North Virginia. Shenandoah Valley............................. 345
Map—M'Clellan's Campaign in Virginia............................... 346
Portrait of General Robert E. Lee.... 348
Map—Pope's Retreat to Washington. 350
Portrait of General Jackson......... 354
Map — Part of Pennsylvania, Maryland, and Virginia................. 355
Union Vessels passing the Vicksburg Batteries.......................... 356
Capture of Lookout Mountain....... 358
Map—Vicinity of Charleston........ 360
Fort Sumter after the Bombardment. 361
Destruction of the Alabama by the Kearsarge......................... 365
Portrait of General W. T. Sherman.. 366
Map—War in the Southwest. Red River Expedition.................. 367
Battle of Atlanta.................... 370
Map—North Carolina, South Carolina, and Georgia................... 371
Portrait of General Thomas......... 371
Siege of Nashville................... 372
Sherman's Army on its March to the Sea............................... 373
A Battle Scene in the Wilderness.... 374
Map — Petersburg and Richmond, 1864–65............................ 376
Map—Shenandoah Valley............ 377
Portrait of General Sheridan........ 377
Farragut entering Mobile Bay....... 379
Grant and Lee signing the Terms of Surrender......................... 383
Portrait of General J. E. Johnston... 384
Portrait of President Johnson....... 385
Portrait of President Grant.......... 390
Early Gold Mining in California..... 392
Three Brothers—Yosemite Valley... 394

HISTORY OF THE UNITED STATES.

CHAPTER I.

EARLY DISCOVERIES AND EXPLORATIONS.

SECTION I.

DISCOVERY OF AMERICA BY COLUMBUS.—THE CABOTS.

1. THERE are writers who tell us that the inhabitants of Iceland visited the most northerly shores of America in the eleventh or twelfth century, and for some time traded with the natives. But if these hardy voyagers ever did this, the very remembrance of America and the route to it soon died out among the Icelanders themselves, and the discovery was not published to the nations of Europe.

2. In the first of the two maps that follow is traced the outline of the world as known to the geographers of Europe in the first quarter of the fifteenth century. This was before the famous navigator, Prince Henry of Portugal, began to send out expeditions to explore the west coast of Africa. In place of the now known shape of that peninsula, the lower part is cut off by a slightly curved line running from Cape Nam—now Nun—on the west, to Juba on the east; the continent of America is wanting; Australia and the East Indies are wanting; and the pictured animals show the nameless terrors of the unknown coasts. In the second map, on the same scale, is the world as known in our own day.

---

1. What is stated by some writers about the first discovery of America? Is this statement denied? If this discovery was made, of what advantage was it to the Icelanders and to Europe?

2. What is shown by the first map on the next page? What is shown by the second? State what parts of the world are wanting in Map I.

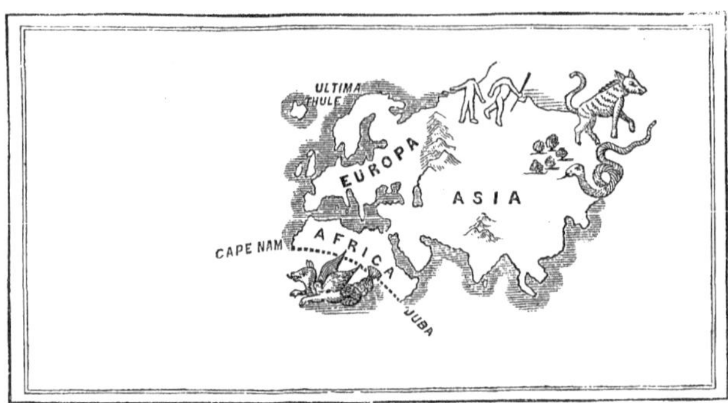

I. THE WORLD AS KNOWN TO EUROPE ABOUT THE YEAR 1418.

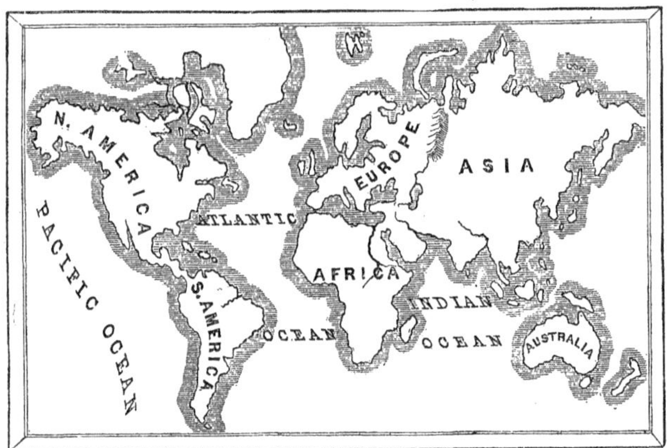

II. THE WORLD AS KNOWN IN OUR OWN DAY.

3. It may therefore be safely said that the continent of America was unknown to the leading nations of the eastern hemisphere, until nearly the close of the fifteenth century. A vast and stormy ocean lay between, and the boldest sailors seldom ventured on its waters, far from the coasts of Europe and Africa.

4. The latter half of the fifteenth century was a time of great activity throughout Europe. The science of navigation had been vastly improved; the art of printing had been

3. What was known of America previous to the year 1492? What separated America from Europe? How had sailors looked on this unknown sea?

invented; books of travel and adventure were eagerly read; and men's minds were thus greatly excited by stories of the wealth of the Indies, of the gold of Cathay or Farther India, and of Cipango (*se-pango*), supposed to be Japan, the gorgeous descriptions of which were to be read in the travels of Marco Polo and other authorities.

5. The trade of the Indies for many centuries enriched every nation that was in turn able to control it. At this time, in Europe, the Italians had held it for many years. But, as the rich goods of India reached Italy only after tedious and expensive transportation on the Red Sea and by caravan, it became a leading idea of those times to find a more direct route to the East. The passage by the way of the Cape of Good Hope had not yet been discovered; though Portugal was making great efforts to reach and pass the Stormy Cape, and thus secure the India trade.

6. Christopher Columbus, an Italian, a native of Genoa (*jen'-o-ah*), but residing at Lisbon, where he made maps and charts, had caught the spirit of the times, and was filled with a desire to discover a shorter route to the Indies. From the age of fourteen he had been a navigator, and had traversed a large part of the world as then known, had voyaged to Iceland, and sailed with the Portuguese explorers along the coast of Africa. While engaged in his business at Lisbon, he carefully studied the charts and accounts of former voyages, and at length came to the conclusion that, as the earth was round, Asia must stretch so far to the east as to be easily reached by sailing westward from Europe. He was probably not less than forty years of age when he began to form this opinion.

7. About the year 1484 Columbus applied to Genoa, his native state, for assistance in preparing an expedition to

4. What is said of the latter half of the fifteenth century? What art had awakened the mind of Europe? What wonderful stories filled men's minds?

5. What is said of the trade of India? What people held this at the close of the fifteenth century? How did the India trade of these times reach Europe? What did these long journeys lead men to desire? Why did they not sail round Africa? What nation was trying to find a route that way?

6. Who was Columbus? What effect had these stories about India produced on his mind? What was his occupation in early life? What was his business in later life, and to what studies did this lead him? At what conclusion did he arrive? How old was he when he arrived at this? Where is Lisbon?

test his theory of a westward passage to India, but was unsuccessful; then to the King of Portugal, who kept him in suspense for some time, and at last disappointed him. Next he sent his brother to the King of England for help. He himself went to the court of Spain in 1486, to ask assistance from Ferdinand, king of Aragon, and his wife Isabella, queen of Castile (*cas-teel*) and Leon (*lā-on*). Here he waited anxiously for five long years; but at last a council of learned men, to whom his petition was referred, decided against his plans. He then turned to France for help; and, while on his way thither, he was persuaded to make another attempt to secure the assistance of the Spanish court, and especially to gain the favor of the queen.

8. Isabella, who was a deeply religious woman, gave him a hearing, and became greatly interested in his plans, especially when, in his enthusiasm, he spoke of the conversion of the natives in those distant yet unknown countries to the

COLUMBUS EXPLAINING HIS PLANS TO FERDINAND AND ISABELLA.

7. Did he apply to England? Where did he himself go? Who at that time ruled over Spain? What was the result of his application? Where did he then conclude to go? What happened after he began his journey?

Christian religion. She at last overcame her husband's indifference, and offered to pledge her crown jewels for the expenses of the expedition. These were not needed. The royal treasurer furnished seven eighths of the cost of the expedition. Columbus and his friends provided the rest.

9. Columbus was nearly forty-eight years of age when he first sought the assistance of Genoa; he was about fifty-six when he received the final approval of Ferdinand and Isabella. He had spent eight years of waiting in weariness, amid mockery and discouragement; but, through all his anxieties, he was supported by a deep religious enthusiasm, because he firmly believed that he was chosen by God to carry Christianity to the Indies.

VESSELS OF COLUMBUS.

10. On Friday, August 3, 1492, he sailed from the port of Palos (*pah'-los*), in Spain, having received from the king and queen the commission of high admiral and the title of viceroy. In addition, he was to be allowed a considerable share of the profits of the expedition. This consisted of three vessels, the Pinta (*peen'-tah*), Santa Maria (*ma-rē-ah*), and Nina

---

8. What was the character of Isabella? What deeply interested her in the plans of Columbus? How did she show her husband what she felt in regard to them? How were the expenses of the expedition met?

9. How old was Columbus when he began to seek help? How old when he obtained it? How many years had he waited? What supported his noble soul during this long period?

(*né-nah*), with their crews, numbering ninety seamen. Columbus stopped at the Canary Islands a month to refit; and thence, on the 6th of September, he struck out westward over the unknown sea. On the 12th of October, 1492, the admiral descried land, and immediately after took possession of it with great pomp and solemnity, in the name of Ferdinand and Isabella. The land he found to be an island, which he named St. Salvador, called by the natives Guanahani (*gwah-nah-hah'-ne*), one of the Bahama Islands. Supposing that this was near the eastern shores of India, he called the natives Indians, a name which was afterward given to the red or copper-colored race over the whole continent.

11. Columbus soon after discovered the great island of Cuba, and coasted along its shores, believing them to be the famous Cipango. Sailing thence, he first saw the island which he named Hispanio'la, now called Hayti (*hā-te*), and here founded a colony. In January, 1493, he returned to Spain to recount his discoveries to the king and queen. He made, in all, four voyages to the "New World." In the third of these, during the year 1498, he reached the main land at the mouth of the River Orinoco, in South America. But he died in the belief that what he had discovered was only the eastern part of Asia.

12. His last days were extremely sad. Through the malice and jealousy of his enemies, he was removed from his government in the year 1500, and sent home to Spain in chains as a criminal. The king and queen, when they saw him, expressed great sorrow for his ill treatment, but he was never restored to his viceroyalty. In the year 1502 he was sent out on his fourth and last voyage. From this he returned in 1504, a disappointed man, to find Queen Isabella, his friend, dying, and Ferdinand cold and forgetful. Two years after this, in 1506, the discoverer of a "New World"

---

10. What commission did Columbus receive? When and from what place did he sail? What was the size of the expedition? Where did he stop, and how long did he remain there? When did he discover land? How many days was this from the time he left the Canaries? What was the land? What name did he give the natives? Why? How far did this name extend?

11. What great island did he discover? What island did he make his residence? How many voyages did he make from Spain? When and where did he reach the main land? Did he know that this was a new continent?

COLUMBUS IN CHAINS.

died, at the age of nearly seventy, poor, and neglected by the monarch whose reign he had rendered forever illustrious.

13. The discoveries of Columbus quickly drew many adventurers to the shores of the new continent. Among them, in the year 1499, came a Florentine named Amerigo Vespucci (*ă-mĕr'-e-go ves-pootch'-ee*), who published the first account of the new regions that was given to the people of Europe. For this reason the continent came by degrees to be called America.

THE CABOTS.

14. The man who first touched the main land of America was neither Columbus nor Vespucci. In the year 1497, John Cabot (*cab'-ot*), a Venetian by birth, with his son Sebastian, left Bristol, England, with one vessel, and sailed along the coast of North America for three hundred leagues

---

12. What happened to Columbus in the year 1500? How did the king and queen receive him on his arrival at court? What happened to him in 1502? What did he find on his return? What is said of his death?

13. What immediate effect was produced by the discoveries of Columbus? Who visited the continent in 1499? Why was the new continent called America?

or more. He discovered the island of Newfoundland, and gave the whole coast that name. John Cabot labored under the same opinion as Columbus, that this was only the eastern coast of Asia, "the land of the Great Cham" (*kam*), the sovereign prince of Tartary. The voyage of the Cabots was in the reign of Henry VII. of England, and under a commission from that prince. Sebastian Cabot the next year, 1498, with two ships, sailed along the coast from Labrador to Florida, touching at several places, and hoping to find an open passage to India. Little attention was paid to these discoveries of the Cabots, because Vasco de Gama (*dä gah'-mah*), under the Portuguese flag, in the year 1498, rounded the Cape of Good Hope, and opened for ships the long-wished-for route to the East.

SECTION II.

THE ABORIGINES, OR EARLY INHABITANTS OF NORTH AMERICA EAST OF THE MISSISSIPPI.

1. At the beginning of the 16th century, North America was inhabited by numerous tribes of copper-colored men, or Indians, the name that Columbus first gave to the natives of San Salvador. Within the present limits of the United States, these tribes were rude and uncivilized. They had no cities, although they sometimes had large but poorly constructed villages, or Indian towns, surrounded by palisades of trees or brushwood. There were no houses, but only wigwams or tents

INDIAN WIGWAM.

14. Who was the first voyager that touched the American continent? When? Who was John Cabot? State what is said of his voyage. What opinion did he hold respecting his discovery? In the reign of what king was the voyage made? Who sailed again from England in 1498? What was the extent of his explorations? What was Sebastian's object? Did these voyages of the Cabots attract much notice? Why was this?

made of the skins of animals, or, in summer, huts made of the branches of trees.

2. They were, for the most part, an unsettled race; yet the wanderings of each tribe, with but few exceptions, were confined to its own hunting-grounds. Their dress was as rude as their dwellings. In summer they had little clothing, in winter they wore the skins of animals. The men were fond of the display of dress and ornament. No civilized fop could surpass an Indian chief tricked out with gewgaws, painted and tattooed with vermilion, with stripes of black, red, and blue from ear to ear, and his head adorned with the beak and plumage of the raven or eagle, or the wing of the redbird.

3. The men, proud of their idleness, left the cultivation of the fields to the women, and spent a large part of their time in eating, or play, or sleep. Their great business was war, fishing, and hunting. Their weapons, which were the work of the men, were bows and arrows, spears, tomahawks or hatchets, and clubs. Their tomahawk and spear heads were made of flint or the hardest stone; their arrows were pointed with flints, shells, or bone, sometimes with eagles' claws. They could bring a tree down only by burning around it. Their canoes, made from the trunks, were hollowed by fire and their stone hatchets. Afterward from the white man they obtained weapons of iron.

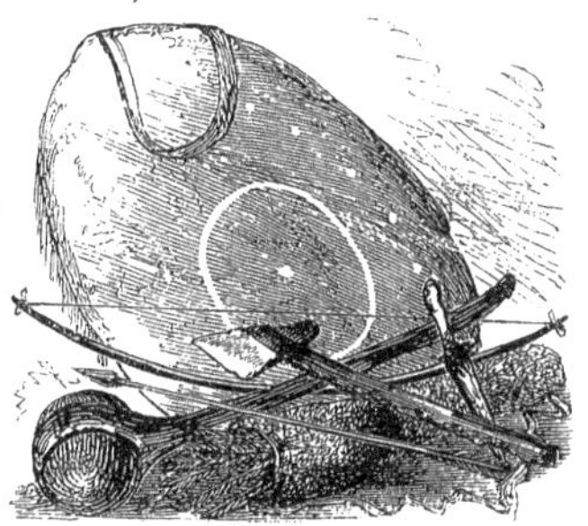
INDIAN SHIELD AND WEAPONS.

4. They had no learning, because they had no written language. But they had a sort of rude picture writing, an example of which is given on the following page.

1. By whom was North America inhabited at the time of its discovery? What was their condition in refinement? How did they live together? Describe their villages and dwellings. What would it have shown had they lived in cities?

2. What habits interfered with the building of houses? What was their usual dress? What is said of their fondness for decoration?

3. On what did they depend for a living? What was the occupation of the men? What were their weapons, and of what were the heads of these made, and why? Give an example of the difficulty produced by the want of metals.

4. Did they have written or printed books? Why was this? What was there in its place?

5. Their records were made up of a few of these on skins or bark, or occasionally belts of beads made of shells were used to keep up the remembrance of treaties. Their traditions consisted chiefly of the stories of brave deeds recited by the father to his sons, or by the older men to the younger.

WESTERN INDIAN PICTURE WRITING.

The chiefs Black Wolf, Raven, Fast Bear, and Standing Bear hold a war council round the fire where grass was high. They dig up the hatchet, have plenty of arrows, and start on foot (moccasin tracks) to a Cheyenne village (Cut-arm, Cheyenne sign) on Beaver Creek, where they expect to have a fight, and stampede the herd of fat ponies.

6. In youth they were taught to throw the tomahawk, to shoot the arrow, and to spear the fish. War was held to be the most honorable and glorious employment. In it they learned to follow their enemies with unquenchable revenge through cold and heat; to fight with cunning and with courage, and, if taken prisoner, to endure any torment, and even death itself, with unflinching and wonderful fortitude.

7. Indolent by nature, and with few wants, they were careless of the future. Perhaps on this account they had not the steady purpose that marks the white race. Although capable of powerful exertions when once roused, they could not be relied on. Yet they were hospitable to strangers, for this they regarded as a sacred virtue; and they seldom forgot a kindness, and never an injury.

8. The condition of the Indian women was very miserable. They raised the fruitful crops of maize, prepared skins

---

5. How did they preserve the remembrance of past events? What is said of their traditions?

6. What was an Indian boy taught? What was regarded as of the first importance? Name some of the required virtues in the warriors.

7. Were they industrious? Why was this? What steady virtue did they cultivate? and what is said of their friendship and enmity?

for clothing, and in their wanderings bore the heavy burdens, besides carrying their papooses or infants. They did all the drudgery at home and abroad, and were little better than slaves. Daughters were purchased in marriage from their parents, and the chiefs had often several wives, who might be dismissed at pleasure.

WARRIOR AND SQUAW.

9. The government of the tribes was patriarchal. The head of the tribe was a chief or sachem, sometimes so by birth, but generally chosen on account of his bravery, or wisdom, or eloquence. His opinion, if supported by a council of the elders, was the only law. But he had no means of enforcing it on those who were unwilling to obey. His influence depended wholly on his personal character. The warriors followed him on a war party only if they chose; there could be no compulsion. Proud as the Indian was in many things, that of which he was most proud was his personal freedom.

INDIANS IN COUNCIL.

10. The god of the red man was the Great Spirit. To the Indian there was an invisible spirit in every thing grand, or terrible, or beautiful; in the sun, the moon, and the stars; in the cataract, the great forest, the thunder, and the tempest; in the water; and in the fire. He believed that after death the warriors or braves only would be taken to the happy hunting-grounds in another world.

---

8. How did they treat their women? Describe their labors and drudgery. What is said of marriage?

9. What was the government? What is patriarchal? State what is said of the head of the tribe, and of his authority.

10. What idea did the Indian have of God? Where did this invisible spirit reside? What was the Indian belief of the state after death?

11. The tribes inhabiting the present limits of the United States are generally grouped under eight families, speaking different languages. The four which were most active in the history of this country were the Algonquin, the Huron-Iroquois, the Cherokee, and the Mobilian. The first and last divided between them almost the entire country east of the Mississippi. The Algonquin family of tribes stretched from Hudson's Bay as far south as Cape Fear River and the mouth of the Ohio, and from the Atlantic to the Mississippi. The Mobilian family occupied nearly all the territory from the southern boundary of the Algonquins to the Gulf of Mexico.

12. Between these two, on the southern slope of the Alleghanies—the highlands of Alabama, Georgia, and Carolina—were the Cherokees, a family of mountaineers. In the heart of the Algonquin tract was the family of the Huron-Iroquois (*é-ro-kwah*), consisting of several confederacies, chiefly, the Hurons, lying north and south of Lake Erie, and the fierce Iroquois, who claimed the country from Vermont to Western New York, south of Lake Ontario, as far as the head waters of the Ohio, Susquehanna, and Delaware. Thus the Algonquins completely surrounded the Huron-Iroquois; the Mobilians and Algonquins, the Cherokees.

13. The Algonquin tribes appear in the early settlements on the coast north of Cape Fear, the Powhatáns in Virginia; the Delawares and Mohégans in the Middle Colonies; the Pequods, Narragansetts, Massachusetts, and others, in New England. The warlike Iroquois, or Five Nations—Senecas, Cayugas (*ki-oóg-as*), Onondagas (*on-on-dáh-gas*), Oneidas (*o-ní-das*), and Mohawks—were actively engaged in all the intercolonial wars and in that of the Revolution. In the settlement of the Northwest, the early settlers had bloody struggles with the Algonquin tribes of Miamis, Illinois, Sacs and Foxes, and others.

---

11. How are the North American Indians generally grouped? Why is this? What four of these were most known in United States history? Which of these had the largest territory? What were the limits of the Algonquins? Give the boundaries of the Mobilians.

12. Where did the Cherokees live? What family did the Algonquins surround? What tract did this occupy?

13. Where do we find the Algonquins in the history of the coast? State what is said of the Iroquois or Five Nations? Where do we meet the Algonquins still later?

14. With the Mobilian tribes the later history is deeply interwoven: the Creeks and Seminoles fought with a bravery that rivaled the Iroquois on the north. The Uchee, Tuscarora, Catawba, and Natchez families residing among or near the Mobilians were feeble in numbers. West of the Mississippi was the wide-spread family of the Dahcōtah Sioux (*si-oo*), of whom little was known.

15. Vast as was the country east of the "Father of Waters" inhabited by these aboriginal tribes, their numbers were exceedingly small. The warlike Iroquois, for example, never exceeded three thousand warriors, and neither the Creeks, nor Cherokees, nor Seminoles reached five thousand. Careful students of Indian history assure us that there is no reason to believe that the entire Indian population east of the Mississippi, at any time since the discovery of the continent, was over two hundred thousand.

16. It was far otherwise on the table-lands of Mexico, in Central America, and on the western plateaus of South America as far as Peru. Here was a teeming population that had reached a far higher state of civilization than the tribes of the North. They had populous cities; they wove cotton cloth; they worked in copper and gold; they labored steadily in the fields; they erected stately buildings of stone, and they had a fixed society, with priests and kings, or hereditary princes. On the islands near the Gulf of Mexico there was an immense Indian population, doomed ere long to be destroyed.

INDIAN RUINS, CENTRAL AMERICA.

17. From what place these red men first came, peopling

14. Where do we meet the Mobilian tribes? What family lay west of the Mississippi, and what northeast of the Algonquins?

15. What is said of the number of the aborigines? Illustrate this from what is known of different tribes. What number is believed to have covered the Indian population east of the Mississippi?

16. How was the Indian population elsewhere? What was their condition? State the different points that showed their advancement.

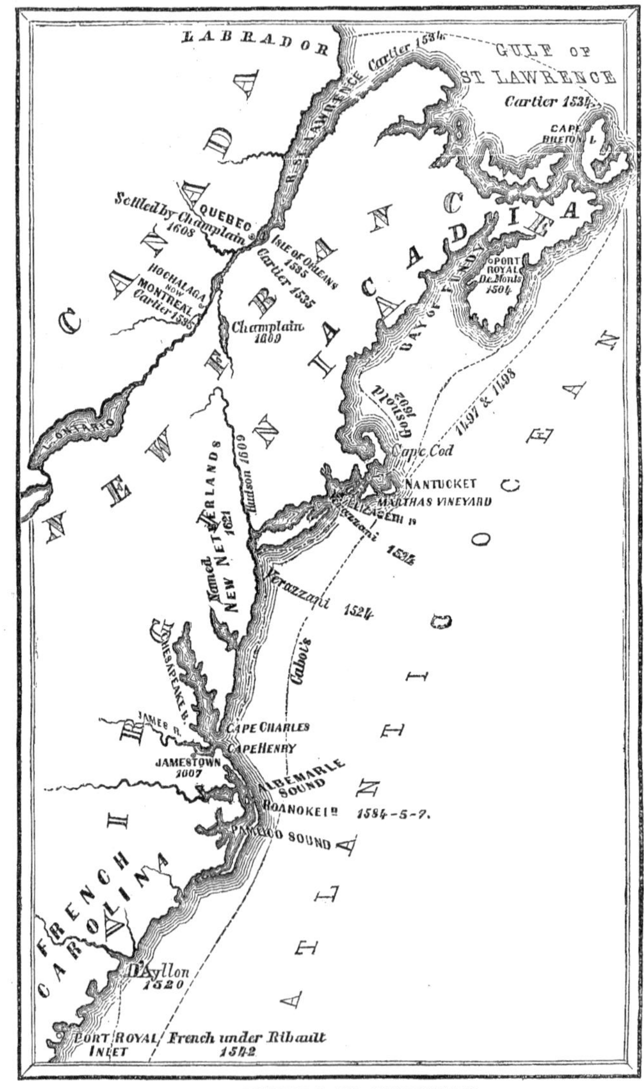

EARLY DISCOVERIES AND EXPLORATIONS.

the continent from the far north to Cape Horn, is not yet ascertained. Some have asserted that the emigration was from the northeast of Asia. But the general opinion seems to be that the Indian is a distinct race from those of the Old World.

18. When the white man first came to these shores he was received by the Indians as a superior being. It was not long before the inhuman conduct of the whites uprooted this feeling of veneration, for we shall presently see that the wrongs of the Indian began soon after the discovery of the continent.

SECTION III.

SPANISH DISCOVERY AND EXPLORATION AFTER THE YEAR 1500.

1. THE Spaniards soon occupied the islands of Cuba, Porto Rico (*reé-ko*), Hispaniola, and Jamaica. From these points it was not a long voyage to the main land in different directions. In 1510, Ojeda (*o-há-dah*), a companion of Columbus, sailed south from Cuba, landed on the isthmus, and settled Darien. From this place, in the year 1513, Nuñez de Balboa (*noon'-yeth da bal-bó-ah*) started with an expedition across the isthmus, and from a height of the Andes first saw the Pacific Ocean in a southerly direction, named by him, on that account, the South Sea. Descending the mountains, he reached its shores, and, wading into its waters, took possession of this sea with great solemnity for the King of Castile. On another account this expedition deserves notice, for Pizarro (*pe-zăr-ro*), who served under Balboa, was present when an Indian chief near the South Sea first told Nuñez of the country of Peru and its wonderful riches.

---

17. Whence did the red man come to America? What different opinions are mentioned about this?

18. What treatment did the first explorers receive from the natives? How was this repaid?

1. What islands were soon occupied by the Spaniards? What was easily reached from these points? What is the first voyage that is mentioned? What settlement? What great discovery was made in 1513? State what is said of it. On what other account is this voyage also worthy of notice? Where is Peru?

2. The year before Balboa's discovery, Juan Ponce de Leon (*ponthā' da lāon*), who had been governor of Porto Rico, sailed northwest from that island to the Bahamas in a vain search for an imaginary fountain of perpetual youth. While he was sailing among the islands, March, 1512, he discovered the main land, which he at first supposed to be an island, on Easter Sunday, called by the Spaniards Pasqua de Flores—the Feast of Flowers. To commemorate the day of the discovery, he named the country Florida.

3. Cordova, another Spaniard, landed and explored the northern coast of Yucatan in 1517. Grĭjal'va (*gre-hahl'-va*) in 1518 explored the southern coast of Mexico. In 1519, Hernan Cortez, sent by Velasquez (*va-lah'-sketh*), Governor of Cuba, at the head of a small body of men, marched into the interior of Mexico. After a severe struggle, marked by great bravery and cruelty on the part of the Spaniards, he overthrew the empire of the Aztecs, and brought it under the dominion of Spain in the year 1521.

4. The expedition of Vasquez d'Ayllon (*vah-sketh dā-ile-yon'*), in 1520, shows the dreadful cruelty of the Spaniards to the Indians. He went to the Bahamas to seize the natives and bring them to the island of Hispaniola to work there in the mines as slaves. A storm drove him on the coast of what is now South Carolina, where he was treated with great kindness by the Indians. While many of these were visiting on board his ships, they were suddenly fastened down under the hatches, and the vessels set sail. Disaster followed the ships. One of them was wrecked, and all on board perished. The Indians on the other preferred death to slavery, and almost to a man starved themselves. D'Ayllon paid the penalty of this atrocious cruelty in 1525, when he went to settle his new province of Chicōra, now South Carolina. The natives, imitating his former treachery, enticed many of his men from the ships and massacred them.

---

2. Who sailed in 1512? In what direction and for what purpose? What discovery did Ponce de Leon make? When? What name did he give to the country, and why?

3. Who first landed on the coast of Yucatan? When and by whom was the coast of Mexico first explored? What expedition was made in 1519? What did Cortez accomplish?

D'Ayllon himself escaped with difficulty, only to return in disgrace to Hispaniola.

5. Pamphilo de Narvaez (*pam-feé-lo du nar-vah'eth*) obtained a grant of land in Florida, and sailed from Cuba to take possession of it, in the year 1528. He landed with three hundred men at Appalachee Bay, and marched inland. After a series of terrible sufferings from hunger, fatigue, and constant skirmishes with the natives, he returned to the coast. Here he built small boats, and embarked to find a Spanish settlement. A storm overtook them, and all but four men were lost. These disastrous expeditions, so far from discouraging the Spaniards, only made many of them more eager to penetrate Florida, the fabled "Land of Gold."

6. Ferdinand de Soto (*da só-to*) entertained a strong belief that in the interior of Florida there was a rich and powerful people like the Peruvians or Mexicans. A renowned companion of Pizarro in the conquest of Peru, he had been made governor of Cuba, and had received an unlimited grant of land in Florida from the Emperor Charles V. He left Cuba for Florida with one thousand men, infantry and cavalry, and landed at Tampa Bay in the month of May, 1539.

7. He marched first north, then westward, and, after two years of wandering and hardship, reached the banks of the Mississippi in 1541, and crossed, as is supposed, into Arkansas. Next spring, 1542, he returned to the Mississippi, and there, worn out and disappointed, died, and was buried in the waters of the river he had discovered. The remnant of his companions floated in rude boats down the Mississippi to its mouth, and, coasting along tho gulf, reached a Spanish settlement.

4. What do we learn from D'Ayllon's voyage? Where and for what purpose did he sail? Where was he driven? How was he treated by the natives? What return did he make for their kindness? What occurred on the homeward voyage? Where did D'Ayllon go in the year 1625? How did the natives repay his former treachery? What became of D'Ayllon?

5. Who next obtained a grant of land in Florida? What attempt did he make to settle it? Where did he land, and then march? What is said of his march? What was the end of tho expedition? What effect did this and the other failures have on the Spaniards?

6. What views did De Soto hold about Florida? Who was he? What grant had he received? What use did he make of this grant? Where and when did he land?

7. What is said of his march? What discovery did he make, and when? What became of him? What became of his companions?

DE SOTO DISCOVERING THE MISSISSIPPI.

8. Still another attempt to settle Florida was made in 1564 by Melendez (*ma-len'deth*), a Spanish noble, who had gained great wealth in America, and had been made governor of Florida by King Philip. He sailed from Spain with 2500 persons, 300 of whom were soldiers. A storm scattered his fleet, and scarce a third of the passengers arrived at Porto Rico. With these he set sail for Florida, and landed on the coast, where he laid out the plan of a town, and named it St. Augustine (*aw-gus-teen'*), September, 1565. This is the oldest town in the United States, and some of the stone houses said to have been built by the Spaniards still remain. A further account of the doings of Melendez will be given under the head of French Discovery and Exploration.

9. In the year 1580, Augustin Ruyz (*rīthe*), a Franciscan friar, with two or three companions, penetrated the wilds

8. Who made another attempt to settle Florida? When? Who was he? Where did he first sail from? What is said of the expedition that he started with? From what place did he finally sail to Florida? Where and when did he land? What is said of St. Augustine?

north of Mexico as far as the upper valley of the Rio Grande (*reo grand*). Next year, 1581, Don Antonio de Espego (*es-pā'-ho*) followed with a band of soldiers, explored the country, and named it New Mexico. He founded the town of Santa Fé (*san-tah fā*) in the following year, 1582. This was seventeen years later than the settlement of St. Augustine, and Santa Fé is therefore the second oldest town in the United States.

SECTION IV.

FRENCH DISCOVERY AND EXPLORATION.

1. THE French were anxious to share the wealth that Spain was gathering in America. Francis I., the French king, sent out an exploring expedition under Verazzani *va-rat-tsah'-ne*), a Florentine, in the year 1524. He sailed northward along the coast, and appears to have entered the harbors of New York and Newport, and to have gone as far as Newfoundland. This voyage of Verazzani, with the subsequent voyage of Cartier (*car-te-á*), formed the foundation of the French claim to the northern part of North America.

2. The French turned their attention to the exploration of this region. An expedition was sent out by the Admiral of France in the year 1534, under James Cartier, who discovered the Gulf and River St. Lawrence. In his second voyage, 1535, he explored the river as far as Montreal, and tried to form a settlement on the island of Orleans (*or'-le-anz*). But the climate was too severe, and in the spring Cartier and his men returned to France, carrying with them the Indian chief whom they had decoyed on board.

---

9. What important exploration was made in 1580? What one was made in the year following? What town was founded? by whom? and when? What is said of Santa Fé?

1. What stimulated the French to make voyages to America? Who sent out an expedition? Who commanded this expedition? What is said of his voyage? When was it?

2. To what part of the continent did the French turn their attention? What Frenchman first went there? What discovery did he make? When? How many years was this after Verazzani's voyage? How soon after his first voyage did Cartier go again? What was said of his attempt to form a settlement?

3. De la Roque (*rōk*), Lord of Roberval, was made viceroy of the new country by the king, and great preparations were made for an expedition, of which Cartier was appointed chief pilot and captain general. Cartier started first with five ships, in 1541, and passed the winter on the island of Orleans. The climate proved so severe, and the Indians, whose chief Cartier had on his last voyage treacherously carried away, kept the settlers in such constant alarm, that, when the river opened, they were glad to make sail for home. Roberval, with three vessels, set out from France in 1542, and met Cartier and his men off the island of Newfoundland (*nū-fund-land'*) on their way home. Roberval pushed on to the St. Lawrence, and, after wintering at the isle of Orleans, he also returned to France. In the year 1549 he made another voyage, but was never heard of afterward.

4. Some French Protestants, called Huguenots (*hū'-gĕ-nots*), being anxious to emigrate to America, John Ribault (*re-bó*) was sent out on a voyage of exploration to Florida in 1562, and, after touching at St. John's River, entered Port Royal Inlet. Here he built a fort, and named it Carolina, in honor of Charles IX., king of France. Leaving twenty-six men in charge, Ribault then returned for supplies. None came; and, after enduring great hardships, they set sail for France in a vessel they had built, and were picked up, when nearly starved, by an English ship.

5. Two years afterward, in 1564, Laudonniere (*lāh-don-yer*), with three ship-loads of Huguenot settlers, landed at St. John's River, and built a fort called also Carolina. They became dissatisfied, and were about leaving, when Ribault arrived with provisions and colonists. Melendez, the Spanish governor, who has already been mentioned, determined to expel the French from his territory. He landed at St. Augustine in September, 1565, and soon after surprised the

---

3. Who was made viceroy of the new territory? What is a viceroy? What was immediately done? What position did Cartier occupy? When did he sail? What success attended the settlement? What part did Roberval take in the expedition? Whom did he meet on his way back? What was Roberval's success? What happened to him in 1549?

4. What Frenchmen were anxious to make a home in America? Who was sent out to begin a settlement? Where and when did he land? What beginning did he make? Where did Ribault go? Who were left in the fort? What became of them?

Huguenot fort, and put nearly all the men, women, and children to the sword.

6. The French king took no steps to avenge this slaughter, but a chivalrous French knight, Dominic de Gourges (*dŭ-goorj*), at his own expense equipped an expedition, and sailed in 1567 secretly to Florida. Here, next year (1568), he surprised and captured two hundred Spaniards at Fort Carolina, and hung his prisoners on trees. De Gourges then returned to Europe.

7. Nothing further was done in America by the French until 1598, when the Marquis de la Roche (*la-rōsh*) sent a colony of forty convicts to the sandy island of Sable, off the coast of Nova Scotia. In a few years the settlement died out. In 1603, De Monts (*dŭ-mong'*), a rich Huguenot courtier, obtained the grant of a large tract of land extending from the 40th to the 46th degree of north latitude, or from a line south of New York as far north as Cape Breton. To this tract was given the name of Acadia, limited afterward to what is now New Brunswick, Cape Breton, and adjacent islands.

8. De Monts, accompanied by the celebrated Samuel Champlain (*sham-plane*), came out, in 1604, with two ships, to explore the country and to form a settlement. A fort was built at the mouth of the St. Croix (*kroī*) River, but he soon abandoned this, and settled finally at Port Royal, September, 1605. This was the first permanent French settlement in America.

9. Champlain, in 1608, on a trading and exploring voyage up the St. Lawrence, established a post which he named Quebec. In the next year, 1609, he pushed south into the interior, and was the first European that saw the lake that bears his name. Other French explorations were made west-

---

5. Who came out again in 1564? Where did he land? How did the settlers like their new home? What kept the colonists from leaving the settlement? Who looked on the French as intruders? Why? What did he do?

6. How did the French king regard this massacre? Who took the quarrel up? Did he have the consent of the king? What did he do when he got to Florida?

7. When and where did the French make the next settlement? What became of it? Who was De Monts? What grant did he receive? What name did he give to it?

8. What was the first use that De Monts made of his grant? Where was the fort built? Did he stay here long? Where did he finally settle? When and where did the French first settle permanently?

ward, and the territory thus opened, together with Canada and Acadia, was known as New France. Canada embraced all the territory watered by the St. Lawrence or its tributaries.

SECTION V.

ENGLISH DISCOVERY AND EXPLORATION PREVIOUS TO THE YEAR 1608.

1. AFTER the year 1492, the commerce of England rapidly increased, and the merchants were anxious to obtain a share of the trade with India. As a western passage seemed hopeless, they directed their efforts to the discovery of a northeast passage through the Arctic Sea. This was given up after several attempts. They then renewed the search for a northwest passage; and in 1576, Martin Frobisher, with this object, entered and discovered the straits that bear his name.

2. In 1579, Sir Francis Drake, a celebrated Englishman, endeavored, from the Pacific side of the continent, to find a passage to the Atlantic. He had sailed north along the west coast of America in pursuit of plunder from Spanish ships, and had explored the coast of Upper California, which he named New Albion. He then entered and explored the Bay of San Francisco, where he passed the winter of 1579–80.

3. Sir Humphrey Gilbert, an English knight, took a deep interest in the discovery of a northwest passage, and was anxious to plant a colony in America. For this purpose he received a patent from Queen Elizabeth, granting him au-

---

9. Who ascended the St. Lawrence in 1608? What post did he establish? What year was this? What noticeable thing did Champlain do in 1609? In what direction did French explorers go? What name was given to all the French claim? What did Canada embrace?

1. What nation was fast rising in commercial importance? What did her merchants greatly desire? In what direction did they try to find a road to India? Why did they attempt this route? Did they succeed? When and in what direction did Frobisher make the attempt? What name on the map of America still points this out?

2. What attempt was made by Sir Francis Drake? When? How did he come to be on the Pacific side? What did he explore and name? What bay did he enter and explore? What did he hope that this would prove to be? When was this?

thority over six hundred miles of territory, unoccupied by the settlers of any Christian prince. In 1583 Gilbert sailed with three ships and reached Newfoundland, of which he took possession in the name of the queen, and soon after sailed for the continent. As he neared the shore, one of his ships struck a hidden rock and was lost. The other two set out for England. On the passage, the vessel in which Gilbert sailed foundered, and all on board perished.

4. Walter Raleigh (*raw'-ly*), half-brother of Gilbert, was a great favorite with Queen Elizabeth, and easily obtained a patent nearly the same as Gilbert's. He immediately sent out two skillful commanders, Am'idas and Barlow. They landed near Cape Fear, North Carolina, and thence went to Roanoke Island, where they were treated by the Indians with great kindness. On their return their vessels were loaded with skins and furs, cedar wood and sassafras bark. When they arrived in England they made a flattering report of the country, and the name Virginia was given to this new and beautiful region in honor of Elizabeth, "the Virgin Queen." The queen herself was delighted, and conferred on Raleigh the honor of knighthood.

5. Raleigh, now Sir Walter, in 1585 sent out seven ships, under Sir Richard Grenville, to Roanoke Island. He left Ralph Lane, with one hundred and ten men there, and then returned to England. Lane and his men nearly starved to death in the year that followed, and were almost in a state of despair, when Sir Francis Drake, on his way home from the West Indies with a large fleet, appeared off the settlement. Drake, who was an intimate friend of Raleigh, treated them with great kindness, and on their urgent entreaty took them back to England with him in June, 1586. They had scarcely gone when a ship with provisions sent by Ra-

---

3. What is said of Sir Humphrey Gilbert? Who was Queen of England at the time? What grant did Gilbert receive? When and what place did Gilbert first land? What did he do here? Where did he then go? Did he land here? What happened to him?

4. Who took up Gilbert's scheme? Who was Raleigh? What grant did he get? Whom did he send out? At what two points did they land? How were they treated by the natives? What was the cargo they brought home? What occurred on their arrival in England? What name was given to the country, and why? How was Raleigh rewarded?

QUEEN ELIZABETH KNIGHTING RALEIGH.

leigh arrived, and a fortnight afterward Grenville came with three more ships. Finding nothing of the colony, he left fifteen men on the island, and then returned.

6. Raleigh was too great a man to be easily discouraged, and he at once prepared another expedition. This time, instead of single men, he sent families, and with them, as governor, John White, to commence the "City of Raleigh." On arriving at Roanoke Island in 1587, they found that the fifteen men left by Grenville had been killed by the Indians.

7. White went back to England in the fall of 1587 for supplies, leaving in the colony 117 persons, men, women, and children. When he arrived home the nation was greatly

5. When and under whom did Raleigh send out the next expedition? Where did he land? Did Grenville remain long? Who were left? How did Lane and the colonists pass the next year? Who fortunately arrived in time? Why did Drake look after the settlement? What did he do? What arrivals came soon after Drake left? What did Grenville do? Where is Roanoke Island?

6. What did Raleigh do when he got the news? When did he send the next expedition? Who commanded it? Of whom was it composed? In what condition did they find Grenville's colony? Give date.

excited on account of a threatened Spanish invasion, and all vessels were forbidden to leave the country. Raleigh at last managed to send off two ships, under White, in 1588, but the latter, instead of proceeding directly to the colony, turned aside to cruise for Spanish prizes, was badly beaten, and compelled to return to England.

ONE OF RALEIGH'S SHIPS.

8. Raleigh had spent a sum nearly equal to $200,000 on the colony—a great sum in those days—and was unable or unwilling to spend more. He therefore assigned his patent, March, 1589, to some Londoners, who did not send help to Roanoke Island until next year, 1590. When the vessel arrived there not one of the settlers could be found, nor was any one of them ever heard of afterward. Although Raleigh had failed in settling Virginia, he was the means of introducing tobacco into England. He himself set the fashion at court, and the habit of "drinking tobacco," as it was called, spread so rapidly, that before many years it created such a demand for the plant as to turn the attention of emigrants to Virginia.

9. The assignees of Raleigh's patent kept up a small trading business with Virginia. Bartholomew Gosnold, master of a vessel sent out by them in 1602, discovered the point of land which he named Cape Cod. He discovered also the islands which he named Nantucket, Martha's Vineyard, and the Elizabeth Islands. In June, 1602, he returned to England with a valuable cargo of sassafras and furs.

10. Gosnold praised the country so highly that some Bristol merchants sent out Martin Pring in 1603 to obtain furs,

7. Why did White leave in the fall? How many did he leave in the colony? What state of things did he find on his arrival in England? When and to what extent did Raleigh find means to send help? What happened to the ships?

8. What amount had Raleigh spent on the colony? What did he do in 1589? When did the assignees send help to Roanoke? What state of things was found when the vessel arrived? What habit was introduced into England from Virginia? By whom? What effect did this have on the future of Virginia?

9. To what use did Raleigh's assignees put the grant? When and what discoveries did Gosnold make? What was the trading return for this voyage? In whose employment was he?

and sassafras which had rapidly grown into use as a medicine; he was also ordered to explore the country. Pring entered Penobscot Bay, coasted as far south as Martha's Vineyard, and returned to England after a successful voyage.

11. King James, in the year 1603, confiscated Raleigh's patent, and this made the previous assignment of no value. In the year 1606 the king granted all the territory between the 34th and 45th degrees north latitude to two companies. From the 34th to the 38th degree was given to the London Company, composed principally of Londoners. To the Plymouth (*plim'-uth*) Company, made up of persons living in the west of England, was given the country between the 41st and 45th degrees. Between the 38th and 41st degrees neither company could settle within one hundred miles of a colony of its rival. A council residing in England was to superintend and make general laws for both colonies; and each colony was to be governed by a council of seven persons residing therein. All these officers were appointed by the king.

12. The London Company made active preparations, and in December, 1606, sent out three ships with 105 settlers, under the command of Captain Christopher Newport. The intention was to land at Roanoke; but a storm drove the vessels north, and they entered Chesapeake Bay. After three weeks' search for a suitable place for a settlement, they ascended the River Powhatan to a spot fifty miles from its mouth. Here, on the 23d of May, 1607, the first permanent English settlement in America was made. It was called Jamestown in honor of the king, and the river was at first named the King's, afterward the James.

---

10. What effect did Gosnold's account of his voyage produce in Bristol? Where is Bristol? What was Pring ordered to do? State what is said of the voyage.

11. What was done by the king in 1603? How did this affect the right of the assignees? What grant did the king make in 1606? What were the names of these companies? How much land was given to each? How were both colonies to be superintended? How was each colony to be governed directly? Who appointed the members of all these councils?

12. What movement did the London Company make? Where did they intend that these colonists should settle? What prevented this? What place did they finally select for a settlement? When was this? What names were given to the settlement and to the Powhatan River? Why were they so named?

SECTION VI.

EARLY DUTCH DISCOVERY AND EXPLORATION.

HUDSON ASCENDS THE RIVER IN THE HALF MOON.

1. CAPTAIN HENRY HUDSON, in command of an English ship, was searching along the American coast, in the year 1607, for a northwest passage to the Pacific. Failing in this, he sailed again in 1608, and sought a northeastern passage between Nova Zembla and Spitzbergen, but was stopped by the ice. In 1609, in the service of the DUTCH EAST INDIA COMPANY, Hudson made another unsuccessful attempt in the same direction. He then crossed over to the American continent, and, entering New York Bay, May, 1609, ascended the river that bears his name as far as the head of navigation. This was the foundation of the Dutch claim in North America.

---

1. What is said of Hudson's first voyage and its success? What is said of his second voyage? Why is his next voyage of great interest to us? State what is said of the voyage of 1609.

2. Hudson's fourth voyage was his last. Next year, 1610, still undiscouraged, and once more in the employment of the English, he went in search of a northwest passage, and entered that inland sea known as Hudson's Bay. Here his crew mutinied and set him adrift in an open boat, with his son and eight of his companions. They were never again heard of.

SECTION VII.

GENERAL REFLECTIONS ON CHAPTER I.

1. The most important voyages connected with the discovery and exploration of the North American continent have already been given. The first Europeans that fixed themselves firmly on the continent were the Spaniards.

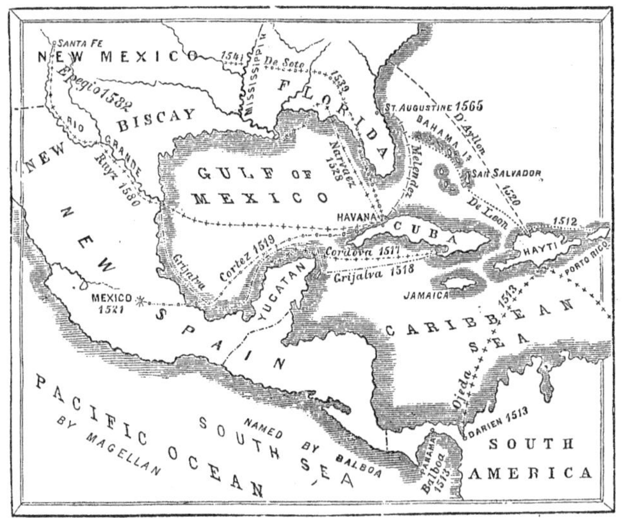

EARLY VOYAGES OF THE SPANIARDS FROM CUBA AND OTHER ISLANDS.

---

2. How many voyages did he make in search of a passage to Asia? Give the dates and flags under which he sailed. What was the object of his fourth voyage in 1610? Describe the voyage and its result.

It is worthy of notice that the land which Columbus first touched lies midway, north and south, on the shores of the Western World. Hispaniola, now St. Domingo, Cuba, Porto Rico, and Jamaica were soon occupied, and from these, as a centre, the Spanish adventurers pushed out in different directions, to South America, to the Pacific, to Yucatan, to Mexico, to Florida.

2. In these early voyages for the exploration of the continent, the leading object was to find gold and silver, and, combined with this, to obtain fresh supplies of Indians to work as slaves in the mines of Hispaniola, and in the other islands. The treatment of the Indians by the Spaniards forms one of the most terrible records in connection with the history of the New World. No language can do justice to the cruelty that the poor and, at first, confiding natives suffered at their hands. They were put into the mines and worked to death; they were tortured, burnt, murdered. The Indians made every effort to escape from this frightful misery, but it was impossible. Families, and often whole villages, committed suicide to avoid the oppression of their taskmasters.

3. To the credit of the rulers in Spain, it must be said that they tried to stop this terrible work. Ferdinand and Isabella both spoke strongly against it. The Church issued orders in condemnation of it, and the bishops in the West India Islands tried to interfere. But the New World in those days appeared much farther away from Europe than in our times with the swift steamer; and the governors, who of course came from Spain, nearly all became cruel tyrants after they began to govern. In the end, whole nations of Indians were blotted out of existence. One million two hundred thousand natives are stated on good authority to have been destroyed in a few years, in Hispaniola alone.

4. By these explorations and efforts, Spain was filled with

---

1. What circumstance connected with the landing of Columbus is worthy of notice? What naturally followed? Give these voyages from the map, page 28.

2. What was the leading object of the early explorers? What object was afterward intimately connected with this? What is said of their treatment of the Indians? Give some idea of the cruelty of the Spaniards.

3. What efforts were made to put a stop to this cruelty? Why did this prove ineffectual? What was the result of this cruel treatment? Give a particular instance.

wealth that she obtained from her new territories. Over these she held entire control, and would allow no other nation to trespass within them. She had grown so powerful that she could easily maintain her claims; and the other European nations, being thus prevented from getting a share of the wealth of Mexico and Peru, became the more anxious to discover a western passage to India. Portugal opened a new route, round the Cape of Good Hope, five years after the discovery of America. Yet this, although a great improvement on the overland journey, was long and perilous; and the southwestern passage to India through the Straits of Magellan, discovered in 1520, was still longer and more dangerous than that by the Cape of Good Hope. A SHORT WESTERN PASSAGE TO THE EAST INDIES remained the anxious wish of maritime nations. It was the hope of discovering this that led to the exploration of the northern part of the continent by Cabot, by Verazzani, by Cartier, by Frobisher, by Hudson, and others. Long afterward, when colonies were planted on the coast, the same hope was still strong that somewhere would be found a passage to the South Sea of Balboa.

5. The FRENCH, with the exception of the Huguenot failures, first at Port Royal Inlet, and next at the St. John's River, confined their explorations to country far north, on and near the St. Lawrence. To this entire claim, one of immense extent, they gave the name of NEW FRANCE.

6. The ENGLISH explorations were limited to Pamlico and Albemarle Sounds, and to the coast of Massachusetts and Maine, with the neighboring islands. To their claim of territory, which was founded on the voyage of the Cabots, extending from Labrador to Florida, the English gave the name of Virginia.

---

4. In what way did Spain grow rapidly great by the discovery of America? What course did she pursue toward other nations? To what did this drive the maritime nations of Europe? What success did Portugal meet with? How was this route regarded? What other route is mentioned? What hope still animated the navigators of Europe? Who are mentioned? How far onward in history did this hope extend?

5. Where did the French confine their explorations? What name did they give to the vast territory they claimed?

6. To what parts of the coast were the English explorations limited? What name did they give to their claim? How far did it extend?

7. The DUTCH, by virtue of the voyage of Hudson, after a time laid claim to a portion of the coast within the limits of Virginia, a claim which the English would never for one moment allow. To this territory, extending from Cape Cod to the Delaware River, the Dutch, some twelve years after Hudson's voyage, gave the name of NEW NETHERLANDS.

8. These three claims—for Florida did not give much trouble—in course of time, greatly interfered with each other. Their boundaries were very indefinite. The French claim overlapped the northern and western part of Virginia; that of the Dutch struck into the middle of it. While the country was only settled at points many miles apart, there was little or no trouble; but as settlements began to increase, these rival claims became a fruitful source of quarrels, which were at last ended mainly by the sword.

CONTEMPORANEOUS EVENTS AND REIGNS.

9. Just before Columbus sailed, the Spaniards had driven the Moors out of Spain, where they had been for eight hundred years. It was at the surrender of Granada (*gran-ah′-dah*), the last strong-hold of the Moors, that Columbus finally obtained the approval of Ferdinand and Isabella for his expedition. At the time that De Soto was struggling toward the Mississippi, the Emperor of Germany, Charles V. of Spain, was the ruler of the mightiest empire in the world. When the French and Spanish were slaughtering each other in Florida, Charles IX. reigned in France; Philip II., son of Charles V., was King of Spain; and the great Queen Elizabeth reigned in England. When Raleigh was making the last attempt to plant his colony on Roanoke Island, Spain was preparing her great Armada to conquer England, an expedition which ended in that terrible defeat so famous in English and Spanish history.

---

7. What is said of the Dutch claim? How far did it extend? What name did they give to this?

8. Why did these claims interfere with each other? In what way did this happen?

9. What great event in Spain happened just before the sailing of Columbus? With what is the surrender of Granada associated? Who was ruler in Spain when De Soto was engaged in his expedition? What names are mentioned as rulers in Europe while Melendez was in Florida? When was this? What was taking place in Europe while Raleigh was busy with his Roanoke colony? When was this?

REVIEW QUESTIONS.—DISCOVERY AND EXPLORATION.

1. State what ideas the Europeans had of the extent of the world previous to the discovery of America.

2. What was the state of the public mind in Europe during the latter half of the 15th century?

3. What can you state about the India trade of those early times?

4. What great idea prompted the discovery of America?

5. Give an account of the struggles of Columbus for assistance.

6. What great events were occurring in Spain while Columbus was soliciting aid?

7. State the connection of Ferdinand and Isabella with the voyages of Columbus.

8. How many voyages did he make, and when?

9. Sketch the painful events that marked the close of his life.

10. Why was America not named after Columbus?

11. Who first touched the American continent? Give an account of his expedition and that of his son?

12. What claim was founded on these voyages?

13. Where, during the first few years after the discovery, did the Spaniards plant colonies?

14. What cruelties marked the early Spanish settlements?

15. What leading expeditions were undertaken by the Spaniards from 1498 to 1545?

16. Which of these belong to the history of the United States?

17. What was the most striking point of De Soto's expedition?

18. What were the notions of the Spaniards as to the extent and value of Florida?

19. How many attempts were made by the Spaniards to explore or settle it?

20. Were any attempts made by any other people: if so, when, by whom, and with what result?

21. What part of the coast besides Florida did the French attempt to settle?

22. What names are connected with the discovery and exploration of the St. Lawrence?

23. Where and what was Acadia? to whom granted, and when?

24. What did these early French and English explorers hope to find?

25. Why were they forced to search for this north of Florida?

26. What names can you give connected with these attempts?

27. What Englishman first explored San Francisco Bay?

28. With what hope did he enter it, and when did he do so?

29. Where and in what years were the principal efforts at settlement by the English previous to the year 1600? Give the story of Sir Humphrey Gilbert.

30. What great Englishman was connected with these attempts?

31. Give a brief sketch of the attempts at Roanoke. What was the original extent of Virginia?

32. With what rulers, and with what great event in European history are these efforts associated?

33. Give the dates of the following: 1, the settlement of St. Augustine; 2, of Santa Fé; 3, the attempts on the St. Lawrence.

34. What bloody event is connected with the settlement of St. Augustine?

35. What can you state regarding Henry Hudson?

36. Who is supposed to have entered New York Bay before him, and how many years?

37. Which is the oldest colony in the United States? Give the date.

38. What division was made of Virginia in 1606?

39. What immediate use was made of these grants?

40. Where is Jamestown? Why so called?

41. How many and what European nations were connected with the North American continent previous to the year 1610?

42. How did their claims interfere with each other?

43. Give an account of the attempts to find a western passage.

CHAPTER II.

SETTLEMENT AND PROGRESS OF THE ENGLISH COLONIES FROM THE YEAR 1607 TO THE BEGINNING OF THE WAR OF THE REVOLUTION.

SECTION I.

VIRGINIA AND MARYLAND.

VIRGINIA.

ARRIVAL AT JAMESTOWN, 1607.

1. THE colonists that settled at Jamestown were for the most part poorly fitted to make a living in a new country. Forty-eight of them were broken-down gentlemen, who despised work, and of the remainder only twelve were laborers, and seven or eight were mechanics. The leading men were Newport, the commander; Wingfield, a London merchant; Gosnold, the discoverer of Cape Cod; and John Smith, a man still under thirty years of age, but who had passed a life of wonderful adventure in the Old World.

1. What was the character of the men who settled Jamestown? Describe them. Who were the leading men? What is said of each?

2. The voyage had been long and wearisome, and this led to discontent, which was increased by jealousy among the chief men. Unfortunately, the names of the council for the colony were unknown; and had been put, by the king's order, into a sealed box, not to be opened until the settlers landed. Smith was charged by Wingfield with the design of seizing the government, and was placed under arrest during the remainder of the voyage.

3. When they arrived in Virginia the box was opened, and the leading men already mentioned, together with Radcliffe, Martin, and Kendal, were found named as the seven councilors. Wingfield was chosen president. Smith, not allowed to take his seat, was soon after brought to trial and acquitted. The jury gave him heavy damages against Wingfield, and he was permitted to take his place in the Council.

4. In the month of June, Newport returned to England. He had scarcely sailed when the settlers began to sicken from want of proper food, from exposure, and from the diseases common to settlers in a new country. By the month of September, fifty had died; among these was Gosnold. To add to their distress, Wingfield was found to be living on the best of the stores while others were starving. For this, and for attempting to desert the colony in a small vessel, he was deprived of the presidency; and he and Kendal, his accomplice, were expelled from the Council.

5. There were but three members left, Smith, Radcliffe, and Martin. Radcliffe was made president; but he was a weak man, and the power fell into the strong hand of Smith. He cheered the spirits of the colonists, and, to keep them busy, persuaded them to erect a fort and to build log huts for the winter. From the Indians he obtained, partly by threats, partly by kind words, supplies of Indian corn; and as winter approached, there came plenty of game. Thus all fear of famine was removed. Smith then proceeded, Decem-

---

2. What is said of the voyage and its effects? What unfortunate thing increased this jealousy? With what was Smith charged? How was he treated?

3. When the box was opened, who were found named of the Council? Who was made president? What is said of Smith's trial and the verdict?

4. What occurred soon after Newport returned to England? How soon was this? How many died? What leading man was among this number? How was this disaster increased? What measure became necessary, and why?

CAPTAIN JOHN SMITH.

ber, 1607, to explore the River Chickahominy, which enters the James River above Jamestown, hoping that this might prove a passage to the South Sea. For this the colonists had been particularly ordered to search.

6. On the expedition he was captured by the Indians, and, after being carried round from one Indian village to another, was condemned to die. As he lay bound, with his head on a stone, awaiting the fatal blow from the Indian club, Po-ca-hon-tas, a young girl ten or twelve years old, the favorite daughter of the chief Powhatan (*pow-hah-tan'*), rushed forward, and, clasping Smith's head in her arms, implored his life. Her prayer was granted, and in a short time he was sent back in honor to Jamestown, after a captivity of seven weeks.

7. When he arrived there he found the settlers in a miserable condition, and wholly disheartened. They were reduced in number to forty persons, some of whom were preparing to escape in the company's bark. Smith persuaded or compelled them to remain; and, by his influence with the Indians, with whom he was now in favor, obtained abundance of provisions.

8. Soon after, Newport arrived from England, bringing supplies and 120 colonists. These were no better fitted for the new country than the first. They were chiefly vagabond gentlemen unused to labor, and a few goldsmiths sent out to seek for mines. Not long after their arrival they found some glittering mica, which they mistook for gold dust; and

5. Who were left in the council? What is said of Radcliffe? How did Smith show his greatness of character? How did they secure their supplies for the winter? How did Smith then busy himself? Where is the Chickahominy?

6. What misfortune befell Smith? Give an account of what followed. How was this prayer regarded? How was he treated after this?

7. How did he find things on his return to the colony? What were they about to do? What was Smith's conduct? In what way did Smith's captivity among the Indians prove a benefit?

one of Newport's ships was sent back laden with this to England.

9. Smith left them to their folly, digging and washing the useless earth, and spent his time exploring the country. In an open boat he examined the shores of the chief rivers that flow into the Chesapeake, sailed more than three thousand miles, and made the first map of the great bay. On his return to Jamestown, in September, he was made President of the Council.

10. The same month Newport brought from England an addition of seventy settlers, and a very angry letter from the Company, who were dissatisfied with the returns they had obtained from the colony. Smith wrote to them that "it were better to send out thirty working men than a thousand like the present colonists." Of so little service had these proved, that Jamestown, at the end of two years from its settlement, was still a mere village, with very little cultivated land around it.

11. A new charter was given to the London Company in 1609. The council resident in the colony was abolished, and Lord De la War, known as Delaware, was appointed governor for life. The Company went to work with new vigor, hoping for better returns; and sent out a fleet of nine ships, with five hundred colonists, under command of Newport. Lord Delaware was not able to go with the expedition; but Newport, Sir Thomas Gates, and Sir George Somers were appointed commissioners to govern the colony until his arrival. Unluckily, these three embarked on the same vessel. A severe storm dispersed the fleet, and drove the vessel in which they sailed on the Bermudas, where they were compelled to remain all winter.

---

8. Who arrived about this time? Describe the new settlers. Into what folly did their ignorance lead them?

9. How did Smith look upon all this? How did he spend his time? What is said of his explorations? What took place on his return?

10. What month did Newport come with fresh settlers? What else did he bring? How did Smith reply to this? What is said of Jamestown at the end of two years?

11. What important event took place in 1609? What changes were made? Did this charter have any effect on the spirits and efforts of the Company? What arrangement was made about the government of the colony? What happened to the vessels of the expedition? Were the commissioners in different ships? What became of the vessel in which they were?

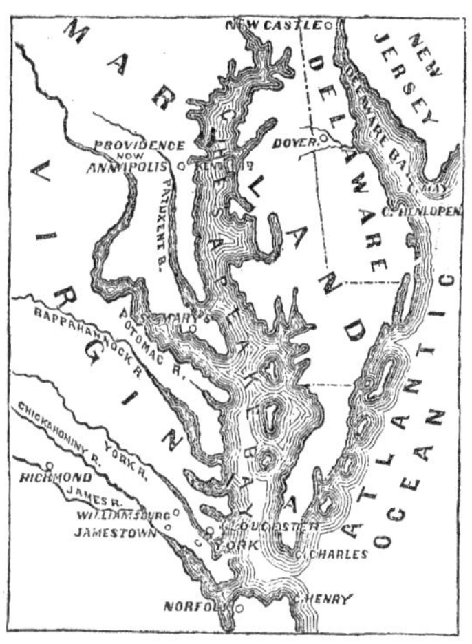

EARLY SETTLEMENTS IN VIRGINIA AND MARYLAND.

12. The other ships, save one which was lost, arrived at Jamestown with their passengers. The most of these were indolent and vicious, fitter "to breed a riot than found a colony." Smith at first had great trouble in dealing with them, because they claimed that under the new charter he was no longer president; but he maintained his authority in the absence of the commissioners, and firmly repressed all disorder. In October he was badly wounded by an accidental explosion of gunpowder, and was compelled to go to England for surgical aid.

13. After his departure the colonists became riotous and idle. They wastefully consumed the provisions, and ill-treated the Indians, who, in revenge, killed several small parties out foraging. Vice, famine, sickness, and the hostility of the natives made so great a havoc among them, that out of five hundred persons in the colony when Smith sailed, there were, in six months, only sixty left. This dreary and terrible winter of 1609–10 was long known in Virginia as "the starving time." Fortunately, Newport, Gates, and Somers arrived from the Bermudas in May, 1610, just in time to save these sixty from starvation.

14. The new comers brought with them only about sixteen days' provisions, expecting to find abundance in the colony. They found only starving men and a ruined settle-

---

12. What became of the remainder of the vessels? What is said of the passengers in them? What success did Smith have in dealing with these men? What occurred in October, 1609?

13. How did this affect the settlers? Describe their bad conduct. What was the consequence of all this? When did this take place, and what was it called? What fortunate arrival saved the remnant of the colony?

ment. As it appeared useless to remain at Jamestown, they all determined to sail for Newfoundland, and obtain help from the fishing vessels there. While they were descending the James River, June, 1610, they met Lord Delaware, who had just arrived from England with three ships containing provisions and settlers. He persuaded them to return with him to Jamestown, where he at once began to arrange the affairs of the colony. While engaged in this he was taken sick, and shortly returned to England.

15. Lord Delaware left about two hundred settlers in the colony. In May, 1611, three ships came out with three hundred colonists. In September of the same year, Sir Thomas Gates, deputy governor, brought out six ships and three hundred and fifty men. What was still needed to place the colony on a firm foundation was families.

16. Gates made a wise regulation that proved of great advantage. Hitherto all the land had been worked in common, and the proceeds put into the public store. Gates ordered that three acres should be set apart to each man to cultivate for his own use. This put new life and energy into the poorer settlers, by giving every man the fruit of his own labor.

17. The London Company had spent a large amount of money on their colony, and had received little or no return. In London the settlement of Virginia was publicly sneered at as a failure, and the stockholders threw the blame on the council in England. To quiet this outcry, the charter was altered in 1612. The governing council residing in London was abolished, and every stockholder was allowed a voice in the weekly meetings of the Company. No change was made in the office of governor, which was held by Lord Delaware, still in England on account of ill health.

---

14. What amount of supplies were brought? By what were they met? What course was determined on? What happened before they had gone out of the river? What did Lord Delaware persuade them to do? How was this interrupted?

15. How many settlers did Lord Delaware leave in the colony? How many arrived in May and September? Who came with the September party?

16. How was the land cultivated previous to the arrival of Gates? What wise regulation did he make? How did this affect the energies of the colonists?

17. What had been the success of the London Company so far? How was Virginia regarded on this account? On whom was the blame thrown? When was the charter altered, and why? What alterations were made? Who still remained governor? Where was he at the time?

18. During the same year, Pocahontas was enticed on board of a vessel by one Captain Argall, and taken to Jamestown. Powhatan demanded his daughter; but the colonists refused to give her back, claiming that the Indians had enticed away the servants of the settlers and stolen some fire-arms. Powhatan was greatly enraged, and vowed revenge, which was fortunately appeased by the marriage of Pocahontas with one of the settlers, in April, 1613. John Rolfe, a young man of good family, asked her in marriage, and Powhatan consented. In the year 1616 Rolfe took his young bride on a visit to England, where she died. She left a son, from whom some of the leading families of Virginia have been proud to trace their descent.

MARRIAGE OF POCAHONTAS.

19. The marriage had a very happy effect on the Indians, and, while Powhatan lived, the good understanding was kept up between them and the colonists. It is worthy of notice that Rolfe's example was not followed. The In-

18. What happened to Pocahontas in 1612? What did her father do? How did the colonists justify their conduct? How did Powhatan receive this? How was a war with the Indians prevented? State what is said of her marriage. What afterward happened to Pocahontas? What is said of her son?

dians were desirous of intermarriage, but the English detested it.

20. During the year 1613, Captain Argall sailed from Virginia to look after the English fisheries at Newfoundland. On Mount Desert Island he found a few Frenchmen, and at once broke up their settlement. Sailing again in a few months, he burned the houses at Port Royal abandoned by the French, who fled to the woods. On his way home he entered New York Harbor, and compelled the Dutch traders on Manhattan Island to hoist the English flag. All these places were claimed to be within the limits of English authority. Argall's successes, however, were only temporary. The French, immediately after his departure, returned to Port Royal, and the Hollanders again hoisted the Dutch flag on Manhattan Island.

21. The cultivation of tobacco, as a staple, was begun in Virginia as early as the year 1615, and spread so rapidly

CULTIVATION OF TOBACCO AT JAMESTOWN, 1615.

---

19. What was the effect of this marriage on the Indians? Was Rolfe's example followed? How was intermarriage looked on by the English and Indians?

20. Who sailed from Virginia in 1613, and for what purpose? What did he do at Mount Desert Island and Port Royal? What happened on his second voyage? Why had Argall dared to act as he did? Was his conduct of any lasting benefit to the English? State what occurred after his departure from Port Royal and Manhattan Island.

that, in a short time, "the fields, the gardens, and even the streets of Jamestown" were planted with tobacco. It readily brought, in 1620, three quarters of a dollar per pound; but the price fell as low as two or three pence per pound in after years. So eagerly did the colonists plant, that they neglected to raise corn, and suffered not a little in consequence.

22. Meanwhile Virginia was ruled by deputy governors, for Lord Delaware was still sick in England. In 1617 the complaints against Argall's conduct as deputy became so serious that the Company besought Delaware to go out to Virginia. He accordingly set sail, but died on the passage at the mouth of the bay, which, from that time, has borne his name.

23. Yeardley was appointed governor, and, on his arrival, found the settlers arranged in "seven plantations." This number he increased to eleven. He then, in 1619, called together an assembly, composed mainly of two representatives from each of these plantations or boroughs. This assembly was called the House of Burgesses, from the word borough, and was the first Colonial Assembly that met in Virginia.

24. In the same year ninety young women of good character were induced to emigrate to Virginia and become wives to the settlers. Previous to this there were but few women in the colony. The price of a wife was fixed at the cost of the passage—one hundred lbs. of tobacco, worth at that time about $75 of our currency. In the year 1621, sixty more were sent out, and the price was raised to 150 lbs. of tobacco.

25. In August of the preceding year, 1620, twenty negroes were brought by a Dutch vessel to the James River and sold as slaves. This was the beginning of negro slavery in the colonies, but it did not extend rapidly for forty years.

21. When was the cultivation of tobacco begun in Virginia? What is a "staple?" How did the cultivation spread? What prices did it bring? What mistake did the colonists fall into in their anxiety to make money on tobacco?

22. How was Virginia ruled at this time? Why was this? What was done in consequence of Argall's conduct? What is further said of Lord Delaware?

23. Who was made governor? How did he find the settlers arranged? What important steps did he take? Of whom was the Assembly composed? What was this called?

24. What important addition was made to the colony this year? What was the price of a wife? When did others arrive? To what was the price raised?

In 1621, the year following, a few cotton seeds were planted as an experiment. The plants throve, yet their farther cultivation was neglected for many years.

26. As the colony increased in numbers, the people began to obtain more liberty. Martial law was abolished, and trial by jury took its place. A constitution, defining their rights, was granted to the colony in the year 1621. To the House of Burgesses, under the name of the "General Assembly of Virginia," was given the power of making the laws. But these could not be put in force until they had been signed by the governor, and had received the approval of the Company in England.

27. The settlements, in the year 1622, had spread to a considerable distance around Jamestown, and every thing began to bear the marks of prosperity. The settlers, grown over-confident in themselves, had learned to despise the wily Indians, who were only waiting an opportunity to wreak their revenge. Powhatan, the friend of the colony, had died in 1618, and Opecancánough, his brother, a bold and cunning man, who hated the English, was now chief.

28. At the same hour of the day, March 22, 1622, the savages fell suddenly on the plantations at a distance from Jamestown, and killed three hundred and forty-seven persons. Jamestown and a few plantations near it were saved by a converted Indian, who gave warning to the settlers the night before the massacre. A bloody war followed, and, at the end of a year, the number of colonists had fallen from 4000 to 2500. The Indians suffered so severely that they remained quiet till 1644. Then came a massacre of five hundred settlers, and war ending in the expulsion of the natives from their lands near the York and James Rivers.

---

25. When did negro slavery begin in the colonies? How did it begin? Did it extend rapidly? What experiment was made in 1621, and with what success?

26. What was the effect of the increase of numbers on the colony? What two great rights were granted the settlers? What new name and powers were given to the House of Burgesses? What was necessary before laws could be put in force?

27. What is said of the settlements at this time? How did the settlers feel about the Indians? Who was now chief of the Powhatans?

28. What was the sad result of their carelessness about the Indians? How was Jamestown and the plantations near it saved? How did the whites act? What was the effect of the war on the colonists and on the Indians? What occurred in 1644? How did the war end?

INDIAN MASSACRE, 1622.

29. The disasters of the colony produced much contention in the meetings of the stockholders in London, and a part of them appealed to the king to examine the affairs of the company. This was what King James wanted. He had been long jealous of it, on account of the patriotic sentiments uttered at its meetings. Examiners were appointed, and their report was as unfavorable to the company as the king could have desired. He thereupon dissolved it in 1624, and declared its charter forfeited to the crown. Thus ended the London Company, after an existence of eighteen years, during which it had spent $700,000 in trying to settle Virginia. For this, a great sum of money in those days, the stockholders had received no pecuniary return.

30. The king, during the brief remainder of his life, did

29. How was the news of these disasters received in England? What did a part of the Company do? Why was this particularly pleasing to King James? What was at once done by the king, and with what result? How long had the London Company existed? How much money had been expended? What is said of the stockholders?

not disturb the colony by any serious changes. His son, Charles I., who succeeded him in 1625, also left the Virginians to manage their own affairs, because he had enough to do in England in trying to crush the patriots who were struggling in and out of Parliament for popular freedom.

31. Civil war broke out between the king and his Parliament in the year 1642, and lasted for seven years. In 1649 the Parliament triumphed, and King Charles was tried and beheaded. During the struggle, Virginia remained loyal to the king; yet, after the restoration of Charles II. to the throne, the colony received a poor return for its loyalty.

32. A Navigation Act was passed in 1660, excluding all foreign vessels from the colonies. This was felt to be so great a grievance in Virginia, that Governor Berkeley (*berk'-ly*) was sent to England in 1662; and 200,000 lbs. of tobacco were appropriated to meet his expenses. Instead of relieving the colonists, the English government, in 1663, passed a still more oppressive act, compelling them to ship their staples to England alone, and forcing them to buy all their European goods there also. This carrying trade was to be done only by English vessels.

33. The colonists were at the same time far from being at peace among themselves. Two parties had sprung up, the aristocratic party, composed chiefly of rich planters and office-holders, and, opposed to this, the party of the people. Berkeley, the governor, belonged to the aristocratic party; and we may learn what its spirit was from what he said in 1671: "I thank God there are no free-schools nor printing-presses here, and I hope we shall not have them these hundred years. God keep us from both."

34. The people began to groan under burdensome taxes

---

30. Did James meddle any farther with the colony? Who succeeded him on the throne? How did he treat the colonists?

31. What took place in the year 1642 in England? How long did the war last? Who triumphed at last? What side did Virginia take? How were they treated for their loyalty?

32. What oppressive act was passed? State the object of this act. How was this received in Virginia? What was done by the colonists? Did the English government relieve them? What did this new act compel them to do?

33. In what condition were the colonists themselves? Describe these two parties. Which side did Berkeley take? What remark of his is given showing the spirit of the man?

raised to pay heavy salaries to office-holders, and to complain that they had no voice in regulating the taxes or their local affairs. The troubles came to a crisis when an Indian war broke out on the frontiers of Virginia in 1675. A large body of the settlers thought that Berkeley and his party did not provide sufficiently for their protection, and they charged the governor with a leaning toward the natives. The colonists at once rallied round a young man, Nathaniel Bacon, as their leader, who, without a commission from the governor, promptly marched at the head of 500 men against the Indians, April, 1676.

35. Berkeley, who was a courageous but wrong-headed man, for this proclaimed him a rebel, and determined to punish him. Bacon had the bulk of the people on his side; and, in the struggle that followed, the governor and his party were expelled from Jamestown, and the village itself was burned. While at the height of his success, the young

RUINS OF JAMESTOWN, 1676.

34. What pressed heavily on the people? Of what did they particularly complain? How did their troubles reach a crisis? Give the date of the war. How did a large body of the settlers feel toward Berkeley? What charge was brought against him? Whom did they choose for a leader? How did Bacon show his spirit?

leader of the people suddenly died. This left his adherents without a head. The armed force gradually retired to their homes, and the rebellion, as it was called by the aristocratic party, ended October, 1676.

36. Governor Berkeley returned to power, and made a terrible use of it. He hanged twenty-three persons, and could scarcely be persuaded to stop here. A great many were fined, imprisoned, or banished. So cruel was his conduct, that when King Charles II. heard of it he said, "The old fool has hanged more men in that naked country than I did in England for the murder of my father."

37. In 1673, three years before the rebellion, King Charles granted the entire colony of Virginia for thirty-one years to Lords Culpepper and Arlington, two profligate noblemen. After the death of Governor Berkeley in England, Culpepper, who had obtained Arlington's share of the grant, was appointed in 1677 governor for life. He came out in 1680, and governed with such tyranny and rapacity that he was deprived of his office in 1684. He then surrendered his patent to the crown, and Virginia once more became a royal province. Its further history, until the year 1754, presents little to attract our notice. When, in that year, war broke out between the French and English colonies, Virginia, as will be seen hereafter, at once assumed a position of the first importance.

MARYLAND.

1. GEORGE CALVERT, an English nobleman by the title of Lord Baltimore, was a member of the original London Company. In religion he was a Catholic, and was anxious to secure a refuge in America for those of his own persuasion at

---

35. What step did Berkeley take against Bacon? How were the people divided? Which party was defeated? What event occurred that put an end to the contest? Give the date of this?

36. What use did Berkeley make of his restored power? What did the king say when he heard of these cruel acts?

37. To whom and when had King Charles assigned the colony? For how long? When did Berkeley die? Who was appointed governor for life? When did Culpepper come out to Virginia? What kind of a governor did he make? What did Virginia now become, and why? What is stated with regard to its further history?

that time persecuted in England. He first attempted to plant a colony in Newfoundland, but the severe climate and the barren soil soon brought it to an end. He then turned his attention to Virginia, which he himself visited in the year 1628. The feeling at that time in the Jamestown colony was very bitter against the Catholics, and he soon returned to England.

2. After his return, he obtained, in 1632, from Charles I., a grant of land lying north of the Potomac; and in honor of the queen Henrietta Maria, he called the country Maryland. Lord Baltimore died before the patent received the king's seal, and it was finally made out in the name of his son, Cecil Calvert, second Lord Baltimore.

3. By this patent he was made proprietor, with full power to frame laws with the consent of the people. It was the first colonial charter that secured to freemen in America a voice in the making of the laws. It also made no distinction in favor of any Christian sect, a provision greatly in advance of the general opinions of the age.

4. The Virginia colony remonstrated against this grant to Lord Baltimore, because Maryland was within the limits of Virginia as granted to the London Company. William Clayborne, a member of the council at Jamestown, especially refused to recognize Lord Baltimore's right. As early as 1632 he had established, under royal license, two trading posts, one on the isle of Kent, in the Chesapeake, the other at the mouth of the Susquehanna. Both of these were within the limits of the Maryland grant.

5. A company of Catholic gentlemen, led by Leonard Calvert, brother of Lord Baltimore, sailed from England in November, 1633, in two vessels, the Ark and the Dove. In February, 1634, Calvert arrived in the Chesapeake, and on

---

1. Who was George Calvert? Why was he anxious to form a settlement in America? Where was his first attempt made? With what result? Where did he then go? In what year was this? Why did he soon return to England?

2. What did he get from the king? When was this? How was it named, and why? In whose name was the patent made out? Why was this?

3. What power was given by this patent? What privilege was it the first colonial charter to secure? What remarkable provision was there in it about religion?

4. How did the Virginia colony look on this grant to Lord Baltimore? Why was this? Who especially objected to the grant? On what grounds did he object?

the 27th of March settled on the site of an Indian village, which he named St. Mary's.

6. Clayborne soon began to quarrel with the colonists, and fitted out a small vessel to annoy them. After a sharp skirmish, in which Clayborne was beaten, he escaped to Virginia. The governor of that colony sent him to England for trial, and his settlement at the isle of Kent was seized by the Marylanders. In 1644 Clayborne returned to Maryland, raised a rebellion, and compelled Governor Calvert to flee to Virginia. In 1646 the governor came back with a body of troops, and Clayborne fled.

7. In order to confirm the right of religious freedom as granted in the charter, the Assembly, in April, 1649, passed the "Toleration Act," securing to all Christians the right to worship God according to their own consciences. Maryland thus became an asylum for all persecuted sects of Christians, a large number of whom came from Virginia. It is not pleasant to know that some of those very men, who had come to Maryland to enjoy this freedom, afterward united to deprive those who had passed the "Toleration Act" of the rights guaranteed by that statute.

8. After the Parliament triumphed over King Charles, they sent out commissioners in 1652 to look after "the plantations within Chesapeake Bay." One of these officers was Clayborne, the old enemy of Maryland. Proceeding partly on his advice, they compelled Stone, who was acting governor, to resign. The Protestant party took sides with the Commissioners, and a decisive battle was fought, March, 1655, in which Stone was taken prisoner, with several of his chief officers. Some of the latter were hanged.

9. During the three years that followed it was difficult to

---

5. Who sailed from England in 1633? When and where did they arrive? Where and when did they settle?

6. What did Clayborne do? What happened to him in Maryland? What became of him when he fled to Virginia, and of his settlement? When did Clayborne return, and what happened to him? How long did this state of things continue?

7. What act was passed by the Assembly, and when? What was its nature? Why was it so celebrated? What did Maryland thus become? In what way did many of these new settlers show their want of toleration?

8. What was done to Maryland by Parliament after it triumphed over the king? Who was one of these officers? What did they proceed to do by his advice? Which party took sides with the Commissioners? What followed?

tell which party was uppermost. There were two governments, one Protestant, the other Catholic; and there was great confusion. In 1658 these disputes were settled, and in 1660 Lord Baltimore was restored by the king to all his rights as proprietor. Philip Calvert was appointed governor. The second Lord Baltimore died in 1675, and was succeeded by his son Charles, third Lord Baltimore. In the year 1691 King William III. deprived him of the right of government in Maryland, and it was made a royal province.

10. Sir Lionel Copley arrived in 1692 as royal governor. Very soon after, the Assembly established the Church of England; and the Catholics soon found themselves disfranchised in the colony they had established. Under Copley, the capital was changed from St. Mary's to Annapolis. For twenty-four years Maryland remained under royal governors. In 1715, the fourth Lord Baltimore was restored to his proprietary rights. These passed by his death the same year to his infant son, fifth Lord Baltimore, in whom they remained undisturbed until the Revolution.

GENERAL REFLECTIONS ON VIRGINIA AND MARYLAND.

1. **Character of the Settlers.**—The early troubles of Virginia arose chiefly from the kind of men that came from England during the first year. They were a worthless class, who despised labor, and meant to live without it. They came with no idea of remaining for life, but only to make their fortunes and then go back to England. They brought neither wives nor families with them, and, without homes, there was nothing to attach them to the settlement. It was for twelve years a colony of men chiefly, with all the vices

---

9. In the years that followed, what was the condition of the colony? When were matters brought to a settlement, and how? How long did the right of government remain at this time in the Baltimore family? What change took place?

10. Who was sent as governor? What did the Assembly do? In what condition did the Catholics ere long find themselves? What is "disfranchised?" Who changed the name of the capital? How long did the colony remain under royal governors? When was Lord Baltimore restored to his original rights? How long did this last? How many Lord Baltimores are mentioned in the history of Maryland?

of such a state. When ninety young women were sent over in the year 1619, and became wives of the settlers, then the permanence of the colony was secured. The settlement of Maryland began long after Virginia had passed through its early trials, and without suffering, with no fear of want, the foundation was peacefully and happily laid.

2. **Their Treatment of the Indians.**—In the treatment of the Indians by the Virginia settlers we see one of the causes of their troubles, and the origin of the dreadful Indian massacres of 1622 and 1644. The natives, it is true, were jealous of the whites, but there was something very brutal in the way the English treated them, as savages who had few or no rights, whose rich lands were to be seized, and, when they resisted, were to be blotted out of existence.

3. Smith, the most active and useful man that came to Virginia, found it difficult to restrain the settlers from acts of cruelty to the Indians. While he remained in the colony they were kept on good terms with the whites. One great cause of Governor Berkeley's unpopularity, as late as the year 1675, at the beginning of Bacon's rebellion, was that he was supposed to have a kindly leaning toward "the doomed Indian."

4. **Industry and Progress.**—Tobacco, for many years the great staple of Virginia, and also its currency, was the first product which brought prosperity and trade to the settlements. The plant needed a rich soil, and wherever this was found, there the colonists grouped themselves near one another for mutual defense, and called the assemblage of farms a plantation. The settlers were thus scattered over a considerable area, making a widely extended agricultural colony.

---

1. What caused the early trials of the Virginian colonists? What was their character? What was their object in going to Virginia? Why had they little to attach them to the colony? What remedied this, and gave stability to the settlement? What is said of the early settlement of Maryland as compared with Virginia?

2. To what cause are the Indian massacres of 1622 and 1644 to be attributed? What is said of the treatment of the Indians by the English settlers?

3. How was the character of Smith distinguished from the others? How is the Virginian hatred of the Indians shown by an incident in the later history of the colony?

4. What was the great staple of the colony? How did its culture affect the mode of life of the settlers? What sort of a colony did it in this way become?

5. The coast of Virginia is deeply indented by large rivers that cut the country into narrow peninsulas, or necks, and which furnished a convenient route by which the planters could get their tobacco and other produce to market. The vessels came up these convenient waters almost to the very doors of the Virginians, and took from them what each desired to send to a distance, bringing back in exchange what articles were wanted. There was no need of any large towns, and they built none. Jamestown, when it was burnt in 1676, had, besides the church and State-house, only some sixteen or eighteen substantial houses.

6. In 1649, forty-two years after the settlement and five years after the Indian massacre of 1644, there were 15,000 Englishmen in the Virginia colony, and 300 negroes. There were several hundred acres of wheat under cultivation, and many fields of tobacco. There were thirty ships trading regularly to the colony. They exported not only tobacco, but also staves, lumber, and heavy timber. Maryland in 1660 had a population of about 10,000.

7. **Religion and Education.**—The established religion of Virginia, which was that of the Church of England, was well provided for. In 1649 there were twenty good churches, the ministers of which each received a salary of £100 a year. Public education was not thought worthy of any great care. We have already seen how Governor Berkeley regarded public schools, and printed books in the hands of the people. The College of William and Mary was chartered in 1691, and established at Williamsburg, the new capital, in 1692.

8. In Maryland at first there was, as we have seen, no established religion. Before the law, all Christian sects believing in the Trinity were equal. This lasted, with some interruptions, until the year 1692, when, in the reign of King William III., Copley being royal governor, the Episcopal

---

5. What is said of the coast of Virginia? Of what advantage did this prove? Describe this in full. How did this peculiarity of surface affect the building of towns? Give an instance.

6. What was the population of the colony in 1649? What is said of the state of agriculture? Of the commerce and exports? What are exports?

7. What was the established religion? Show what provision was made for its support. To what extent was public education cared for? Do you remember what Governor Berkeley said about this?

Church was established by law. In the year 1713, seventy-eight years after its settlement, Maryland adopted a school system, the most liberal, in its provisions, of any colony except those of New England.

9. **Growth of Political Liberty.**—The political history of the colony of Virginia divides itself naturally into two parts—the first, under the London Company, from 1607 until 1624, a period of seventeen years; the second, under a royal government, from 1624 until the Revolution, broken by a short interval of eleven years under Culpepper. The first period under the London Company is by far the most important, short as was the time; because during these seventeen years the colony was planted, the habits of the people were formed, and the foundation of their future liberty was laid.

10. The Virginians were fortunate in this, that in the early years of their settlement—that is, under the London Company—the party of liberty in England had begun their great struggle with James I. for political rights, which ended forty years after in the beheading of his son Charles I. The majority of the stockholders of the London Company were of this party, and they granted to the colonists those rights for which they themselves were struggling in England.

11. From this we see the great work which the London Company did for Virginia, although the stockholders sunk all the money they had invested in it. The colony never lost the good effects of the efforts of their English friends; for amid all the changes of charters and governors until the time of the careless Charles II., the liberties of the colonists were in the hands of all freemen without exception. It was the same in Maryland.

---

8. What was the established religion in the early settlement of Maryland? How were all Christian sects treated? By what sect was it settled? How long did this religious freedom last? What is said of public schools in Maryland?

9. Into what parts is the political history of the colony divided? Which of these is by far the most important, and why? How long did it last?

10. What circumstance was very favorable to early Virginia liberty? How did this circumstance affect Virginia?

11. What do we gather from this? State what is said of these efforts of the English stockholders. Do you remember how much money the London Company expended on Virginia?

12. Then came a period of oppression. The Navigation Act was a deadly blow at the welfare of the colonists; but this did not crush out their free spirit. That which is called Bacon's Rebellion was really a struggle commenced by the people, under Bacon, against the aristocratic party in the Colonial Assembly for rights denied them. The chief of these rights was the right to vote how much money should be spent, and who should spend it.

13. The Navigation Act and other oppressive measures brought good with them. They weaned the settlers from their love and attachment to England, and prepared the way for those feelings that burst out in the American Revolution. The seed of liberty was thoroughly planted in Virginia, and also in Maryland; and neither foes from without nor Royalists from within were able to prevent its growth into a goodly tree.

REVIEW QUESTIONS.

1. What were the limits of South Virginia in 1607?
2. When and under whose auspices was the colony of Jamestown settled?
3. What class of persons came over during the first year or two?
4. How many periods of disaster befell the colony during the first four years?
5. Who saved it repeatedly from ruin?
6. Give a sketch of Smith's services to Virginia.
7. How was the loss of his remarkable energy felt at Jamestown?
8. Who was Pocahontas, and what influence did she have on the fortunes of the colony?
9. What important addition of immigrants in 1619 first gave stability to the colony?
10. Can you tell why this produced such a result?
11. When was the cultivation of tobacco begun, and what effect did its cultivation produce on the settlement of the country?
12. When and where did negro slavery commence in the United States?
13. What plant was first raised as an experiment about this time?
14. How rapidly did its cultivation spread?
15. How many charters did the London Company receive?
16. State in what these charters differed.
17. What great misfortune befell the colony in 1622?
18. To what important change did this lead, and how?
19. How long did the London Company rule Virginia?
20. What was its success as a company?
21. What nobleman was intimately connected with the settlement of Virginia?
22. To what was his name given, and for what reason?
23. Under what charter was this?

---

12. What act shows the oppression of King Charles II.? From what do we see the spirit of the people? What was the great right for which the colonists struggled?

13. What were the good effects of the Navigation Act and the other oppressive measures?

24. What prevented the King of England from meddling much with Virginia after the London Company ceased?
25. What side did the Virginians take in the quarrel between the king and his Parliament?
26. How were they rewarded for this?
27. Describe the main features of the Navigation Act.
28. What two parties arose in Virginia?
29. What were the complaints of the people?
30. Who was governor at the time?
31. By what can we judge of the opinions of the aristocratic party?
32. What brought the quarrel between parties to a crisis?
33. Give an account of Bacon's rebellion.
34. How did Governor Berkeley act when he returned to power?
35. To whom was Virginia granted in 1673, and for how long a time?
36. Give a sketch of the government.
37. What led the colonists to settle in groups called "plantations?"
38. To what was it owing that there were no large towns in the colony?
39. What was the size of Jamestown just before it was burned?
40. How long had it then been in existence?
41. Give an account of the size and enterprise of the colony in 1649.
42. What was the most important period in the colonial history of Virginia?
43. Why was this? State this fully.
44. Sketch the effect of this training in what is called Bacon's rebellion.
45. What influence was produced by the Navigation Act on the spirit of the people?
46. Under how many kinds of government was Virginia from 1607 to 1776?
47. What led to the settlement of Maryland?
48. To whom was the grant made?
49. Give a sketch of the connection of the first Lord Baltimore with America.
50. What was remarkable in his patent?
51. How was this grant regarded by Virginia?
52. Under whom and where was Maryland first settled? Give date.
53. Who gave the first settlers of Maryland a great deal of trouble?
54. Describe the celebrated act passed by the Assembly in 1649.
55. In what way did the termination of the civil war in England affect the Marylanders?
56. How were these troubles arranged?
57. How was the arrangement disturbed?
58. In what way did the Catholics suffer by the change?
59. Under what form of government was the Maryland colony during the most of its existence?
60. When did the Baltimore connection with Maryland end?
61. State briefly the different circumstances under which the colonies of Virginia and Maryland were settled.
62. Give the principal events in the history of Virginia, with dates.

SECTION II.

NEW ENGLAND COLONIES.

Massachusetts.

EXPLORATION OF PLYMOUTH BAY, 1620.

1. By King James's charter of 1606 North Virginia was given to the Plymouth Company. In August, 1607, they sent out two ships, with forty-five colonists, under Raleigh Gilbert, younger son of Sir Humphrey Gilbert, as admiral, and George Popham as president of the council. Gilbert landed on a small island at the mouth of the Kennebec, and there built a rude fort. The winter was long and severe; the president died; and the colonists were so disheartened that they all returned to England in the spring.

2. For some years after this, the coast of North Virginia was only visited by vessels on private trading and fishing voyages. In one of these, Captain John Smith, celebrated in

1. What was the first attempt made by the Plymouth Company to settle North Virginia? Where did Gilbert land? What is the further history of the colony?

South Virginia history, commanded two vessels that lay near the Penobscot River in the year 1614. Leaving the ships, in a boat with eight men he explored the shore from the Penobscot to Cape Cod, drew a map of it, and named the country New England. In the year 1615, Smith, with the help of several members of the Company, twice tried to plant a colony on the coast. On his second attempt he was left by his crew in the hands of French pirates. He was then taken to France, but escaped to England from the harbor of Rochelle (*ro-shĕl*) in an open boat.

3. As soon as he arrived he published a description of New England. This energetic man then traveled through the West of England, stirring up the merchants and gentry by his descriptions of the beauty of the new country. The North Virginia Company, moved by Smith's flattering accounts, applied for a new patent, and a charter, known as "the Great Patent," was given them by the king in the year 1620.

4. By the terms of this instrument, the whole country between the 40th and 48th degrees of north latitude, westward to the Pacific, was granted to forty noble and influential persons, under the name of the Council of Plymouth. Within this vast territory, which was named New England, and which covered more than a million of square miles, the Company had full power to make settlements and laws, and to carry on trade.

PLYMOUTH COLONY.

5. The first settlement in New England was not made by the Council of Plymouth, but by a small band of persecuted "Puritans," without the knowledge of the Council or the king. The Puritans were so called at first in derision, be-

2. What visits were made to the coast during the next few years? What remarkable man now reappears? How was he employed? State what he did. When was this? What took place next year? What occurred on his second attempt? How did he escape?

3. What did he do on his arrival in England? How did he further show his regard for this "New England?" With what success did his efforts meet? How did the king regard their application?

4. What was the extent of the grant in the great patent, and to whom was it made? What name was given to the territory? What was its area in miles? What powers were granted to the Company?

cause they set up claims to live a pure, religious life. A portion of them left the Church of England, to which they belonged, and, being persecuted, fled to Amsterdam, in Holland, in 1608. In the following year they removed to Leyden (*li'-den*). Being exiles from their own country, and having no fixed home, they took the name of "Pilgrims."

6. At Leyden they lived for several years in religious freedom, under the care of their minister, John Robinson. But they were very poor; they were in a strange land, and they dreaded the influence of the Dutch manners on their children. These things led them to turn their minds to America, and in the year 1619 they obtained a grant of land from the South Virginia or London Company. Some London merchants advanced the money for the voyage, and were to receive, for seven years, a large share of the profits of the venture.

7. A small Dutch vessel was bought, which they named the Speedwell, and brought to Delfthaven, on the coast of Holland. Here it took on board a part of the Leyden congregation, and sailed for Southampton, England. At Southampton they found the Mayflower, a ship hired for the voyage, and a small band of "pilgrims" from London. In these two vessels the whole party was distributed, and they then set sail. The Speedwell proved old and leaky, and twice both vessels put back—the last time to Plymouth. The Speedwell was here condemned as unseaworthy, and the Mayflower, crowded with one hundred persons—men, women, and children—set sail September 16, 1620.

8. The Pilgrims intended to reach some place not far from the Hudson River, within the limits of South Virginia; but, when they first saw land near Cape Cod, they had been at

---

5. Did the Council of Plymouth make the first settlement? Who did? Did they have any permission to settle there? How did they receive the name of Puritans? Give the story of those that fled to Holland until they arrived at Leyden? Why did they assume the name of "Pilgrims?"

6. What is said of their life at Leyden? What led them to turn their attention to America? What did they get in 1619? How did they raise money to meet the expenses of the voyage? and on what terms?

7. What preparation was made for the voyage? Who sailed in the Speedwell from Delfthaven? Who joined them at Southampton? What happened on the first attempt? What vessel finally sailed, and when? Why did the Speedwell not go? How many persons went on board of the Mayflower?

sea sixty-three days, and the voyage had been very stormy. They had suffered so long and so severely from their crowded condition, and, besides, the season was so late, that they determined to anchor in Cape Cod Harbor.

9. In the cabin of the ship, before landing, they signed a "compact" or agreement that every settler should have equal rights, and that they would obey the laws they should make for the common good. They then chose John Carver

SIGNING OF THE COMPACT ON BOARD THE MAYFLOWER.

governor for one year. Such was the first form of government in New England. The names of all the signers have been preserved. The most distinguished of them were Carver, Bradford, afterward governor, Brewster, a leading elder, Standish, the brave soldier, and Edward Winslow.

10. The place where they at first landed was bleak and sandy, and they spent five weeks in exploring the neighbor-

8. To what place did they intend to go? Where and when did they first see land? How long had their voyage lasted? Where did they determine to anchor? What was their reason for this?

9. What remarkable agreement did they make before landing? Whom did they choose for governor? What were the terms of this "compact?" What form of government was this? Who were the most celebrated of these signers?

ing country. On the 21st of December, 1620, a party sounded Plymouth Harbor, and, finding it good for shipping, went ashore and chose a place for a settlement. This is the day kept as the anniversary of the Landing of the Pilgrims. In "kind remembrance" of the place from which they last sailed, they named the spot chosen New Plymouth.

11. The winter was a mild one, but the sufferings they had already endured from exposure began to wear on their health. Within the first five months after they landed they lost half their number from colds and lung diseases. Fortunately, no Indians troubled them during the winter. In March, 1621, Massasoit (*mas-sas'-o-it*), chief of the Wampanoags (*wom-pa-nó-ags*) living north of Narragansett Bay, came to visit the Pilgrims. He was treated with great kindness, and Governor Carver made a treaty of friendship with him.

12. In the month of April, 1621, Carver died from the effects of exposure, and Bradford was chosen governor. In February, 1622, Canon'icus, chief of the Narragansetts, sent a bundle of arrows tied with a rattlesnake's skin to New Plymouth, by way of defiance. Bradford sent back the skin stuffed with powder and ball. The Indians in the interior, taking this for a fatal charm, sent it around from village to village, and then returned it to New Plymouth. The governor's firmness effectually overawed the Narragansetts.

13. The harvest of 1621 proved a failure, and the colonists were compelled to live on half allowance for six months. Strong men staggered with weakness from want of food. They would have perished had they not obtained scanty supplies from the Indians, and from the fishing vessels off the coast. The colony progressed slowly. At the end of four years, although it had received several companies of

---

10. How long did they spend exploring the country? Why did they not settle at once? What place did they finally select? When was this? How is the day kept among New Englanders? What name did they give the new settlement, and why?

11. What name did they give the new settlement? Why? What is said of their sufferings during the next five months? What caused these? What trouble did they have from the natives? What tribe of Indians was not far from them? Who visited them, and what was the result of his visit?

12. What important man died in April? Who succeeded him? Tell how he cowed the Narragansett Indians.

settlers, it numbered only one hundred and eighty-four inhabitants. There had been spent, thus far, about 34,000 dollars, and the London adventurers would advance no more. They were glad to sell out their entire interest to six of the leading colonists for 9000 dollars, November, 1627.

14. Till the year 1630 the settlers had no grant of the lands they occupied. In this year they obtained from the Council for New England a grant of territory embracing New Plymouth, but without any rights of government therein. These could only be exercised under a charter from the crown, and this they were unable to obtain. The colonists therefore continued to make such laws as they needed without royal authority.

MASSACHUSETTS BAY COLONY.

15. The Council for New England, in the year 1628, granted to John Endicott and five associates a belt of land stretching from the Atlantic to the Pacific, and extending three miles south of the Charles River and Massachusetts Bay, and three miles north of every part of the River Merrimac. Endicott came over the same year with seventy settlers, and, after landing at Naumkeag (*nahm-ke-ág*), explored the head of Massachusetts Bay.

16. A number of persons of rank joined the associates in England, and in 1629 obtained a royal charter in the name of the Governor and Company of Massachusetts Bay in New England. Endicott was made governor of the colony. The same year two hundred Puritan settlers arrived at Naumkeag, named by them Salem, and about one hundred of these founded Charlestown.

17. In the charter given to the Company, it was originally

13. What is said of the harvest of 1621? What followed from this scarcity? What good fortune befell them? What had been the success of the colony at the end of four years? How much had been spent on the settlement? What were the feelings of the adventurers? What became of their interest?

14. Under what grant was the colony settled? When and from whom did they obtain one? What right were they unable to get? How did they manage without this?

15. What grant was made in the year 1628? When and by whom was the first attempt at settlement made? What is said of his landing, and the exploration that followed?

16. How was the association in England increased? What did they obtain? Who was made governor of Massachusetts Bay Colony? What settlements followed?

arranged that the governor and his assistants should reside in England. It soon became plain that the affairs of the colony would best succeed if the government and charter were transferred to New England, and placed in the hands of the settlers there. This change was accordingly made in September, 1629, and produced great results. A great number of persons determined to emigrate. Many of these were of the best Puritan families of England, well educated, and in good circumstances, who longed for that religious freedom they could not obtain at home.

18. In June and July, 1630, not far from 1500 settlers, chiefly Puritans, arrived, some at Salem, and others at Charlestown. John Winthrop had been chosen governor from among them before they left England. Presently the governor and several families removed from Charlestown to the peninsula of Shawmut, and laid the foundation of Boston. The rest settled principally at Dorchester, and at Watertown on Charles River. The colonists did not escape the usual fate of early settlers. Before December passed, two hundred of them died from the effects of exposure in tents and the diseases of the climate.

19. Although the Puritans had come to America to enjoy religious freedom, they were not willing to allow the same liberty to any who differed from the religious opinions of the majority. Among those who found the rule of the Massachusetts churches hard to bear was Roger Williams, the young minister of the church at Salem, who had fled from persecution in England, and had arrived in the colony in the beginning of the year 1631.

20. Among other doctrines, he preached that no power could bind the conscience of men in religion, or deprive them of "soul liberty," as he called it. His sermons aroused the great body of the churches and ministers against him;

---

17. Where was it originally intended that the governor and his associates should reside? What change was found necessary? When was the change made? What immediate result followed? What class of persons were these from?

18. How many came over in 1630? Who was chosen governor? What led to the settlement of Boston in 1630? What other places were settled? What is said of the hardships endured by the settlers?

19. How did the Puritans treat those who differed from them in opinion? Who was Roger Williams? What is said of him?

and in the year 1635, he was, after trial, ordered to leave the colony within six weeks. He found refuge with Mas-sas'oit, the Indian chief, and, soon after, with five companions, settled within the limits of the present state of Rhode Island.

21. During the same year, 1635, three thousand settlers arrived in Massachusetts Bay, many of whom brought with them extreme notions with regard to the right of free speech that were very displeasing to the Massachusetts ministers. One of these new arrivals, Mrs. Hutchinson, a very remarkable woman, held meetings of her own sex, where she preached very plainly about the ministers from whom she differed on religious points. She was strongly supported by Governor Henry Vane, and some of the leading men; but the ministers generally, and very many of the "judicious" settlers, opposed her. After a long controversy, she was tried, and, in the winter of 1637, sentenced to be banished from the colony.

22. The colonists knew the value of education, and made provision for it at a very early date. In 1636, the "General Court," as the assembly of freemen was called, set apart one thousand dollars to found a seminary or college at Newtown. Two years after, in 1638, John Harvard, a minister, died, and left to this school his library and the sum of £800. It then received the name of Harvard College, and, in honor of the University in England where many of the settlers had been educated, the name of Newtown was changed to Cambridge.

UNION OF NEW ENGLAND COLONIES.

23. Besides the colonies of Plymouth and Massachusetts Bay, those of New Haven and Connecticut, both settled

---

20. What was one of the particular doctrines he advanced? What was the effect of his preaching? How did they deal with him? With whom did he find refuge, and when and where did he settle?

21. How many settlers arrived in 1635? What is said of their opinions? What remarkable woman was among these new-comers? What is said of the course she pursued? Who were her supporters? Who opposed her? How did they deal with her?

22. What appropriation was made in 1636? How was this amount increased in 1638? Why was the college named Harvard? Why was the name of Newtown changed?

principally from Massachusetts, had meanwhile grown into importance. These four colonies, in the year 1643, formed a union for mutual protection against the Dutch, French, and Indians. Two delegates from each colony were to meet at least once every year and consult for the common good. Their decisions did not bind any of the colonies, each of which voted whether it would adopt the measures proposed. This union lasted for more than forty years. Rhode Island was refused admission because it would not acknowledge the authority of Plymouth colony.

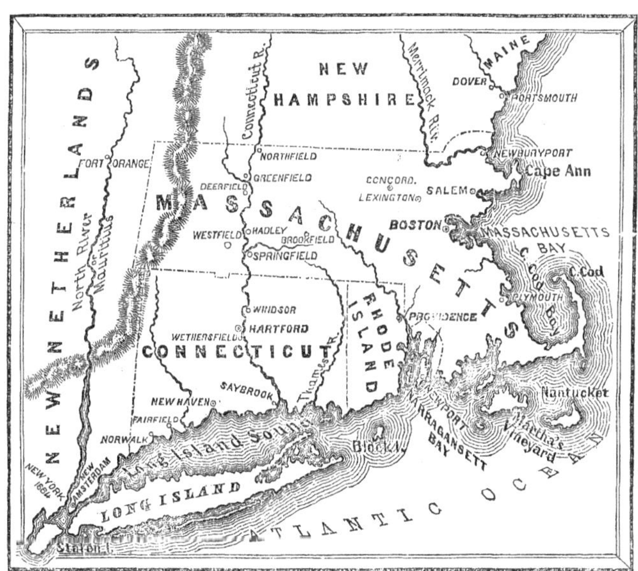

NEW ENGLAND COLONIES AND PART OF NEW NETHERLANDS.

24. Notwithstanding the banishment of Roger Williams and Mrs. Hutchinson, with their adherents, the Massachusetts magistrates had fresh trouble from a new set of opinions. In 1656 the Quakers first arrived from England. They

23. What colonies in New England had grown into importance besides Massachusetts Bay and Plymouth? In what important agreement did these four colonies unite? Why was Rhode Island excluded? What was the plan of union? What veto was there on their proceedings? How long did the union last?

believed in an "inward light" as a guide, in freedom from all Church control, and in the doctrine of non-resistance. The magistrates first tried banishment from the colony, but this did no good, for the Quakers came in greater numbers. Then laws were passed against them so severe that they might perhaps be called cruel. Still the Quakers persisted in coming, particularly to Boston, where the prison was crowded with them, glorying in their sufferings.

25. As a last resort, the Commissioners of the New England Union recommended that all banished Quakers returning to any of the colonies should be put to death. A law to this effect was passed in Massachusetts, and four were hung. This excessive severity, however, brought public opinion over to the side of the Quakers. Before long the persecution ceased, and they were allowed to live in peace.

26. The Navigation Act of 1660 has been already mentioned in the history of Virginia. It pressed with great severity on the people of Massachusetts, for there was a large and active shipping trade belonging to the colony which was entirely broken up by this oppressive act.

KING PHILIP'S WAR.

27. The Wampanoags for nearly forty years faithfully kept the treaty of peace that was made with the Plymouth colony in 1621. Yet, though quiet, they were far from being contented, because they saw themselves gradually pushed out of their hunting-grounds on the east side of Narragansett Bay.

28. Massasoit, the prudent friend of the whites, died in 1659; and in 1661, his younger son, called by the colonists King Philip, of Mount Hope, near Bristol, Rhode Island, be-

---

24. What new trouble did the Massachusetts magistrates now suffer from? When did some of this new sect arrive? What were their opinions? What measures were first tried against them? What was next resorted to? How far did this prevent them from coming to Boston?

25. What was recommended as the last resort? To what extent was this put in force? How did this excessive severity operate on the public mind? State what followed.

26. What was the Navigation Act? See history of Virginia. How did it affect the people of Massachusetts? Why was this?

27. How had the Wampanoags kept their treaty? How did they look on the conduct of the English meanwhile?

THE GREAT SWAMP FIGHT IN RHODE ISLAND. Page 66.

came chief of the tribe. In the year 1674, a converted Indian, employed by Philip, told the Plymonth magistrates that he had discovered a plot on the part of the chief to unite the New England Indians and destroy the whites. Not long after, this informer was found drowned. The colonists seized three Wampanoags on suspicion, and hung them for the murder.

29. Exasperated by this, the Indians attacked Swanzey, thirty-five miles southwest from Plymouth, and killed some of the people, June, 1675. The Plymouth settlers, assisted by Massachusetts men, promptly marched to the Wampanoag villages near Mount Hope, intending to surprise and capture Philip; but he had received notice of their approach, and escaped before they arrived. In a short time he persuaded the other New England tribes to join in a war against the whites.

---

28. What took place in 1659 and 1661? What startling report was made to the Plymouth magistrates? What was the fate of the informer? What did the colonists do on hearing of the murder?

29. How did the Indians revenge this, and when? What did the settlers do? How did Philip defeat this plan? What league did he form?

30. The colonists at first thought they could easily chastise the "insolent savages," but they soon found out their mistake. The war spread rapidly along the frontier settlements. Brookfield, Northfield, Deerfield, Hadley, and Springfield, outlying northerly villages on and near the Connecticut, were attacked in August, September, and October, 1765, and some of them burned. Even small bands of armed settlers were surprised and massacred.

31. The New England men determined to strike the Narragansetts, who had broken their treaty with the whites, before they could join Philip in the spring. In December, 1675, fifteen hundred colonists suddenly attacked three thousand of them, posted in the middle of a swamp in Rhode Island, where they had laid up a large store of provisions for the winter. This "Swamp Fight" was a bloody affair for the colonists, for six captains and two hundred and fifty men were killed or wounded. Of the Indians over a thousand warriors were killed, and several hundred were taken prisoners. Six hundred wigwams were burned, and the provisions were destroyed.

32. This proved a heavy blow to the Indians, but it did not end the war. Philip made fresh exertions, and in the spring of 1676 it burst with greater fury over three hundred miles of frontier. Nor was the war confined to the outposts. The Indians attacked villages within twenty miles of Boston; Warwick, Rhode Island, was burned, and Providence partially destroyed; the whole colony of Plymouth was overrun: the Indians seemed every where. This lasted till June. Then the Indians began to grow weary of fighting; their resources failed, and the colonists pressed them with energy. Some of them submitted, and were sold as slaves; others fled to Canada; hundreds were tracked by the colonists and shot down.

---

30. How did the colonists at first look on the war? Give some account of how it spread. Tell from the map, page 53, the location of these villages.

31. What tribe did the colonists fear would join the Wampanoags? What did the colonists determine to do? What attack was made? What is said of the battle, and the losses on both sides?

32. Did this defeat end the war? What took place in the spring of 1676? Describe the extent of the Indian movements. How long did this last? What took place after June?

33. Philip himself would not submit. He went back to his old home at Mount Hope in July, and was at last shot in August, 1676, by a traitorous Indian who had guided the whites to his hiding-place. His wife and little son had been previously taken prisoners, and the latter was sent to the Bermudas and there sold as a slave. Thus ended King Philip's War. The Wampanoags and Narragansetts were blotted out of existence as tribes.

DEATH OF KING PHILIP.

34. A tract of land embracing the territory of Maine and New Hampshire had been granted to Gorges and Mason in 1622. In the year 1677, Massachusetts bought out the rights of the heirs for six thousand dollars. New Hampshire did not remain long in her possession, for Charles II. in 1680 made it a royal province. Six years after, Massachusetts also became a province. An officer of customs, while enforcing the Navigation Act at Boston, had been resisted, and forced to return to England. King Charles II. eagerly seized on this as an excuse for annulling the charter, but he died before the arrangements were completed.

33. Where was Philip during this time? What happened to him? What became of his wife and his little son? What Indian tribes were destroyed?

34. How did Massachusetts increase her territory in 1677? How large was the tract? How long did Massachusetts retain possession of it? What befell the colony in 1686? What led to this?

35. In 1686, after his death, the charters of all the New England colonies were declared forfeited, and King James II. sent over Sir Edmund Andros as first royal governor of New England. His rule, which was very tyrannical, lasted three years. When, in 1689, the news arrived that King James had been expelled from the English throne, the people of Massachusetts rose against Andros, and sent him under arrest to England. The New England colonies then quietly resumed their old form of government.

KING WILLIAM'S WAR.

36. When James II. fled to France in 1688, William, Prince of Orange, was called to the throne of England. The French king, Louis XIV., took up the cause of the exiled king, and declared war against England in 1689. The contest spread at once to the colonies in North America, the French uniting with the Indians against the English settlers.

37. A body of French and Indians, in the year 1690, attacked different posts on the frontiers of New York and New England, and committed great barbarities. Massachusetts, in return, fitted out a fleet, and sent seven hundred men with it, under Sir William Phipps, to ravage the French settlements. He captured Port Royal, in Acadia, and obtained plunder enough to pay the expenses of the expedition.

38. This success led the colonies of New York, Massachusetts, and Connecticut, the same year, to fit out a land, and also a naval expedition for the conquest of Canada. But both failed miserably, and proved so costly that no other important expedition was attempted by these colonies during the war. It lingered along until the year 1697, when it was terminated by the treaty of peace signed at Ryswick (*riz'-wik*), in Holland.

---

35. What sweeping measure was adopted in 1686 by the new king? Who was appointed governor of all New England? What is said of his rule, and how was it brought to an end? What kind of government followed throughout New England?

36. Who succeeded James on the throne of England? How did the French king regard this? What followed in Europe and America?

37. What colonies suffered severely? What did Massachusetts do in return? What was Phipps's success? Where was Acadia?

38. To what did the success of Phipps lead? What was the success of these expeditions? How long did the war last, and how did it terminate?

39. In the year 1692, Phipps had been sent to England for assistance, but could get none. The colonies were left to defend themselves. He had better fortune for himself, for he returned the same year with a royal charter, including Massachusetts colony, Maine, and Nova Scotia in one province, under the name of Massachusetts, of which he was made royal governor. From this time onward to the Revolution, Massachusetts remained a royal province.

40. On his arrival at Boston, Phipps found great excitement on the subject of witchcraft. There were nearly one hundred persons in prison charged with this crime. Acting on "learned advice," he ordered a "special court" for their trial. This court hanged twenty of the prisoners. One of the hanged was a clergyman. When the delusion reached its height, eight persons were under sentence of death, the jails were full of prisoners, and new accusations were made every day. No one was safe; even Lady Phipps, the wife of the governor, was suspected. In 1693 reason began to resume its place; the "special court" was abolished; and Phipps ordered that all those in prison on the charge of witchcraft should be set at liberty.

QUEEN ANNE'S WAR.

41. The French and English colonies were not permitted to remain long at peace. In the year 1701, James II., the dethroned king, died an exile in France, and his son was proclaimed King of England by the French monarch. The English at once resented this as an affront to Queen Anne, their reigning sovereign, and war was declared in 1702. This was known in America as Queen Anne's War; and in Europe, from causes that involved Spain as well as France, the War of the Spanish Succession.

---

39. For what purpose was Phipps sent to England? How far was he successful? What was the extent of the new province? How long did Massachusetts remain a royal province?

40. What disturbance had sprung up during Phipps's absence? How many had been imprisoned? What measure did Phipps adopt? What immediately followed? What was the state of things when the delusion was at its height? When did the delusion end? State what was done.

41. How many years did the colonies remain at peace? What led to war in Europe? When was war declared? By what names is this war known?

42. In America, the weight of hostilities fell on South Carolina and New England. The operations of the former will be noticed hereafter under the history of that colony. The middle colonies remained unharmed during the war. New York, which was particularly exposed, was fortunately saved by a treaty of neutrality that the Five Nations had concluded with the French of Canada. On the north, the French guided the Canadians and Maine Indians in barbarous attacks on the frontiers of Massachusetts.

43. To revenge these barbarities, a thousand men sailed from Massachusetts, June, 1707, against Port Royal, in Acadia, which had been restored to France by the treaty of Ryswick. This expedition failed; but in 1710, New England, assisted by an English fleet, compelled it to surrender. The name was changed to Annapolis, in honor of the queen.

44. This success encouraged the English government, in 1711, to attempt the conquest of Canada by means of two expeditions, one by land, the other by sea; and a powerful fleet and army was sent from England to co-operate with the colonial troops. The fleet, badly handled while proceeding against Quebec, was wrecked in the St. Lawrence, with the loss of eight vessels, and 884 men drowned. This disaster compelled the return of the naval expedition, and the abandonment of the movement by land against Montreal. Hostilities were at last brought to an end by the treaty of Utrecht (*u-trekt*) in 1713. By this Acadia was ceded permanently to Great Britain, and became a province under the old name of Nova Scotia.

KING GEORGE'S WAR.

45. For thirty years peace reigned between the rival French and English colonies. In 1744, war arose in Europe out of disputes about the succession to the throne of Aus-

---

42. How was the contest felt by the colonies? How was New York saved from Indian incursions? What happened on the New England frontier?

43. What did Massachusetts do in return? State the success. Where was Port Royal? What other Port Royal is mentioned in the earlier history? What happened in 1710? What was Port Royal named, and why?

44. What expedition was next planned, and where? With what success did it meet? When did the war end? What permanent accession of territory did England gain?

tria. England and France took opposite sides in the contest, and this involved the colonies. In Europe it was known as the War of the Austrian Succession, in America as King George's War.

46. The principal event in the struggle on this continent was the capture of the strong and important post of Louisburg, on the island of Cape Breton. Massachusetts, New Hampshire, Rhode Island, and Connecticut agreed to furnish men and ships for the expedition; New York sent some money and cannon, and Pennsylvania gave provisions. The chief burden of the enterprise fell on Massachusetts. In April, 1745, over three thousand men, under Sir William Pepperell, sailed from New England, and on their way were joined by a large British fleet and additional troops. On the 11th of May, to the surprise of the garrison, they anchored within sight of Louisburg, and, so spirited were the movements of the 4000 combined troops in the ensuing siege, that the French surrendered on the 28th of June.

47. The colonial forces were greatly rejoiced at their success. The expedition had been planned in New England, the great body of the troops were from New England, and they had done the most of the work in the siege; but the English fleet got the glory and the prize-money. The war was ended in 1748 by the treaty of Aix-la-Chapelle (*akes-la-sha-pél*), in Prussia. The capture of Louisburg, accomplished at so much expense on the part of the colonies, proved of no permanent value. It was given back to France by the treaty.

48. These three wars laid the foundation of bitter hatred between the French and English colonies. This, together with the disputes about territory, was the cause of that long and bloody contest that followed not seven years after,

---

45. How long did peace last between the French and English colonies? When did war break out in Europe, and what was the cause? By what names is the war known in Europe and America?

46. What was the principal event of this war in America? What did the different colonies contribute to the carrying on of the war? What is said of the force sent against Louisburg? State what is said of the siege, and the result.

47. How did England regard the success, and why? Who were rewarded? How was the war ended? Did the capture of Louisburg prove of any permanent value?

known as the French and Indian War, and which involved all the colonies from New Hampshire to the Carolinas.

CONNECTICUT.

1. IN the year 1630, a tract of land, extending one hundred and twenty miles along the coast west of Narragansett River, and from the Atlantic westward to the Pacific, was granted to the Earl of Warwick ([illegible]) by the Council of Plymouth. Next year he transferred his grant to Lord Say-and-Seal and Lord Brooke, in company with other Englishmen. The territory embraced within its limits the present State of Connecticut.

2. The Dutch claimed that the Connecticut Valley was a part of New Netherlands, and in 1633 built a block-house in the south part of what is now the city of Hartford, naming it Good Hope. The same year some traders from New Plymouth sailed up the river past the Dutch fort—the commander of this threatening to fire upon them as they went by—and built a trading-house at Windsor. Two years after this, in 1635, sixty immigrants came across the country through the wild forest from Massachusetts Bay colony, and settled near the New Plymouth trading-house.

3. In 1635 the agents of the English proprietors sent a small party from Boston to the mouth of the Connecticut, who there built a fort, which was named, in honor of the proprietors, Say-Brook. This became the foundation of the Saybrook colony, and completely prevented the Dutch from any further attempts to take possession of the river. During the summer of 1636, one hundred persons, under the Reverend Thomas Hooker, from four towns around Boston, came across the country, and settled chiefly at Hartford, Windsor,

---

48. What was the effect of these wars on the French and English colonists? To what did this hatred eventually lead?

1. Describe the tract of land granted in 1630. To whom was it granted, and to what parties was it afterward transferred? What state was embraced by that grant?

2. What claim did the Dutch make to a portion of this? Why? What did they proceed to do? Where is Hartford? Who interfered with the claims of the Dutch at this time? How did the Dutch resent this? When did other immigrants arrive, and where did they settle?

and Wethersfield. These settlements were under the protection of Massachusetts, and known as CONNECTICUT COLONY.

PEQUOD WAR.

4. The new settlements were scarcely planted when war sprang up with the Pequod Indians, living on Long Island Sound east of the Connecticut River. Charged with several murders of the whites, an expedition was sent against them from Massachusetts, which burned their villages and ravaged their country, August, 1636. Thirsting for revenge, they tried to persuade the Narragansett Indians to join them in an attack upon the English settlements. Fortunately, Roger Williams heard of this, and, forgetting all the wrongs the Massachusetts people had done him, went to the Narragansett chief while the Pequod messengers were still there. At the risk of his life, he succeeded in persuading the Narragansetts not to take sides against the English.

5. The Pequods meanwhile lurked about Fort Saybrook, and killed or captured several persons. During the winter they killed several settlers as far up the river as Wethersfield. These murders roused the Connecticut towns, and in May, 1637, they met at Hartford and declared war. Massachusetts sent twenty men, under Captain Underhill, to help them. Captain Mason, with sixty Connecticut troops, making, with Underhill's men, some eighty whites, together with several hundred friendly Mohegans and Narragansetts, started out rapidly to attack the Pequods.

6. Mason, learning that they were collected in two rude forts a few miles east of the Pequod River, now called the Thames, landed near one of them at nightfall on the 4th of

---

3. Who sent the next party of immigrants, and where did they locate themselves? What name did they give to their fort? What did this eventually become? How did this affect the claims of the Dutch? When and by whom were the next settlements made? Under what protection were these made?

4. What occurred to disturb the peace of the new settlers? Where did these Indians live? What cause had they for this bad feeling? What alliance did they attempt to enter into against the whites? How was this alliance prevented? Why is this to be considered a very generous act on the part of Williams? What do you remember of his treatment by the people of Massachusetts?

5. Did the Pequods still persist in their hostilities? What did the Connecticut settlers do? Who assisted the latter? What forces were raised, and who were the leaders?

INDIANS ATTACKING THE SETTLERS.

June, 1637. At daybreak next morning he moved on the enemy, and in one hour burned the fort and killed some five or six hundred of the warriors, together with a number of old men, women, and children. Only seven of the Indians fell alive into the hands of the colonists.

7. The Indians were allowed but little time to recover from the effects of this terrible blow. Fresh troops came to the help of the Connecticut men from Massachusetts. The wretched Pequods, hunted and broken-spirited, fled to the swamps. There many were surrounded and shot; some surrendered, and were enslaved by the English; some escaped and joined other tribes. By the close of the year 1637 nearly nine hundred Pequods had perished, and the tribe itself was exterminated.

8. The Colony of New Haven was founded in the year 1638 by a body of wealthy emigrants from London, who arrived at Boston in 1637 under the leadership of John Davenport, a Puritan minister, and Theophilus Eaton, a London

---

6. Where did Mason find them? When and where did he make his attack? Describe what followed. How did the result show the bitter feelings of the colonists?

7. What energetic measures followed? What is said of the sufferings of the unhappy Pequods? How and when was the war terminated?

merchant. Land was purchased from the Indians, and the plan of the city of New Haven was laid out. The new settlers were soon joined by others from England and from the Connecticut colony. During the first year little government was needed, but in 1639 the settlers agreed that the Bible should be adopted as the law of the colony, and that only Church members should be freemen. They then chose Eaton as governor.

9. Earlier in the same year 1639, the towns of Hartford, Windsor, and Wethersfield agreed on a very liberal form of government, and, in remarkable contrast with that of the New Haven colony, they allowed all residents of good character to be freemen. The power was thus left in the hands of the whole people. The Connecticut colony is, therefore, the first example of a pure democratic government in America.

10. There were at this time three colonies in what is now the State of Connecticut—Saybrook, at the mouth of the river, governed by the proprietors; the towns of Hartford, Windsor, and Wethersfield, called Connecticut, independent; and New Haven, with adjacent towns, also independent. Next year, 1644, the only remaining proprietor of the Saybrook colony sold his interest in it to the Connecticut towns, and it became a part of that colony.

11. The disputes about the boundary-line between New Netherlands and Connecticut several times threatened to end in a war with the Dutch. This was one of the causes that led to the formation of the New England Union in 1643. In the year 1650 a boundary was agreed on, and the matter was put at rest.

12. In the year 1662 the Connecticut colony obtained a royal charter, which included New Haven, and from the

---

8. When and by whom was the New Haven colony founded? Who were the leaders? How did they procure their land? Who soon joined them? What is said of the government during the first year? What was finally adopted as the law of the colony? Who was chosen governor?

9. What towns are spoken of as having agreed on a remarkable form of government? What was its main feature? Of what is the Connecticut colony an example?

10. How many colonies were there at this time in Connecticut? Name them, and state their forms of government. What union was formed, and when? How was the Saybrook colony united to this?

11. What danger now threatened the colony? In what way was the matter settled?

year 1665 the latter ceased to have a separate existence This was the most liberal charter that had yet been granted to any colony. It secured to the whole people all the rights of free government that had been agreed upon by the Connecticut towns in 1639. So perfect was it, and so liberal, that it remained the constitution of the State of Connecticut long after the American Revolution.

13. When Andros was appointed governor of New England in 1687, he was anxious to get possession of this famous charter. For this purpose, he went to Hartford while the Assembly was in session, and demanded it from the members. It was brought out and laid on the table. The members, who were determined to keep it, spoke so long about their right to do so that the debate was carried on until evening. As the discussion drew to an end, suddenly the

THE DISCUSSION OVER THE CHARTER.

---

12. When did Connecticut obtain a charter? What was included in this? When did the existence of the New Haven colony terminate? What is said of the charter? How long did it remain in force?

lights were extinguished. When they were relighted the charter had disappeared. A trusty hand had carried it off, and hid it in the hollow trunk of a tree, which was afterward known as the "Charter Oak."

14. Andros, however, declared the charter government at an end, dissolved the Assembly, and with his own hand wrote the word "finis" at the end of the minutes of the last meeting. His triumph was very short, for in 1689, after he was arrested in Boston, the charter was taken from its hiding-place, and the colony quietly resumed its old form of government.

15. Connecticut took a firm stand for its rights under the charter in the year 1693, during King William's War. Fletcher, the governor of New York, had received a royal commission to order out the Connecticut militia for service. This was resented by the colony as a violation of the charter, which provided that the militia could only be called out by the General Court. Fletcher went to Hartford, and ordered out the militia to hear his commission read.

16. When the reading began, Captain Wadsworth, in command of the company, ordered the drums to be beaten to drown the voice. Fletcher ordered silence, and the reading again began, only to be once more drowned by the drums. When Fletcher again ordered silence, Wadsworth very firmly told him that if he repeated that order "he would make the sun shine through him in a moment." The governor gave up the attempt, and returned to New York.

17. In the year 1701, the General Court, instead of meeting entirely at Hartford, was ordered to meet alternately at Hartford and New Haven. This was the foundation of the two capitals. In the same year, a school for the education of ministers was established at Saybrook. It was afterward

13. What attempt was made to deprive the colony of this charter? Give an account of the proceedings in the Assembly with regard to it. In what way were the charter taken care of?

14. What did Andros persist in doing? How long did the charter remain hid? What event brought it from its hiding-place? Did the colony continue a royal government?

15. What offensive requisition was made by the Governor of New York in 1693? How was this resented? What did Fletcher do?

16. How was the reading of the commission received? How was Fletcher finally forced to yield?

removed to New Haven, and named Yale College, after Elihu Yale, its first patron.

18. Connecticut, as a colony, continued to enjoy her rights under the charter and to elect her own governors. She was not compelled, like Massachusetts, to endure the tyranny of governors appointed by the crown. She bore her share in all the intercolonial wars, and, as a part of New England, vigorously supported Massachusetts. We shall find her again active in the French and Indian War.

Rhode Island.

FINAL LANDING-PLACE OF ROGER WILLIAMS ON THE PAWTUCKET.

1. In November, 1635, Roger Williams, the minister of the Salem church, was banished from the Massachusetts Colony. He started in the depth of winter, and, after wandering fourteen weeks in the woods without a guide, he found a shelter and a welcome among the Narragansett Indians. From them he received a grant of land at Seekonk, on the east side of the Seekonk or Pawtucket River, which flows into Narragansett Bay.

2. He had just begun to plant corn here in 1636, when Governor Winslow, of the Plymouth Colony, advised him to

17. What change was made with regard to the place of meeting of the General Court? What do you understand by the General Court? In what year was this? What school was established this year? Where was it removed to, and what was it named?

18. What rights did Connecticut enjoy? In what respect was she better off than Massachusetts? What is finally said of Connecticut?

1. What is said of Roger Williams? Give an account of his wanderings. What did he procure from the Indians? Where is the Seekonk River?

remove, as the land was within the limits of the Plymouth grant. To be entirely free, he and five companions went to a place on the west side of Pawtucket River, and, in remembrance of "God's merciful providence to him in his distress," he named the new plantation Providence.

3. Shortly after he began this settlement he was asked by Governor Vane, of Massachusetts Colony, to use his influence with the Narragansetts against the Pequods. We have already seen how prompt and how successful he was in doing this. The kindness of Williams met a poor return from the Massachusetts ministers and magistrates. In 1638 the latter forbade all trade with the Providence people, and threatened to arrest them if found within the limits of Massachusetts.

4. In the year 1637, the husband of the celebrated Mrs. Hutchinson, together with William Coddington and others, by the advice of Williams came to Narragansett Bay. Coddington, through the influence of Williams, bought the island of Aquiday from the Indians, and named it the Island of Rhodes, a name afterward changed to that of Rhode Island. He settled at Portsmouth, on the upper end. Newport, at the lower end, was not settled until the year 1644.

5. Mrs. Hutchinson joined her husband and friends at Portsmouth, when she was banished in 1638. This greatly persecuted woman was not permitted to remain long on Aquiday Island. Coddington, in 1641, began to talk about making friends with the magistrates of Massachusetts. Thinking herself not safe here, she, being now a widow, removed near what is now New Rochelle, within the limits of New Netherlands. Soon after her arrival there, the whole family of eighteen persons except one—a daughter carried off prisoner—were massacred by the Indians in the Dutch and Indian war under Governor Kieft.

---

2. Why did he find it necessary soon to leave this place? Where did he finally settle? What name did he give this "plantation?"

3. How was his influence used for the benefit of the Massachusetts Bay Colony? How was this requited?

4. What persons settled on Narragansett Bay by the advice of Williams? How did they procure land? What name was given to this land? Where did Coddington settle? When was Newport settled?

5. When did Mrs. Hutchinson join them? Did she remain long here? Why did she not feel safe? What became of her?

6. In the year 1643 the Massachusetts rulers showed their dislike of the free principles prevailing in the Providence and Rhode Island plantations by refusing to admit them into the New England Union. This they did under the plea that these two settlements had no charter, and that they were within the limits of the Plymouth and Massachusetts grants. To terminate these disputes, Williams determined to go to England and solicit a charter.

7. He was not allowed by the Massachusetts magistrates to visit Boston, and there embark, but was compelled to go to Manhattan, and take passage by way of Holland. Vane, the former governor of Massachusetts, and a friend of Williams, was at this time a man of great influence in England. Through his assistance, Williams obtained, in 1644, a charter for the two plantations, uniting them in one colony. The two plantations did not come together without some difficulty. It was not until the year 1647 that they met and elected a governor and officers. They then agreed on a set of laws, the greatest of which was that celebrated act which granted freedom of religious faith and worship to all sects.

8. Like Connecticut, the colony received a new charter from Charles II. in the year 1663, securing to the people all the liberties guaranteed by the first. When Andros was made royal governor of New England, Rhode Island submitted, but resumed her own form of government when he was expelled. No further event of striking importance marks the history of the colony until the Revolution.

New Hampshire.

1. Sir Ferdinand Gorges and John Mason, in 1622, obtained from the Council for New England a tract of land, which they named Laconia, stretching from the Merrimac to the Kennebec River, and extending westward to the St.

---

6. How did the Massachusetts rulers show their dislike to these settlers? How did they justify themselves in this? What did Williams determine to do?

7. Where was he obliged to go to take passage? Was he successful in his undertaking? When did the two plantations unite to form one colony? What is said of their laws?

8. When was their charter renewed? When did Rhode Island submit to a royal governor? How long did this last?

Lawrence. A colony of fishermen was sent out next year, 1623, and settled, part of them at Little Harbor, near Portsmouth, and part at Dover, eight miles up the river. These were nothing but fishing stations, and for several years had a very feeble life.

2. In 1629, the country between the Merrimac and Piscataqua was given to Mason alone. This tract was called New Hampshire, after Hampshire in England, where Mason lived. It was soon subdivided by grants, passing into the hands of several proprietors, and creating constant litigation. In the year 1641 the people put themselves under the protection of Massachusetts. Against their will, and to please the heirs of Mason, they were placed under royal government in the year 1680.

3. Mason's grandson came over next year, 1681, and sought to enforce his claim to the soil. The courts sustained his right, but the people resisted, and neither he nor his heirs could recover any thing. They were at last compelled to allow the actual settlers to enjoy their farms undisturbed.

4. The two colonies of Massachusetts and New Hampshire were so closely united that they have almost a common history. Three times they either voluntarily, or by royal order, were joined under one government, and as often were changed back to separate provinces. In 1741 they were finally separated, and New Hampshire remained under its own royal governor until the Revolution. It suffered severely from the Indians during the intercolonial wars. Lying north of Massachusetts, her people were greatly exposed to the inroads of the savages and the French. The villages were laid waste, and the settlers murdered; but she had a hardy, courageous, and persevering race, who rallied with renewed energy after every trial.

---

1. When and to whom was the first grant of land given? What were its limits? What was the first attempt at settlement? What is said of these settlements?

2. When did Mason get a separate portion? What name did he give this part? What eventually caused great strife? What protection did they place themselvos under? What change was afterward made?

3. Who set up a claim to this land? How was this received? How did it end?

4. What is said of New Hampshire in connection with another colony? When did they finally separate? From what did New Hampshire suffer? Why was this? In what did her strength consist?

GENERAL REFLECTIONS ON THE NEW ENGLAND COLONIES.

1. **Character of the Settlers.**—The first settlers of New England were very different from the men who first arrived in Virginia. The Puritans came with their families to make homes in which they could live in peace, worship God in their own way, and govern themselves for the common good. They endured hard trials soon after their first settlement; but these were principally owing to the severe climate, and to the exposure arising from their new life in so wild a country.

2. **Treatment of the Indians.**—In the New England colonies we find a great deal of the Virginian mode of dealing with the natives. Although their treatment by the New England governments, except in war, was in the main just and honorable, yet the individual settlers were too often regardless of their rights. They wanted the lands of the red men, and bargained for these when they were able; but they seldom hesitated to drive the Indians from the territory when the latter could not be persuaded or cajoled into a bargain.

3. Still, it is to be borne in mind that the Indians, at a very early day, became jealous of the whites, and this not only in New England, but in nearly all the other colonies. They saw the pale faces steadily increasing in numbers; they were, besides, inwardly conscious of the superiority of the latter; and the oldest and wisest men of the tribes foresaw—what soon happened—that they must be driven westward from their hunting-grounds by the energy of the whites.

4. That the settlers regarded the Indians as an inferior race is plain from what took place after the Pequod, and especially after King Philip's War. At these times a number of the captives were sold to slavery in the Bermudas, or were divided as slaves among the colonists. Notwithstanding all this, there was also a strong mixture of kindness in

---

1. How did the early New England settlers differ from the first settlers at Jamestown? State what you remember about the latter. What is said of their trials?

2. What different treatment did they experience from the magistrates and from individuals? Give the mode of dealing with the red men in reference to their land.

3. What is said of the ill feeling on the part of the Indians, and its cause? How did the old men look on this?

their treatment of the aborigines, for the Puritans felt that the natives had souls to save; and the story of the labors of Eliot and other Puritan ministers among the Indian tribes furnishes some pleasing pages in New England history.

5. **Industry, Trade, and Commerce.**—The chief business of the earlier New England colonists was agriculture. Their farms were for the most part small, and the lives of the settlers were hard and laborious. The name "Plantations" was used in the early years of New England, particularly in Rhode Island, but was soon dropped. A few settlers quickly turned their attention to commerce, for in 1631, the year after Boston was founded, we learn that they had built and launched the first vessel. In 1641 they had seven ships trading to Virginia alone, besides a number sailing to the West Indies and Europe.

6. Then they had the mackerel fisheries of Maine within their own borders, and they were not far from the great cod fishing ground lying close to Newfoundland. The fish they cured, and sent chiefly to Spain and Portugal, and to the West Indies, from which they brought back in exchange the products of these warmer climes. In 1690 they commenced the whale fishery. In New Hampshire there was considerable ship-building, and great quantities of pine-tree masts and spars were shipped to England annually. As the people traded, they collected more and more into towns near the coast, and in this they formed a striking contrast to the settlers in Virginia and Maryland.

7. Money was for many years very scarce in New England, as it was in all the colonies. The chief supply was obtained from the immigrants who arrived from the Old World. In the year 1635 it was so scarce that the General Court of Massachusetts ordered that musket bullets should pass in place of farthings, not more than twelve in one pay-

---

4. What was the general feeling toward the Indians? What instance is given of this? How far was this an unmixed feeling?

5. What is the chief employment of New Englanders? How soon, and to what other mode of livelihood, did they soon turn their attention? What is said of the progress in this?

6. In what other way were the people busy? What addition to their means of getting a living was made in 1690? In what respect did these settlements differ from Virginia?

ment. In Virginia tobacco was the chief currency. In New England it was principally corn and other grain, and beaver skins.

8. Grain was made a legal tender for debts, at prices fixed by law; but beaver skins held the next place to coin, on account of these being easily transported to any distance. A more convenient currency than beaver skins for small amounts was found in the Indian wampum. This was made of beads half an inch long, of two colors, white and bluish black, manufactured out of sea-shells and strung together. These strings of wampum were of different lengths, to represent different sums of money; but their value steadily declined as the colonies increased in trade.

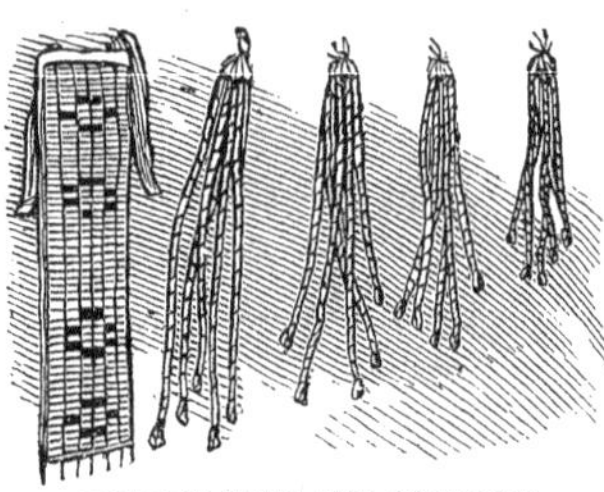

WAMPUM BELT AND CURRENCY.

9. The taxes were paid in "kind," that is, in what was raised or manufactured by the people; and the tax-gatherer often found it difficult to dispose of the beef and pork he took in this way. The town of Hingham, in Massachusetts, in the year 1687, compounded for its taxes in milk-pails. Money, in small amounts, was coined in New England as early as the year 1652. The pine-tree shilling of that date is still preserved. Throughout the colonial times, and un-

PINE-TREE SHILLING AND OTHER CURRENCY.

---

7. What is said of the abundance of money? What curious currency was authorized in Massachusetts? What was the common currency in Virginia, and what in New England?

8. What was made a legal tender for debts? What stood next to this as a tender in trade? What was the currency for small amounts? Describe this wampum. What is said of their value?

til after the close of the Revolution, the English currency —sterling money—was chiefly used in business.

10. **Dress and Customs.**—The dress of the country people was mostly home made, spun from the wool of their own sheep; in the towns it was richer, and obtained by trading with other countries. In the early times they had few luxuries. Four-wheeled carriages were not much seen until after the Revolution. The roads were poor, and the usual mode of land travel in all the colonies was on foot or on horseback.

11. The great annual feast of New England—"Thanksgiving Day"—which is now kept throughout the United States, had its origin at Plymouth in 1623. Governor Bradford, after the gathering of the harvest that year, sent out men to get game, who brought it home in abundance. A feast was made, and to it were invited Massasoit and ninety of his Indians. The colonists, with overflowing and grateful hearts, "thanked God for the good things of this world," and there they kept the first thanksgiving.

12. **Religion and Government.**—We can only obtain a correct idea of the early government of the New England colonies by noticing the difference in this which prevailed among them for a number of years. In the early history of Massachusetts, Plymouth, and New Haven, the Puritan churches, in fact, governed the people, and the ministers were nearly equal to the magistrates in political influence. Only Church members were allowed to be freemen. This was very severe on the male settlers, a large proportion of whom, as the colonies increased in numbers, were not Church members, and were thus deprived of the rights of citizenship. Nor would the churches permit any other religious sect among them. Out of this sprang the banishment of

---

9. How were the taxes paid? and what was often the situation of the tax-gatherer? What instance is given of this payment "in kind?" What mention is made of coined money in New England? In what denominations of money were accounts kept in all the colonies until after the close of the Revolution?

10. What is said of the dress of the people in the country and in the towns? What instances can you give of their simple habits in travel? To what, besides their poverty, was this owing?

11. When and where did the feast of "Thanksgiving" have its origin? State the circumstances under which the first was made.

Roger Williams, of Mrs. Hutchinson, and also of the Quakers.

13. In the year 1662, Charles II. sent orders to have the religious test of citizenship abolished, but this order was not obeyed. When the charter of Massachusetts was taken away in 1686, and a royal governor was appointed, the power of the ministers and churches began to wane. Other religious sects were allowed to build houses of worship, and greater religious freedom prevailed. Finally, in the year 1692, under King William's charter, the religious test of citizenship was entirely abolished.

14. The government of Connecticut and Rhode Island colonies was in striking contrast with that of the others. Here every male adult of good moral character, without reference to Church membership, was allowed to be a citizen. Rhode Island was particularly remarkable for toleration from the very first; and when New Haven was merged in Connecticut by the charter of 1655, that instrument secured to the enlarged colony the entire political freedom which the Connecticut River towns assumed for themselves in the year 1639.

15. Much has been said against the severe laws of New England. But severe and cruel laws were not peculiar to these colonies: they were the custom of the times, in Europe as well as America. In New England, in the year 1641, the offenses punishable with death were twelve in number. In Virginia, in 1611, only thirty years before this, the number of a like sort was seventeen.

16. **Education.**—If the ministers and churches were strict in religious matters, they deserve praise for their care of education. The public school or seminary at Newtown, now

---

12. How can we best understand the early government of New England? What was the state of things in Massachusetts, Plymouth, and New Haven? How did this affect the great body of male settlers? In what other way was this exclusiveness felt?

13. In what way did King Charles II. interfere? What broke the power of the churches of Massachusetts? How was this shown? When and how was freedom of citizenship obtained?

14. What difference was there in Connecticut and Rhode Island? What is said of Rhode Island in particular? How was New Haven colony affected by its union with Connecticut?

15. State what is said of the so called "severe laws" of New England. What comparison is made between the death code of New England and Virginia?

known as Harvard College, was provided for 1636, six years after the first settlement of Boston. This school was so dear to the people that the ministers in 1645 easily persuaded each family in the colony to give one peck of corn or one shilling in cash to the college.

17. Free schools were begun as early as 1635 in Boston, and the other towns soon followed. In 1665 every town had a free school, and, if over one hundred families, a grammar school. In Connecticut, in 1665, they punished every town that would not keep a school for three months in a year with a fine of £5 for each offense. The early schools were partly supported by free contributions and partly by tax; but it was expressly provided that the children of the poor should be taught free.

18. **Love for Civil Freedom.**—The "town meetings" which were held throughout the New England colonies for the settlement of local matters were assemblies where every thing was discussed with great freedom. There young and old met together, and the rich and poor were on an equal footing if they were citizens. These were the great schools of New England liberty. Meeting in this way, the people grew up independent, bold, and self-helpful.

19. Being Puritans, they were left to themselves, and were not disturbed by the Long Parliament or by Oliver Cromwell. After the king came to the throne they suffered in common with other colonies from oppression and commercial restrictions; but, in spite of this, we have already seen with what spirit they sent off Governor Andros to England when they could no longer endure his tyranny. During the intercolonial wars with the French and Indians, the great weight of the struggles fell on the New England colonies. This made them still more hardy and determined; and when

---

16. For what do the ministers and churches deserve praise? When was Harvard College established? What instance is given showing how the settlers regarded this seminary?

17. When and where were free schools begun? How long was this after the settlement of Boston? What was the state of education in 1665? What rule was put in force in Connecticut in regard to education? How were the early schools supported? What excellent provision was made?

18. What is said of the town meetings of New England? What took place at those meetings? How did they affect the spirit of the people?

the tyranny of England showed itself after the close of the French and Indian War, the New England men met it, in common with their brethren in Virginia and the other colonies, like men who knew how to fight and to die for their rights.

REVIEW QUESTIONS.—NEW ENGLAND COLONIES.

1. Whose name is linked with the settlement of Virginia and the exploration of the coast of New England?
2. By whom was it named New England?
3. Give the circumstances under which Smith was connected with the exploration of the latter, and date.
4. In what grant was it?
5. State the extent of this grant.
6. What are known as the New England colonies?
7. Which of these was first settled, and when?
8. What was the origin of Plymouth colony?
9. What grant of land did it have at first?
10. When did it get any, and what was its extent?
11. What is there remarkable about its compact of government?
12. How far was it a successful colony?
13. When was it united to Massachusetts?
14. What was the name of the leading colony of Massachusetts?
15. When and where were the first settlements?
16. What was the extent of the grant?
17. State the origin of the settlement of Rhode Island.
18. Did Williams have at first any grant from the Plymouth Company?
19. Why was he compelled to get one, and what was its extent?
20. What colony sprang from Massachusetts in 1635?
21. What and how many colonies are embraced in the earlier history of Connecticut?
22. How and when did these become united under the name of Connecticut?
23. Give the origin of these different colonies.
24. Under what government was New Hampshire settled?
25. How many of the early New England colonies were at first under this form?
26. What was the character of the great body of the settlers of New England?
27. What had they come to this country chiefly to obtain?
28. How far did they grant this freedom to others in their new settlements?
29. Give a sketch of three leading instances of persecution in the early history of Massachusetts, and the dates.
30. Sketch the history of Mrs. Hutchinson.
31. Name the early Indian wars in New England.
32. Give the cause and duration of the first of these.
33. What was its effect on the Indian tribe?
34. Give the cause and duration of King Philip's War.
35. What tribes were engaged?
36. What was the result?
37. State an incident at the close of this war showing how the early New Englanders regarded slavery.
38. When and for what purpose did the first union of colonies in America take place?

---

19. How were they treated by the English Puritan government? How by the king? How far did this repress their spirit? What wars fell most heavily on the New England colonies? What effect did these produce on the spirit of the people?

39. How long did it last, and what were its power and influence?
40. What side did the New England colonies take in the struggle between the English king and his Parliament?
41. Sketch the early history of New Hampshire.
42. When was New Hampshire made a royal province?
43. From what did the principal troubles of New Hampshire arise?
44. When and under what circumstances was Massachusetts first made a royal province?
45. How long did it remain at that time under a royal governor?
46. When was it made a royal province a second time?
47. How long did this last?
48. For what was the charter of Connecticut so famous?
49. State briefly her spirited struggles with Andros about this charter.
50. Under what government did Connecticut and Rhode Island remain after the expulsion of Andros?
51. How many intercolonial wars were there before the year 1750?
52. What was the cause, duration, and termination of King William's War?
53. State any important event connected with it.
54. Give the origin, duration, and termination of Queen Anne's War.
55. Mention any important events connected with it.
56. How and when did King George's War begin, and how long did it continue?
57. Name the principal events of this war.
58. What was the effect of these three intercolonial wars on the colonies?
59. Why is their story told in connection with the New England colonies?
60. What were the three leading pursuits of New England?
61. How was one of these affected by the Navigation Act?
62. State some facts showing the early and deep interest taken by these colonies in education.
63. Give some account of the primitive habits of the people.
64. What can you state regarding the rude currency of early New England?
65. What was necessary to become a citizen in some of the New England colonies?
66. What colonies formed a marked exception to this?
67. On what great principle was the settlement of Rhode Island based?
68. How did the early New England laws compare with those of Virginia?
69. To what extent did their religious views interfere with their love for and defense of civil liberty?
70. State in what way civil liberty was cultivated among them.

THE CHARTER OAK.

SECTION III.

MIDDLE COLONIES.

New York.

BLOCK AND HIS COMPANIONS ON MANHATTAN ISLAND BUILDING A VESSEL.

1. During the year 1610, the year after Hudson's discovery, the Dutch sent out ships to trade with the Indians on the new river, which they named the Mauritius. To shelter the men engaged in this trade, huts were built in several places. In 1613, one or more of these was at the south end of the island of Manhattan. It was this point that Captain Argall, of Virginia, visited in 1613, and there compelled the Hollanders to pull down their flag. In 1615 there was a fortified trading-house a little below the present site of Albany.

---

1. What use did the Dutch make of Hudson's discovery? What was the origin of the first European settlement on Manhattan Island? Who was Captain Argall? Can you tell why he interfered with the Dutch traders? See History of Virginia.

2. In the year 1614, an Amsterdam Company sent out five vessels on an exploring voyage. Adrian Block, one of the commanders, starting from Manhattan Island, sailed through the East River, which he named Helle-gat. He then explored the north shore of Long Island Sound, discovered the Housatonic and Connecticut rivers, and sailed as far as Cape Cod. Block Island was one of his discoveries. Captain Mey, a companion of Block, after exploring the southern shore of Long Island, entered the South Bay, now known as Delaware Bay. His name was given to its northern cape.

3. The English, who claimed all this country, remonstrated with the States of Holland about their conduct. The latter paid no attention to this remonstrance, and in the year 1621 granted the territory from Cape Henlopen to Cape Cod, already known as New Netherlands, to a powerful association called the Dutch West India Company.

4. In 1623, the company sent out two vessels, one of which was commanded by Captain Mey, who was made the director of New Netherlands. With him came a number of families, some of which settled Manhattan Island. Mey ascended the South River, now the Delaware, and built Fort Nassau, a few miles below Camden. During the same year, Fort Orange was built near the place where Albany now stands, to protect the Indian traders on the north.

5. Peter Minuits arrived as director in 1626. Among the first settlers were some Walloons—Protestants from Holland, descendants of exiled French Huguenots. These settled finally at Wahle-bocht, or Foreigner's Bay, now known as the Wallabout, on the East River, probably in 1626. This was the beginning of the Dutch settlement of Long Island. Bruekelen — Brooklyn — was first settled about the same time. After his arrival, Minuits purchased the island of

---

2. What expedition was sent from Holland in 1614? Who first sailed through the East River, and when? What were his discoveries? Who was Captain Mey? In what direction, and how far did he sail from Manhattan? What point still retains his name?

3. How did the English regard the conduct of the Dutch? How far were the Hollanders hindered from proceeding through fear of the English? What was the name of the Dutch claim in America?

4. What steps did the West India Company take to occupy their new grant? What forts were built in the year 1623?

Manhattan from the Indians for about twenty-four dollars. A block-house, surrounded by a palisade, was immediately built at the southern extremity, and named Fort Amsterdam. Round this, for shelter, houses were gradually built, and a little village grew up, named New Amsterdam, now supplanted by the great city of New York.

LANDING OF THE WALLOONS.

6. The West India Company were anxious to settle the country. They offered large tracts of land, with extraordinary rights and privileges, to any of their members who should, within four years, plant colonies thereon of fifty persons over fifteen years of age. The members who received these grants were called Patroons, signifying patrons or protectors, a name which was in use for more than two hundred years afterward.

5. What important arrivals took place in the year 1625? Where did they finally settle? How is this settlement to be regarded? Why? What great city was first settled about this time? What important purchase was made in 1626? What use was at once made of the purchase? What further remarks are made regarding it?

6. How did the Dutch Company show their anxiety to settle New Netherlands? What were the persons called, and why so named, who availed themselves of these grants?

7. Minuits was recalled in 1632, and Wouter (*woo-ter*) von Twiller came over as director in 1633. In a short time a dispute about territory arose between the Dutch and English on the Connecticut River. The former had built a fort, named the "House of Good Hope," near Hartford. The English, disregarding this, erected a trading-house a few miles above the Dutch post. Presently an English fort was built at the mouth of the river commanding its entrance.

8. In the south of New Netherlands also there was trouble. The Swedes, in 1638, sent out a body of settlers under Minuits, who had left the employment of the Dutch Company, and taken service under the Swedish king. Minuits (*min-yu-its*) erected a fort on Christiana Creek, near what is now Wilmington, Delaware. The new Dutch director, Sir William Kieft (*keeft*), sent word to them that this was within the limits of New Netherlands, but the Swedes paid no attention to Kieft or the Dutch claim.

9. The Dutch governor had now as much as he could take care of nearer home. The Algonquin Indians around Manhattan Island had been growing uneasy, and Kieft, by his inhuman cruelty, early in 1643 drove them almost to desperation. The Dutch farms or boweries extended thirty miles east, and from ten to twenty miles north and south of New Amsterdam. On these settlements the Indians fell suddenly, burning and slaying without mercy. The frightened colonists, from all sides, fled to New Amsterdam. After a time the revenge of the Indians was satisfied, and they made proposals for peace, which were gladly accepted. But, in the interim, the war broke out anew, and continued, with all its horrors, until the year 1645. It was in this war that the unfortunate Mrs. Hutchinson, and all but one of her family, were murdered by the natives.

---

7. Who succeeded Minuits? When, where, and with whom did trouble spring up? What measures were taken by the Dutch? What was done by the English?

8. In what way did their former governor give the Dutch Company trouble? What notice did the Dutch take of this? What attention was paid to Kieft's remonstrance?

9. Why was Kieft prevented from taking active measures to expel the Swedes? Describe the exposed state of the Dutch settlements, and the Indian massacre that took place. How was the war terminated for a time, when was it recommenced, and how long did it continue? What interesting incident is connected with the horrors of this war?

10. Kieft, who had grown very unpopular, and whose conduct had mainly brought on the Indian War, was recalled by the Dutch Company at the request of the colonists. He sailed in 1647, taking with him a rich cargo of furs; but the ship was cast on the rocks of Wales, and Kieft and others were drowned.

11. Peter Stuyvesant (*sti-ve-sant*), the new director, who arrived in 1647, was a very different man—a brave soldier, and a person of great spirit and energy. One of the first things he did was to settle the boundary-line between Connecticut and New Netherlands. This being done, he turned his attention to the Swedes, and built Fort Casimir, on the Delaware, five miles below the Swedish fort at Christiana Creek.

12. The Swedes shortly after surprised and took Fort Casimir; and in due time a letter came from the Company in Holland ordering Stuyvesant to expel them from the South River and Bay. Accordingly, he went from New Amsterdam in 1655, to the Delaware, with six hundred men; and so overwhelming was his force, that every Swedish post at once submitted to his authority. Thus ended the Swedish colony, after an existence of seventeen years.

13. There was, however, no quiet for Stuyvesant. A number of emigrants, principally from England, had settled in and around New Amsterdam. They began to ask that the laws should be made by the consent of the people, and this idea soon spread among the Dutch settlers. Stuyvesant, who hated popular government, resisted these demands as well as he could, but was kept in constant trouble by them until the year 1664.

14. In that year a British fleet, under Colonel Nichols, appeared in front of Fort Amsterdam, and demanded its surrender in the name of the Duke of York, the brother of

---

10. When and for what reason did Kieft's directorship terminate? What is said of his unhappy end?

11. Who succeeded Kieft, and what was his character? What is said of his movements? What did he next do?

12. What befell Stuyvesant's fort? How did the Company in Holland look on this? What spirited movements followed? How long had the Swedish colony existed?

13. What settlers gave Stuyvesant a great deal of trouble? What opinions did those settlers hold? How did Stuyvesant act?

Charles II. The king had granted his brother the whole territory from the Connecticut to the Delaware. Stout-hearted Peter Stuyvesant, now sixty-two years old, tried hard to get his council to refuse the demand of Nichols and fight, but in vain. The Dutch were lukewarm, and the En-

THE WRATH OF PETER STUYVESANT.

glish settlers favored the English demand. The magistrates signed a treaty of surrender, and, at the last moment, Stuyvesant, in great sorrow and chagrin, added his own name. The English flag rose over New Amsterdam September, 1664, and over Fort Orange, changed to the name of Albany, in October following. The entire province, as well as the city, was named New York, in honor of the proprietor. Thus ended, after an existence of forty years, the supremacy of the Dutch West India Company in New Netherlands.

14. What important event occurred in 1664? Upon what claim was this demand founded? How did Stuyvesant act in the crisis? What was the conduct of the magistrates? What changes took place on the surrender of Fort Amsterdam?

NEW YORK UNDER THE ENGLISH.

15. Colonel Nichols was the first governor of the province of New York, and proved both a wise and kind ruler during the three years he was in power. He was followed by Lovelace, who oppressed the colonists, and, when they complained and protested, ordered their protest to be burned by the common hangman.

16. A war between England and Holland broke out in the year 1672. In July, next year, 1673, a Dutch squadron appeared in the harbor of New York, and the city surrendered at the first summons. The authority of the Dutch continued only fifteen months. In the month of November, 1674, after peace had been proclaimed, it was restored to the English, according to the terms of the treaty.

17. Major Edmund Andros came out as governor in 1674, but did not find a very submissive colony. He ruled with an iron hand, and attempted to extend his authority over New Jersey, which had been granted by the Duke of York to Lord Berkeley and Sir George Carteret. Complaint was made by the governor of New Jersey, and Andros was recalled in 1680. This was the same Andros who was expelled for his tyranny from New England nine years later.

18. The governors who succeeded Andros were severe rulers, and when the Duke of York was declared king, under the title of James II., in 1685, they became, by his tyrannical order, more and more severe. When the news arrived, in 1689, that he had been expelled from the throne of England, a portion of the citizens placed themselves under the command of Jacob Leisler (*līs-ler*), a merchant, and seized the fort in the name of the new king, William III.

19. Nicholson, the governor, fled to England, and told the

---

15. What was the character of the new governor? What is said of his successor, and of his treatment of the people?

16. What war broke out in Europe in 1672? How long did this affect New York? How long did it remain in the possession of the Dutch? In what way did it return under English control?

17. What well-known colonial governor first appears as governor of New York? What was his character and conduct? To what did this lead?

18. What is said of the governors that followed? What important event occurred in England in 1689? How did this affect the colony of New York?

king that Leisler was an arch rebel and renegade. In 1690, King William appointed Colonel Sloughter (*slaw-ter*) governor, and sent out Captain Ingoldsby in command of a small body of soldiers. Ingoldsby arrived at New York early in 1691, before Sloughter, and demanded of Leisler the surrender of the fort. Leisler refused to give it up until the arrival of the governor. When Sloughter did arrive in 1691, Leisler and his son-in-law, Milborne, who had acted as his deputy, were thrown into prison, and, after trial, condemned as traitors and rebels.

20. Sloughter was unwilling to order them to execution; but Leisler's enemies of the aristocratic party invited the governor to a dinner-party, and it is said that, when he was intoxicated, they obtained his signature to the death-warrant. Leisler and Milborne were taken out of prison in the

SLOUGHTER SIGNING THE DEATH-WARRANT.

19. How was King William's mind poisoned against Leisler? Who was appointed governor? Who preceded him? What occurred on his arrival at New York? What happened on the arrival of Governor Sloughter?

early morning following, and executed, May, 1691. The mass of the citizens were greatly excited by the execution of their favorite leader. He was styled the people's martyr, and his cruel death divided the colony into two parties, that long regarded each other with the most bitter hatred.

21. During Leisler's government, and for some time after, the French and their Indian allies bore heavily on the northern frontier. This was in King William's War, a sketch of which has been given in the history of Massachusetts. As early as 1690, Schenectady, a frontier village on the Mohawk, was burned by the French and Indians. Sixty persons were killed with barbarous cruelty, and thirty were made prisoners. In Queen Anne's, and also King George's War, the colony bore its full share of the expense and suffering. We shall shortly see that, in the French and Indian War, her frontier territory became the scene of bloody conflicts.

22. In 1741, the citizens of New York were thrown into great excitement by a report that the negroes had formed a plot to burn the city and murder the inhabitants. The wildest rumors prevailed, and, on very slight suspicions, thirty persons were executed, some of whom were whites. It took some time for common sense to resume control, but the citizens came at last to be ashamed of the cruelty of which they had been guilty. New York suffered much from the oppression of the royal governors. The struggles of the people for their rights developed the spirit of liberty, which fitted the New Yorkers to take a very active part in the events that preceded the American Revolutionary War. Until the close of that contest, a large part of the colony remained a royal province.

---

20. What delayed their execution? What means did their enemies take to reach this? What followed? How was the execution regarded by the people? How did it affect the future of the colony?

21. What intercolonial war was raging during Sloughter's government? What event occurred on the frontiers during this war? What is said of the colony during the other colonial wars?

22. What excitement broke out in the city of New York in 1741? State what is said of it. From what did New York suffer? What good result came out of this? How long did England retain control of the colony?

NEW JERSEY.

1. NEW NETHERLANDS embraced within its limits the country lying between the Hudson and the Delaware, now known as New Jersey. A few of the Dutch from Manhattan Island crossed the "North" River, so named to distinguish it from the "South" River, or Delaware, and formed a small settlement at Bergen about the year 1620. But the active settlement of New Jersey did not begin until the year 1664. In that year the whole of New Netherlands passed, as we have seen, into the possession of the Duke of York.

2. Nichols, the duke's governor, on his arrival at New Amsterdam, granted lands lying west of the Hudson to some Long Islanders and New England men, and they, the same year, 1664, settled Elizabethtown. This is the first settlement of New Jersey by the English. In the mean time, the duke, in England, had sold a large tract between the Hudson and the Delaware to Lord Berkeley and Sir George Carteret. This was then named New Jersey, after the island of Jersey, in the English Channel, of which Carteret had been governor.

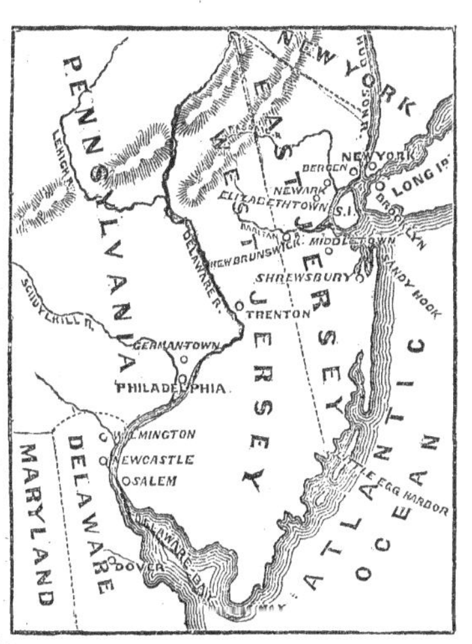

MIDDLE COLONIES.
For part of New Netherlands, see Map, page 63.

3. Philip Carteret, the brother of Sir George, was sent over as governor in 1665, and made Elizabethtown his resi-

---

1. What did New Netherlands embrace within its limits? What was the earliest settlement made here? When did the active settlement of New Jersey begin? What important event occurred that year?

2. What grants were made on the territory west of the Hudson? What settlement was made the same year? What disposition had meanwhile been made of a large part of the territory? What was it named, and why?

dence. Colonists began to flock into the province, and Newark, Middletown, Shrewsbury, and other places were rapidly settled. The climate was mild, the soil in many places was rich, the proprietors charged no rents for the land for five years, and there was no danger from Indians.

4. At the end of five years, the settlers who had received their grants from Nichols refused to pay the quitrent of a halfpenny per acre demanded by the proprietor, and, in the disturbances that followed, the governor was compelled to leave the colony in the year 1670. Afterward, in 1675, some concessions were granted to the settlers, and he quietly resumed the government.

5. Lord Berkeley sold out his right to Fenwick and Byllinge (*bill-inj*), two Quakers, in the year 1674. Next year Fenwick came over with a number of immigrants, and settled Salem, at the head of Delaware Bay. Byllinge became unfortunate in his business, and his interest in Berkeley's grant was assigned, for the benefit of his creditors, to three trustees, who divided it into ninety shares, and sold them. As Carteret was still half owner of the original grant of New Jersey, it was agreed, in 1676, to divide the territory into East and West Jersey. Carteret took the eastern part; Fenwick and the trustees of Byllinge took the western. The same year upward of four hundred Quakers from England settled at Burlington, on the Delaware. These were soon followed by others, and West Jersey in this way became distinctively Quaker.

6. In the year 1678, Major Edmund Andros, as governor of New York under the duke, claimed, as we have already seen, that the whole of New Jersey was included in his government. In enforcing this claim, he carried Philip Carteret prisoner to Manhattan Island in the year 1680. Next year,

---

3. Who was sent over as governor in 1665? What was made the capital of the province? What places were settled? What is said of the soil and climate, and the encouragement to settlers?

4. What trouble occurred in the colony at the expiration of the five years? When were these troubles settled, and how?

5. What change in proprietors took place about this time? When, where, and by whom was a settlement soon after made? What other change in proprietors occurred shortly? How and why was New Jersey divided? What kind of settlers came to West Jersey?

1681, the Duke of York relinquished all claim to the Jerseys, and the proprietors were restored to their rights.

7. Sir George Carteret dying, his heirs, in the year 1682, sold East Jersey to William Penn and eleven other Quakers. The government did not not move very smoothly here on account of disputes about land titles, and it was the same in West Jersey. There were too many proprietors, and they could not always agree among themselves as to who had a right to grant a title to the purchasers. Wearied out in disputes with the tenants, who seemed to think that the government of the proprietors was mainly for the purpose of extorting quitrents, the latter, in 1702, gave up their right of government to the crown; they, however, retained their private rights to vast tracts of land, some of which titles have descended through their heirs to the present time.

8. In 1702, the whole of New Jersey was united with New York under one governor; they had, however, separate Assemblies. This arrangement continued twenty-six years, and then, on the earnest petition of the people, New Jersey obtained a royal governor for itself. Under this separate government it remained until the Revolution.

Delaware. Pennsylvania.

1. Delaware was first settled by the Swedes, under Peter Minuits, on Christiana Creek, near the present city of Wilmington, in the year 1638. The tract of land lying around the settlement, purchased from the Indians, was named New Sweden. In 1643 they built a fort on Tinicum Island, in the Delaware, a few miles below Philadelphia. This was, therefore, the first settlement in what is now the State of Pennsylvania.

---

6. What claim was set up by the Governor of New York? What high-handed act did Andros perpetrate? How was the contest about government settled?

7. What disposition was made of East Jersey in 1682? What interfered with the peace of the settlement? What was a principal cause of these disputes? How did the settlers gain the victory? What did New Jersey thus become? What did the proprietors retain, and what is stated in regard to these titles?

8. What union took place in 1702? How long did this last? What change took place, and how long did this remain in force?

1. By whom and where was Delaware first settled? By whom, where, and when was Pennsylvania first settled?

2. The Dutch regarded the Swedish posts on the Delaware as an intrusion on their territory of New Netherlands, and, as we have already seen, compelled the settlers to submit to their authority in 1655. But these settlements on the west bank of the river continued to flourish long after the Swedish power there had ended, and from time to time were increased by Dutch and English immigrants from New York and New England.

3. In the year 1681, William Penn, a son of the celebrated English Admiral Penn, obtained a grant of land in America, west of the Delaware, from Charles II. of England, in payment of a debt due to his father. This tract, called Pennsylvania by the king, was increased by a grant to Penn from the Duke of York of all that territory now forming the State of Delaware, and presently named "the territories or three lower counties on the Delaware." This gave Penn the western and southern shore of the river and bay, and also an outlet to the ocean for his new province. Being himself a Quaker, his desire was to provide a home in the New World for oppressed "Friends," as the Quakers called themselves, that they might here enjoy their religion in peace.

4. In 1682, Penn himself came over with a hundred immigrants, and in the same year twenty-three vessels with settlers sailed from England, all of which arrived safely. Penn landed at Newcastle, November, 1682, and was received by the settlers on the Delaware, as well as those who had preceded him in 1681, with great respect. Early in 1683 he laid out the city of Philadelphia, on land purchased from the Swedes, which they had bought from the Indians. It progressed so rapidly that by the close of the year there were eighty substantial houses.

5. Penn's treatment of the Indians—with whom, soon aft-

---

2. What colony treated these settlements as trespassing on its territory? Do you remember who compelled them to submit? How far did this break up the Swedish settlements? How were they increased?

3. Who was William Penn? In what way did he become connected with the history of America? What was the new province named, and by whom? What further grant did he obtain? How was this addition known? Of what advantage was this to the province? To what denomination did Penn belong? How did he design to use the grant of land that had been given to him?

4. When did Penn himself first come over? What immigration came in the same year? Where did Penn land, and how was he received?

PENN'S ARRIVAL AT NEWCASTLE.

er he landed, he made a treaty of love and friendship under an elm-tree near Philadelphia — was so kind and truthful, that the natives always trusted one in the dress of a Quaker. The consequence was that the early settlers of Pennsylvania were not troubled by the Indians for many years. He was equally liberal to the colonists, both Swedes and English. He freely gave them the right to elect all the subordinate officers of the colony, and all the law-making was placed in their hands. Entire religious freedom was also secured by law.

6. Lord Baltimore from the very first disputed the boundaries of Penn's grants, and claimed that the northerly line of Maryland ran west from the Delaware above the Schuylkill. This claim covered the three lower counties, and also included the city of Philadelphia. Penn, unable to agree with Baltimore about the boundaries, went to London in

---

5. How did Penn secure the love of the Indians? How was this shown in the early history of the colony? What is said of his treatment of the early settlers?

1684 to have the dispute settled. It was there decided that Penn should have half the territory between the Chesapeake and the Delaware lying north of Cape Henlopen.

7. When Penn went to England he left a deputy, with a council of five, to take charge of the colony. In 1691 this council gave great offense to the three lower counties on the Delaware, and the latter set up a separate government. Penn "sorrowfully" sent word from England to let them have their way, and appointed a deputy governor over them. Next year, 1692, the province and the territories were taken from him, because he was thought to be a firm friend of the deposed King James, and were united to New York; but in 1694 all his rights were restored to him.

8. In 1699 he came out from England, and found the people angry and dissatisfied. There was no good reason for their complaints. Penn had been very kind to them, and their lives had been entirely free from the troubles that had befallen the early settlers in nearly all the other colonies. Penn, always anxious for the welfare of the people, gave them a new "Charter of Liberties," but this did not satisfy the three lower counties.

9. Meanwhile news was brought from England that an attempt was in progress to bring all the proprietary governments in the colonies under the crown. This led Penn, in 1701, to return to England, whence he wrote to his province that he would allow the lower counties to have a separate Assembly. A final agreement of separation was accordingly made in 1703; but both colonies until the American Revolution remained under one governor. After Penn's death in England in 1718, they were governed by his descendants or deputies. In the year 1779, the State of Pennsylvania, grateful to the memory of its founder, paid to his

---

6. With whom was Penn involved in disputes? What were the rival claims of Lord Baltimore? What was Penn compelled to do? What was the result?

7. What occurred during Penn's absence in England? How did Penn act when he heard the news? What great change took place in 1692, and why? When and in what way was justice done to Penn?

8. When did he return from England? What did he find on his arrival? What is said of the grounds which the settlers had for this discontent? How did Penn show his benevolent feelings? How far did this satisfy them?

heirs nearly five hundred and eighty thousand dollars as an equivalent for their proprietary rights.

10. The history of one of the very greatest of American patriots and philosophers, Benjamin Franklin, is closely connected with the later colonial history of Pennsylvania. Born in Boston in 1706, he settled, when a youth, as a printer in Philadelphia, where he gradually rose to the first honors in the province. Here he made his famous discoveries in electricity, and here he gained a great reputation for sagacity and skill in the management of public business. We shall meet him in the history of the French and Indian War and of the American Revolution.

9. What attempt important to Penn was being made in England? How did he meet this? What concessions did he make? When was this concluded? How were Delaware and Pennsylvania governed after the separation? When and where did Penn die? What eventually became of the rights of his heirs?

10. What great man was a resident of Philadelphia during its colonial history? What is said of his character?

GENERAL REFLECTIONS ON THE MIDDLE COLONIES.

DUTCH FAMILY SCENE.—NEW AMSTERDAM.

1. **Early Settlers.**—In the middle colonies—New York, New Jersey, Pennsylvania, and Delaware—we find the settlers differing in language and in race much more than in Virginia or New England. Among them were to be found DUTCH, SWEDISH, GERMAN, FRENCH, and ENGLISH colonists. The Swedes had only a very limited influence on the lower Delaware; the Dutch left a very powerful and lasting impression on New York and on East Jersey; the Germans settled principally in Pennsylvania, where their influence was confined to their own communities—Germantown, for example, was settled by a band of German Quakers; the French were to be found in considerable numbers in New York.

2. The English were the most numerous throughout these four colonies, and, after the conquest of New Netherlands,

1. What comparison is made between the early settlers in the middle colonies and those in Virginia and New England? From what nations did they come? What is said of the Swedes? the Dutch? the Germans? the French? the English?

overshadowed all the others. The English Quakers spread over Pennsylvania, West Jersey, and Delaware. The New England men settled the east part of Long Island, and worked their way in among the Dutch of Manhattan, very much to the annoyance of the Dutch governors and the settlers. They crossed over also into East Jersey, where soon came a large number of Scotch Presbyterians, whose influence has come down to our own time.

3. **Their Relations with the Indians.**—With the exception of the quarrels with the proprietors and others about land titles under conflicting land grants, New Jersey, after the English settlement, was remarkably free from every thing that could disturb the settlers. Nearly surrounded by the other colonies, it was almost entirely sheltered from the Indians, and the early inhabitants endured no such privations from exposure or want of food as the settlers of Virginia and New England.

4. Pennsylvania was equally fortunate. Penn's kind treatment of the Indians, from the very first, won their confidence. It is to be borne in mind, however, that these Delawares of the Algonquin family were a feeble remnant, and very different from the Eastern Indians or the fierce Iroquois. The settlers in the "three lower counties on the Delaware," and in West Jersey in particular, were as happily situated as the Pennsylvanians. It may be said safely that no body of people ever enjoyed more abundant blessings in peace, comfort, and moderate freedom, than the early settlers in West Jersey, Pennsylvania, and the Territories. There are no very striking events in the history of these colonies, because there was among them so much solid happiness. It is out of oppression and wars that what are generally called the great events of history arise.

---

2. Where did the Quakers settle? Where do we find the New England men? How were these immigrants regarded in the New Netherlands? Where else did they find their way?

3. What is said of the early condition of New Jersey? How was it saved from the Indian massacres? In what other thing are the settlers to be considered fortunate?

4. How was Pennsylvania saved from Indian troubles? What is said of the "three lower counties?" What general statement is made regarding the happiness of the settlers? Why are there very few striking events in the history of New Jersey, Pennsylvania, and Delaware?

5. The early history of New York was different. The Indian wars, at an early day, carried destruction among the settlers. Not only on the north were they exposed to the fury of the Indians, but the neighborhood of Manhattan Island suffered severely. For these massacres the Dutch had themselves to blame. Governor Kieft's cruelty to the Indians produced the effect that might have been expected on the jealous and revengeful natives.

6. **Industry of the People.**—All these colonies were for a long time agricultural. The climate was temperate, and the soil yielded in abundance maize, wheat, and other grains, much of which was exported, particularly from Pennsylvania. But the industry of the settlers was not confined particularly to farming. The foundations of two great mercantile cities were laid, New York and Philadelphia.

7. New Amsterdam, admirably situated for commerce, at a very early day did a considerable business with the Indians in skins and furs, which were exported to Europe; but the Dutch town grew slowly. In the year 1656 there were only 1000 inhabitants. After it passed into the hands of the English, New York increased more rapidly, for in the year 1700 there were nearly 6000 residents.

8. Philadelphia, on the other hand, grew quickly and vigorously from the very first. In 1684, two years after its settlement, it was estimated to contain 2400 inhabitants, and for many years was greatly in advance of New York. It carried on an active commerce, and, having a rich country near it on both banks of the Delaware, occupied by thrifty farmers, it soon became a place of considerable business. The manufactures of the people will be alluded to hereafter in some general remarks on colonial commerce and manufactures, and the restrictions imposed on them by the English government.

---

5. What contrast is to be found in the history of New York? What was the cause of this?

6. What was the chief occupation of the settlers in the middle colonies? What is said of this? What other calling was pursued?

7. What is said of the business of New Amsterdam, and its growth? Why is it so well situated for commerce? What was its population in 1656 and in 1700?

8. What is said of the growth of Philadelphia? What is stated of its commerce and local business?

9. **The Proprietary Governments and Land Grants.**—In these middle colonies we see a full trial of the proprietary plan of government. There was much civil freedom, but the administration of authority did not work happily for the proprietors. Even Penn, who said he desired nothing so much as the happiness of his colonists, became in time very weary of their sturdy opposition. They wanted constantly more of their own way, and this he was not always ready to grant. Then there were bitter disputes in New Jersey, as well as New York, about land titles. The proprietors either sold their lands in small farms or leased them perpetually at low rents. But the titles of these proprietors were often conflicting, and the rents were not paid when they became due, no matter how small the amount. The whole arrangement did not work well for the proprietors, and in the end they were happy to give up their powers of government to the crown.

10. The system practiced by the West India Company of granting great tracts of land in New Netherlands to patroons proved very oppressive. The troubles these grants produced have descended almost to our own times, breaking out into armed resistance to the claims of proprietors as late as the year 1842. These were called the "Anti-rent Troubles," and occurred in some of the Hudson River counties in New York. The same system of land grants was pursued under the English governors. As an instance, Livingston Manor, a large tract below the present city of Hudson, extending twelve miles on the river bank, and stretching with increasing width as far as the Massachusetts line, was granted by Governor Dongan to Robert Livingston, a Scotch immigrant.

11. These enormous grants in New York helped greatly to produce an aristocracy, and the chief power of the colony was thus held in the hands of a few leading families and their friends. That greatest event in the early history of

---

9. What form of government was fully tried in the middle colonies, and how did it operate for the governors and the governed? How is this shown in Penn's experience with his settlers? What was the state of things in New Jersey about lands?

10. What is said of the grant made by the Dutch West India Company and the troubles that proceeded therefrom? What were these troubles called, and where did they take place? What instance is given of the system of English grants?

the colony of New York, the political murder of Leisler, sprang from this. Leisler was the leader of the people, and lost his life when the aristocracy triumphed, the Livingston mentioned above being one of his prominent enemies.

12. After his death the struggle became more bitter between the party of the people and their enemies, continuing for more than a quarter of a century; and this contest fitted the people to take the bold stand they did against the mother country in Revolutionary times. Nowhere throughout the colonies was there a more active spirit shown against England than by the "Sons of Liberty" in New York City in 1774.

13. **Religion and Education.**—It is interesting to notice how many of the colonies were founded by persons escaping from religious persecution. We have already seen Maryland, Massachusetts, and Rhode Island first settled from this cause. The middle colonies were also the refuge of the persecuted. No religious sect was called on to endure more reproach and persecution than the Quakers, and no people was at last more happily situated than they were in West Jersey and Pennsylvania.

14. To New Netherlands, also, came the Walloon families from the South Belgic provinces—exiles from France for religious persecution, and really Huguenots speaking the French language. The persecuted Waldenses, exiled from Piedmont to Holland, were early settled on Staten Island. Fifty years after the arrival of the Walloons there was a large addition of Huguenot families of the first character, many of whom settled on and near Manhattan Island, others in what is now Ulster county. New Rochelle, in Westchester county, settled in 1689, still points out, by its French name, an early Huguenot settlement.

---

11. What did these grants tend to produce? What event sprang out of this? What leading man was closely connected with the execution of Leisler?

12. How far did Leisler's death put an end to this contest? How did it educate the people? In what way was this spirit shown in later times?

13. What is stated as worthy of particular notice? What colonies already mentioned were settled from this cause? How was it in Pennsylvania and Jersey?

14. Who were among the first settlers of New Netherlands? What were they? Who were the Waldenses? What can you say of the Huguenots and their early settlements?

15. The Protestant settlers of New Amsterdam brought with them from Holland the church of their choice. They soon added to this the school and the schoolmaster, because they understood the value of education. One of the most urgent and constant demands made by them to the West India Company was that the directors should send competent schoolmasters from Holland, and the settlers freely offered to be taxed for their support and for that of a public school. In the year 1659, a Latin school was established by the directors at their earnest solicitation, and a learned professor was sent from Europe to conduct it. This school became so successful that in 1662 children were sent to it from as far south as the Delaware River and Virginia.

16. After New York passed into the hands of the English in 1664, the subject of education was greatly neglected. This was owing, among other things, to the intermixture of languages, races, and sects. The same causes operated powerfully in Pennsylvania, where, though Penn had granted a charter for a high school as early as 1689, it was owing to the vigorous efforts of Benjamin Franklin that an "academy" was established in 1749. This became in a short time a college, and finally the University of Pennsylvania. By Franklin's influence, there was added, in 1752, a free school, where all poor children were taught reading, writing, and arithmetic.

In conclusion, we see that among the early settlers of these middle colonies there were the elements that form a vigorous, liberty-loving, industrious, and intellectual people. They came from the sturdiest and most advanced nations of Europe, and in this new land their children displayed in due time the sterling virtues which they inherited from their ancestors.

---

15. How early did the settlers attend to education in New Netherlands? How is this shown? Give an account of the establishment of the Latin school. What is said of its success?

16. What is said of education after 1664? To what was this greatly owing? What was the state of things in Pennsylvania? When and through whom was a free school established in Philadelphia?

What is said in general of the settlers in the middle colonies?

REVIEW QUESTIONS.—MIDDLE COLONIES.

1. From what European nations did the first settlers of the middle colonies come?
2. Which was the first of these colonies?
3. What were the limits of New Netherlands, and to whom granted?
4. Why was the Hudson River called the North River?
5. What was the South River?
6. Where and when was the first occupation of this colony?
7. Where, and by whom, and when was it first settled?
8. What people from the north of Europe settled in New Netherlands?
9. When and where did they settle?
10. How long were they a separate colony?
11. When and how did it end?
12. Which of the middle colonies did the English first settle?
13. How long did the Dutch maintain their authority in New Netherlands?
14. Who was their last governor, and what was his character?
15. When and how did the Dutch supremacy come to an end?
16. How much territory did the Duke of York claim to be within his grant?
17. In what way did this claim influence the settlement of New Jersey?
18. Where and when was it first settled by the English?
19. By whom was the eastern end of Long Island first settled?
20. To whom did the duke assign a large portion of his territory?
21. When and why was it afterward named New Jersey?
22. By whom was West Jersey principally settled?
23. Tell from the map, page 124, the boundaries of East and West Jersey?
24. What trouble did the settlers have with the proprietors?
25. How did such troubles generally end?
26. What grant was made to William Penn? Who was he?
27. What colony did Pennsylvania originally embrace within its limits?
28. Why did it separate from Pennsylvania?
29. Give the particulars of the early settlement of Pennsylvania?
30. What sect formed the great bulk of the settlers there?
31. When and how did the colonizing of Delaware begin?
32. What colonies were to a large extent first settled by Friends?
33. How many of the middle colonies had proprietary governments?
34. What was their experience under this form of government?
35. Which of these colonies were first settled out of religious persecution?
36. What tragical event is deeply interwoven with the early politics of New York?
37. State briefly the particulars of this.
38. Who were the patroons, and how did they affect the comfort of the colony?
39. Where did the Germans settle?
40. Were there any French Protestants in any of these colonies? If so, where?
41. Who were the Walloons and the Waldenses?
42. In what respect did Penn and the Dutch differ in their treatment of the Indians?
43. How did Penn and his colonists treat each other?
44. What is said of the condition of the early settlers of West Jersey and Pennsylvania?
45. Give the dates of the different settlements, and state by whom they were made.

SECTION IV.

EXTREME SOUTHERN COLONIES.

NORTH CAROLINA.

1. UNDER his Virginia grant, Raleigh, it will be remembered, made several unfortunate attempts to settle on Roanoke Island. These were the first efforts at settlement within the present limits of North Carolina. The country remained unnoticed until the year 1630, when Charles I. of England granted an immense tract of land south of the Chesapeake to Sir Robert Heath; but he did not make any settlement on the territory, and the grant thus became void.

2. About the year 1651, a few emigrants from Virginia settled near the mouth of the Chowan River. Ten years later, some New England people settled on the Cape Fear River, near the present site of Wilmington. The land there was very barren, the Indians were hostile, and the colony soon went to ruin.

3. In 1663, Charles II. granted to Lord Clarendon and seven noblemen, out of the territory originally given to Heath, a new province, which was named Carolina, in honor of the king. A party of settlers from Virginia, under a governor appointed by the proprietor, settled, in the year 1664, on the Chowan River, near the old settlement of 1651, and the colony was named Albemarle, in honor of one of the proprietors.

4. The proprietors as well as the settlers supposed this to be within the limits of the Carolina grant. They soon found they were north of it, and new boundaries were granted. The present southern boundary of Virginia became the line on the north, and the southern line took in more than one half of Florida. About the year 1665, Sir John Yeamans brought a number of emigrants from Barbadoes, who settled

1. Where and by whom were the first attempts made to settle North Carolina? Was this attempt successful? When and to whom did King Charles I. grant land? What use was made of the grant?

2. What settlement was made in the year 1651? What was made ten years later? What was its success?

3. When was the next grant given, and to whom? From what place did the settlers come, and when? Where was the first settlement made? What was it named?

near Wilmington. This was named the Clarendon County Colony.

5. Earl Shaftesbury and John Locke, two celebrated Englishmen, on behalf of the proprietors, drew up a plan of government for Carolina. It provided for the creation of an order of nobility, who were to govern the people and make the laws. This aristocratic government was, perhaps, suited to an old and populous country, but not to a wild territory, where the settlers were few and widely scattered. After being tried for more than twenty years, it was found to produce nothing but constant heart-burnings, and was finally given up.

6. Clarendon County Colony did not succeed. The country around it was barren, and the settlement was nearly abandoned in 1671. Albemarle County Colony flourished in numbers, but there was constant discord between the settlers and the proprietors, arising partly out of the scheme of government, and partly out of the old and troublesome question of yearly rents for their lands.

7. The same state of things existed in North Carolina as in nearly all the other colonies under proprietors—the people were unwilling to pay these rents, and the proprietors found it impossible to collect them. The trouble that this occasioned in the province was increased by the bad governors that were appointed. Things went on in this unsettled way until the year 1729, when North Carolina passed under royal government, and so remained a royal province until the American Revolution.

---

4. Where did these settlers suppose themselves to be? How were the boundaries finally arranged? Where did the next settlers come from? What was the name of this colony?

5. Who drew up the first form of government? How were the people to be governed under this form? Did this prove suitable at that time? Did it finally prove successful?

6. What is said of the Clarendon County Colony? Was the Albemarle County Colony more successful? From what did their troubles arise?

7. What trouble did North Carolina have in common with other colonies? How was this increased? How long did this state of things last? How did it finally end?

SOUTH CAROLINA.

1. JOHN RIBAULT, as has been already stated, attempted to settle a colony of Huguenots at Port Royal in the year 1562, but was driven off by the Spaniards.

2. The proprietors under Clarendon's grant turned their attention to the southern part of their territory, and sent out some colonists, who settled first at Port Royal, but afterward removed to the Ashley River, and founded old Charleston, 1670. The settlement was named the Carteret County Colony. In 1680, the old Charleston settlers removed to the junction of the Cooper and Ashley Rivers, and laid the foundation of the present city of Charleston.

3. Religious persecution in France drove a large body of Huguenots to seek a home in South Carolina about the year 1686. They were not well received by the colonists, who were at first disposed to drive them out of the country. The French exiles bore all this with great patience, and so won on the better feelings of the English by their industry and integrity, that they were, after some time, admitted to the full rights of citizenship. From this Huguenot stock there descended many of the most powerful and well known families of South Carolina.

4. The people of the colony were no more submissive to authority than in the northern settlements. They quarreled with the proprietors about rents, taxes, and their rights; resisted the famous scheme of government already alluded to, and went so far as to banish one of their governors.

5. The Spaniards at St. Augustine, in Florida, were their nearest neighbors on the south. When war, known as Queen Anne's, was declared in 1702 by England against France and Spain, South Carolina raised an expedition, and sent it

---

1. Who made the first attempt at settling in North Carolina, and when?

2. What was the next attempt? Where did they finally remove to? In what year was old Charleston settled?

3. What event in France caused a great many people to seek a home in South Carolina? How were they received? How did the exiles bear this treatment? What was the result of their forbearance? What effect on the colony did this Huguenot immigration eventually produce?

4. What is said of the submissiveness of the South Carolinians? What did they quarrel about? How far did they carry their resistance to the government?

against St. Augustine, in Florida. The Spanish fort was found too strong, and the Carolina troops were compelled to return without effecting their object. In the year 1706, a French fleet from Havana attacked Charleston, but was repulsed, with the loss of three hundred men, and one of the ships, which was captured.

6. The Indians on the borders occasioned them great trouble at different times; but in 1715 a severe battle was fought, and the natives were driven into the swamps of Florida. When the Indian War ended, the expenses that had been incurred produced discontent, which broke out in open rebellion, and the settlers a second time expelled the governor. In 1720 the king declared the charter forfeited, but paid the proprietors about $80,000 for their rights. Thus ended the proprietary government, and South Carolina became a royal province.

GEORGIA.

1. THE present State of Georgia formed a portion of the great Carolina grant of Clarendon. This southern portion remained unsettled until the year 1732, at which time all the land between the Savannah and the Altamaha Rivers was granted to James Oglethorpe and others.

OGLETHORPE.

2. Oglethorpe was a man of fortune, an officer in the English army, and a member of Parliament. The interest we feel in the history of the settlement of Georgia centres in this very remarkable person. He was possessed of a very

---

5. Who were their nearest neighbors on the south? What did South Carolina do when war was declared between France and England? What was the result of this? What attack was made on them after this, and with what success?

6. What caused them much trouble? How was this put an end to? What new trouble arose out of this Indian war? What was done by the king? What did South Carolina thus become?

1. In what grant was the present State of Georgia included? How long did this remain unsettled? What grant was made in that year?

benevolent nature, and had made his name well known by his efforts to abolish imprisonment for debt, and the cruelties of the prisons in England. His object in establishing the colony of Georgia was to provide a home for suffering poor people, and for such discharged prisoners as might desire to live a better life in a new country. For this purpose, the tract was conveyed to twenty-one trustees for the period of twenty-one years.

3. Oglethorpe settled with the first immigrants at Savannah, at the mouth of the [illegible] in the year 1733. The class of poor persons that he brought out with him was badly chosen. It was composed of bankrupt tradesmen unused to labor, very helpless and complaining. In the following year some 600 settlers came over, but they were of that class which poverty had made lazy and vicious. Oglethorpe went back to England, and brought over 221 poor persons from England at the trustees' expense. Meanwhile the colony was increased by an arrival of a party of sturdy Scotch Highlanders and a considerable body of industrious German emigrants.

4. The Spaniards looked on th[illegible]lony as an intrusion on their territory of Florida, and Oglethorpe very soon saw that it would be necessary to provide means to defend the settlements. In 1736 he went to England to ask for help, and returned in 1738 at the head of a regiment of soldiers.

5. In the early part of the year 1740, soon after the beginning of [illegible] George's [illegible] Oglethorpe, at the head of twelve hundred whites, five hundred of whom were from North Carolina and Virginia, and twelve hundred Creek Indians, marched against St. Augustine; but he found the fort stronger than he expected, and this, together with sickness among his troops, obliged him to return home.

---

2. Who was Oglethorpe? How had he distinguished himself in England? What was his object in settling Georgia? To whom, and for what purpose, was this tract conveyed?

3. Where and when did Oglethorpe first settle? Of what class of people were the emigrants composed? Describe those who came the following year. What did Oglethorpe next do? How had their numbers been increased in the mean time?

4. How did the Spaniards look upon this colony? What discovery did Oglethorpe make?

5. What did he next proceed to do? How far was this movement successful?

6. In 1742, the Spaniards, in turn, fitted out at Havana an expedition of three thousand men against the coast of Georgia. Frederica, a small town on St. Simon's Island, was attacked in June; but the Spanish general managed the business so badly, and Oglethorpe was so watchful and active, that the expedition returned to Cuba in July without effecting any thing.

7. While Oglethorpe was active in protecting the colony from the Spaniards, the settlers had been busy in sending a messenger to England with complaints against him. Oglethorpe went there to meet his accuser in 1743. It is pleasing to know that this good man was highly trusted by the government; for all the charges, after a fair hearing, were dismissed, and the accuser was punished for making false complaints. Oglethorpe was made a major general in the English army, and did not again return to Georgia.

8. The settlers continued to complain against the trustees in the same way that they had complained of Oglethorpe. After twenty years' efforts, and at a cost of $700,000, there were only three small towns, seventeen hundred white inhabitants, and four hundred negroes. The colonists wanted the rights the Carolinians had, and especially the right to own slaves, which the trustees had forbidden. Wearied with the complaints of the people, the trustees at last resigned their rights to the crown in 1752, and Georgia became a royal province.

REVIEW QUESTIONS.—NORTH AND SOUTH CAROLINA, AND GEORGIA.

1. In what original grant was North Carolina included?
2. What do you remember about Roanoke Island?
3. How did the grant in 1606 affect North Carolina?
4. Who first settled it? when and where?
5. Who settled South Carolina? when and where?
6. Under what grant was this?
7. What was its extent?

---

6. What is said of the movements of the Spaniards? Why did they fail in this enterprise?

7. While Oglethorpe was thus active, what were the settlers doing? What did he do? Were his accusers successful in their charges against him? What is finally said of Oglethorpe?

8. Were the colonists any more contented? What had been the success of the colony? What rights did settlers want? What special permission did they desire that had been forbidden them? How did the trustees meet these complaints?

8. What plan of government was prepared for both colonies?
9. How did this operate?
10. How many settlements called colonies can you name within their limits?
11. Give their respective histories.
12. How far were they connected with any intercolonial wars before 1750?
13. What was the government of these colonies?
14. When was this changed, and why?
15. Under what grant, and for what purpose was Georgia settled?
16. Who was the founder of the colony, and what is said of his previous life?
17. Give a sketch of Oglethorpe's energetic operations in its behalf.
18. How far was the colony a success at first?
19. What was the cause of this?
20. Under what government was it conducted?
21. How was he treated by the colonists and by the English government?
22. How long did the trustees' government continue, and why was it abandoned?

SECTION V.

FRENCH EXPLORATIONS AND SETTLEMENTS IN THE WEST AND SOUTHWEST.

1. Samuel Champlain, the French explorer and governor of New France, entered the northern part of what is now New York in 1609, to assist the Algonquin and Huron tribes against the Iroquois, or Five Nations. By his help the Iroquois were defeated, and he gained for the French the inveterate hostility of that great confederacy. The French missionaries, who not long after settled among tribes near the Iroquois, were seized by the latter, put to torture and murdered, and the missions were broken up.

2. Prevented in this way from exploring the country to the south, the French penetrated along the north shore of Lake Ontario in 1626. The explorers were chiefly Jesuit and other Catholic missionaries, whose object was to plant Christian missions among the natives. In the year 1634 we find these remarkable men as far west as Lake Huron, with several missions established on Georgian Bay. In 1664 they explored a considerable distance on the shores of Lake Superior, where they first learned of the great copper region near the lake; and in 1668 the mission of St. Mary was established, the oldest European settlement in Michigan. In

1. Who was Champlain, and of what territory was he the first explorer? What was his chief object and the result of his expedition? In what way were the French made to feel this?

1672 the missionaries visited Milwaukee, Chicago, and St. Joseph's, and planted missions among the tribes on Lake Michigan. From these Indians they heard vague accounts of a great western river.

3. Next spring, the missionary Marquette (*mar'-ket*), in company with Joliet (*zho-lĕ-ā*), a trader from Quebec, and five other Frenchmen, floated in canoes down the Wisconsin River, and discovered the Mississippi, or "Great River," in the month of June, 1673. They then sailed down its waters as far as the mouth of the Arkansas. In the early part of the next year they ascended the Mississippi, and, having discovered the mouth of the Illinois, went up this river as far as it was navigable, and then crossed by land to Chicago, whence they paddled their canoes to the mission at Green Bay.

4. La Salle, a famous French adventurer, and celebrated as the explorer of the Lower Mississippi, was a man of extraordinary energy. As early as 1670 he had been engaged in trying to find in Canada an overland western passage to China. As a reward for the sagacity and energy he displayed in exploring Lakes Ontario and Erie, the French king had granted to him Fort Frontenac, at the outlet of Lake Ontario, together with a large tract of the adjacent country. His imagination was so inflamed by the accounts he had received of the newly-discovered "great river," that he went to

LA SALLE.

---

2. In what direction did the French then turn their attention? Who were these explorers? Where do we find them in 1634? Where in 1664? Where were they in a few years after? What did they learn while there?

3. When did they make an attempt to see this river? Who were the explorers? What was their success? To what point did they go on its waters? Describe their return.

France in 1677 and obtained a commission from the French king to continue the exploration.

5. Returning to Canada and Fort Frontenac in 1678, he built, near the present site of Buffalo, on Lake Erie, a bark, the Griffin, of sixty tons, and in the following year sailed through the great lakes as far as Green Bay. From this place he sent back his vessel, laden with furs, for supplies; while he, with some companions, sailed up Lake Michigan in birch-bark canoes to the mouth of the St. Joseph's, and there built a fort.

6. On a branch of the Illinois they built another fort, called by La Salle Crève-cœur (*krāve-kur*)—"Heart-break," on account of his disappointment at the non-arrival of the Griffin with supplies. To obtain these, La Salle, with fearless energy, took with him three companions, and struck through the wilderness to Fort Frontenac in the spring of 1680. While he was gone, Father Hennepin, by his orders, explored the Upper Mississippi as far as the Falls of St. Anthony. In 1680 La Salle returned to Lake Michigan.

7. In 1682 he descended the Mississippi to the Gulf of Mexico, and named the country on the banks of the great river Louisiana, in honor of Louis XIV., king of France. Ascending the Mississippi, he returned to France in 1683 to enlist his countrymen in his plans for the settlement of the new territory. He was successful in this, and toward the end of the year 1684 La Salle left France with four ships and 280 persons, well supplied with all the necessaries to plant a colony at the mouth of the Mississippi. But the entrance of the "great river" was hard to find: La Salle missed it, went westward, and early in 1685 landed his colony at Matagorda Bay, as is supposed, in Texas, where he built Fort St. Louis.

---

4. Who was La Salle? What was he doing in 1670? How and for what was he rewarded? Why was he not contented to remain on his grant?

5. What were La Salle's movements in 1678? What important steps did he take?

6. What incident shows the disappointment he endured? How did he try to meet these difficulties? What explorations were made during his absence? When did La Salle return?

7. What took place in 1682? With what name is La Salle forever associated? Where and for what object did he go in 1683? How far was he successful in this? What is said of the sailing of the expedition? Where did the vessels land? Why was this?

8. In little more than two years the colony was reduced by disease and suffering from 250 to 36 persons. La Salle, despairing of help from France, started with 16 men to go north to Canada by land in 1687. His wonderful skill, energy, and courage might have carried him through, but on his journey he was murdered by two of his companions. Five of them, who kept together, after six months' wandering, reached a small French post on the Mississippi near the mouth of the Arkansas. The twenty men left at the fort in Texas were never again heard of.

9. In 1699, twelve years after La Salle's death, D'Iberville, a native of Quebec, came from France with an expedition, and built huts on Ship Island. Taking with him fifty men, he sailed up the Mississippi as far as Red River, and returned by way of Lakes Maurepas (*mó-re-pah*) and Pontchartrain, so named by him in honor of two ministers of the French king. Soon after he left a colony on the Bay of Biloxi, at the mouth of the Pascagoula, Mississippi, and sailed for France, May, 1699.

10. Toward the end of the year he returned to the Mississippi, and early in 1700 went up as far as the present site of Natchez, where he marked out a settlement named Rosalie (*rōz-a-lee*). In 1702 he came a third time from France, and removed the colony from Biloxi to Mobile, which became the capital of Louisiana; but it did not flourish. During ten years its population never increased beyond 200 persons, and it was only kept alive by supplies from France and the island of St. Domingo.

11. While these attempts were in progress in Louisiana, the French were active in the West. Detroit was founded in 1701, and about the same time the villages of Kaskaskia and Cahokia grew up round the missionary stations on the east bank of the Mississippi, above the mouth of the Ohio.

---

8. What was the fate of the colony? What resolution did La Salle form and put in execution? What prevented him from fulfilling it? What portion of his companions escaped? What became of those left at Fort St. Louis?

9. When and by whom was the next attempt made to settle Louisiana? Where did he first land? What were his next movements? Where, before his return to France, did he plant a colony?

10. When did he return to Louisiana? Where and when did he then go? What is said of D'Iberville's third voyage? What was the success of the colony at Mobile?

Yet the French population in America did not increase rapidly. In 1690 Canada had not more than 1200 inhabitants; Acadia had scarce 1000. In the whole of Louisiana, in the year 1702, there were not more than 30 families.

12. The designs of the French were, however, of the grandest sort. They looked to the formation of a mighty empire in the valley of the Mississippi, stretching from the great lakes to the Gulf of Mexico. This hope was not destined to be realized. In Louisiana, notwithstanding a lavish expenditure of money in colonizing it, the repeated efforts of the government and of individuals met with little but misfortune, from the unhealthiness of the climate, and nearly constant wars with the Natchez and Chickasaw Indians. Although in 1722 the colony was firmly planted, its population in 1740 did not exceed 5000 whites and half that number of blacks.

13. It is impossible not to admire the remarkable enterprise and activity of the French. While the English settlements were confined to a strip of territory east of the mountains, the French had pushed thousands of miles into the interior. They had explored the great lakes; they had examined the Fox, the Wisconsin, the Illinois, the Maumee, and Wabash Rivers—the Ohio they had comparatively neglected—and they were familiar with the shores of the Mississippi from the Falls of St. Anthony to its mouth.

14. Before the year 1750 they had more than sixty military stations, at intervals from Lake Ontario, by way of Green Bay and the Illinois, the Wabash, and Maumee Rivers, down the Mississippi to New Orleans. At the principal posts were regular garrisons, relieved once in six years. All this had been done in the face of most bitter Indian wars waged against them by their old enemies the Iroquois, and also by the Chickasaws and the Natchez on the Lower Mississippi. In addition, they, in the year 1748, traversed the

---

11. What settlements were meanwhile made in the West? What is said of the French population in Canada? In Acadia? In Louisiana?

12. What great designs had the French formed? What is said of the success of their efforts? How is this shown by a comparison of dates?

13. Where were the English during these active movements of the French? What explorations had the French made?

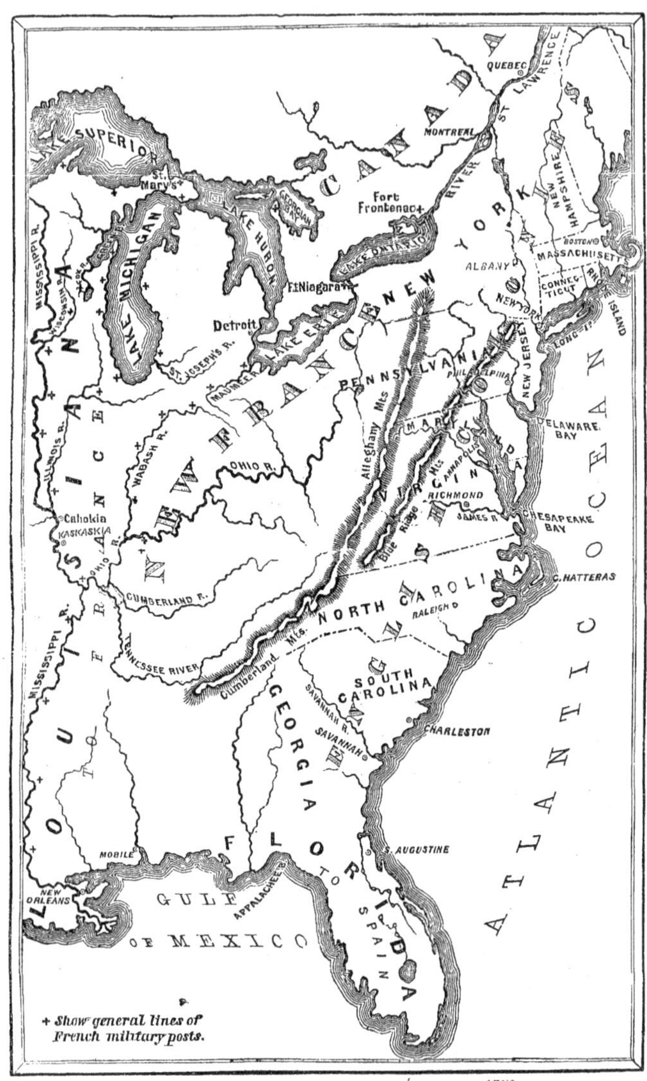

ENGLISH, FRENCH, AND SPANISH OCCUPATION.—1750.

country south of Lake Erie east to the mountains, and took formal possession of it by burying, at important points, leaden plates with the arms of France engraved thereon.

15. It was on such vigorous efforts at occupation that the French based their claim to the valley of the Mississippi and the country watered by its tributaries. According to the usual custom prevailing among rival European nations on this continent, the French could scarce have held the new territory by a much stronger title. That claim was soon put to a test at the cannon's mouth in the French and Indian War.

SECTION VI.

FRENCH AND INDIAN WAR.

Events immediately Preceding the War.

1. The three intercolonial wars left intense hatred between the French and English in America. A fresh source of quarrel soon arose out of rival claims to territory. In the year 1749, only a year after the close of King George's War, a grant of six hundred thousand acres of land west of the Alleghanies, on and near the Ohio River, was made to some Londoners and Virginians, under the name of the Ohio Company.

2. As the French considered this to be a part of their territory, they treated the Company's surveyors as intruders, made them prisoners, and broke up the trading-posts. They acted with still greater vigor in 1753. In that year twelve hundred men were sent from Montreal, who built a fort at Presque Isle (*pres-keel*), on the southern shore of Lake Erie, now the present town of Erie. The same year they advanced south from this, and built two forts—one, Fort le Bœuf (*buf*), at the present town of Waterford, and Fort

---

14. Describe their line of posts. How many did they have? What is said of their garrisons? In what other way had they claimed possession of a large tract of country? What is said of the opposition they had met with?

15. On what, then, was the French claim to the Mississippi Valley based? What is said of the justice of this claim? How was this claim tested?

1. What was the feeling between the French and English colonies? What new quarrel arose? Describe the grant made in 1749.

Venango, on French Creek, which flows into the Alleghany River.

3. Dinwiddie, lieutenant governor of Virginia, alarmed at the movements of the French, sent a messenger to the French commander of these posts, asking their removal. The person he chose to carry this message was George Washington, a native of Virginia, then a young man of two-and-twenty. On the 30th of October, 1753, the very day on which he received his credentials, he left Williamsburg, and, pushing through the wilderness, arrived at Fort Venango Dec. 4. At Le Bœuf he at last found St. Pierre (*pe-are*), the commandant, who received his letter, and treated him with marked kindness. In the course of Washington's stay the French officers talked with great frankness, said that they were there by

WASHINGTON ON HIS HOMEWARD JOURNEY.

2. How did the French claims interfere with those of the English? In what way did they treat the servants and property of the Company? What active measures did they take to keep possession of the territory?

order of the king, and should remain there so long as he commanded them to do so.

4. St. Pierre's written reply to Dinwiddie was given to Washington, who at once commenced his long and fearful journey of four hundred miles to Williamsburg. Snow had fallen; the rivers had risen, and were filled with ice; the horses broke down at the very commencement, and the journey had to be made on foot. The Indians were far from friendly, and once Washington was shot at from a distance of not more than fifteen paces. Through all these dangers he made his way home unharmed, January, 1754, and delivered St. Pierre's letter, which contained a polite but firm refusal to give up the posts.

EVENTS OF 1754.

5. **Commencement of Hostilities.**—Early in 1754, the Ohio Company sent out a small party to erect a fort at the junction of the Alleghany and Monongahela Rivers, and Dinwiddie dispatched a captain's command to protect them. In addition to this, in March, a regiment of six hundred men was raised in Virginia, of which Frye was colonel, and Washington second in command. They quickly commenced their march to the new fort, intending to occupy it. While on their way, they learned that the French had surprised and driven off the Company's men, and had then completed the works, naming them Fort du Quesne (*doo-kane*).

6. Washington was sent on in advance to reconnoitre, and fell in with a small body of French under Jumonville (*zhoo-mong-veel*), at Great Meadows, about forty-five miles from Fort du Quesne. Washington surprised this party on the night of May 28, and in the attack Jumonville was slain, and nine of his men. This was the first blood shed in the war. Frye died about this time, and Washington assumed

---

3. What was done by the English? Who was chosen to carry this message? Describe Washington's journey to the French post. How was he received, and what was said by the French officers?

4. How long was Washington's journey back? Describe its difficulties. What answer did St. Pierre send to Governor Dinwiddie?

5. What measures did the Ohio Company take to protect their claims? What help did they at first get from Dinwiddie? What additional troops were raised? What news met them while on their way?

the command. The rest of the troops soon joined him at Great Meadows, where he built a stockade, which he called Fort Necessity.

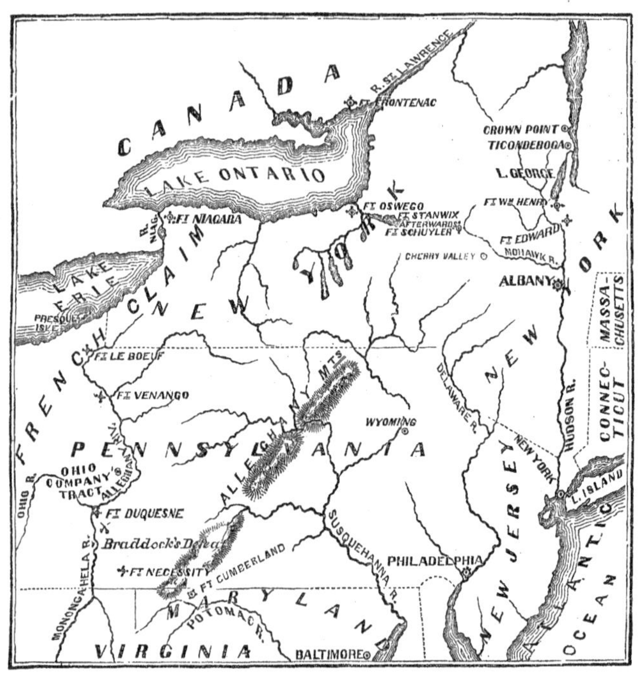

CHIEF SCENE OF OPERATIONS. FRENCH AND INDIAN WAR.

7. Here he was attacked in July by De Villiers (*vil-yerz*) with 1500 French and Indians. At the end of ten hours' hard fighting, Washington surrendered the fort on condition that his troops should be allowed the honors of war. This expedition under Washington was the commencement of the great struggle between the French and English for the possession of the North American continent. All the previous intercolonial wars sprang from disputes in Europe, which involved the French, English, and Spanish colonies.

---

6. What happened to Washington? What did he do? What was his success? How did he get the command? Where did he encamp and build a fort?

This began in America itself about territory. There was, as yet, no formal declaration of war between the two nations, nor was any made till nearly two years later.

8. The English government was anxious that their colonies should take the most active part in the contest, and urged them to unite on some plan of defense. While Washington was fighting in the wilds of Virginia, a convention of delegates from seven of the colonies assembled at Albany to see what could be done. The first object they had in view was to secure the friendship of the powerful Iroquois on the northern borders. This they succeeded in doing.

9. They then debated and adopted a PLAN OF UNION for mutual defense, subject to the approval of the colonies and the English government. The author of the plan was Benjamin Franklin, a delegate from Pennsylvania. It never went in force, because it pleased neither the king nor the colonies. The king thought it gave the people too much power, the colonies thought it gave the king too much. The probability is, therefore, that Franklin's plan was nearly correct.

EVENTS OF 1755.

10. The plan of union not having been adopted, the English government determined to carry on the war with such help as the colonies might feel inclined to furnish. In February, 1755, General Braddock was sent out from England to the Chesapeake, as commander-in-chief, with two regiments of British troops. At Alexandria, Braddock met a convention of colonial governors, and, with their advice, decided on the campaign for the year. Braddock, in person, was to march against Fort du Quesne; Governor Shirley, of Massachusetts, to lead an expedition against Fort Niagara; and William Johnson, an influential man with the Iroquois,

7. What attack was made, and when? Which party was successful? What may this be called? How does this differ from the other intercolonial wars? Was there any formal declaration of war?

8. How did the English government show their interest in this? While Washington was fighting, what was done elsewhere? What was the first object? How did they succeed in this?

9. What was the next proceeding? Who was the author of this? Why did this never go in force?

was to attempt, with their assistance, the capture of Crown Point.

11. Besides these three expeditions planned by Braddock, still another, against the French settlements at the head of the Bay of Fundy, had been previously arranged in Massachusetts. They were defended by two French forts, and were considered by the English to be within the limits of Nova Scotia. In the month of May, Colonel John Winslow, at the head of three thousand New England men, left Boston to attack these posts. On his arrival at the Bay of Fundy, Colonel Monckton, with three hundred British regulars, joined him, and assumed the command. The forts were soon taken with little bloodshed, and the whole territory was now completely in the hands of the English.

ACADIA, CAPE BRETON ISLAND, AND NOVA SCOTIA.

12. The French settlers or Acadians, twelve thousand or more in number, were a simple-hearted people, devoted to their farms and their country pleasures, and attached to the French rule by language and religion. They would have

---

10. What was the determination of the English government? Who was sent out with troops? Whom did he meet? What was decided on? What was the plan of the campaign?

11. What other expedition had been previously arranged? and by what colony? Why was this undertaken? What was the size of the expedition? What was its success?

been glad to have seen the French authority established throughout the old limits of Acadia, but they were far from being troublesome to the English.

13. Under false pretenses, the Acadians were induced to assemble in large numbers at different points; and, without warning, with scarce an opportunity of bidding farewell to their homes, seven thousand of them were thrust on board of English vessels, and were scattered throughout the English colonies. Wives were separated from husbands, children from parents; and, in misery and wretched exile, this once happy people lingered out a weary life. To add to this dreadful cruelty, the country was laid waste, the farm-houses were burned; the growing crops were destroyed, in order to starve any who might still be lurking in the woods, and this beautiful and fertile tract was for a time reduced to desolation.

14. **Braddock's Expedition against Fort du Quesne.**—Braddock's force at Alexandria had been increased by the arrival of Virginia troops, and, in the month of May, numbered 2500 men. In the beginning of June he left Fort Cumberland, on the extreme frontiers of Virginia, and, with his whole army, proceeded against Fort du Quesne. Impatient at the slowness of the march, he ordered General Dunbar to follow him with the baggage, and pushed on with 1200 light troops. This was done at the advice of Washington, who was one of his aids-de-camp.

15. Washington had already earnestly warned him of the Indian mode of fighting; and Benjamin Franklin, who visited the general at Frederickton, did the same. But Braddock was a vain man, and held the provincial troops and the Indians in contempt. His self-confidence proved his ruin. When he was less than seven miles from Fort du Quesne, he was suddenly attacked on the 9th of July by

---

12. What was the character of the Acadians? Why did they prefer French rule? How far did this feeling make them troublesome to the English?

13. What method did the colonists take to drive them from their country? How far was it successful? What cruel measures were taken to prevent their return?

14. How had Braddock's forces been increased? What was the object of the expedition? From what point did he finally set out? How did he hasten his march?

WASHINGTON WARNING GENERAL BRADDOCK IN HIS TENT.

about 800 Indians and a few Frenchmen, commanded by an officer no higher than the rank of captain.

16. The enemy were posted chiefly behind trees. The English were in open ground, without shelter, exposed to a deadly fire. It was in vain that the English officers again and again led their men against their unseen foe. They themselves were shot down. Braddock, after showing the greatest bravery, was at last mortally wounded and carried from the field, and the troops fell into confusion. Washington did every thing in his power to restore order. He was repeatedly shot at, and was the only mounted officer that escaped without a wound. At last he was able to rally the Virginia troops, and in this way cover the retreat of the regulars.

15. What warnings did he receive? How did Braddock treat these? What was the consequence of this imprudence?

16. Give an account of the first part of the battle. What was the fate of Braddock? How did Washington conduct himself in this terrible defeat? What did he succeed in doing? What is said of Dunbar?

17. The day had been most disastrous to Braddock. Out of the 1200 engaged, nearly 800 were killed or wounded, and of these, 62 were officers. Dunbar, who was coming on slowly with the baggage and the rest of the army, on learning the disaster, destroyed his wagons and made a hasty retreat, or rather flight, with the wreck of his army, first to Fort Cumberland, and then to Philadelphia.

18. **Expedition against Niagara.** — Governor Shirley, in command of the expedition against Niagara, had only reached Oswego by the month of August. The news of Braddock's defeat, together with sickness among his men, and the desertion of his Indian allies, so discouraged him that, after building two forts at Oswego, and leaving 700 men to garrison them, he returned to Albany. By the death of Braddock, Shirley became commander-in-chief of all the forces in America.

19. **Expedition against Crown Point.**—In July, 1755, General Lyman was in command of six thousand provincial troops assembled on the Hudson, at the head of boat navigation, fifty miles north of Albany. While waiting the arrival of Johnson, he threw up a strong fortification, named at first Fort Lyman, afterward called Fort Edward. In August, General Johnson joined him with the stores and artillery, and then advanced to Lake George, fifteen miles distant.

20. On his arrival, he learned that two thousand French and Indians from Montreal, under Baron Dieskau (*de-es-ko*), governor of Canada, were on their way to attack him. He at once sent out Colonel Williams with a thousand Massachusetts men, and Hendrick, a Mohawk chief, with his Indians, to intercept him. About three miles from Johnson's camp, Williams and Hendrick fell into an ambuscade, and were both slain. Their troops retreated to the camp, pursued by the French.

---

17. What is said of Braddock's loss? What assistance did Dunbar render? To what points did he retreat?

18. What is said of Shirley's expedition? What events conspired to alter his plans? Who succeeded Braddock as commander-in-chief?

19. What was the position of Lyman in July? How did he employ his time? Who joined him? To what post did they advance?

20. What news awaited him? What measures did he take to prevent this attack? What was the fate of these men? How did the troops save themselves?

21. Dieskau promptly led his troops to the assault, but was driven back by the deadly fire of the colonists from behind the breastworks. The Indians fled, and left the French alone, who fought bravely. Dieskau was severely wounded and made prisoner, and the French fell back to Crown Point after losing their baggage and a thousand men. General Lyman, as Johnson was wounded early in the action, really fought and won the battle. The latter did not follow the enemy, but contented himself with building Fort William Henry near his encampment. Late in the fall, he left garrisons in this and also in Fort Edward, and then went to Albany, where he dispersed his army. For the defeat of Dieskau he was rewarded with the honors of knighthood and £5000; General Lyman received nothing.

Events of 1756.

22. In December, 1755, Shirley met with the colonial governors at New York, and decided that there should be three expeditions in 1756—one against Niagara, the others against Fort du Quesne and Crown Point. In June, General Abercrombie arrived from England with troops, and relieved General Shirley from his command. Lord Loudoun, the commander-in-chief, did not reach America until July, and nothing was done until his arrival.

23. Loudoun, who was a pompous and slow man, went to Albany and took charge of 7000 men preparing to move against Ticonderoga and Crown Point. While he was idle at Albany, the Marquis of Montcalm, successor of Dieskau, at the head of 5000 Canadian regulars and Indians, crossed Lake Ontario, and attacked the forts at Oswego. One of these was at once abandoned by the garrison, and the other, after a short bombardment and the death of the commander, Colonel Mercer, was surrendered August 14th.

24. Montcalm obtained by this over 1000 prisoners, 135

---

21. Was the fort attacked? How was it defended? How did the Indians behave? What was the result to the French? Who really commanded in this battle? Who reaped all the honors?

22. What plans were decided on for this year? Who relieved Shirley? By whose conduct were operations delayed?

23. What did Loudoun first do? How did the French employ the time wasted by Loudoun? Where is Oswego? What was their success?

cannon, an immense quantity of military stores, and a fleet of boats and larger vessels that Shirley had made ready the year before for his Niagara expedition. Montcalm destroyed the forts, and thus for a time secured the favor of the native tribes, who had looked with great jealousy upon the erection of these posts by the English.

25. Loudoun sent out some troops, under Colonel Webb, to Oswego, but they were dispatched so late that they were met on their way by the disastrous news, and returned in haste to Albany. Nothing came of Loudoun's expedition against Crown Point. The main body of the troops did not leave Albany. The expeditions planned against Fort du Quesne and Niagara were also failures.

26. The Ohio Indians fell on the outlying settlements in Pennsylvania and committed great devastations. Expeditions were sent against them. At Kittáning the natives received a severe defeat, and were compelled to retire farther west; but scalping-parties continued to penetrate within 30 miles of Philadelphia.

Events of 1757.

27. In January, 1757, it was arranged at Boston that there should be but one expedition this year, and that this should proceed against Louisburg. The frontier posts were to be defended, especially Fort William Henry and Fort Edward. Washington, with provincial troops, was employed to watch the outposts of Virginia, a very laborious and a very difficult duty so long as the French held Fort du Quesne.

28. **Expedition against Louisburg.**—Lord Loudoun sailed from New York with 6000 regulars against Louisburg. At Halifax he was joined by a fleet of 11 men-of-war and 6000 troops. While Loudoun, with his usual slowness, hesitated,

24. What did Montcalm gain by this victory? How did he secure the favor of the Indians? Why did the destruction of the forts do this?

25. What did Loudoun undertake to do? Why was this a failure? How far was he successful against Crown Point? What is said of the other expeditions of the year?

26. What trouble was made by Indians? What did the settlers oblige them to do? Did this quiet them?

27. What was the arrangement for 1757? What posts were to be defended? How was Washington to be employed?

a large French fleet entered the harbor of Louisburg and made an attack hopeless. Nothing was left for the English but to sail back to New York.

29. **Capture of Fort William Henry.**—Montcalm, as we have seen, was a very different man from Lord Loudoun—prompt, active, and vigorous. Suddenly he moved up Lake George from Ticonderoga, and laid siege to Fort William Henry, garrisoned by 2000 troops under Colonel Monroe. General Webb was at Fort Edward, fifteen miles south, with 4000 men, but made no effort to assist him. The siege lasted six days, and Monroe then capitulated with the honors of war. The Indians, greedy for plunder, in spite of the strenuous efforts of the French officers, attacked Monroe's baggage and killed some of the prisoners. Montcalm, satisfied with his success, did not proceed farther, but destroyed Fort William Henry and returned to Crown Point.

30. The close of the year found the French in possession of all the territory they had before the war except the settlements on the Bay of Fundy. The English had suffered greatly. They had lost the Oswego forts and an immense quantity of supplies. Fort William Henry had also been destroyed. Around the borders, the Indian allies of the French, all the way from Massachusetts to Virginia, penetrated by scalping-parties into the interior, and kept the settlers in constant alarm.

Events of 1758.

31. The mismanagement of American affairs created in England a strong feeling against the government. This compelled the king, George II., to form a new administration, and William Pitt, afterward Lord Chatham, was made prime minister. The entire management of the war was placed in his hands, and he immediately went to work with

---

28. What movement was made by Lord Loudoun? How were his forces increased? How were his plans frustrated? What were the English forced to do?

29. How did Montcalm differ from Loudoun? What energetic movement did he make? How was this fort garrisoned? What is said of Webb? What was Montcalm's success? What was the conduct of the Indians? Did Montcalm undertake any thing further?

30. What was the condition of the French at the close of the year? What had been the losses of the English? How had the settlers been annoyed?

great spirit. He persuaded the colonies to raise 28,000 men, and to these he added 22,000 regulars from England, making in all 50,000 troops. Lord Loudoun was recalled, and General Abercrombie was appointed commander-in-chief. The plan of the campaign was to attack Louisburg, Ticonderoga, and Fort du Quesne.

32. **Expedition against Louisburg.**—An army of 12,000 men, under General Amherst, with a fleet of 37 ships, under Admiral Boscawen, appeared before Louisburg on the 8th of June. The fortress, somewhat dilapidated, was vigorously defended by less than 3500 men, and by 11 ships of war that lay in the harbor. After a severe bombardment, in which the works were reduced to ruin, the French surrendered on July 27. With Louisburg, Cape Breton Island and St. John's, now Prince Edward's Island, fell into the hands of the English. The hero of the siege was the brave young General Wolfe, who was killed next year at Quebec. Richard Montgomery, also killed there fighting for the patriot cause in 1775, served as an officer in Wolfe's brigade.

33. **Expedition against Fort Ticonderoga.**—Early in July, Abercrombie, the commander-in-chief, with 15,000 men, advanced to the lower end of Lake George. When near Fort Ticonderoga, the advanced guard, under young Lord Howe, fell in with a French scouting-party. An engagement followed, and Howe was slain, July 7. He was greatly beloved by the New England troops, and his death proved a serious loss to the army. Abercrombie, without waiting for his artillery to come up, ordered an assault on the following day, July 8, and was repulsed with the loss of 2000 in killed and wounded. He then fell back hastily and in disorder to the head of the lake, and there built Fort George, near the ruins of Fort William Henry.

31. What was the effect of these disasters in England? What change was made in the government? What power was given Pitt? How did he increase the army? Who was placed in command? What was the plan?

32. What movement was now made? Describe the condition of the fortress. What was the success of the English? What did the English gain with Louisburg? What officers distinguished themselves in this siege?

33. What advance was made by Abercrombie? What took place on the march? What followed? How was this loss regarded? What hasty movement did Abercrombie execute? What was the effect of this haste? Where did they retreat? What fort was built?

34. While encamped here, he sent Colonel Bradstreet, with 3000 men, against Fort Frontenac, on Lake Ontario. The place was easily taken, nine vessels were captured, and the fort, with a large store of provisions, was destroyed. We shall presently see that this affair of Fort Frontenac proved to be of no small importance. Abercrombie was relieved of his command on account of his want of success at Ticonderoga, and Amherst, who had captured Louisburg, was made commander-in-chief.

35. **Expedition against Fort du Quesne.**—The expedition against Fort du Quesne, composed of 7000 men, 5000 of whom were from Pennsylvania and Virginia, was led by General Forbes. Washington, who commanded the Virginia troops, advised him to take the old Braddock road, but he chose to build a new one at great expense of labor, and, what was more precious, of time. So badly did he manage, that, though he started in the early part of September, the beginning of November found him, with his whole army, little more than two thirds on his way, and fifty miles from Fort du Quesne.

36. He had, besides, lost 300 men of an advance corps, surprised by the French. The army was weakened by desertion and dispirited by sickness, and winter was approaching. A council of war was held, and it advised that the enterprise should be given up. Fortunately, the British general heard, through some deserters, that the spirits of the French at the fort were greatly depressed by the capture of Fort Frontenac and the destruction of the stores intended for their use. In consequence of this loss they had been deserted by the greater part of their Indian allies.

37. Forbes, encouraged by this information, pushed on more rapidly. The French abandoned the works on his approach, and the advanced guard, under Washington, took

---

34. What was undertaken while they lay here? What was their success? Did this prove of much consequence? Why was Abercrombie relieved? Who was made commander-in-chief?

35. How many men were engaged in this expedition? Who led a large part of them? What was Washington's advice? What did he prefer to do? How did this delay him?

36. What discouragement was he laboring under? What was advised? What news reached them at this crisis?

possession November 25. The name was changed to Fort Pitt, in honor of the prime minister. The capture of Fort du Quesne, although so long delayed, was of great importance, because it at once broke the spirit of the Indians in that quarter, who had hitherto been on the side of the French. The frontiers of Virginia and Pennsylvania were thenceforth relieved from Indian incursions during the war.

CAPTURE OF FORT DU QUESNE, 1758

EVENTS OF 1759.

38. The English minister, Pitt, put forth fresh efforts in the year 1759. Three expeditions were again planned—one against Quebec, under General Wolfe; another, under Amherst, against Forts Ticonderoga and Crown Point; a third, under General Prideaux (*prid-o*), by way of Oswego, against Fort Niagara. Amherst and Prideaux, after capturing the

37. How did this news affect Forbes's movements? What was his success? How was the fort named? Why was the capture of this fort of great importance?

forts assigned to them, were to join Wolfe on the St. Lawrence, opposite Quebec.

39. **Expedition against Niagara.**—General Prideaux was killed soon after the siege of Fort Niagara began, and Sir William Johnson succeeded to the command. On July 23 the French surrendered the fort; but Johnson, encumbered by prisoners, was unable, from want of provisions and of boats, to move down the St. Lawrence to the help of Wolfe, as was originally arranged.

40. **Expedition against Ticonderoga.**—When General Amherst and his army reached Ticonderoga, they found that this fort, and also Crown Point, had been abandoned by the French. As was the case with Johnson's army, Amherst's troops could not co-operate with Wolfe, because vessels had not been provided to carry them down Lake Champlain.

41. **Expedition against Quebec.**—On the 26th of June, General Wolfe arrived in the St. Lawrence, opposite the isle of Orleans. He had with him 8000 troops and a fleet of 22 ships of the line, besides frigates and smaller vessels. This immense fleet had entire command of the river; and Wolfe found it easy to erect batteries on Point Levi, opposite Quebec. The city was composed of two parts, the upper and the lower town. Wolfe's guns easily destroyed the houses along the river, but could do no harm to the citadel in the upper town. For miles above the city the rocks rose precipitously from the river bank, and every landing-place at their foot seemed to be guarded by cannon or floating batteries.

42. The lower side of the city was protected by the Rivers St. Charles and Montmorenci, and between these the French had an intrenched camp. In the month of July, Wolfe crossed the St. Lawrence with a portion of his army and attacked

---

38. What were Pitt's plans for this year? Name the expeditions and the officers in charge of them. What further orders did Amherst and Prideaux receive?

39. What was the fate of Prideaux? Who took his command? What success attended this? Was he able to join Wolfe?

40. What discovery did Amherst make on reaching Ticonderoga? Why was he unable to go to the assistance of Wolfe?

41. When did Wolfe arrive in the St. Lawrence? What forces had he? How did this fleet greatly assist him? How was the city divided? What effect did his guns have? How was the upper town guarded?

these intrenchments, but was repulsed with the loss of 500 men. To crown his disappointment, no help came from the Niagara expedition nor from Amherst, and he himself, sick with a slow fever, was left, with his diminished army, to gain Quebec as he could.

43. The Plains or Heights of Abraham lay west of the city, and there was a narrow path up their face scarce wide enough for two men abreast, leading from a small cove on the river. By this path, Wolfe, under the advice of his officers, determined to ascend with his army to the plains. He first sailed up the river several miles above the landing-place, now known as Wolfe's Cove, Sept. 12. That night, flat-bottomed boats, containing the soldiers, dropped down the river and landed them at the cove. Slowly they climbed to the top, and early in the morning they were there drawn up ready for battle. Montcalm saw that he was now compelled to fight, and at once moved against them. The battle was hotly contested, and was decided in favor of the British, but not until Wolfe and Montcalm were both mortally wounded.

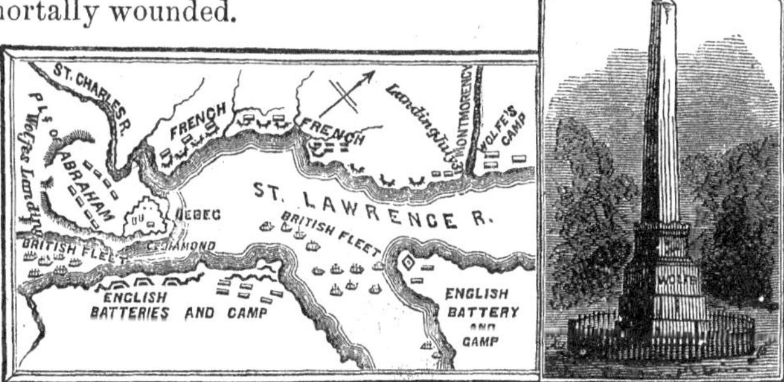

OPERATIONS AROUND QUEBEC, 1759. MONUMENT TO WOLFE AND MONTCALM.

44. Five hundred French were killed and 1000 made prisoners. The loss of the English was 600 in killed and wounded. Wolfe died on the field of battle just as the French had

---

42. How was the lower side protected? When and with what success did Wolfe attack them? What added to his disappointment? What was he forced to do?

43. How did the Plains of Abraham lie? Describe the passage of the face of these heights. What did Wolfe undertake to do? What was his first step? What was done at night? Where did morning find them? What was Montcalm forced to do? What was the result of this battle and fate of the leaders? When was it fought?

BATTLE OF THE HEIGHTS OF ABRAHAM.

begun to retreat. Montcalm died next morning in Quebec. Five days after, on September 18, the city and garrison surrendered to General Townsend, the successor of Wolfe.

EVENTS OF 1760.—CLOSE OF THE WAR.

45. In April, 1760, De Levi left Montreal with 10,000 men to attack Quebec before the arrival of re-enforcements from England. Murray, who was in command at Quebec, marched out with scarce 3000 men to give him battle. A severe engagement followed, April 26, in which Murray lost 1000 men, and fled back to the city, leaving all his artillery. Quebec was at once besieged by the French, but, fortunately, the English fleet arrived May 9, and De Levi retreated in a few days to Montreal.

---

44. What were the losses on both sides? When did Wolfe and Montcalm die? When and to whom did the city surrender?

45. What occurred in April of this year? How was he received? Who was beaten in this engagement? What did the French proceed to do? What proved fortunate for the English?

46. The English made extraordinary efforts during the summer, and in September three powerful armies were united under General Amherst in front of Montreal. The force was so great that the French governor at once surrendered, and with Montreal, all the posts in Canada were given up. There were no further hostilities in America, but the war continued elsewhere until the year 1763.

47. On the 10th of February, 1763, a treaty of peace was signed at Paris. By this treaty, Great Britain obtained all the French territory east of the Mississippi, with the exception of the island of New Orleans, bounded on the north by the Rivers Iberville and Amité, and Lakes Maurepas and Pontchartrain. From Spain she received Florida in exchange for Havana. As some recompense to Spain, France ceded to her the island of New Orleans, and all Louisiana west of the Mississippi.

48. Two nations now claimed the North American continent, the Spanish and the English; the French had not retained a foothold. The whole vast region east of the Mississippi, with the exception of the island of Orleans, from the Gulf of Mexico to the Arctic Ocean, was under the British flag. Florida was divided by the English government into two provinces, East and West Florida; and the River Apalachicola was made the dividing line. The Mississippi formed the western boundary of West Florida. At the same time, Canada was erected into the province of Quebec.

49. **Pontiac's War.**—After the treaty of peace was concluded, the British were not quietly permitted to hold possession of the vast territory on the north and west. The Indian tribes friendly to the French were unwilling to submit to the English rule, and organized a formidable league in 1763 under Pontiac, a famous chief of the Ottawas. Ev-

---

46. What great preparations were made for the fall by the English? What effect did these energetic measures have on the French? What was involved in the surrender of Montreal? Did this end the war?

47. What took place in February? What was given to Great Britain by this treaty? What was given to Spain? What exchange was made between Spain and Great Britain?

48. What two nations now claimed the North American continent? What part was under the British flag? How was Florida divided? What formed the western limit? What did Canada become?

ery post west of Fort Niagara, with the exception of Detroit and Fort Pitt, was captured or destroyed, and their garrisons made prisoners or massacred; these two posts were closely blockaded, and only saved by re-enforcements sent by Amherst. Many settlers were killed, and the rest fled eastward for protection. In 1764, the Indians, overawed by the preparations made to put them down, sued for peace. Thus ended what is known as Pontiac's War.

GENERAL REFLECTIONS ON THE FRENCH AND INDIAN WAR.

1. THE French and Indian War settled the question whether the North American continent was to be French or English in language, laws, and manners. This mighty result had been achieved by means of armies small in comparison with the immense armies engaged in wars of more modern times. Yet the issue of the struggle could never have been very doubtful. The French must have been finally crushed out by mere weight of numbers.

2. In the year 1758, when Pitt, the English prime minister, undertook the management of the war, he raised at once 50,000 men. This was nearly twice the number of all the French in America able to bear arms. The whole population of Canada, New France, and Louisiana scarcely reached 100,000; the population of the English colonies was nearly 1,500,000.

3. In spite of the vast superiority in numbers, the English for three years—1755, 1756, and 1757—had little but disaster, and this was owing mainly to the obstinacy and conceit of the English generals. On the other hand, it was the quickness and spirit with which the French moved, together with the assistance of the Indians, that made them so for-

---

49. Were the English able to hold their possessions without dispute? Why were the Indians unfriendly? What preparations did they make for war? How far were they successful? How was this ended? What was this rising of the Indians called?

1. What was the great result gained by the French and Indian War? How had this been achieved? What might have been anticipated at the beginning of the struggle?

2. What great minister infused energy into the management of the war? What comparison is made between the men he raised and the French population? What was the population of the French and of the English colonies?

midable. It must be owned, therefore, that the French, with the means at their disposal, made a very gallant struggle in a war stretching over so great an extent of territory; for there were in those days no railroads nor steam-boats to carry men and supplies from point to point. Nearly every thing was to be done through a wild country, without roads, over immense distances, and with great labor.

4. This war has been called the French and Indian War; but the English, as well as the French, employed Indians. Sir William Johnson, of New York, rose to influence entirely on account of the power he had with the Iroquois, now known as the Six Nations. The English used all the means in their power to gain the help of the other Indian tribes, but the French were generally far more skillful than the English in gaining and keeping the regard of the natives.

5. **Cost and Extent of the War.**—The contest originally begun for supremacy in America, in a few years extended throughout the world. It raged in the West Indies, in Europe, and on the plains of Hindostan. At its close England was every where triumphant. She was in possession of a large number of the West India islands, had laid the foundation of her great East Indian empire, and was mistress of North America east of the Mississippi. But, in acquiring so much, she had enormously increased her national debt.

6. In their share of the struggle in America, the colonies had spent $16,000,000, and were repaid only $5,000,000 of this by the English government. Thirty thousand of their vigorous young men had died from wounds, or exposure, or on the battle-field. In addition to this, the sufferings of the settlers from the Indians, on the exposed frontiers for hundreds of miles, had been frightful.

---

3. What was the success of the English during the first three years? Why was this? What made the French so successful at first? State what is said of the struggle made by the French. What makes their efforts appear so remarkable?

4. Is the name French and English War strictly correct? What is said about this? What is said of the French mode of dealing with the Indians compared with that of the English?

5. What is said of the extent of the war? What was England's success at its close? What drawback was there to all this glory?

6. What had it cost the colonies in money? What was the loss in men? What is said of the suffering on the frontiers?

7. **Advantages of the War to the Colonies.**—As an offset to all this, the colonists reaped considerable benefits from the war. Great Britain spent a great deal of money among them, particularly in the northern colonies, for the support of her fleets and armies; and she paid for the food of the provincial troops as well as the regulars. War makes busy times, and the Americans in this way gathered considerable amounts of money during these six years. Then, too, they had been united in a common enterprise, and had learned their strength, and what they could accomplish by union. Franklin's plan for a federal union indeed failed in 1754, but the colonies worked on in a united way without it, sending supplies of men, money, and materials for the common use. Thus they were better prepared to act together when the Revolutionary War began.

8. The treatment of the provincials by the English troops was another thing that served to unite the former more closely. The English sneered at the awkward ways of the young farmer-soldiers. During the war, nearly every important command in the army was given to British officers. The provincial officers, with scarce any regard to rank, were thrust aside to make room for young British subalterns. But many of the future leaders in the Revolutionary War were trained in this long war—Washington, Gates, Morgan, Montgomery, Stark, Putnam, Arnold, and others.

9. **Gain in Liberty.**—The liberties of the colonists were more firmly settled at the end of the war, because the royal governors found it next to impossible to enforce arbitrary laws while the war was going on. The English needed the help and money of the colonists, and the Colonial Assemblies would have refused to grant such assistance had the governors been tyrannical. When the colonies voted supplies of money, they did it with great caution, and kept the control of the purse in their own hands. In this way, much was gained in showing the people where their power lay,

---

7. What advantage had the colonies reaped in business during the war? What greatly important lesson had the war taught them? For what was this a preparation?

8. What cemented the colonists still more closely? What is said of this favoritism? In spite of all this, what training sprang out of the war?

and, when the war ended, the royal governors found it impossible to go back to their old arbitrary modes of government.

REVIEW QUESTIONS.—FRENCH EXPLORATIONS. FRENCH AND INDIAN WAR.

1. What drove the French westward in their explorations?
2. To what class of men did these explorers belong?
3. Who first discovered the Upper Mississippi and explored it, and when?
4. Give the general direction of the French exploration from 1609 to 1675.
5. What was the great object of these explorations?
6. When and by whom was the territory called Louisiana named and partially explored?
7. Give a brief account of La Salle's labors.
8. What idea do you form of his character?
9. What do you know of Father Hennepin?
10. Describe briefly D'Iberville's expedition.
11. What contrast is drawn between the activity of the French and that of the English?
12. What was necessary to complete the line of French occupation from the east end of Lake Erie to the Mississippi?
13. How did the French posts affect the English settlements?
14. What portion of North America was occupied by the English?
15. Give the claims of the two nations to territory and what they were based on.
16. What and where was the first grant of lands to the English beyond the Alleghanies?
17. How did this interfere with the French plan?
18. What directly brought on the French and Indian War?
19. Why was it so called?
20. What was the comparative population of the French and English at the beginning of the war?
21. How did actual hostilities commence, and in what year?
22. What great man first appears in history just before the commencement of hostilities, and in the performance of what service?
23. What event in Braddock's ill-fated expedition had a powerful influence on the future history of America?
24. When was Braddock's expedition, and what was its object?
25. Why was the possession of this so desirable?
26. State the general plan of the expeditions for each year of the war.
27. Give the leading events of each year.
28. In connection with what event is Benjamin Franklin mentioned in 1753? Give an account of this.
29. In what does his name appear in 1754?
30. To the efforts of what great English statesman was the final overthrow of the French in America greatly owing?
31. In what year was Fort du Quesne taken?
32. Give an account of its capture, and of the expedition of which it formed a part.
33. What closing event marked the conquest of Canada?
34. Did the French make any attempt to recover it? If so, give an account of it.
35. How long did the war last?

---

9. In what way were the liberties of the colonists benefited? How did they hold their royal governors in check? In what, then, did they find that their power lay? How did all this affect the future conduct of these governors?

36. Why was the war not ended until the year 1763?
37. What names connected with the French and Indian War occur to you as the most remarkable, and why?
38. What names of places, and why?
39. Who was the most distinguished Frenchman, and state for what elements of character he was most remarkable?
40. What was the great battle-ground in the northern part of New York?
41. What made this advanced post so valuable?
42. When and where was the treaty of peace proclaimed?
43. Give the terms of this so far as relates to possession in North America.
44. What great question did the war settle?
45. By what were the military movements of the French marked as compared with those of the English?
46. What was the cost of the war to the colonies in money and men?
47. What advantages, on the other hand, did the war bring to the colonies—1, in reference to union among themselves? 2, in the training of military officers? 3, in confidence in their own powers? 4, in colonial independence?

SECTION VII.

CAUSES OF THE AMERICAN REVOLUTION.

1. THE treaty of Paris secured to the Anglo-Saxon race the control of North America east of the Mississippi; but England was not destined long to remain mistress of this vast region. The treaty was scarcely ratified when the renewed oppressions of the mother country brought on a struggle with the colonies, which ended, twelve years later, in the War for Independence.

2. The more remote causes of the American Revolution are to be found in the oppressive enactments made by England at an early day to cripple or destroy colonial commerce. The celebrated Navigation Act of 1660—for the early act of 1651 was aimed chiefly at Dutch commerce with America—with the additional restrictions of 1663, was passed for this purpose, and was felt severely throughout the colonies, but particularly in commercial New England. It sought to keep the Americans dependent on the mother country, making England the only place where colonial products could be sent for a market, and whence the colonists should wholly draw their supply of foreign merchandise.

1. What remark is made in the beginning of the first paragraph? What occurred soon after the treaty of 1763?
2. What were the remote causes of the American Revolution? What is said of the Navigation Acts? What formed an important part of the plan in these acts?

3. From this it naturally followed that England earnestly strove to discourage the manufacture in the colonies of all such goods as could be provided by her own manufacturers. We can judge what were the settled feelings of the government and people of England on this point when, some years after the French and Indian War, Lord Chatham, late William Pitt, a friend of the colonies, said in Parliament that "the British colonists of North America had NO RIGHT to manufacture even a nail for a horse-shoe." Even as early as the year 1691, the current English idea was that the colonies existed only for the consumption of English commodities and the production of merchantable articles for the English trade.

4. The Americans, on the other hand, strove to encourage manufactures within their own borders. Iron-works were established in Massachusetts as early as 1643; and in 1721 there were in New England six furnaces and nineteen forges. The production of iron was still greater in Pennsylvania, whence it was exported to the other colonies. The British iron-masters the same year tried to prevent the production of iron in America, but failed at that time. In 1750 the Americans were prohibited by act of Parliament from sending pig-iron to England, and from manufacturing steel and bar-iron for home use. This act shut up all such works, and any built thereafter were liable to destruction as "nuisances."

5. Parliament in 1732 prohibited the transportation of American woolen goods from colony to colony; and hats, the making of which was already a thriving business, were placed under the same restriction as woolen goods. As an argument for this, it was asserted that, from the abundance of beaver and other furs in America, the colonists, unless restrained, would soon supply all the world with hats. The act of 1732 was followed, in 1733, by a law known as the "Molasses Act," imposing a duty on rum, molasses, and sugar imported from foreign colonies into any of the Brit-

3. What naturally followed from this? By what can we learn the settled views of the English on this point? What were their opinions as early as 1691?

4. What is said of manufactures in the colonies? In New England? In Pennsylvania? State the efforts of the English to put a stop to this.

ish plantations. This was passed to protect the West India colonial productions at the expense of the North American colonies.

6. The various acts of trade brought in their train a large number of custom-house officers, who applied to the colonial courts in 1761 to grant them "writs of assistance"—warrants to search when and where they pleased for smuggled goods, and to call in others to assist them. This was felt to be a grievous and dangerous power, and the issue of the writs was opposed with so much energy that, though they were granted, they were so unpopular as to be seldom used.

7. Regardless of the state of feeling in America, the English ministers brought forward, in the year 1763, a proposition to tax the colonies. It was claimed that the debt of England had been largely increased by defending them, and that it was only right they should defray a share of the expense by paying a tax to the English government. In the month of March, 1764, the House of Commons resolved "that Parliament had a right to tax America;" and in April an act was passed levying duties on certain articles imported into America, and adding iron and lumber to a list of "enumerated articles" which could be exported only to England. The preamble of this act avowed the purpose "of raising a revenue for the expenses of defending, protecting, and securing his majesty's dominions in America.

8. The colonies protested against this as an attempt upon their liberties, proclaiming that they had borne their full share in the various wars for their defense, and were now able to protect themselves, and affirming that "taxation without representation was tyranny." But armed resistance was not yet hinted at. Boston, under the leadership of Samuel Adams, was the first to move against this new plan of taxation, and instructed her delegates in the

---

5. What occurred in 1732? What is said of hat-making in the colonies? What was the "Molasses Act?" What was its object?

6. What did these acts of trade bring along with them? What were "writs of assistance," and what trouble did they produce in the colonies?

7. What important measure was proposed by the English ministry soon after the treaty of Paris? On what grounds was this based? What followed in March, 1764? Describe the act of April, 1764, and its purpose.

Massachusetts House of Representatives to remonstrate against it.

9. This body resolved "that the imposition of duties and taxes by the Parliament of Great Britain upon a people not represented in the House of Commons is absolutely irreconcilable with their rights." A letter was sent to the agent of the colony in London, urging him to protest vigorously against the scheme of taxation, in which letter were the remarkable words, "If we are not represented we are slaves." The Massachusetts House also ordered that a committee should correspond with the other colonies.

10. Connecticut, New York, Rhode Island, and Virginia followed the example of Massachusetts, and dispatched remonstrances to England. New York sent one so strongly expressed that no member of Parliament could be found bold enough to present it. All this produced no effect. The Stamp Act, the other part of the taxation scheme, passed the House of Commons, March, 1765, by a vote of five to one, and the House of Lords were so agreed that there was no division. This act imposed a duty on all paper, vellum, and parchment used in the colonies, and declared all writings on unstamped materials to be null and void.

11. Another act passed by Parliament was more irritating to the Americans than the Stamp Act. This was known as "the Quartering Act." A standing army was ordered for the colonies, and the people, wherever these troops were stationed, were required by this enactment to find quarters, fire-wood, bedding, drink, soap, and candles for the soldiers.

12. The Virginia Assembly was in session when the news of the passage of these acts arrived in May. The aristocratic leaders of the House were afraid to take any action;

---

8. How did the colonies show their dislike to these measures? Did they at first contemplate armed resistance to England?

9. What is said of the conduct of Boston? What spirited resolution was passed by the Massachusetts House of Representatives? State what is said of the letter sent by the House to its agent in London.

10. How was the conduct of Massachusetts regarded by the other colonies? What effect did all this produce on the English ministry? Describe the Stamp Act. When did this pass Parliament?

11. What other act was passed at the same time? Why was this so disagreeable to the people?

PATRICK HENRY, 1785.

but Patrick Henry, a young lawyer, presented a series of resolutions denouncing the acts as destructive to British as well as American liberty. The resolutions, supported by Henry's wonderful eloquence, passed, notwithstanding great opposition, and copies were sent at once to the different colonies. Before the Virginia resolutions reached Massachusetts, her representatives had recommended that committees from the several colonies should meet at New York in October, to consult on what was to be done.

13. The people seemed scarcely inclined to wait for the meeting of this Colonial Congress, but took matters into their own hands. In New York, as early as June, the Stamp Act was hawked about the streets as "The Folly of England and the Ruin of America." In Boston the citizens had frequent meetings under a tree, which they named "Liberty Tree." Upon this they hung in effigy those persons who were supposed to favor the English government. In August a mob attacked the house of a stamp distributer and destroyed the furniture. They also attacked the house of Lieutenant Governor Hutchinson, and, dragging out his furniture, made bonfires of it. Clubs, called "Sons of Liberty," sprang up all over the North, and spread south as far as New Jersey.

14. Such was the excitement when delegates from nine colonies met in New York in October, 1765, and appointed Timothy Ruggles, of Massachusetts, president. After a session of three weeks, they agreed on a "Declaration of the

12. Why was Virginia the first to take action on these tyrannous measures? Who was the leader there, and state what occurred in the Assembly? Which was the next colony to move? What important recommendation was made?

13. What occurred in New York early in June? How did the people show their feelings in Boston? What is said of the riot there? Who were the "Sons of Liberty?"

Rights and Grievances of the Colonies;" and a petition to the king and memorials to each house of Parliament were also prepared. In the "Declaration of Rights," they took the new ground that representation of the colonies in Parliament was impossible on account of distance, and that the different colonies could only tax themselves.

15. When the 1st of November arrived, the day appointed for the Stamp Act to go into operation, not a stamp was to be seen, and the stamp distributers, every where unpopular, had deemed it wise to resign. In New York the Sons of Liberty burned Governor Colden in effigy, and so far frightened him that he delivered the stamps to the mayor and corporation on the 5th of November.

16. Next day, November 6, at the same place, a committee drew up an agreement to import no more goods until the Stamp Act was repealed. This non-importation agreement was soon signed by the leading merchants in New York, Philadelphia, and Boston. At the same time a combination was entered into for the wearing of American cloths. Business, interrupted for a short time by the want of stamps, was presently resumed, and the courts ere long ceased to regard the Stamp Act in their proceedings.

17. In February, 1766, Benjamin Franklin, of Pennsylvania, agent in England for some of the colonies, was summoned before the bar of the House of Commons to answer questions regarding the condition of the colonies. In this trying position that great man displayed wonderful calmness, readiness, and practical wisdom. His answers in relation to the operation of the Stamp Act, and the temper of the Americans should it be enforced, greatly surprised the officers of the crown and promoted the cause of his countrymen.

14. When and where did the first Colonial Congress meet? Who was the president? How many colonies were represented? What was the result of their deliberations? What was the spirit of the "Declaration of Rights?" In what did this ground differ from that previously held by the colonists?

15. When was the Stamp Act to go into operation? What was the state of things when that day arrived? What happened at New York?

16. What spirited agreement originated in New York soon after? How was this received throughout the colonies? How was business affected by the want of stamps? How far were stamps used in the courts?

17. What remarkable event took place in February, 1766? What is said of his behavior in presence of the House of Commons? What is said of his answers, and their influence?

18. The English government showed signs of alarm; for the British merchants and manufacturers felt seriously the full weight of the non-importation agreement. Pitt, who was the friend of the Americans, nobly defended them in the House of Commons; and in March, 1766, Parliament repealed the Stamp Act by a decisive majority. At the same time, the right to tax the colonies was asserted by a bill which declared the right and power of Parliament "to bind the colonies in all cases whatsoever."

19. The English rulers soon showed that they had not yielded much. In January, 1767, a new bill to tax the colonies was introduced into Parliament, in which tea, paints, paper, glass, and lead were made subject to duty. This was passed in June. A board of revenue commissioners for America was also established, with its head-quarters at Boston.

20. On the receipt of this news, the excitement, which had been allayed by the repeal of the Stamp Act, broke out with fresh fury. The colonial newspapers, twenty-five in number, were filled with stirring and patriotic articles. The non-importation agreement, which had for the time been forgotten, was again adopted in Boston, Providence, New York, and Philadelphia. The Massachusetts General Court, in February, 1768, sent a circular letter to the other Colonial Assemblies urging co-operation and consultation.

21. In June, 1768, the revenue officers at Boston seized a sloop on the charge of smuggling a cargo of wine, and a riot at once broke out. The officers fled for protection to the barracks on Castle Island, in the harbor; and the House of Representatives took no notice of the affair. The English government, in July, ordered the Massachusetts House to rescind their circular letter to the other colonies; but they stoutly refused to rescind, and were dissolved. Some

---

18. How had the opposition of the Americans already affected the English government and the merchants there? What great Englishman was particularly the friend of the colonies at this time? What followed, and give the date? How was this repeal made unsatisfactory to the Americans?

19. In what way did the English government show that they had not yielded much? When was this new tax bill passed?

20. How was the news of the passage of this act received by the people? by the press? by the merchants? What action was taken by the Massachusetts Assembly?

of the Colonial Assemblies that had cordially answered the Massachusetts circular were also dissolved by the governors.

22. To overawe the inhabitants, four regiments were ordered to Boston in September; but the authorities spurned the Quartering Act, and refused to provide for the troops. Some of them encamped on the Common, and Faneuil Hall was used as a temporary barrack. General Gage, hastening from New York, was compelled to hire for quarters some houses obtained with great difficulty, and to provide for the men out of his own military stores; Boston would supply neither bedding nor fuel. In New York the Assembly also firmly refused to comply with the requisitions of the Quartering Act, and was dissolved.

23. In Boston, the ill feeling between the people and soldiers broke out into open quarrels, and on March 5, 1770, a picket-guard of eight men, provoked by the taunts of the crowd, fired, killing three persons and wounding eight others. Next morning Faneuil Hall was filled with an excited crowd; the anger of the people rose throughout the day to a tremendous height, and only the removal of the regiments from the city, in compliance with a positive demand, appeased the citizens. The captain of the guard and the soldiers were afterward tried for murder, but were acquitted on the ground of self-defense.

24. The non-importation of British goods again began to influence public feeling in England, and a bill was passed by Parliament in May, 1773, repealing the tax on all articles except tea, on which there was a nominal duty of threepence a pound. The spirit of the Americans was thoroughly aroused, and they scorned this concession. It was not the amount of the tax, but the attempt to tax them without their consent, of which they complained. The non-importa-

21. What riot occurred in Boston in June, 1768? State what is said of it. What order came to the Massachusetts Assembly from the English government in July? How was this received, and with what result? What followed in some of the other colonies?

22. How did the English attempt to overawe the Bostonians? How did the latter show their hatred of the troops? In what way were the soldiers provided for? At what other place was there the same trouble?

23. What was the state of things in Boston between the people and the soldiers? What happened in March, 1770? What was done to the troops who fired on the people?

tion agreement was so far modified as to apply only to tea, and the merchants at the different ports were earnestly warned against receiving it on consignment.

25. The first of the tea-ships arrived at Boston November 25, 1773. A mass meeting of citizens at Faneuil Hall ordered the vessel to be moored at the wharf, and appointed a guard of 25 men to watch her, and see that no tea was landed. Presently a committee, on which were the active patriots John Hancock, Samuel Adams, Josiah Quincy, and Joseph Warren, obtained a promise from the captain and the owner of the tea-ship that the tea should be carried back to England; but Governor Hutchinson would not grant a permit, and without this the vessel could not pass the fort and ships of war in the harbor.

SAMUEL ADAMS.

26. As soon as the refusal of the governor became known, some 40 or 50 men, dressed like Mohawks, on the night of December 16 boarded the tea-vessels—two more of which had meanwhile arrived—and, in presence of a great but orderly crowd, emptied, in two hours, 342 chests of tea into the water. At New York and Philadelphia the people would not permit the tea to be landed. That which arrived at Charleston was stored in damp cellars, and soon became worthless.

27. When the news of the tea-riot reached England it produced much angry feeling there, which showed itself in

---

24. What concession did the English government make in May? What produced this concession? How did the Americans regard it, and why? How was the non-importation agreement modified? What is said of the people and the tea-merchants?

25. When and where did the first of the tea-ships arrive? What measures were taken by the Boston committee? Name some of the most active men. What success did the committee meet with?

26. What took place at Boston in December? What occurred at other sea-ports?

a determination to punish Boston. Parliament thereupon passed the Boston Port Bill, shutting up the harbor of the town, and removing the port of entry and the seat of government to Salem. In addition, some of the most tyrannous acts were passed; among these, a new act for quartering troops on the people. Boston was chiefly dependent on commerce, and the destruction of her trade produced great distress among her people. The inhabitants of Salem and Marblehead nobly came to their assistance, and offered the use of their wharves to the merchants of Boston; and the colonies sent liberal contributions for her poorer citizens.

28. Virginia was among the first in expressing her sympathy for Massachusetts. Her Assembly was dissolved by the governor in May, 1774, for appointing the 1st of June—the day when the Boston Port Bill was to go into operation—as a fast-day. It met, however, next day, notwithstanding his opposition, and declared that an attack on one colony was an attack upon all; and advised calling a Congress to consider the grievances of the people. The other colonies joined in this recommendation, and it was agreed that a Congress should meet in September.

29. This second Colonial Congress—the great Congress of the Revolution—composed of delegates from all the colonies except Georgia, met at Philadelphia September 5, 1774. Peyton Randolph, of Virginia, was appointed president, and Charles Thomson, of Philadelphia, secretary. The delegates passed a declaration of rights, together with addresses to the king and people of England, and recommended the suspension of all commercial intercourse with Great Britain. It then adjourned, to meet May 10, 1775.

30. Before Congress met in September, General Gage, now governor, had begun to fortify Boston Neck, the only ap-

27. How was the news of this received in England? How did Parliament show its desire for vengeance? How did the Boston Port Bill affect Boston? In what way did the Salem and Marblehead people show their sympathy?

28. Which was the first Colonial Assembly that manifested its sympathy for Boston? How did it show this? What spirited measures did it recommend? How was this received by the other colonies?

29. When and where did the second Colonial Congress meet? What colony was not present by her delegates? Who were the first president and secretary? What important papers were passed? To what time did it adjourn?

proach by land to the town; he had also seized some powder stored by the provincials at Cambridge On the other hand, the Massachusetts Assembly, which had been dissolved by Gage, met in October, 1774, as a Provincial Congress, called out the militia, ordered them to train and be ready at a minute's notice—hence called "Minute-men"—voted £20,000 for military expenses, and made preparations for the worst.

REVIEW QUESTIONS.—CAUSES OF THE REVOLUTION.

1. What were the remote causes of the American Revolution?
2. Mention some of the oppressions on commerce and manufactures.
3. Show in what light the English regarded the colonies.
4. State what an English statesman said in Parliament.
5. What act passed in 1733 produced very ill feeling in America? Why?
6. What were the "writs of assistance?" State their origin.
7. How were the feelings of the Americans still further irritated?
8. How long was this after the French and Indian War?
9. What was the first of the revenue acts?
10. By what general protest, on the part of the colonies, was this met?
11. Which was the first colony to take public action? State what was done.
12. What other colonies followed?
13. How did all this affect the conduct of the British government?
14. When was the Stamp Act passed, and what were its provisions?
15. Describe the character of the act passed about the same time.
16. What two colonies took almost simultaneous action when the news of the Stamp Act arrived in America?
17. What recommendation followed?
18. How did the colonists show their feelings before the meeting of Congress?
19. When and where did the first Colonial Congress meet?
20. What was done at it?
21. What was the ground taken in the "Declaration of Rights?"
22. How was the operation of the Stamp Act nearly nullified before November?
23. In what way did people transact business without the use of stamped paper?
24. What effect did this produce on the British government?
25. State the service done to the colonists by their countryman in England.
26. To what tyrannical claim did the English government still adhere?
27. When and what, as a consequence of this, was the next act of Parliament?
28. What high-handed measure was adopted by the English in 1768? What produced this?
29. How was Boston particularly made to feel the displeasure of England?
30. What concessions shortly followed, and how far were these successful?
31. Show the spirit of the people in the matter of the tea-ships.
32. How was Boston punished for this?
33. What was the conduct displayed by other cities and colonies?
34. Describe particularly the conduct of Virginia?
35. When and where did the second or great Continental Congress meet?
36. What measures did it adopt?
37. When and what were the warlike movements of Gage?
38. What preparations did Massachusetts make?
39. Simply name and give the dates of the leading events in the section.

---

30. What important movements were made by General Gage before the meeting of Congress? What active warlike measures were adopted by the Massachusetts Assembly?

CHAPTER III.

WAR OF THE REVOLUTION.

SECTION I.

EVENTS OF 1775.

1. BY the beginning of April, 1775, the British troops in Boston had been increased by orders of the British government to 3000 men. Meanwhile the Americans had collected a quantity of ammunition and public stores at Concord, 16 miles from Boston. To destroy these, and perhaps capture John Hancock and Samuel Adams, who were lodging in that neighborhood, General Gage secretly dispatched 800 troops, under Colonel Smith, before midnight on the 18th of April.

JOHN HANCOCK.

2. The movement was, however, discovered; the alarm was swiftly given to the country, and when the British arrived before sunrise at Lexington, within six miles of Concord, they found some 70 or 80 minute-men assembled on the green. Major Pitcairn, at the head of the British column, advanced on them rapidly, and called on them, as rebels, to throw down their arms and disperse. Not being in-

1. What was the state of the British army at Boston in the spring of 1775? What movement was made by General Gage in April? Where is Concord?

stantly obeyed, he ordered the troops to fire, and seven of the minute-men were killed and several wounded; the remainder dispersed. The British then proceeded to Concord and commenced to destroy the stores, but were attacked by fresh bodies of minute-men and compelled to retreat.

THE FIRING AT LEXINGTON. [From an old cut.]

3. The country was now thoroughly aroused. Young and old, with such arms as they could collect, flocked to the scene of action. From behind trees, walls, and fences, they kept up such a galling fire on the enemy during their retreat, that, had the latter not met at Lexington a re-enforcement of 900 men and two field-pieces, under Lord Percy, sent by Gage to their assistance, they would have been destroyed or captured to a man. The British continued their retreat to Charlestown, harassed by the Americans. When they arrived here, utterly worn out, they had lost, in killed, wounded, and missing, nearly 300 men. The loss of the pro-

2. How was Gage's movement anticipated? What happened at Lexington Green? What took place at Concord?

vincials was about 90. The skirmish at Lexington, April 19, 1775, was the beginning of bloodshed in the Revolutionary War.

4. General Gage soon found himself closely shut up in Boston by an army of 20,000 provincials, who hastened to that point on the news of the battle of Lexington. A line of intrenchments, extending nearly 20 miles, was formed from Roxbury to the River Mystic, and the greatest activity prevailed among the Americans. In May large re-enforcements arrived from England, under Generals Howe, Burgoyne, and Clinton; and the army of Gage was now increased to more than 10,000 men. Thus strengthened, he issued a proclamation declaring martial law, and offering a pardon to those rebels who would lay down their arms. From this offer he excluded by name John Hancock and Samuel Adams, as persons whose crimes were too great to be overlooked.

5. The provincials encamped around Boston consisted of New England men, chiefly from Massachusetts, commanded by General Ward. To blockade the British more completely in the town, Colonel Prescott was sent with 1000 men, on the night of June 16, to fortify Bunker Hill, which commanded the great northern road out of Boston across the peninsula of Charlestown. By some mistake, Prescott passed by Bunker Hill, and went on to Breed's Hill, much nearer the town, and there threw up intrenchments.

6. When the morning broke, the British were surprised to see earth-works so near them, and from the ships and a battery on Copp's Hill opened fire, which did not disturb the Americans. Gage then determined to carry the works by assault. About three o'clock in the afternoon, 3000 picked

---

3. What made the situation of the British so critical? What is said of the running fight and retreat? What saved the British from destruction? How long did the battle continue? Why is it called the battle of Lexington? What was the loss on each side?

4. What was the situation of the troops in Boston soon after the battle? What was the extent of the American intrenchments? See map, page 162. To what extent was the British army increased in May? When Gage found himself thus re-enforced, what did he do? Who had the honor of being excluded from this offer? Why?

5. What American troops were in the intrenchments in front of Boston? Who was sent to fortify Bunker Hill? Why was this deemed necessary? Where did Prescott go, and why?

British troops left Boston, under Generals Howe and Pigot, and, having landed, began to ascend the hill, while the cannon from the ships played on the American works. From the neighboring heights, and from the roofs and steeples of Boston, thousands of spectators watched anxiously the approaching battle.

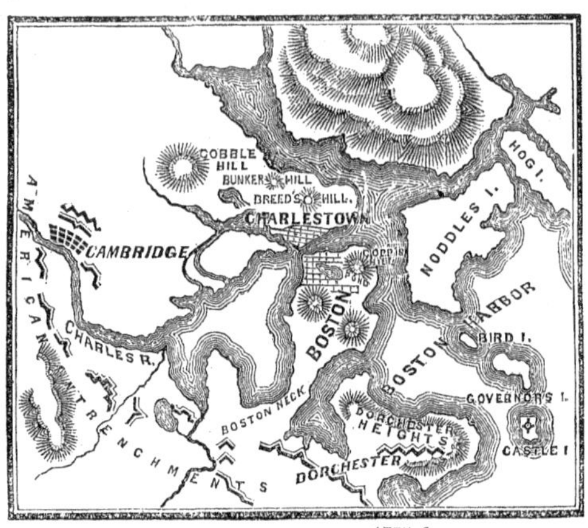

BOSTON AND VICINITY, 1775–6.

7. The Americans remained quiet till the British were within 150 yards of the works, and then delivered their fire so steady and well directed that the enemy fell back in disorder to the foot of the hill. A second time they advanced, but with the same result. It was some time before they could be prepared for a third attack, and in the mean time they were re-enforced by 1000 fresh troops from Boston, under General Clinton. General Gage ordered the houses of Charlestown to be set on fire, and, under cover of the smoke, they were again led up the hill. The powder of the Americans had begun to fail, and the royal troops pushed in at one end of the redoubt, and planted light field-pieces. These raked the breastwork from end to end, and at the same time some British grenadiers swept over the works at the point

6. What were the first movements made by the British when they discovered the works on Breed's Hill? What important movement followed in the afternoon? Who anxiously watched the result of this movement? Where were they?

of the bayonet. The Americans clubbed their muskets, and fell back fighting across Charlestown Neck to a place of safety.

JOSEPH WARREN.

8. The British had won the hill, but at a terrible sacrifice. They had lost over 1000 in killed and wounded, more than a third of their troops engaged. The provincial loss was 450, but among these was the young and ardent patriot General Warren, a loss which the British joyfully thought was worth five hundred men.

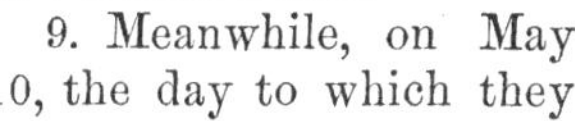

9. Meanwhile, on May 10, the day to which they had adjourned, the delegates to the Continental Congress reassembled at Philadelphia, John Hancock being president, and Charles Thomson, the Quaker schoolmaster of Philadelphia, secretary. They resolved that Great Britain had begun hostilities; they also expressed a great desire for peace, and declared that they had no wish to throw off their allegiance. At the same time, they voted that the colonies should be prepared for war, and that nothing but superior force would compel them to submit to British taxation. It was as yet chiefly in New England that the idea of independence was freely spoken of; it found little favor in the Middle and Southern Colonies.

10. On June 15, Congress unanimously appointed George Washington, who was then present as a delegate from Virginia, commander-in-chief. He accepted the appointment in

---

7. How many attacks did the British make? Describe the first and second attacks. Describe the third.

8. What was the loss on the part of the British? What was the loss on the provincial side? Why was the death of Warren thought so important by the British?

9. Where and when did the Continental Congress reassemble? Who were the officers? Do you remember any thing of this Hancock? What did they resolve? What recommendations did they make to the colonies? To what extent was the question of independence entertained?

a modest speech, in which he declined to receive any compensation but the payment of his expenses. A fortnight after the battle of Bunker Hill, Washington arrived at the American camp, and took command July 2. During the remainder of the year he was fully occupied in bringing the army into a state of steady discipline, in providing for its wants, and in watching the British shut up in Boston. The right of his line was commanded by General Ward, and the left by General Charles Lee. Washington himself commanded the centre. Lee was formerly a British officer, who had espoused the patriot cause, and was made a major general by Congress.

11. On the 10th of May, the day on which Congress met, some Connecticut militia, under Ethan Allen and Benedict Arnold, captured the British post at Ticonderoga. Two days after, Crown Point was captured by Colonel Seth Warner, with 150 cannon and a large amount of ammunition and stores, which proved of great service to the Americans.

12. **Invasion of Canada.**—The road to Canada lay open by the capture of Ticonderoga and Crown Point, and it was determined to attack the British power in that quarter. Toward the end of summer, Generals Schuyler and Montgomery, the latter already noticed as a companion of Wolfe in 1758, with one division, went by the way of Lake Champlain and St. John's; and Colonel Benedict Arnold was sent with 1100 men, by way of Maine, to join the other division in front of Quebec.

13. Schuyler fell sick, and Montgomery, assuming the command, captured St. John's, on the Sorel River, after a spirited resistance, November 3, and entered Montreal without opposition on the 13th. In the beginning of a Canadian

---

10. Who was appointed to the command of the army, and when? What was his salary? Why was he not present at the battle of Bunker Hill? When did he arrive in front of Boston? How was Washington occupied during the remainder of the year 1775? Who assisted Washington in the command before Boston? Who was Lee?

11. What important event took place on the same day that Congress met? What took place soon after? Why was the capture of Crown Point of so much importance at this time?

12. To what expedition did the capture of these two places lead? How many divisions did the expedition embrace? What route did each take, and who were the respective commanders? Where did Montgomery figure in 1758?

winter, with his force reduced to 300 men, ill clad, and without proper supplies, he moved toward Quebec to join Arnold's division. That officer, after crossing the northern wilderness of Maine, and overcoming fearful difficulties from hunger and fatigue, reached the St. Lawrence, and climbed the Heights of Abraham in November. Finding his force, which was reduced to 750 men, too small to attack the city, he went up the river 20 miles and waited for Montgomery. On the arrival of the latter, they had together less than 1000 men, and with this small band Montgomery laid siege to Quebec, December 5.

14. The American troops made no progress with the siege because they had no heavy artillery; and, as a last hope, an assault was ordered, December 31. Montgomery, at the head of one division, was shot down. Arnold, while leading another, was severely wounded, and gave up the command to Captain Morgan, a celebrated officer in the later years of the war. Morgan entered the city, but was overpowered by numbers and compelled to surrender. Arnold then fell back, with some 500 men, to a position three miles above Quebec, where he remained all winter.

15. In April, 1776, General Wooster, with re-enforcements, took command, and made another attempt on Quebec, but without success. He was succeeded by General Thomas in May, who fell back, leaving the sick, together with the stores, in the hands of Carleton, Governor of Canada, who had been heavily re-enforced. By the month of June, the American force, utterly broken down by sickness and want, the mere skeleton of an army, reached Ticonderoga. Thus ended the useless attempt to invade Canada.

16. While these events were transpiring at the North, the patriots were active in Virginia. In the month of April,

---

13. What places were taken and occupied by Schuyler's division? Was Schuyler at the capture of these places? Why not? To what point did Montgomery march after entering Montreal? What was the number and condition of his men? What difficulties had Arnold's division met with? Why did he not attack Quebec? Where did he go? What was determined on after the arrival of Montgomery?

14. What progress was made in the siege? What attempt was made on the last day of the year? Give an account of this. Who took the command after the failure of the assault? Where did he encamp for the winter?

15. Who arrived in the following April? How long did he retain command? Who succeeded him, and what did he do? What is said of the close of the expedition?

Governor Dunmore seized a quantity of powder, and placed it on board an armed vessel. Patrick Henry, at the head of a band of citizens, immediately demanded and received full pay for the same. In June, Dunmore was driven from his government, and forced to take shelter on board a British man-of-war in York River. Toward the close of the year, having collected a body of regulars, royalists, and fugitive slaves, he attacked the Virginians near Norfolk, December 9, and was defeated. In revenge, January, 1776, he burned the town, then the richest and largest in Virginia, and containing 7000 inhabitants. During the summer of that year he committed great depredations along the rivers, plundering plantations, burning houses, and carrying off slaves. Finally, with his booty, he retired to Florida.

17. As early as May, 1775, the people of North Carolina threw off the yoke of the mother country, and organized an independent government. In that province, and, indeed, throughout the Southern Colonies, there were a great many influential royalists, who, incited by the government, were already very active for the English cause. In South Carolina and Georgia the spirit of independence animated the patriots, and they rose against the authority of the royal governors.

SECTION II.

Events of 1776.

1. In the month of January, the British in Boston were busy preparing a secret expedition to be sent off under Sir Henry Clinton. Washington had reason to suspect that this was intended against New York, and sent General Lee to collect volunteers from Connecticut and march to the defense of that city. Lee accomplished this so rapidly that he entered New York on the same day, February 4, that Clin-

---

16. What is said of Dunmore and Patrick Henry in Virginia? What happened in June? What occurred in December? What did Dunmore do in revenge? State what is further said of Dunmore's operations.

17. What took place in North Carolina? How was public opinion divided there? How far did this extend? What is said of South Carolina and Georgia?

ton arrived in the harbor. Being thus disappointed, Clinton soon after sailed away to Virginia, but there the patriots were prepared to receive him. He then went to Cape Fear, where he awaited the arrival of a squadron from England.

2. During the winter, the British were shut up in Boston and watched closely by Washington, whose army, January 1, did not amount to 10,000 men. Gage had been superseded, on account of the battle of Bunker Hill, by Sir William Howe. Washington hoped to be able to make an attack on the British when the harbor was frozen, but the winter was a very open one, and nothing could be done in that way.

3. Resolute in his purpose to drive the enemy from the city, Washington, on the night of the 4th of March, marched to Dorchester Heights, and, before morning, threw up earth-

VIEW OF BOSTON FROM DORCHESTER HEIGHTS IN 1774.

works which completely commanded Boston. Howe, feeling that he must dislodge the Americans from the heights or evacuate the city, made immediate preparations for an assault; but a severe storm delayed him, and by the time it

1. In what preparations were the British in Boston busy in January? Against what point did Washington suppose these were intended? How did he prepare to meet this plan? In what direction did Clinton then sail? Did he accomplish any thing here? Whither did he then go, and why?

2. What was the situation of the British army during the winter? Who was now the British general? Why was Gage displaced? What did Washington hope to do during the winter? Why was this not done?

subsided the works had been made too strong to be easily taken. Nothing was left for the British but to evacuate Boston; and on March 17th they embarked on board the fleet, taking with them some 1500 royalists, and sailed for Halifax. This bloodless victory was hailed with joy throughout the colonies. Congress passed a unanimous vote of thanks to Washington, and ordered a gold medal to be struck in remembrance of the event. Washington, being anxious about New York, sent off the main body of his army to that place.

4. The first point of attack proved to be, not New York, but Charleston, South Carolina. A British squadron, under Admiral Parker, came from Ireland, and was joined at Cape Fear by Clinton. After some delay, they sailed to attack Charleston, and appeared off the harbor June 4.

5. The Carolina patriots, notified of their danger, had thrown up some works on Sullivan's Island, and placed Colonel Moultrie there with a regiment. When the British ships attempted to enter the harbor, June 28, they became entangled in the shoals, and were met by so furious a fire from the fort that they were compelled to retire with heavy loss. One of their vessels was abandoned. The British soon after sailed for New York, to join the troops that were assembling in that neighborhood.

6. On the same day that Fort Moultrie was attacked, General Howe landed on Staten Island from Halifax with the Boston army and other re-enforcements. Admiral Lord Howe, the brother of the general, arrived from England shortly after with more troops, raising the number to 30,000 men. A large part of these were Hessians, hired by the English from the Duke of Hesse-Cassel in Germany.

---

3. What unexpected movement was made on the 4th of March? What did Howe do? Why was he prevented from making the attack? What was the result? How was the news of the evacuation of Boston received in the colonies and by Congress? To what point did Washington send the bulk of his army?

4. What was the first place attacked by the British? Give the particulars of the force sent against it.

5. What preparations had been made by the Carolinians to receive them? Describe the attack. Where did the British sail after their repulse?

6. What general arrived near New York on the very day of the attack on Fort Moultrie? What troops did he bring? Who arrived soon after? How many British were on Staten Island? What soldiers formed a large part of Admiral Howe's re-enforcements?

ATTACK ON FORT MOULTRIE, SOUTH CAROLINA.

7. Washington in the mean time was not idle, having fortified Manhattan Island at several points. Defenses were also thrown up on a range of hills on Long Island, south of Brooklyn, and here was an intrenched camp, at first under General Greene, and afterward under General Putnam. The American forces in and around New York were about 25,000, but scarcely 17,000 were fit for duty on account of sickness.

8. The British crossed over from Staten Island to Long Island, and, on the morning of the 27th of August, advanced in three divisions. Two of these occupied the attention of the Americans in front, while Clinton, with the other, marched by a wide circuit and struck the Americans in the rear. For a time the latter fought well; but, finding themselves nearly surrounded, they retreated with great loss within the intrenchments at Brooklyn.

---

7. How was Washington prepared for the attack on New York? What preparations were made on Long Island? What force was there to meet the British?

8. What was the first movement of the British? Describe the movements of the 27th of August. What was the result of the battle?

9. Washington crossed over to Brooklyn during the action, and saw, with indescribable agony, the destruction of his "brave fellows." The Americans had suffered severely. They had lost 2000 out of 5000 men engaged. Had the British followed up their success, and attacked the intrenched camp, the Americans must have been utterly destroyed; but Howe waited till the following morning. Fortunately for the Americans, the next day, the 28th, was one of drenching rain, and the enemy did nothing but break ground for a battery. On the 29th a dense fog covered the island, but news reached Washington that the British ships were preparing to move up into the East River and thus cut off his retreat.

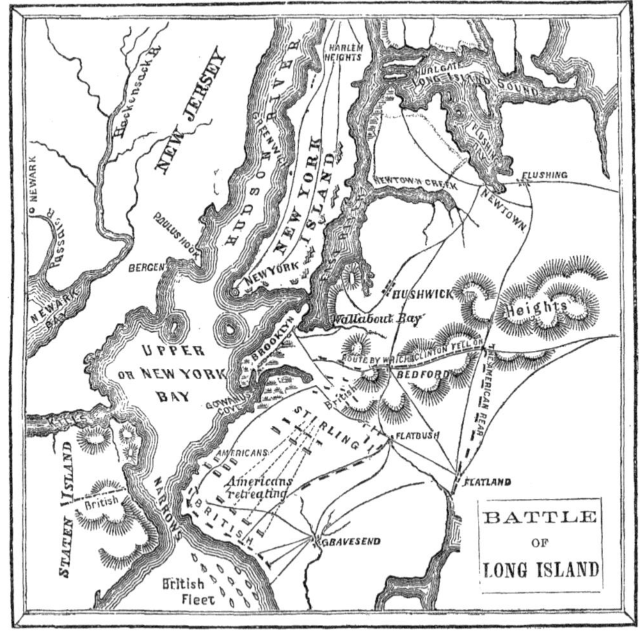

BATTLE OF LONG ISLAND

9. Was Washington present in the battle? What were his feelings during the engagement? What was the loss of the Americans? What blunder did the British general make at the close of the battle? Did Howe attack next day? Why not? What prevented him on the 29th? What important news did Washington meanwhile receive?

10. In this state of affairs, with the enemy so near his works that he could hear them in their camp, he accomplished one of the most brilliant operations of the war. On the 29th he collected what boats he could find on the East and North Rivers, and during the night moved his whole army across to New York. During all this time a heavy fog prevailed on Long Island, concealing the movements of the Americans from the British, while, at the same time, the weather was quite clear on the New York side. Howe was greatly chagrined to find that his enemy had escaped from Brooklyn, and secretly made preparations, with the assistance of his ships, to surround Washington in New York.

11. The American officers, in a council of war, held September 12, decided that the city could not be held, and the main body of the army was withdrawn on the 14th to the northern part of the island, the most southern point of defense being on Harlem Heights. Washington was anxious to learn what were the designs of the British, and Nathan Hale, a young captain in a Connecticut regiment, volunteered to ascertain them. He accordingly crossed over to Long Island, and, having obtained the necessary information, was on his way back, when he was arrested on suspicion and taken to Howe's head-quarters, now, September 21st, on New York Island. Without even the form of a trial, he was next morning hanged as a spy, September 22. He met his death with great firmness, regretting that he had only one life to lose for his country.

12. On the 15th of September, the British crossed in force from Long Island, and landed, with trifling opposition, about three miles above the city. They presently occupied a line stretching across New York Island from Bloomingdale to the East River. On the 16th a severe skirmish took place, in which the Connecticut troops behaved with great valor, and drove back the enemy. In the affair Colonel Knowlton was killed. This success raised the spirits of the troops,

---

10. How did he prepare to meet this? State what was his success. What greatly assisted him to accomplish this? What is said of Howe after the escape of the Americans?

11. What important movement was now made by Washington? Why? Who was Nathan Hale? For what duty did he volunteer? What was his fate?

which had been much depressed since the battle of Long Island.

13. Howe now tried to get to the rear of the American army. Leaving his own lines in front well guarded, he landed the main body in East Chester, while the fleet went up the North River on the west side. Washington saw Howe's plan, and, having left 3000 men to defend Fort Washington, on the heights overlooking the Hudson, fell back to the line of the River Bronx, with his head-quarters at White Plains. Here he was attacked on October 28th, and compelled to retire to the heights of North Castle.

14. Howe was unwilling to follow him farther, and returned with the main body of his army to Dobbs's Ferry, on the Hudson. Washington left Lee at North Castle, and, after providing for the defense of the Highlands, crossed the river at King's Ferry with a portion of his army, and entered New Jersey, where he joined General Greene at Fort Lee, November 13. While he was here, 5000 Hessians, under General Knyphausen, assisted by some English troops, attacked Fort Washington, defended by Colonel Magaw. The place was taken by storm, November 16, with a loss to the assailants of nearly 1000 men, chiefly Hessians. Over 2000 Americans were made prisoners.

15. Four days after, November 20, Lord Cornwallis was sent across the Hudson into New Jersey, at the head of 6000 men, to follow Washington. On his approach, Fort Lee was abandoned by the Americans, together with all the baggage and military stores. Washington retreated across New Jersey at a rapid rate, followed so closely by Cornwallis that the vanguard of the latter was often within cannon-shot of the Americans.

16. The condition of the latter at this time was very dis-

12. Describe the movements of the British, Sept. 15th. What position did they occupy at its close? What occurred here? What good effect did this affair produce?

13. What was Howe's next movement? In what way did Washington disappoint the plans of the British general? What battle occurred on the 28th of October? What followed?

14. Where did Howe go after the battle of White Plains? What important movements did Washington make? Where was Fort Washington situated? What important event occurred here? Where is King's Ferry? See map, page 198.

15. By what was this promptly followed up? What places fell into the hands of Cornwallis? What is said of Washington's retreat?

tressing. Many of the militia went quietly to their homes. Those that remained were wretchedly clothed, ill fed, and utterly worn out. On the 8th of December, with scarcely 3000 men, Washington crossed the Delaware into Pennsylvania, and Cornwallis and his troops went into quarters on the New Jersey side of the river.

17. During this long and painful retreat, Washington sent repeated and positive orders to Lee at North Castle to cross the Hudson and join him with his troops. The latter hesitated, and moved so slowly to the support of his commander that he was no farther than Morristown on the 8th of December. On the 13th, while lying carelessly quartered apart from his troops, in a small tavern at Baskenridge, he was surprised and made prisoner by a troop of British cavalry. The command then devolved on General Sullivan, who joined Washington a few days afterward.

18. The army was now considerably increased, and Washington determined to strike a sudden blow before the term of a large part of the troops should expire. A body of 1500 Hessians at Trenton, under the command of Colonel Rahl, was chosen as the object of attack. On the night of December 25, Washington, with 2400 of his best men, crossed the Delaware with great difficulty nine miles above Trenton. Two other divisions, crossing at different points, were to co-operate with him, but were prevented by the floating ice. Amid a storm of rain and sleet, Washington pushed on, and at eight o'clock in the morning fell suddenly on the enemy. Rahl was mortally wounded; thirty or forty Hessians were killed; about 500 escaped to Bordentown; and the remainder, to the number of 1000, threw down their arms and surrendered. In the evening Washington re-entered Pennsylvania with his prisoners.

---

16. What was now the condition of Washington's army? How was his retreat ended? Give the line of this retreat from map, page 179.

17. Where was General Lee during the early part of the retreat through the Jerseys? What is said of his conduct? What happened to him on the march? Who took command of his division? Where is Morristown?

18. What blow did Washington determine to strike, and why? Where is Trenton from Philadelphia? What was the amount of Washington's force? How was he disappointed in assistance? Describe his movements. What was the result of the attack? How far did Washington advance into New Jersey?

SURPRISE OF THE HESSIANS AT TRENTON.

19. The spirits of the people were raised to a very high pitch by this successful movement, executed with so much energy and so little loss, at a time, too, when their affairs seemed sunk to the lowest point. Several regiments whose term of service was about to expire were persuaded to remain six weeks longer, and Washington recrossed the Delaware on the 30th of December and took post at Trenton. The British, astonished and alarmed at the activity of the Americans, broke up their scattered encampments on the Delaware, and assembled at Princeton; while, at the same time, Howe ordered Cornwallis, who was about to embark for England, to resume his command in New Jersey.

20. **Civil Transactions. Growth of Public Opinion.**—The beginning of the year 1776 brought a great change in the feelings of the American people toward England. Hither-

19. How did the battle of Trenton affect the spirits of the patriots? What was Washington's next movement? What were the movements of the British troops? Who was ordered to New Jersey? Where is Princeton?

to they had been fighting simply for their rights, and had not thought of breaking away from the mother country. But now it began to be seen that these rights could only be secured by separation from England, and this view rapidly spread throughout the country. Those who still adhered to the king, and were therefore opposed to independence, were known as "Tories," a name drawn from English politics. They were much more numerous in some parts of the country than in others, and comprised many of the wealthiest and most influential persons in the community.

21. As the year 1776 progressed, they were often very harshly treated. In some places, where the patriots greatly outnumbered them, they were tarred and feathered, and carted round as a spectacle. Congress tried to prevent this by appointing local committees to watch over, and, if necessary, protect them; but these committees proved of very little service. Not a small number of the more ardent patriots regretted that the tories could not be exterminated.

22. The ravages of Lord Dunmore, the governor of Virginia, and the activity of the tories in the South, particularly in North Carolina, turned the minds of the people of the Southern provinces strongly toward independence; the battles of Lexington and Bunker Hill, and the evacuation of Boston, produced the same feeling at the North. Early in March, Congress took decided steps toward entire separation from England. It granted letters of marque and reprisal against British commerce—that is, established privateering—and sent Silas Deane as an agent to France to seek assistance. Still further, in May, it recommended the colonies to disregard the royal governments, and appoint patriotic rulers in all cases where this had not already been done.

---

20. What is said of the feelings of the colonists toward England previous to the year 1776? What change had now begun to take place? Who were the king's friends, or "Tories?" Whence came the name of "Tories?" Were these persons numerous in the colonies?

21. How were they treated where they were in a minority? Was any thing tried to prevent this? What is said of the feelings of some of the more ardent patriots?

22. What had turned the attention of the people of the South toward independence? What events had done the same thing at the North? When did Congress take the first steps toward independence of England? What measure did it adopt against British commerce? What approaches did it make toward foreign powers? What important recommendation did it make to the colonies in May?

23. The most decided action on the question of independence came now from Virginia. Her Assembly, on the 15th of May, instructed her delegates in Congress to offer resolutions in favor of this. She was almost immediately followed by Massachusetts, the delegates from which were likewise instructed, May 30, to support the movement in Congress. On the 7th of June, 1776, Richard Henry Lee, of Virginia, seconded by John Adams, of Massachusetts, offered a resolution "that the United Colonies are, and ought to be, free and independent states, and that their political connection with Great Britain is, and ought to be, dissolved." This was earnestly debated and passed, not without great opposition—seven colonies in favor and six opposed.

24. In accordance with this resolution, a committee was appointed to draw up a declaration of independence. The committee was composed of Thomas Jefferson, John Adams, Benjamin Franklin, Roger Sherman, and Robert R. Livingston. They presented their draft of the paper on the 28th of June, and on the Fourth of July the Declaration of Independence was adopted, and copies were immediately sent throughout the country. The Thirteen United Colonies thenceforth became the Thirteen United States of America. At the time the committee was appointed to draft the Declaration, another committee was ordered to prepare Articles of Confederation. Their report, presented in July, was not adopted until 1777; the Articles were not ratified by all the states until the year 1781.

25. On the 12th of July Admiral Howe arrived from England, empowered, with his brother the general, to offer to the colonies terms of submission and reconciliation. Disappointed, but not discouraged by the adoption of the Declaration of Independence a few days before his arrival, he sent a

---

23. From what colony came the first decided action on independence? What did this colony do, and when? By what colony was she immediately followed? When? What two colonies were they that took the lead in independence? Give an account of the important movement made in Congress June 7. How was this received by Congress?

24. What followed? Who composed this celebrated committee? When was the Declaration of Independence presented and adopted? Under what name did the new nation begin? What other committee was appointed at the same time? What became of their report?

circular letter to the colonies, offering pardon to those who would submit, and threatening those who refused. Congress published this circular, and scattered it among the people, to show the patriots how little they had to expect from the mercy of Great Britain.

26. Soon after Howe landed at Staten Island he tried to open communication with Washington by a letter addressed George Washington, Esq., etc., etc., not giving him his title of commander-in-chief. This Washington declined to receive; and, after some slight efforts on the part of Howe, the attempt was abandoned. After the unfortunate battle of Long Island, thinking that the Americans would be in a more compliant humor, Howe sent to Congress asking a committee of conference. A committee was appointed, which met him at Staten Island; but, after a long and courteous meeting, the conference ended without success. There was, after this, no hope of settlement but by the sword.

27. Meanwhile, Congress was taking active measures to obtain assistance from Europe. Benjamin Franklin, Silas Deane, and Arthur Lee in place of Thomas Jefferson, who declined the appointment, were sent, December 30, as commissioners to the French court. That government was not prepared to go to war with England; and for this reason gave money privately, which was expended in the purchase of war material, that was then sent to the United States. It was arranged that the money given in this way should be repaid by Congress through a mercantile house in remittances of tobacco and other articles of produce.

---

25. Who arrived from England in 1776 with power to make arrangements with the revolted colonies? Who was associated as commissioner with him? What did he do? How did Congress treat this circular of his?

26. What attempt did Howe make after he landed on Staten Island? How was this received by Washington? In what did this attempt result? What further efforts did Lord Howe make a short time after to promote reconciliation? Did Congress take any notice of this? How did it all end?

27. What was Congress busily engaged in doing while all this was going on? Who were appointed commissioners? How did France give assistance? Why was this done privately? How was the money spent? How was this money to be repaid by Congress?

REVIEW QUESTIONS ON THE YEARS 1775 AND 1776.

1. Where and under whom were the British at the beginning of 1775?
2. How did hostilities begin?
3. Describe the battle of Lexington.
4. What effect did the battle of Lexington produce throughout the colonies and on the British troops?
5. What were minute-men?
6. By what colonial troops was this battle fought?
7. What led to the battle of Bunker Hill? Describe it.
8. Why was Washington not present?
9. Between whom had the struggle been carried on up to this time?
10. How had Washington become known enough as a soldier to receive the nomination of commander-in-chief?
11. How old was he when appointed?
12. Give a brief sketch of the operations in the North in 1775.
13. How was Washington occupied during the fall and winter?
14. Mention the important events of 1775?
15. By what success did Washington signalize the month of March, 1776?
16. What foothold did the British have in the colonies?
17. What saved New York from being occupied by them in the early part of 1776?
18. When and where did they attempt to gain a footing in the South, and with what success?
19. Against what point did they direct their efforts, and what were their preparations?
20. Why was New York so necessary to the British?
21. How was Washington prepared to meet them?
22. How did Washington's first pitched battle of the Revolution terminate?
23. State how far Washington was connected with the battle. Who had the chief command?
24. In what way did Howe lose the full benefit of the battle of Long Island?
25. Sketch rapidly the movements of the two armies after the battle.
26. What was Howe's plan, and when did he give it up?
27. After Howe returned, where did Washington move?
28. What was Washington's idea in this?
29. Why was Philadelphia so important?
30. How was the retreat through New Jersey terminated? When did it begin and end?
31. What brilliant action terminated the campaign of 1776?
32. When and by what act did the colonies become a nation?
33. How many and what were the original United States?
34. What is said of the important measures taken by Congress in March?
35. When and by whom was the subject of independence first broached in Congress?
36. When and how did the desire for independence come to be generally entertained?
37. For what at first were the colonies fighting?
38. What efforts did the British make toward reconciliation during this year?
39. At what particular time were they made?
40. Who were the commissioners authorized to propose terms of reconciliation?
41. Give an instance of the spirit of Congress in reference to Howe's proclamations.
42. What steps to obtain foreign aid were taken by Congress in 1776?
43. State the general result of the war at the end of the year 1776.
44. Name the leading military events of 1776.

SECTION III.

EVENTS OF 1777.

1. WASHINGTON, while encamped at Trenton, was informed that the British were assembling in the neighborhood of Princeton for a movement toward the Delaware. By his urgent order, Generals Mifflin and Cadwallader joined him on the 1st of January with 3500 men. Toward sunset on the 2d, General Cornwallis, with the van of the British army, arrived at Trenton, and made repeated attempts to pass the little stream that runs through the town, but was as often repulsed by the artillery of the Americans. Cornwallis therefore concluded to wait for his re-enforcements, and renew the attack on the following day.

2. The situation of Washington was most critical. In front was an approaching army of 7000 men; in the rear was the Delaware, impassable by reason of floating ice. From this position he determined to extricate his troops by a bold and rapid maneuvre. During the night he sent his heavy baggage down to Burlington, and, leaving his camp-fires burning to deceive the enemy, marched his little army by a roundabout road toward the British post at Princeton. On the morning of the 3d, his advance guard, under General Mercer, met about 800 British near that place on their way to join Cornwallis, and a sharp engagement followed. The Americans were at first

SEAT OF WAR IN NEW JERSEY.

1. What was the situation of the two armies at the beginning of 1777? How was Washington re-enforced? Describe Cornwallis's movements. What did he determine to do?

worsted; but Washington, coming up, routed the enemy with the loss of 100 killed and 300 prisoners. General Mercer was mortally wounded.

3. Cornwallis, who heard the firing, came rapidly up from his camp at Trenton; but he was too late to take part in the battle. Washington, destroying the bridges behind him, fell back to the heights of Morristown, while Cornwallis, anxious for the safety of the stores at New Brunswick, pushed swiftly to that point. Though Washington had but the shadow of an army at Morristown during the winter, he displayed so much activity, and so harassed the British, that by the beginning of spring they had abandoned every post in New Jersey except New Brunswick and Perth Amboy.

4. Toward the end of April, General Howe dispatched General Tryon, ex-governor of New York, at the head of 2000 men, to destroy a large quantity of American stores collected at Danbury, a small town in the western part of Connecticut, 23 miles from the Sound. Tryon landed, April 26, between Fairfield and Norwalk, marched to Danbury, destroyed the stores without hindrance, and set fire to the town. On his retreat, which commenced before daylight on the 27th, and continued two days, he was attacked by the militia, under the command of Generals Wooster and Sullivan, and also Benedict Arnold, who volunteered as a leader. At length the British were able to reach their shipping with the loss of nearly 300 men. The Americans lost the brave General Wooster, a veteran in his sixty-eighth year. Arnold, who had two horses shot under him, displayed so much daring gallantry that he was made a major general by Congress.

5. The burning of Danbury was revenged by the Connecticut troops in the following month. Colonel Meigs, with 120 men in whale-boats, crossed the Sound to the east end

2. What is said of Washington's situation? How did he extricate his army from this? What engagement followed? Describe the battle of Princeton.

3. How did Cornwallis act? What were Washington's movements after the battle? How did he employ his army during the remainder of the winter? What was the situation of the British in the spring?

4. What expedition was sent from New York in April? Where is Danbury? How far was Tryon successful in his object? By whom was he opposed, and name the commanders? State what is said of the fight. How was Arnold rewarded?

of Long Island on the 23d of May, destroyed a great quantity of stores and 12 vessels at Sag Harbor, took 90 prisoners, and returned in 25 hours without the loss of a man. An exploit still more daring, and equally successful, was the capture of General Prescott, the commander of the British forces in Rhode Island, in the month of July, by Colonel Barton and 40 men. In the silence of the night of the 10th they crossed Narragansett Bay, passed by the British guard-ships unchallenged, landed, and surprised Prescott at his own quarters in bed. Barton then returned unmolested with his prisoner to the main land. Washington had now in his hands a general that could be exchanged for General Lee, captured very much in the same way by the British.

6. Principally through the efforts of the American commissioners in France, there arrived in 1776 and 1777 a large number of foreign military officers who offered their services to Congress. Washington complained that they were so numerous he did not know how to find employment for them; and he hinted that their appointment by Congress to places of higher rank than those given to faithful American officers was producing very ill feeling in the army. Several of these foreigners, who became afterward well known, were the famous Kosciusko and Count Pulaski, two young Polish officers and patriots; Conway, an Irishman by birth, but 30 years in the French army, and, after entering the American service, one of the most unprincipled of Washington's enemies; the young French Marquis de Lafayette, who purchased a ship, and, in opposition to the wishes of the French government, came over, together with Baron de Kalb and others. Later came Baron Steuben, a Prussian general trained under Frederick the Great, who did great service to the American army in perfecting its discipline.

7. On the 12th of June General Howe left New York and went to New Brunswick. From this point he tried to get

---

5. In what way did the Connecticut militia revenge the attack on Danbury? When was this? What other daring exploit occurred in July? Describe it. In what way did the capture of Prescott benefit the Americans?

6. What persons arrived in America about this time? What did Washington say of many of these new arrivals? Name some of these officers. What was peculiar in the coming over of Lafayette? Of what great benefit was Baron Steuben?

to the rear of the American army and bring on a general engagement. Baffled in this, after several attempts, he then, on the 30th of June, crossed over with his entire force to Staten Island, leaving no British troops in New Jersey. At Sandy Hook General Howe found his brother, Lord Howe, with his fleet. On board this he embarked 18,000 men, and sailed to the head of Chesapeake Bay, where he landed his troops near Elk River, in Maryland, 60 miles south of Philadelphia, August 25. Howe then advanced northward to the capital as far as the Brandywine River.

8. Washington, who had not understood Howe's object until he was well on his way, by forced marches reached the Brandywine before the arrival of the British, and at Chad's Ford was prepared to resist their crossing, September 11. General Knyphausen, at the head of the Hessians, was ordered to make a feint as if he were about to try the ford. Meanwhile Cornwallis, with a large portion of the army, crossed higher up, and, falling on Washington's flank, compelled him to retreat with the loss of 1200 men. For his bravery in this battle, Count Pulaski was made a brigadier general. To complete the disaster at the Brandywine, General Wayne, a few days after, September 20, while watching the British, was himself so suddenly surprised near Paoli Tavern that he lost 300 men. The loss of the enemy was only seven.

9. As the British continued to advance, Washington gave up the hope of saving Philadelphia, and fell back to Pottsgrove, on the Schuylkill. Congress left the city, and, after a few days, assembled at York, Pennsylvania. Howe entered Philadelphia September 26, and stationed the bulk of his army in camp at Germantown, at that time a small village about ten miles distant. Washington, having received re-enforcements, on learning that two detachments of British had been sent away, left his camp on the Schuylkill, 14

7. What was Howe's first movement in June? What was his object? Where did we leave Washington encamped during the first part of this year? What was Howe's success? Who was at Sandy Hook? On what expedition did Howe move? Where and when did he land? Where did he march?

8. Where, when, and by whom was he opposed? By what maneuvre was Washington defeated at the Brandywine? What other misfortune befell a portion of the American army soon after?

miles above, marched all night, and at sunrise, October 4, fell suddenly on the British at Germantown. The enemy were taken by surprise, and at first driven in disorder. Victory seemed within the grasp of Washington; but, in the fog of the morning, the American lines became broken and separated by the stone fences that lay near the village. A portion of the British made a stand in a stone house; the rest of the army recovered from its surprise, and in turn drove the Americans back, with the loss of 1000 men.

10. Howe was in possession of Philadelphia, but the Americans still held command of the Delaware, principally by means of Fort Mifflin on Mud Island, and Fort Mercer at Red Bank, opposite; there were also obstructions placed in the channel of the river. These effectually prevented the British ships from bringing supplies to Philadelphia. On October 22, Count Donop, with 1200 picked Hessians, attacked the fort at Red Bank, held by Colonel Greene, while the British ships opened fire on Fort Mifflin. Donop's attack was repulsed, and he himself killed, together with nearly 400 of his men. Two British ships were destroyed, and

9. In what way did Howe's advance influence the movements of Washington and of Congress? When did Howe enter Philadelphia? Where did he station the bulk of his army? What attack did Washington plan and execute? What prevented his success in the battle? What was the American loss?

the rest retired, badly injured by the fire of the American guns.

11. The British, soon after this repulse, erected batteries on a small island in the river, and on September 10 opened a severe cannonade on Fort Mifflin. The bombardment, in which the fleet joined, continued until the close of the 15th, when the works were nearly demolished; the garrison was withdrawn during the following night. Two days after, the fort at Red Bank was abandoned, and thus the river was open to the British. Washington established his winter quarters at Valley Forge, on the Schuylkill, 20 miles from Philadelphia, while Howe kept his army within a strongly-fortified line extending from the Delaware to the Schuylkill.

12. **Events in the North. Burgoyne's Invasion.** — In the spring of 1777, the British planned an expedition to move from Canada to the Hudson by way of Lake Champlain. Its object was to obtain control of that river, and thus cut off New England from the Middle and Southern States. Accordingly, General Burgoyne, with a brilliant army of 8000 men, appeared before Ticonderoga, commanded by General St. Clair, on the 2d of July. On the 5th the British guns were planted on a steep hill called Mount Defiance, that commanded the fort, and which had been left unguarded. St. Clair at once saw that defense was hopeless, and that his only safety was in instant retreat. Sending his baggage and stores by water up the lake to Skenesborough, he ordered the troops to march by land and join them at that point. Burgoyne dispatched General Fraser in pursuit of the enemy, while he himself, by rapid movements, captured the stores at Skenesborough. Fraser overtook the rear of St. Clair's force at Hubbardton on the 7th of July, and inflicted on it severe loss.

---

10. What prevented Howe's communication with his ships? How did he try to remedy this? What was the success of these attempts?

11. What is said of the next attack on Fort Mifflin? How did the enemy get possession of Fort Mercer? Where did they pass the winter? Where was Washington encamped?

12. What expedition was planned in the North in 1777? What was its object? Who commanded it? Where did he first appear with his army? What was his success? Who was the American general? How did he manage to escape? What happened at Skenesborough? at Hubbardton?

13. Schuyler had command of the Army of the North, and was at Fort Edward, on the Hudson. His force was made up of raw militia, amounting to about 5000, many of whom were unarmed, and there was, besides, great scarcity of ammunition and provisions. Schuyler was soon joined by the wreck of St. Clair's troops. It was 24 miles from Burgoyne's army at Skenesborough to Fort Edward, and Schuyler quickly obstructed the road through the wilderness by destroying the bridges and felling trees in the way. So thoroughly did he do this work that it cost Burgoyne nearly a fortnight to reach the Hudson. On his approach, Fort Edward was abandoned, July 29th, and the American army retired, first to Saratoga, and then to Stillwater, near the mouth of the Mohawk.

BURGOYNE'S CAMPAIGN.

14. As the British army was drawing near Fort Edward there occurred the murder of Miss M'Crea, an event which exerted a baneful influence on the future career of Burgoyne. This young lady was betrothed to an American loyalist officer in Burgoyne's army, and was stopping with a friend near Fort Edward. A marauding party of Indians, after sacking the house, carried off Miss M'Crea; and, in a quarrel as to whose prize she was, one of them, in a rage, killed her on the spot, and carried her scalp into the British camp. Burgoyne, when he heard of this bloody deed, was struck with the greatest horror, and promptly disavowed it; but the

13. Who had command of the army that was to oppose Burgoyne? What was its condition? What wise measures did Schuyler take to hinder the advance of the British? How was the wisdom of these measures shown? To what point was the American army withdrawn? Where was Fort Edward?

people of the frontiers were powerfully excited, and flew to arms to protect their families and firesides from their cruel enemy.

15. While Burgoyne was moving up Lake Champlain in June, he sent Colonel St. Leger, with a mixed force of regulars, tories, Canadians, and Indians, into the valley of the Mohawk. On the 3d of August St. Leger laid siege to Fort Schuyler, the present site of Rome, commanded by Colonel Gansevoort. A few days after this, the garrison was cheered by the intelligence that General Herkimer, at the head of 800 militia, was on the march to their aid. About six miles from the fort, at a place called Oris'kany, Herkimer fell into an ambush, August 6, and was mortally wounded; but the garrison at nearly the same time, by a successful sally, repulsed a portion of St. Leger's force. The British colonel soon after retreated on news of the approach of Arnold, who had been sent by General Schuyler to the relief of the fort. St. Leger made his way by Oswego to Canada with what remained of his command.

16. In the beginning of August, Burgoyne, being greatly in want of provisions and horses, sent a party of 800 men, under Colonel Baum, to Bennington, to seize the stores collected there by the Americans. Colonel Stark, at the head of the New Hampshire militia, met and defeated Baum about five miles from Bennington. Colonel Breyman, with another body of British, arrived just as Baum's corps had been defeated; but, fortunately, a fresh body of Americans also arrived, under Colonel Warner, and Breyman was compelled to retreat. The loss to the British in both engagements was 200 in killed, 600 prisoners, 1000 muskets, and four pieces of artillery. The American loss was 14 killed and 62 wounded. This, together with the news of St. Leger's defeat, was a great disaster to Burgoyne, and put a stop to any hopes

---

14. What event occurred about this time? Why was this important? Who was Miss M'Crea? Describe the circumstances of her capture and death. How did Burgoyne look on the act? What effect did it produce on the Americans?

15. What expedition was sent off by Burgoyne before he appeared in front of Ticonderoga? What place did St. Leger attack? What help was sent to the garrison? What happened to this body of militia? In what way did the garrison help themselves? What was the end of St. Leger's attempt on the fort? In what direction did he go?

he had of penetrating the country by way of the Hudson; but he could not retreat, for the militia had now begun to collect in large numbers in his rear.

17. Loud complaints having been made against General Schuyler for his conduct of the campaign, Congress removed him from his command just when he was about to reap the reward of his labors, and General Horatio Gates was appointed in his stead. Burgoyne, having received a fresh supply of provisions, crossed the Hudson to the plains of Saratoga, where he encamped and threw up intrenchments. Gates left his position on the islands at the mouth of the Mohawk, and fortified himself on Bemis's Heights, not far from Burgoyne.

18. On the 19th of September an alarm was sounded in the American camp that the British were advancing, and a spirited engagement followed. Many times both armies advanced, and each in turn was driven back; but the battle ended with the British troops in possession of the ground. The vigorous attack and defense by the Americans were greatly owing to the bravery of Arnold. Two weeks of inactivity followed the battle, during which the two armies were within cannon-shot of each other. Meanwhile the militia from the country had entirely cut off Burgoyne's communication with the lake, and his hopes of supplies. In this desperate state of affairs, he risked another engagement on the 7th of October, and was beaten with the loss of 400 in killed, wounded, and prisoners, and a portion of his intrenched camp.

19. In the night he withdrew his troops to some heights in the rear. When, two days after, he fell back to Sarato-

---

16. Against what point did Burgoyne send a part of his army in August? For what object? By whom were they first met? How many engagements were there on the same day? Give the particulars of the second. What was the loss on each side? What effect did this and St. Leger's (led-jer) defeat have on Burgoyne's plans? Why, then, did he not retreat?

17. What complaints had been made against General Schuyler? How was Schuyler treated? What were Burgoyne's movements? What were the movements of Gates? Who was Kosciusko?

18. What occurred on the 19th of September? Describe the battle of Bemis's Heights. Who acquired great glory in the battle? What occurred during the next fortnight? What is said of Burgoyne's situation? What did he do? What was the result of the second battle?

ga, his whole effective force was not more than 4000 men. Yet he still kept a bold front, and hoped to receive help from General Clinton, who was pushing up the Hudson from New York to his assistance. Meanwhile his provisions were reduced to a three days' supply; and his men being worn out with hunger and fatigue, and hemmed in by thrice the number of Americans, who were constantly increasing, he was forced to surrender his army, with the honors of war, October 17. Nearly 6000 prisoners, a large number of brass cannon, 5000 muskets, and a great quantity of ammunition, were the trophies of this great success.

SURRENDER OF BURGOYNE.

20. Had Burgoyne known what Gates well knew, or had he been able to hold out for a few days longer, fortune might have taken a very different turn; for Clinton had captured Forts Clinton and Montgomery, which commanded the High-

19. By what movement did he show that he had been fairly beaten? Where did he go? State the condition of his army. What hope buoyed him up? How did it all end? Give the particulars of the surrender.

lands, October 6. On learning the news of Burgoyne's surrender, he collected his army, dismantled the forts that he had captured, and descended the river, taking with him all the cannon and stores to New York. The capture of Burgoyne's army sent joy throughout the country, raised the spirits of the people, and increased the number of volunteers. It also completely relieved the Americans from any fear of an invasion from Canada.

SECTION IV.

EVENTS OF 1778.

1. THE American army, in their huts at Valley Forge, spent a very wretched winter amid the snow, many of them being without shoes, half clad, and all of them suffering from want of provisions. The officers, as well as the men, were without pay, and Congress had no means of paying them. The distress of the army was so great that Washington was authorized to seize provisions wherever he could, and give bills on Congress for the amount. This was a harsh, though necessary measure; but it, in some degree, improved the condition of the army. This period is considered the gloomiest in the war.

2. During the winter occurred the famous plot, known as the Conway Cabal. After the surrender of Burgoyne, the reputation of Gates rose very high. While this was at its height, a few officers of the army, headed by Generals Conway and Mifflin, to whom were joined some members of Congress, formed a plan to destroy the military reputation of Washington by charging him with want of energy and success. In this way they thought to compel him to resign, and then to elevate Gates to the command of the army.

---

20. What possibility was there that Burgoyne might have been saved? What did Clinton do when he heard of the surrender? Where were Forts Clinton and Montgomery? See map on page 198. How was the news of Burgoyne's surrender received in America? What effect did it produce?

1. Where did Washington and his army spend the winter of 1777? What was the condition of the army while there? In what way did Congress attempt to remedy this? How is the winter of 1777 generally regarded?

The plotting was very active and malignant while it continued, but Washington held too firm a place in the confidence of the people and the army to be easily shaken from it. The country was aroused; his enemies were baffled, and his popularity rose to a greater height than ever before.

3. The spring of 1778 opened with a more cheerful state of things in the army and in Congress. The news of Burgoyne's surrender had produced widely different feelings in France and England. The French court still remembered with bitterness the loss of its American colonies a few years before, and now saw with joy that England was likely to suffer in the same way. By the English government the news was received with astonishment and alarm, which were increased by the knowledge that France was disposed to assist the colonies. The English ministry, therefore, felt the necessity of offering terms to the Americans; and accordingly, in January, 1778, two bills were passed in Parliament —one, renouncing all intention to levy taxes in America; the other, appointing five commissioners, with full powers to treat with the colonies for the restoration of the English authority.

4. Fortunately, soon after the news of the offer of these propositions in Parliament reached America in April, there arrived, in a French frigate, the intelligence that, in the month of February, France had agreed with the American commissioners on two treaties with the United States—one, of friendship and commerce; and the other, of defensive alliance in case Great Britain should declare war against France. No peace was to be made without mutual consent, and not until the independence of the United States had been acknowledged by England. These treaties, speedily ratified by Congress, strengthened the confidence of the American patriots; and when the English commissioners arrived in

---

2. What was started during the winter of 1777–78? What is said of Gates? What was the plot, and who formed the cabal? What did they hope to do? What was the result of their schemes?

3. How did next spring open? What was now the state of feeling at the French court? What news produced this? How did the English government receive the same news? What other information increased their alarm? What did this prompt the English government to do? State the nature of these two bills. Which of these seems the more important?

June, Congress declined to treat with them unless the independence of the colonies was first recognized, and the fleets and armies of England were withdrawn.

5. In this determination Congress was still farther strengthened by what was occurring at Philadelphia. Sir Henry Clinton, on the 11th of May, took command there in place of General Howe, who was recalled. Orders were also received from England to withdraw the troops from Philadelphia, and the British fleet from the Delaware, as a large French fleet for the assistance of the Americans might be expected on the coast at an early moment.

6. Clinton, soon after his arrival, made active preparations for the evacuation of the city, and, on the 18th of June, with his army of about 12,000 men, he left Philadelphia, crossed the Delaware, and commenced his march through New Jersey to New York. Admiral Howe had already sailed with his fleet from the Delaware, and anchored inside of Sandy Hook, ready for the arrival of Clinton. Washington, informed of Clinton's movements, crossed the Delaware in pursuit on the 24th of June. Lee, who had been exchanged for General Prescott, was second in command. The progress of the British was hindered by the great quantity of baggage, and by the intense heat of the weather. Washington, who moved more rapidly, came up with Clinton, near Monmouth Court-house, on the 27th of June, and determined to give him battle.

7. On the 28th of June, Lee, with the advance body, moved forward to the attack; but the enemy were in greater force than was supposed, and Lee fell back, in some disorder, to higher ground. Washington came up with the main body, and prevented serious disaster; and the day closed, after se-

---

4. What intelligence came from France in May? What was the purport of these two treaties? How were they received by Congress and the country? How were the English received in June?

5. Who had assumed command of the British army at Philadelphia in May? What orders had he received from England? What then was the first-fruit of the French alliance?

6. How soon was Clinton prepared to evacuate Philadelphia? What is said of his leaving? What meanwhile were the movements of the British fleet? What were Washington's movements? Who was his second in command? How was the British army hindered in its march? Where and when did Washington overtake Clinton?

vere fighting, without any positive advantage on either side. Washington intended to resume the battle in the morning, but before sunrise Clinton's army was far on its way toward the Highlands of Navesink. The Americans were so worn out with rapid marching, and the fatigue and intense heat of the previous day, that it was decided to abandon the pursuit; and, after a day's rest, they were marched to New Brunswick, where they encamped. Arriving at Sandy Hook, the British were met by Lord Howe's fleet, and were conveyed to New York. Clinton's retreat had cost him, in killed, wounded, and by desertions, more than 2000 men.

8. When Lee was falling back at the battle of Monmouth, Washington rode up in great haste, and, being deeply irritated at what he saw, addressed Lee in angry terms. The latter was greatly offended at Washington's public rebuke, and, after the battle, addressed two haughty and offensive letters to his general, in which he demanded a speedy trial. Washington at once ordered him to be arrested and tried by court-martial for disobedience of orders; for having made an unnecessary, shameful, and disorderly retreat; and for disrespect to his commander in the letters he had written. He was acquitted of the most serious part of the charges, but was sentenced to be suspended from his command for one year.

GENERAL LEE.

9. He thereupon retired to his estate in Virginia, in the Shenandoah Valley. Shortly after the expiration of the period of his sentence, he addressed a hasty and insolent let-

---

7. Who led the attack? What was his success? What prevented serious disaster? How did the battle of Monmouth terminate? What prevented a renewal of the battle next day? Did Washington continue the pursuit? Why was this? How did Clinton finally reach New York? What was his loss during this retreat?

8. What took place at the time of Lee's retreat at Monmouth? In what way did Lee receive this? What immediately followed? What is said of the trial?

ter to Congress; and for this his name was promptly ordered to be struck from the rolls of the army. Brave, able, and a well-educated soldier, Lee's chief faults seem to have been an excessive opinion of his own abilities, and a too great readiness to criticise the military conduct of Washington. But there is no evidence that he ever joined the cabal of Gates, Conway, and others, to ruin the commander-in-chief.

10. The French fleet, under D'Estaing (*dĕs-tang*), with 4000 troops on board, arrived too late to find Admiral Howe in the Delaware. The latter was safe in Raritan Bay, where the heavy French ships could not reach him. A combined movement against the British army in Rhode Island, under General Pigot, was arranged, in which the American troops, under General Sullivan, were to be assisted by the French fleet and army.

11. On the 29th of July, D'Estaing's fleet arrived in Narragansett Bay. On the 8th of August it entered the harbor, and passed the British batteries with little injury. This delay of a week was caused by the non-arrival of the American troops; but it proved fatal to the enterprise, because it gave the brave and active Lord Howe time to arrive off the harbor of Newport, on the 9th, to the assistance of General Pigot. D'Estaing promptly sailed out on the 10th to give Lord Howe battle. Before the ships could engage, a terrible storm scattered and disabled both fleets. Howe made his way back to New York, and D'Estaing's fleet returned to the bay in a very forlorn condition, but soon sailed to Boston to refit.

12. Sullivan, in command of the American forces, to the number of 10,000 men, performed his part of the plan by advancing toward the British lines at Newport. Here he waited for the co-operation of the French fleet and army that were to unite with him in an attack on the British works.

---

9. Where did Lee go after his trial? What happened to him after the expiration of his sentence? What is said of his character?

10. What re-enforcements arrived from France? With what disappointment did they meet? Where was Lord Howe? Against what point was a combined movement planned? Who were the commanders of this?

11. What were the movements of D'Estaing's fleet? Why did the fleet not enter the harbor sooner? What was the effect of this delay? What occurred after the appearance of Howe's fleet? What were the fleets compelled to do?

When D'Estaing got back to Newport, he informed Sullivan that he was about to sail to Boston to repair damages. Sullivan remonstrated, and asked him to remain two or three days, before the end of which time the place must fall; but D'Estaing remained firm to his purpose. Still again Sullivan asked that the French troops might be left. This also was refused.

13. Thus left to his own resources, Sullivan was compelled to fall back to the north end of the island, pursued by the British. On the 29th, an obstinate engagement was fought at Quaker Hill, but the advantage remained with the Americans. Meanwhile rumors had reached Sullivan that assistance to Pigot was on the way from New York. There was no time for delay. On the night of the 30th, the American army, with great skill and without loss, was transported to the main land. It was not too soon. Next day Clinton arrived at Newport, in a light squadron, with a re-enforcement of 4000 men.

14. Clinton made use of the troops that had arrived a day too late in sending them, under Major General Grey, to ravage the coasts to the eastward. This was the same energetic but merciless officer that surprised General Wayne at Paoli Tavern, in Pennsylvania. Grey made terrible havoc among the shipping on the coasts; laid waste New Bedford, Fair Haven, and the island of Martha's Vineyard, and returned, with a great amount of plunder, to New York.

15. The conduct of Grey had already been far surpassed in Pennsylvania. In the beginning of July, about 1100 tories and Indians, under Colonel John Butler and the Indian chief Brandt, entered the Valley of Wyoming, on the Susquehanna. After defeating an armed body of settlers, they laid waste the fields, burned the houses, and murdered the inhabitants under circumstances of great cruelty. Nearly

---

12. How far did these movements of D'Estaing affect those of Sullivan? What did D'Estaing conclude to do? How did Sullivan act when he heard of this, and with what result? What favor did Sullivan finally entreat of him?

13. In what situation did this conduct of D'Estaing place General Sullivan? What happened on the 29th of August? What rumors reached Sullivan? How did Sullivan extricate himself? Why was he fortunate in this?

14. In what way did Clinton make use of these troops? Who was Grey? What were the results of this expedition?

the same dreadful atrocities were perpetrated at Cherry Valley in November following. The country for miles around was a scene of murder and bloodshed.

16. Toward the end of the year, Clinton sent an expedition to Georgia, under Colonel Campbell, to attack Savannah. This was fortified and held by a garrison of about 1000 men, under General Robert Howe. After severe fighting, the British took possession of the city on the 29th of December. During the winter the French fleet was in the West Indies, whither Admiral Howe had followed it.

17. The war had now lasted four years, and the British, after tremendous exertions, held, in the North, only New York Island and Narragansett Bay. In the South they had only gained a foothold in Georgia; while, on the other hand, the Americans had become more formidable than ever by means of the French alliance. Yet the American cause was still laboring under great difficulties. Congress had very little specie, and had issued so much paper money that it had become nearly worthless. Every thing must have gone to ruin had it not been for the exertions of Robert Morris, a member of Congress from Philadelphia, in which city he was a leading merchant. He borrowed large sums of money on his own credit, and lent them to the government. This he continued to do until the close of the war. Notwithstanding all this, the army were still heavy sufferers from want, not only of their pay, but of the necessaries of life.

---

15. What raid was made by the enemy in Pennsylvania this year? State what was done. At what other place were like cruelties perpetrated?

16. To what point did Clinton turn his attention toward the end of the year? Whom did he send thither? Who commanded the place? What was the result of the expedition? Where was the French fleet?

17. State the situation of the British at the end of four years' warfare? What was the military condition of the Americans? What was producing great injury to the American cause? What saved the country from nearly total financial ruin? In what way? Did this put a stop to the suffering of the army?

SECTION V.

Events of 1779.

1. In the beginning of January, 1779, the British, to the number of 3000, were at Savannah, under the command of General Prevost. He moved against the American post at Sunbury, which surrendered at his appearance, January 9. Prevost then sent Colonel Campbell to Augusta, which was occupied without resistance. The tories were very numerous in that region, and very active. Seven hundred of them, under Colonel Boyd, while on their march to Augusta to join the British, were attacked at Kettle Creek, February 14, by a patriot force under Colonel Pickens, and defeated with severe loss. Five of the prisoners were hung as traitors.

SCENE OF OPERATIONS IN THE SOUTH 1779 - 1781

2. Lincoln, the American general, sent General Ashe to threaten Augusta, and Campbell fell back to a small stream, called Brier Creek, about half way to Savannah. Ashe, who

1. What was the situation of the British army at the South in January, 1779? Against what point did Prevost move? and with what success? What was the next movement of the British? How did a large part of the population regard the British? What befell a large party of them? What instance after the battle gives an idea of the bitterness between the patriots and tories?

was over-confident, was surprised there, March 3, by Campbell, and nearly his whole force destroyed or dispersed. Prevost, encouraged by the defeat of Ashe, marched to Charleston to demand its surrender. Lincoln heard of this, and, having been re-enforced, followed him, by rapid marches, so closely, that Prevost was forced to retire to the island of St. John, opposite the main land. At the crossing to the island, called Stono Ferry, the British erected a redoubt. This Lincoln attacked on the 20th of June, but was repulsed with considerable loss. Some time after, Prevost fell back into Georgia, and the weather became so hot and sickly that all military operations in the South were suspended for some months.

3. In the month of September, D'Estaing, with his fleet, arrived off the coast of Georgia from the West Indies. He and Lincoln agreed to lay siege to Savannah, September 23, and every thing bade fair for success; but D'Estaing became impatient at the delay of a regular siege. To gratify him, an assault was ordered; and the French and Americans were signally repulsed, on the 9th of October, with the loss of several distinguished officers, the chivalrous Pole, Count Pulaski, being one of this number. D'Estaing, alleging the lateness of the season and the dangers of the coast, would not consent to make a second attempt, although entreated to do so. He soon after sailed away, and Lincoln was compelled to fall back into South Carolina. This closed the campaign in the extreme South during the year 1779.

4. In May, Clinton sent 2500 men, under General Mathews, from New York to the Chesapeake. They sailed up Elizabeth River and the James, burnt the shipping, destroyed property to the amount of two millions of dollars, and brought away some three thousand hogsheads of tobacco.

---

2. In what way did the American general meet the movements of the British? With what success at first? What happened to Ashe? What advantage did Prevost take of this? How did Lincoln attempt to check Prevost? With what success? What was there at Stono Ferry? What occurred here? What stopped operations for some time?

3. When were operations resumed? Who arrived off the coast at that time? What plan was arranged? Why were the operations unfortunately hastened? What was the result? What distinguished foreigner was killed? How did the whole business end?

4. What expedition was sent from New York in May? State what it accomplished.

5. **Events in the North.**—The Americans had begun to construct two forts on opposite banks of the Hudson, some distance below West Point, and commanding the river at King's Ferry. These two forts were at Stony Point on the west, and at Verplanck's Point on the east. In the month of June, General Clinton captured Stony Point, which was still unfinished, without resistance, and Verplanck's Point soon after surrendered. After Clinton's return to New York, General Tryon, late governor of New York, was sent, early in July, to Long Island Sound to plunder the coast towns. He ravaged New Haven, burned Fairfield and Norwalk, and then visited Sag Harbor. While he was preparing to make a descent on New London, he was recalled to New York by Clinton, who was alarmed at the retaking of Stony Point by the Americans.

THE HUDSON—NEWBURG TO NEW YORK.

6. Washington had deeply felt the loss of Stony Point, as this compelled him to send his supplies, east and west of the Hudson, by a tedious route through the Highlands. In the month of July, General Anthony Wayne was ordered to capture the fort at all hazards. At midnight on the 15th, his troops, in two columns, entered the works from different sides, and carried them at the point of the bayonet. While he was making preparations against Verplanck's Point, the British came up the river in force, and he was compelled to abandon Stony Point. A month later, June 18, Major Lee surprised the British post at Paulus

5. What important Ferry was then on the Hudson, and where? How did Washington show his sense of its importance? What happened to the forts in the month of June? Who was General Tryon? What duty was assigned to him by Clinton? How did he succeed? What put a stop to his farther depredations?

Hook, now Jersey City, a little after midnight, and took 159 prisoners.

7. These brilliant exploits were counterbalanced by a severe disaster that happened to the American arms as far east as the Penobscot River. A Massachusetts expedition of 1500 militia, and 19 armed vessels, under General Lovell, was sent to destroy a British post that had been erected on the river. The works were found too strong to be taken by assault, and Lovell sent to Boston for Continental troops. In the mean time five heavy British ships of war ascended the Penobscot, and destroyed or captured nearly the whole flotilla, August 13. The Americans escaped into the woods; and, after wandering, in great suffering, for nearly a hundred miles through the wilderness, they finally reached some frontier settlements.

8. To revenge the massacres of Wyoming and Cherry Valley in the previous year, and to punish the Indians belonging to the Six Nations, General Sullivan, with 3000 men, was sent to Western New York about the beginning of August. Joined by General James Clinton, at the head of 2000 men, he attacked and defeated 1700 Indians and tories at Newtown, now Elmira, August 29. Sullivan then pushed into the heart of the Indian country as far as the Genesee River, destroying the orchards and corn-fields, burning the villages, and laying waste the country. The Indians fled westward for shelter to Fort Niagara; but the punishment, although severe, did not prevent them from renewing their hostile attacks as soon as Sullivan retired.

9. This year was marked by a most desperate naval battle, fought by John Paul Jones, a Scotchman by birth, but an American by adoption, and a commissioned officer in the American navy. He was cruising near the British coast in

---

6. How did Washington regard the loss of Stony Point? What steps did he take to remedy it? Give an account of Wayne's exploit. How long did he keep possession of it? What other dashing enterprise took place in the following month?

7. Where did the American arms meet with a reverse? What were the Americans doing there? What success did he meet with at first? What occurred before help came?

8. What American general headed an expedition in August? What was the object of this? By whom was he joined? What followed? What severe punishment did he administer in the Indian country? What permanent effect did it produce?

September, in command of a small squadron of three ships, fitted out in France, and fell in with two powerful English frigates with a convoy of merchant vessels. The battle began at seven in the evening. During its progress, Jones lashed his own vessel, the Bon Homme Richard, to the English ship Serápis, and the combat was continued with the muzzles of the guns of the two ships almost touching each other. The vessels were on fire several times. At ten o'clock the Serapis surrendered, and soon after the other frigate did the same. Jones's ship was so badly injured that it sank next day.

REVIEW QUESTIONS.—1777, 1778, 1779.

1. What two campaigns mark the year 1777?
2. State briefly the movements of the opposing armies in New Jersey.
3. Why did the British not go up the Delaware?
4. With what events in this campaign did the active movements of the year begin and end? Give dates.
5. What two prominent points were held by the British at the end of the year?
6. Where did Washington winter?
7. Sketch briefly the movements of Burgoyne without describing the battles. Give dates.
8. When did they begin, and describe the events at its close.
9. What effect did the surrender of Burgoyne have on the future of the war?
10. What Americans were in France at a very early time endeavoring to get French assistance?
11. Who was the most distinguished of these?
12. What did England do when she began to see that France was about to assist America?
13. What came of these offers?
14. Give the principal events of 1777.
15. What were the movements of both armies in Pennsylvania and New Jersey in 1778?
16. How far had French assistance compelled these movements?
17. Where had the British made a lodgment in the Eastern States?
18. What efforts were made to drive them out of this, and with what success?
19. What other sea-port fell into their hands toward the end of the year?
20. Where did Washington's army winter in 1778-79?
21. State the position of the British at the end of the year 1778.
22. Of what assistance had the French army been during the year?
23. What was the condition of the finances of the country?
24. Who was of the greatest assistance, and what is said of him?
25. Give the principal events of 1778.
26. To what point were the more active operations of the war transferred in 1779?
27. What persons formed a large part of the population of Georgia?
28. State, without describing the battles, the movements of both armies in Georgia and its vicinity during 1779.

---

9. Up to this time had there been many naval battles? By whom was the great naval battle of this year fought? Where did he get his ships? What was the force opposed to him? Describe the battle. What became of the Bon Homme (*bon-om*) Richard?

29. What reason had General Lincoln to be dissatisfied with the French?
30. At what other point in the South were the British busy?
31. State what was done.
32. Sketch briefly the movements in New York and on Long Island Sound.
33. What new enemy united themselves to the tories in the North?
34. How, where, and by whom were they punished?
35. What disaster occurred on the Penobscot?
36. Had the United States any navy of importance? Why not?
37. What brilliant but terrible battle took place off the coast of France in 1779?
38. Give the principal events of 1779.

SECTION VI.

EVENTS OF 1780.

1. THE main body of the American army was in huts among the hills around Morristown, in New Jersey, during the winter of 1779–80. The winter was the most severe ever known in the country. New York Bay was frozen over firm enough to bear the heaviest artillery. The sufferings of the troops for want of provisions and clothing would, in the most moderate winter, have been distressing, but, with such a season, were terribly increased. Washington had to resort to the same severe measures as were adopted the previous year in order to save his army from starvation.

2. The paper money of Congress had sunk so low that, at the beginning of the year, it passed at the rate of thirty Continental dollar bills for one dollar of silver. It was natural that the farmers should be unwilling to part with their produce for a currency which was every day growing of less value; nor did they think more highly of the bills on Congress, which Washington compelled them to take. It was still worse, if possible, with the army. Neither men nor officers could get their pay even in this currency, comparatively valueless though it had become.

3. At the close of the year 1779 Clinton sailed south, with the main body of his army, in the fleet of Admiral Arbuthnot, leaving General Knyphausen in command at New York. In the month of February, 1780, the British landed at St.

1. Where was the American army during the winter? Why was the suffering of the troops rendered more severe this winter? How were they fed and clothed?
2. What was the condition of the finances? What made Washington's measures seem harsh to farmers? Was it any better for the army in money matters?

John's Island, 30 miles below Charleston; and, while Clinton moved by land to the banks of the Ashley, opposite the city, the fleet sailed round to enter Charleston Harbor. The approach of the British was so slow and cautious that Lincoln, the American general at Charleston, had time to strengthen his works, and to add to his garrison of regulars a number of militia from the surrounding country. It was not until April that the British fleet, with little damage, passed the fire of Fort Moultrie, on Sullivan's Island, and took a position off the city. A few days before, Clinton had thrown up works, and commenced preparations for a regular siege.

4. At different points, some miles north of the city, there were stationed bodies of American militia to keep open the communications with the country. Against these posts active British officers were sent soon after the siege began. On the night of April 14, Colonel Tarleton fell suddenly on a body of 1400 American cavalry, under General Huger, at Monk's Corner, 30 miles north of Charleston, and defeated them with severe loss, capturing a great quantity of military stores. Other American posts were also taken.

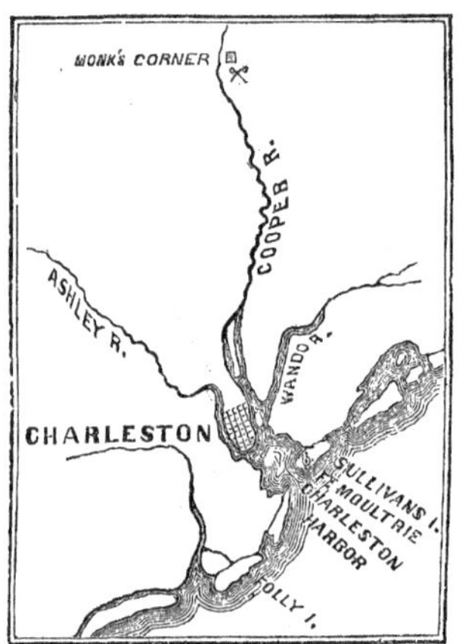

CHARLESTON AND VICINITY.

5. Clinton pressed the siege of Charleston with vigor, and Lincoln's situation became every day more and more distressing. His works were destroyed by the enemy's cannon, which approached very close; his communications with the country were cut off; and, seeing no hope of relief, he surrendered the city and the

3. To what point was the seat of war transferred? Who was left to take care of New York? Where did the British land? State their movements after landing. Who was in command at Charleston? What preparations were made there to receive the British? Show how slow were the movements of the latter. What was the position of their fleet and army?

4. What important posts were there north of Charleston? What was done by the British? Mention what is said of the most important of these posts.

garrison on the 12th of May. The prisoners, including every male adult in the city, amounted to about 6000.

6. After the surrender, Clinton sent off three expeditions to overrun and subjugate South Carolina. One of these, commanded by Tarleton, overtook at Waxhaw Creek, May 29, a regiment of Virginia troops, under Colonel Buford, which had retreated into North Carolina after the fall of Charleston, and put nearly all of them to the sword. The other expeditions met with no resistance. South Carolina was brought so completely under British rule, that Clinton set sail in the early part of June for New York, leaving Cornwallis to secure its conquest. The Carolinas abounded in tories, who now joined the British forces in large numbers. On the other hand, there were bands of American patriots in those states, called partisan corps, who were very active under such leaders as Marion, Sumter, and Pickens. At Hanging Rock, east of the Wateree River, Sumter defeated a large body of regulars and tories, August 6th.

7. To make a rallying-point for the formation of a regular army, Washington sent Baron De Kalb, with two regiments, to the South; and Congress dispatched General Gates, the conqueror of Burgoyne, to take the command of operations in the Carolinas. In a short time Gates was able to draw a considerable force around him. With this he unexpectedly met the British, under Cornwallis, at Sanders's Creek, near Camden, Aug. 16. The battle was short and violent. At the first charge of the British the American militia fled; but the regulars, under De Kalb, stood firm, although attacked in front and flank. De Kalb at last fell mortally wounded; and then the battle became a disorderly retreat, the pursuit by the British continuing for nearly 30 miles. The Ameri-

5. What was Lincoln's situation in a short time? What was he compelled to do? How many prisoners were surrendered?

6. What did the surrender of Charleston enable Clinton to do? What is said of these expeditions? What was the condition of South Carolina? What effect did the success of the British produce on many of the inhabitants? Was all resistance at an end? How did it show itself? What occurred at Hanging Rock?

7. Who was sent by Washington to the South? For what purpose? Who was appointed commander in the South? What was he successful in doing? Where and when did he fall in with the British? What lost Gates the battle? What instance of steady bravery is mentioned? State the extent of the disaster to the American army.

can army was completely dispersed. Two or three days after, Gates and a few of his officers rested at a point 80 miles distant from the field of Camden.

8. To sum up the disasters to the American cause, Tarleton meanwhile had surprised Sumter on the 18th of August at Fishing Creek, on the west bank of the Catawba, and nearly destroyed his whole partisan corps. All united resistance to the British in South Carolina was for a time at an end. Gates, after several attempts, was unable to draw together more than 1000 men; and Congress, dissatisfied with his management, removed him from the command. On Washington's recommendation, General Nathaniel Greene was appointed in the place of Gates. Cornwallis used his power with great severity. He hanged some of the patriots and imprisoned great numbers. This roused a feeling of vengeance among the people, and started partisan warfare into new life. Marion came from among the swamps, whither he had retired, and Sumter raised a fresh band.

9. In September Cornwallis marched his main body into North Carolina as far as Charlotte, and dispatched Major Ferguson to rally the tories in the interior among the mountains. On his route Ferguson was attacked in camp at King's Mountain, October 7, by a large body of backwoods riflemen, under Colonel Campbell, and himself, with some 150, was killed; the remainder were taken prisoners. The tories in Ferguson's band had been guilty of great cruelties, and had deeply exasperated the inhabitants. After the battle, the North Carolina backwoodsmen hanged a number of the tory prisoners on the spot. Cornwallis, when he heard the news of Ferguson's defeat, fell back into South Carolina, between the Broad and Saluda Rivers. Here he remained until the close of the year.

---

8. What other disaster happened to a partisan corps about the same time? What was now the condition of the patriot cause in the Carolinas? How did Congress regard Gates's conduct? Who succeeded Gates? What is said of the conduct of Cornwallis? What did this produce?

9. In what direction did Cornwallis move? Who was dispatched to rally the royalists? With what disaster did he meet? What occurred after the battle that shows the bitterness of feeling between the patriots and tories? How did Ferguson's defeat affect the movements of Cornwallis? What other movements were made by him during the balance of the year?

10. The suffering in the American camp at Morristown continued to increase as spring opened. In May there was absolute famine among the troops. To such a point of desperation were the soldiers driven, that two regiments of the Connecticut line avowed their purpose to march home or gain subsistence at the point of the bayonet. It required all the influence of Washington to restore order, and to obtain supplies of food for the soldiers. So serious was the danger that Congress authorized him to declare martial law.

11. While Clinton was in the South, Knyphausen, hearing of the state of things in the American camp, determined to strike a blow. On the 6th of June he landed with 5000 men at Elizabethtown, and advanced toward Springfield. He experienced serious resistance; and, after burning the village of Connecticut Farms, returned to Elizabethtown. Clinton arrived with the fleet and part of the army from the South on June 7. Knyphausen again moved forward toward Springfield, and on the 23d attacked the Americans, under General Greene, who, after a sharp fight, fell back in good order to the heights. The British, checked by Greene's spirited resistance, after burning Springfield, marched back to Elizabethtown.

LAFAYETTE.

12. Lafayette, who had spent the winter in France, was successful in persuading the French court to send a new fleet and army to the help of the Americans, and brought over the good news in April. Accordingly, in July, the fleet, under Admiral De Tiernay, arrived at Newport with an army of nearly

10. What was the condition of the troops at Morristown as the winter came to an end? What did this state of suffering produce? How was order restored? What powers were granted by Congress?

11. What advantage did the British attempt to take of the feeling in the American camp? What was Knyphausen's success? Who arrived to Knyphausen's assistance? What movements followed? How did it end?

7000 men, under the command of Count De Rochambeau. Great expectations were formed from this assistance; but, unfortunately, the British fleet on the American coast was heavily re-enforced. This prevented the French ships from leaving Narragansett Bay, and for a time banished the hope of any combined operations with the fleet and army, that Washington and the nation had deeply at heart.

13. **Arnold's Treason.**—At the very time that Washington was absent at Hartford, Connecticut, consulting with De Tiernay and De Rochambeau on the best plan to render useful the French fleet and army, treason was plotting to put into the hands of the British West Point, the strongest fortress in the country. The traitor was Benedict Arnold. The wounds he received before Quebec and at Saratoga had rendered him unfit for active duty in the field, and through the influence of Washington he was placed in military command of Philadelphia after its evacuation by Clinton in 1778. Here he lived expensively and far beyond his means; or, as was asserted, far from what befitted a republican general.

BENEDICT ARNOLD.

14. In his command he was somewhat overbearing, and quarreled with the Pennsylvania authorities, who made complaints to Congress against him for abuse of his high position by embezzling or misusing public property. On this charge he was tried, and sentenced to be reprimanded by Washington, who, notwithstanding all this, still retained the highest confidence in his personal honor and bravery. Arnold's pride was, however, greatly wounded by the sentence.

---

12. What is said of Lafayette's efforts? When and where did the French land? What prevented the French from giving active assistance to the American cause?

13. What occurred while Washington was absent from the Northern Army? Where was Washington? Where is West Point? What was Arnold's reputation as a soldier? Why and through whose influence was he placed in command at Philadelphia? What facts are mentioned about his life here?

In August, 1780, after earnest solicitation, he obtained from Washington the command of West Point, and at once entered into a correspondence with Clinton at New York with reference to the surrender of that important place to the British. The person who conducted the correspondence with Arnold on the part of Clinton was Major André (*andra*), under the assumed name of John Anderson.

15. When the affair had been sufficiently understood by letter, André went up the Hudson in the sloop of war Vulture, and was met near Haverstraw on the west bank by Arnold, September 22. Here all the arrangements for the surrender were completed. Meanwhile, the Vulture, commanded by the Americans, had dropped lower down the river, and André, with a pass from Arnold under his assumed

CAPTURE OF MAJOR ANDRÉ.

---

14. What charge was made against him while in command here? Was the charge sustained? To what extent did all this affect Washington's confidence in Arnold? How did Arnold receive his sentence? In what way did Washington show that his regard for Arnold still continued? What use did Arnold make of this kindness? In what way was the correspondence conducted by Clinton?

name, was compelled to return by land on the east side. When he had ridden as far as Tarrytown, at a turn of the road his horse's reins were suddenly seized by one of three militiamen, and, being for the moment surprised, he did not at first use his pass. He was searched, and the plans of West Point were found concealed in his boots. He then offered his purse, his watch—any reward, indeed, that they might demand, if they would let him pass, but they refused. They took him to the nearest American post, and the commander thoughtlessly permitted André to write to Arnold telling him that Anderson was taken. Immediately on receipt of this letter, Arnold escaped in his own barge down the river, and was taken on board the Vulture.

16. André was tried by court-martial as a spy. When before the court, he stated his connection with the whole affair with the utmost frankness. On these statements he was condemned to death, and was hung at Tappan, near the Hudson, October 2, 1780. Congress voted each of the militiamen—Paulding, Van Wart, and Williams, a pension of 200 dollars a year for life, and a silver medal. Arnold received for his treachery the appointment of brigadier general of the British army, and £10,000 sterling; but his conduct was detested by the great bulk of the British officers nearly as much as by the American patriots.

17. The American cause had made a narrow and most fortunate escape from disaster. The loss of West Point would have proved an almost irreparable injury to the country. It would have given the British the command of the Hudson, thereby separating the Middle States from the Eastern, and for a time would have completely disarranged all the plans of Washington.

---

15. Describe André's movements. When and where did he and Arnold first meet? Why did not André go back by the Vulture? How then did he return? What happened to him at Tarrytown? How did the militiamen display their patriotism? What unfortunate blunder was committed by the officer in whose hands he was first placed? What was the result?

16. What is said of André's bearing before the court? What was his fate? How were the militiamen rewarded? What were their names? What reward did Arnold receive?

17. Why was West Point of so much consequence to the American cause?

SECTION VII.

Events of 1781.

1. A LARGE part of the American army spent the winter of 1780–81 at Morristown, under General Wayne. They were better provided with food than in the previous winter, but they still suffered much from want of pay and clothing. The troops from Pennsylvania had an additional grievance. Many of them had enlisted to serve for three years or the war. The three years had ended, and their discharge was refused on the ground that by the war was meant a longer time than the three years, should fighting continue; whereas the men contended that it meant a shorter time than three years, if the war ended before that time.

2. On the 1st of January, the Pennsylvania line, to the number of 1300, under arms, left the camp at Morristown and commenced their march to Philadelphia, to demand redress from Congress. General Wayne interposed, but they threatened to bayonet him if he used force. In an attempt on the part of the officers to repress the mutiny, several were wounded and a captain was killed. They halted at Princeton, where British agents from Clinton met them with inducements to join the British service. The Pennsylvanians showed their patriotism by seizing these men and delivering them up to General Wayne as spies.

3. Congress was alarmed, and a committee of that body, and another from the Pennsylvania Assembly, proceeded to meet the troops. An agreement was entered into discharging those who had served three years, and making provision for back pay and clothing. These concessions on the part of Congress produced an injurious effect on the rest of the army. The troops at Pompton, New Jersey, mutinied on the 20th of January, but Washington sent a detachment

---

1. Where was a large part of the army during the winter? What improvement was there in the situation of the soldiers? What grievance was complained of by the Pennsylvania troops encamped there?

2. What step did they take to obtain redress? What brave officer attempted to prevent them? With what success? What other attempt was made? What proof did they give of their loyalty to the American cause?

from West Point which quickly reduced the mutineers to obedience. Such disturbances showed plainly that extraordinary exertions were demanded to relieve the sufferings of the troops, otherwise the cause would be lost. Congress acted with vigor. Direct taxation was resorted to; money was obtained from Europe; a national bank was established; and full power was placed in the hands of Robert Morris to adopt what measures he deemed best to restore the well-nigh ruined finances of the country. These exertions were partially successful.

4. In the beginning of January, the traitor Arnold, now in the service of the British, at the head of 1500 men, principally tories, ascended the James River, plundered the plantations, and burned many public and private buildings in Richmond. Governor Thomas Jefferson called out the militia, and Arnold fell back to Portsmouth. A plan was laid by Washington for his capture at this place. Lafayette was ordered to move with 1200 men by land, and the French fleet, sailing from Newport, was to prevent the escape of Arnold from Elizabeth River. The plan failed. Admiral Arbuthnot, with a British fleet, followed, and defeated the French off the entrance to the Chesapeake, compelling them to return to Newport. General Philips presently arrived from New York with 2000 British troops, threw up works at Portsmouth, and assumed the command. Arnold then returned to New York, while Philips proceeded to ravage the country.

5. Early in January, Cornwallis set his troops in motion toward North Carolina. Tarleton was dispatched with a cavalry force to get between Greene and Morgan, who commanded a part of the American army, and came up with the latter at the Cowpens, January 17. Tarleton, dashing

---

3. How did Congress look on these movements? What agreement was entered into? How did this operate on the rest of the army? Mention an instance of this, and how it was met. What good effect did these mutinies produce on the country? What measures were adopted? What praise is given to Robert Morris? Who was he? See page 195.

4. How did Arnold show his activity after he joined the British army? Did he meet with any resistance? State what. For what was Washington anxious while Arnold lay here? What plan was laid? Why did it fail? What military officer soon after came tc Arnold's assistance?

forward impetuously, as was his custom, at first swept every thing before him; but Morgan turned suddenly on the British when they were disarranged in pursuit, and defeated them with great loss. Cornwallis, when he heard of this, moved with great speed to cut off Morgan's retreat into Virginia, but reached the Catawba River a few hours after the latter had crossed. Cornwallis waited until morning, and in the night the river became swollen with the rain, and prevented his crossing for several days.

The enemy being put to flight, captured, or killed at the Cowpens.

MEDAL GIVEN TO MORGAN BY CONGRESS.

6. Determined on pursuit, he burned all his heavy baggage, and spared nothing but what was absolutely necessary. Morgan pushed on to the Yadkin River, and was there joined by General Greene, who took command and crossed. Cornwallis reached the western bank just in time to see Greene's troops marching away from the other side. Here again the rain raised the water so high as to prevent the immediate crossing of the British. The retreat and pursuit were continued from the Yadkin to the River Dan. Both armies made the most unsparing exertions. The track of the Americans was marked by blood from their shoeless feet, but they were able to reach and cross the Dan a few hours before Cornwallis arrived. The British general, disheartened at his ill success, gave up the pursuit, and slowly made his way back into North Carolina. Greene received great honor for his skillful retreat.

---

5. Where did Cornwallis move in January? What active force was dispatched elsewhere, and for what object? What happened? What steps did Cornwallis take to retrieve this disaster? Why was he not successful? What hindered him?

6. What vigor did Cornwallis display? Where did Morgan push? By whom was he joined? Show the energy of the pursuit. What again saved the Americans? What is said of the pursuit and sufferings of the Americans? What saved them? How did this affect Cornwallis? What is said of Greene's conduct?

7. Being re-enforced, he in a short time resumed the offensive, and advanced into the Carolinas to watch Cornwallis. On the 15th of March he made a stand at Guilford Court-house, where he was attacked by Cornwallis, and

driven back several miles. His defeat was nearly equal to a victory, for the British loss in the battle was so very heavy that they were compelled to fall back to Wilmington, near the sea-coast. Greene then turned his attention to the British forces in South Carolina, under the command of Lord Rawdon, at Camden, and encamped at Hobkirk's Hill, about a mile from the British camp. Here, on the 25th of April, he was surprised and defeated. The loss on both sides was nearly equal, and Greene was able to retire in good order. The victory was of no value to Lord Rawdon; for, being unable to bring on another general engagement with Greene, and becoming anxious for the safety of the posts between Camden and the coast, he retreated first to Nelson's Ferry, on the Santee, and then to Monk's Corner.

8. So active, meanwhile, were the American partisan offi-

7 How did Greene show his activity? What stand did he make? What was the result of the battle? Where is Wilmington? Who was in command of the British forces in South Carolina? To what point did Greene turn his attention after Cornwallis retreated? What occurred at Hobkirk's Hill? What use was Rawdon able to make of his victory? Where did he go, and why?

cers, Marion, Lee, and Pickens, that, by the month of June, 1781, only three important strong-holds were held by the British in South Carolina—Charleston, Nelson's Ferry, and Fort Ninety-six, near the Saluda. In Georgia, Augusta was surrendered on the 5th of June to Lee and Pickens, after a close siege of seven days. Greene himself marched against Ninety-six, defended by Carolina loyalists; and Rawdon, on learning this, moved rapidly to their relief. Greene received notice of his approach, and concluded to assault the fort before he arrived, but was repulsed, June 18th, with severe loss, and abandoned the siege.

9. After the beginning of July, the active movements of the two armies were suspended for a time on account of the intense heat of the sultry season. The partisan corps of tories and patriots still kept the field, rifling houses, killing each other, and sometimes not sparing women and children. The unavoidable horrors of war were thus greatly increased; and the desire for vengeance was rendered still more bloodthirsty by the execution of Colonel Hayne, a distinguished citizen of Charleston.

10. When the city was surrendered, he had given his parole of honor that he would not serve in the American ranks. The British commander, greatly in need of re-enforcements, demanded his services in the army. Hayne refused, alleging that this demand was not within the meaning of the parole. He then headed a partisan corps, and was taken in arms and hanged, August 4, in spite of the earnest entreaties of his fellow-townsmen. In retaliation, Greene felt compelled to ex-

GENERAL NATHANIEL GREENE.

8. In what way was it seen that the Americans were gaining ground? Where were these posts situated? What important point in Georgia was surrendered by the British? What check did Greene meet with? Describe it. Where is Augusta?

9. What put an end for a time to the active movements of both armies? How was the contest still kept up? What is said of the effect of these barbarities? How were the feelings of both parties still more embittered?

ecute as deserters all those prisoners who had formerly served in his own army; and it was not always possible to prevent the American partisan troops from shooting the British officers who fell into their hands.

11. Rawdon went to England, and left the command of the troops to Colonel Stewart. Greene, now re-enforced, and having been joined by Marion and Pickens, marched with 2500 men against him, and compelled him to fall back to Eutaw Springs. Here he was attacked by Greene on the 8th of September; and, after severe fighting, Stewart's left wing was driven in every direction. Unfortunately, the American troops stopped to plunder the British camp; this gave the enemy time to recover from their confusion and make a stand. Greene then drew off his troops, and left the field to the British; but the latter were unable to improve this advantage, because they had lost nearly one third of their force, and during the following night they retreated in great haste.

12. Greene, after following them as far as Monk's Corner, returned with his barefooted and half naked troops to the high hills of Santee. The result of the campaign in the Carolinas gave great satisfaction to Washington and to Congress. With limited means, and under the most trying difficulties, General Greene had repeatedly fought the enemy; and, although he never gained a decisive victory, yet, even when defeated, he obtained, to a considerable extent, the object for which he fought. In the end, he was able to wrest South Carolina from the British, and restore that state to the American Union.

13. On the 20th of April Cornwallis left Wilmington, and on the 20th of May arrived, with scarce any resistance, at Petersburg, Virginia. At this point he was joined by Philips and his troops, who had just been plundering on the

---

10. What led to his execution? What measures were taken by General Greene in retaliation? What was the feeling among the partisan troops?

11. Who succeeded General Rawdon in the command? Where did Greene come up with him? What is said of the first part of the battle? What interfered with Greene's success? What was the effect of the battle on the British?

12. What were Greene's movements after the battle? What was thought of his operations? Why did they think so highly of him? What great result did he achieve?

James River. Clinton, afraid that the combined French and American forces were about to attack New York, ordered Cornwallis to move near the coast, that the latter might the more easily help him if this attack should be made. Accordingly, Cornwallis, in the month of August, chose Yorktown and Gloucester Point, on opposite sides, at the mouth of York River. Here he threw up fortifications, and occupied them with 8000 men, the main body of which was at Yorktown.

14. During the summer, Washington had been hoping, with the help of the French fleet and army, now increased to 7000 men, to make a combined attack on New York; but he was unable to bring it about. Washington then turned his attention to operations in Virginia, and persuaded Admiral De Grasse and General De Rochambeau to unite with him in an attack on Cornwallis. The plan was to blockade the Chesapeake with the fleet, and at the same time invest Yorktown with the army. Washington, who was in the neighborhood of New York, moved with so much caution, and so completely deceived Clinton as to his intentions, that, before the British general understood his plans, the army was well on its way to Virginia.

15. As soon as Clinton penetrated the designs of Washington, he saw that it was useless to attempt to overtake him. Hoping to draw the latter back for the defense of New England, he sent General Arnold, with a large body of troops, to attack New London. On the 6th of September it was captured, and the shipping, together with a large part of the town, was burned. Fort Trumbull had been evacuated on his approach. He then assaulted and took Fort Griswold, on the opposite side of the Thames, and basely massacred the commander, Colonel Ledyard, and 60 of the garrison, after the surrender. Arnold's expedition failed in its great object. Washington kept on his march toward the

---

13. What were the movements of Cornwallis in April and May? Who joined him here? Where was he ordered to go by Clinton? Why? What position did he choose? What was his whole force?

14. What combined attack had Washington failed to bring about during the summer? What expedition was finally arranged? What was the plan of operations? What is said of the skillful movements of Washington?

south, and left New England to defend itself. The militia collected, and did this so well that Arnold became alarmed for his own safety, and made his way back to New York.

16. On the 28th of September, the allied army, to the number of 16,000 men, encamped before Yorktown, and the French fleet blocked up the Chesapeake. Works were soon thrown up, and on the 9th of October the bombardment began. Two advanced redoubts of the British were stormed and taken on the 14th. Additional batteries were erected by the allies, and the ramparts of the enemy rapidly crumbled beneath the destructive fire; his guns were dismounted; his ammunition failed him; and on the 15th he saw that the place could be held only a short time longer.

SIEGE OF YORKTOWN.

17. On the night of the 16th he determined on the desperate alternative of attempting to cross over to Gloucester Point, and then, forcing his way through, to push for New York by rapid marches. His boats were actually collected for the crossing; but a violent storm came on suddenly, scattering the boats, and compelling him to abandon his purpose. Nothing was left but to capitulate; and on the 19th Cornwallis surrendered his entire army of nearly 7000 men prisoners of war. The ships and naval stores, together with 1500 seamen, were given to the French.

18. The news of the surrender of Cornwallis was received with great rejoicing throughout the country. Every where it was felt that this must end the war. It was the second

---

15. What conclusion did Clinton arrive at? What counter movement did he arrange? What was his object in this? What did Arnold accomplish? What effect did this produce on Washington's plans? With what success did the New England men defend themselves?

16. When did the fleet and allied army arrive before Yorktown? How rapid were their operations? Describe the progress of the siege.

17. To what desperate alternative was Cornwallis about to resort? When was this? What prevented? What was he at last compelled to do? Give the particulars of the surrender.

time that the English had lost an entire army by capture. In England the news produced great astonishment and mortification. Sensible men saw that any further struggle to keep possession of the American colonies must be useless; but the English king and the Parliament, which met in November, still showed a determined and warlike spirit.

SECTION VIII.

Events of 1782–83.—Close of the War.

1. In England, as spring approached, a disposition more favorable to America began to extend rapidly. In the month of March, the House of Commons voted to end the war; and on the 20th of the same month, a new ministry, in favor of peace, came into office. Probably the most stubborn man in the kingdom was old King George III.; but he himself finally yielded, and orders were sent out to the British generals to cease fighting. A stop was thus put to active war movements; yet it took a long time to arrange definitive terms of peace.

2. The American cause was in the greatest danger from the distresses of the army. The troops were without pay, and the different states, already heavy sufferers by the war, were careless, and perhaps unable to provide the means for the payment of their defenders. During the year 1782, the bulk of the army was encamped at Newburg, on the Hudson. In the month of May, the troops became very restless and impatient under their wrongs, and a letter was sent to Washington urging that he would take the government into his own hands as king, and redress the grievances of the troops. Washington at once, and with great firmness, rebuked the writer for daring to communicate such a proposition.

---

18. How was the surrender of Cornwallis received and regarded in America? How was it looked at in England by many? Who did not share this feeling?

1. What great change in English feeling took place? How was this change seen in March? What is said of King George III.?

2. What state of things produced great anxiety in America? Where was the bulk of the army encamped? What important request was made of Washington? What was his answer?

3. Congress meanwhile took no steps for the relief of the army. It could, in fact, do nothing, for it had nearly ceased to have any influence over the states. The officers, after petitioning in December, waited through the winter, hoping for some redress; but none came. In March, 1783, an anonymous letter was circulated in the camp, calling on them to organize for the purpose of enforcing their demands. Washington still retained a powerful influence over the army, and was able to persuade the officers to trust to the justice of the country. Through his efforts, the officers obtained full pay for five yea[illegible] gross sum, instead of half pay for life.

4. Meanw[illegible]782, a preliminary treaty of peace was [illegible] English commissioners at Paris. [illegible]al until the English and French [illegible] treaty; because, by the terms of [illegible]nce and the United States, neither could [illegible]e treaty of peace with England. In January of the next year, 1783, the French and English governments agreed on terms of peace; and in March, 1783, the American Congress ratified the treaty made by their commissioners the year before. Every thing, however, was not finally arranged until September, 1783, when a definitive treaty was signed by all the nations who had taken part in the war—by England on one side, and France, Spain, Holland, and the United States on the other.

5. On the 25th of November, the last of the British troops in the United States evacuated the city of New York. General Washington immediately entered and took possession. On the 2d of November, Washington issued his farewell address to the army, and on December 4 took leave of his officers at New York. He then went to Annapolis, and on December 23, under circumstances of great solemnity, resigned his commission to Congress, which was assembled there. He

---

3. How did Congress act in this alarming state of affairs? Why was this? What course was taken by the officers? How was this plan discouraged, and finally broken up?

4. When and where was a preliminary treaty of peace signed? Why was this not brought to a prompt and final settlement? When did the French and English agree on a treaty? How soon after did Congress ratify their own treaty? Did these treaties bring things to a prompt settlement? Why not?

immediately retired to his estate at Mount Vernon, on the bank of the Potomac River, in Virginia.

WASHINGTON BIDDING FAREWELL TO HIS OFFICERS.

SECTION IX.

FROM THE TREATY OF PEACE TO THE ADOPTION OF THE FEDERAL CONSTITUTION.

1. WHEN Congress declared the United States independent in July, 1776, it agreed to recommend a plan of government to be called ARTICLES OF CONFEDERATION. These were to be approved by the states before they could become the constitution of the country. Five years passed before the states gave their assent, and in the mean time Congress

---

5. What place witnessed the final leaving of the British troops? By whom was it at once occupied? State the closing important events connected with Washington and the army, giving dates of each.

was compelled to act, as has been already stated, doing what it could to gain the contest for independence.

2. The Articles of Confederation went into operation in July, 1781. It was hoped that they would give the Continental Congress greater power to enforce all necessary laws; but a very short time proved that the government could not be strengthened in this way. The public creditors remained unpaid; the states treated the orders of Congress with indifference, and it was fast sinking by its weakness into contempt. Commerce was deranged, and needed regulating. The states interfered with each other in taxing imported goods—that is, one state admitted these at a lower duty than neighboring states. In addition to this, they could not even enforce the collection of taxes within their own borders.

3. What made matters worse was the feeling among many of the people that it was dangerous to give Congress the power to levy money, and to spend it without the assent of the states. They were jealous of the liberty which they had just gained, and they wished to keep the power of levying taxes in their own hands. It was a very trying time in the history of the country, and many wise and good men doubted whether the government would survive it. In Massachusetts, the discontent of the people broke out in open rebellion in the autumn of 1786. The leader was Daniel Shay, and the disturbance, known as Shay's Rebellion, was only put down by a powerful armed force. These troubles excited great attention throughout the country, and men began to see that a stronger central government was necessary.

---

1. When did Congress recommend Articles of Confederation? What was the object of these Articles? What was necessary before they could go in force? How long was it before the states gave their assent? Under what powers did Congress meanwhile act?

2. When did the Articles of Confederation go into operation? What did they accomplish? What is said of the public creditors, and the way the states treated the orders of Congress? In what was commerce deranged? How did the states show their own weakness?

3. What made matters still worse? What produced this state of feeling? How was the condition of the country regarded by the leading patriots? In what way did the discontent of the people show itself? How did the rebellion end? In what direction did the people turn for a remedy for this almost anarchy?

4. In the month of September, 1786, delegates from the states met at Annapolis to devise some plan to regulate commerce and the revenue. They concluded to recommend the assembling of a convention to revise the Articles of Confederation. In May, 1787, delegates from all the states met in convention at Philadelphia, and George Washington was unanimously chosen as its president. Instead of revising the Articles of Confederation, they, after a few months' deliberation, agreed on a Constitution, which was sent to the states for their approval. It was decided that it should go into operation on March 4, 1789, if nine of the thirteen states gave their assent. By the end of 1788, eleven states had ratified it, and the establishment of the CONSTITUTION OF THE UNITED STATES was thus secured. North Carolina did not give its assent until November, 1789, and Rhode Island stood aloof until May, 1790.

5. While the Convention was in session at Philadelphia, Congress was sitting in New York. The session of 1787 was distinguished by an act worthy of lasting remembrance. Virginia, Connecticut, and Massachusetts, by their original charters, had an indefinite western boundary, which became, by the treaty of Paris in 1763, the Mississippi River. Virginia ceded her claim to this vast region in 1784, and in this cession was soon followed by the other two states; and also by New York. In July, 1787, Congress passed the famous Ordinance for the government of this region north of the Ohio, under the name of the Territory of the Northwest.

6. This measure had a wonderful effect on the development of that region. It is especially celebrated for the provision that slavery should never be allowed to exist within the territory, or in states to be formed out of it. Perhaps no single statute ever had so powerful an influence over the

4. What meeting took place in 1786? What was its object? What did they determine? Where and when did this new Convention meet? Who was chosen president? What did this Convention at first intend to do? What did they finally recommend? How long were they in session? When and under what agreement was it to go in operation? When did it get the approval of a sufficient number? What two states were not then ready? How long was it before they ratified?

5. What is said of the Virginia, Connecticut, and Massachusetts charters? How was the western boundary limited by the treaty of Paris? What did Virginia do in 1784? Was she alone in this liberal movement? How did Congress act in relation to it?

MAP OF THE NORTHWEST TERRITORY.

destinies of the United States as this; and in importance it ranks second only to the Constitution itself. It originally emanated from the active mind of Thomas Jefferson as early as 1784; at which time the territory would have been organized had it not been for the opposition that arose on account of Jefferson's provision to exclude slavery from its limits.

7. To the same distinguished man is to be ascribed the honor of presenting the simple plan of our present decimal currency. Congress finally adopted this in August, 1786, and thus abolished the use of English money, universal in the states. The old habit of reckoning by shillings and pence, however, long remained common among the people. A mint was established soon after the adoption of this cur-

6. What effect did this have on the territory itself? What remarkable provision was there in the "Ordinance?" What is said of its importance? From whom did the plan emanate?

rency, but Congress was so poor that only a few tons of copper cents were coined.

8. In September, 1788, Congress, sitting at New York, appointed the first Wednesday of January, 1789, for the choice of presidential electors by the people, and New York as the place where the new government should go into operation on the 4th of March following. That city became, therefore, the first capital of the country under the Constitution. George Washington was unanimously chosen President of the United States, and John Adams, of Massachusetts, Vice-President. On the 3d of March, the great Continental Congress, which for some months had only been kept alive by the attendance of a few members, quietly went out of existence without public observation. All eyes were turned to the new order of things, and the immense services of that departing body were for the time forgotten. Posterity, however, does not forget them, and the best monument to their value is the simple story of the REVOLUTIONARY WAR.

GENERAL REFLECTIONS ON THE WAR FOR INDEPENDENCE.

1. THE war which commenced in the year 1775 between England and her American colonies continued for three years to be purely a struggle between these two contending parties. Important as it was to America, it formed, however, but a part of the extended contest which began in the year 1778, through the alliance of France with the United States. At the close of that year the war had assumed immense proportions; and wherever the forces of France and England met and engaged, on land or sea, there was fierce fighting and great loss of life.

---

7. What other important measure was proposed by Jefferson? When did Congress finally adopt this? Did it stop the reckoning by means of shillings and pence? What is said of the United States mint?

8. What did Congress do in September, 1788? What place was made the capital of the country? Who were chosen President and Vice-President? What is said of the closing days of Congress?

1. What is said of the Revolutionary War during the first three years? When and by what was the theatre of war vastly extended? What is said of its extent at the close of 1778?

2. This gigantic struggle increased still more when, in the year 1779, Spain formed a treaty of alliance with France to assist the United States. Shortly after this was signed, the Spanish laid siege by sea and land to the strong fortress of Gibraltar, originally belonging to Spain, but then in possession of England, and commanding the entrance to the Mediterranean. This was one of the most remarkable sieges of modern times, and lasted for nearly three years. During its continuance, France joined Spain with a fleet and army; but the English at last destroyed the war-ships and floating batteries of the allies, and the siege was raised.

3. In 1781, the Spanish captured Pensacola, and then West Florida fell into their hands. Toward the end of the year 1780, Great Britain declared war against Holland, and severe fighting ensued between them at sea and in the West Indies. In addition to this, she was for a time threatened by an alliance of the Northern powers—Sweden, Denmark, and Russia. Thus we see that England was fighting, single-handed, not only the United States, but the most warlike part of Europe, during the Revolutionary War; and, though she inflicted great damage on France, Spain, and Holland, she herself suffered severely.

4. We have seen what was the patriotism of the American troops; how wonderfully, winter after winter, and year after year, the soldiers fought on, ill fed, ill clothed, and nearly always without pay. The patience, the firmness, the courage, the energy of Washington, were of immense importance. The vigor and perseverance of Congress are worthy also of the highest praise. Yet it is doubtful whether, without the French alliance, all these would have gained the independence of the colonies.

---

2. What event occurred in 1779? What was the first great movement made by Spain? Where is Gibraltar? What is said of the importance of this siege? Did Spain carry it on alone? What was the result?

3. What conquest was made by Spain in North America? What other nation was added to the list of England's enemies in 1780? In what way was she threatened in addition to this? What was the situation of England during the Revolutionary War? What was her success during this struggle with her European enemies?

4. What is said of the American army? Of Washington? Of Congress? What remark is made of the probable success of all these unaided in the struggle with England?

5. The man to whose exertions and great reputation, more than to any single individual, the country was indebted for the French assistance, was Benjamin Franklin. In the year 1776, he was appointed one of three commissioners to the court of France to solicit help. His fame as a philosopher

FRANKLIN AT THE COURT OF FRANCE.

and a sage preceded him; and, on his arrival in France, his simple yet winning manners, his venerable and dignified appearance—now seventy years of age—his great knowledge of the world, and his charming powers of conversation, won the regard of the French people, and gained him the ear of the chief men of that nation. He became so great a favorite, that portraits of him were every where to be seen, and his busts abounded in the shop-windows of Paris.

6. It was to Franklin's influence that the treaty of alliance with France was mainly due; and through the same influence she sent money, clothing, arms, ammunition, fleets, and armies. The money, which she sent in the form of specie, was of the greatest importance, on account of the wretched state of the American finances. In the matter of money, the French troops were also of very great advantage; for, during the two years and a half they were in the country, they paid regularly for their supplies in cash. But we should remember that France and Spain did not love "America and Freedom." They hated the power of England, and saw that, by helping her colonies to independence, they could deal a deadly blow against her, and cripple her power. France, particularly, had not forgotten her own expulsion from Canada in 1763.

7. It is to be remembered, also, that all the people of the colonies were not patriots. In the Middle Colonies, but far more in the Carolinas and Georgia, a large part of the population were tories. There was bitter and bloody fighting between them and the patriots—far more bloody, fierce, and unforgiving than between the latter and the English. At the end of the war, many of these tories fled to Nova Scotia or the West Indies; but in course of time a number returned, and many of them received back their estates, which had been confiscated by the government.

8. If the people of the colonies were not all patriots, neither were all the people of England opposed to the Americans. There was a small but very active party in the English Parliament that constantly opposed the war measures

---

5. To whom and to what extent was the country indebted? What other honor was bestowed upon him in the year 1776? Why is he called a philosopher? Mention the different things that influenced the French people in his favor. Give an illustration of his great popularity.

6. What great measure was mainly due to his influence? What else did he accomplish? What remark is made about the money which France sent? Can you tell from what is stated elsewhere why specie was so important? On what grounds did France and Spain help the United States?

7. What source of weakness to the American cause was there in the colonies? Where did the tories most abound? How did the tories and patriots treat each other? Where did many of the first go after the war?

of the government, and praised the stand taken by the Americans. This party grew stronger and stronger as the war went on, and finally their views triumphed.

9. **Effects of the War on Commerce and Industry.**—The seven years' contest destroyed the commerce of the states. English ships of war swept their vessels from the ocean, and the fisheries, one of the main stays of New England, were broken up. But large fortunes were made by privateering. A great number of English merchant vessels and their cargoes were captured. Three hundred and fifty of them were sold as prizes in French courts, and brought some $5,000,000. This business, however, only benefited the few who were engaged in it.

10. Another small portion of the people became rich by selling supplies to the army. Still the war left the bulk of the inhabitants wretchedly poor; and by far the greater part of those who served in the army could find nothing to do when they were discharged. We shall see before long that this extreme poverty produced great discontent with the new government, and helped to create alarm as to its stability.

11. **Settlement during the War.**—Early in the year 1775, a large tract of land south of the Lower Kentucky was bought by one Henderson from the Indians for a few wagon-loads of goods. In the same month that the battle of Lexington was fought, Daniel Boone was sent across the mountains with a number of adventurers into this tract, and built a wooden fort at what is now called Boonesboro', on the bank of the Kentucky River.

12. Other settlements were made about the same time, and in May the settlers organized under the name of the Assembly of Transylvania. Soon after, they sent a delegate to the Congress at Philadelphia, asking admission. As the

8. State what is said regarding the feeling in England toward the colonies. How was this shown in Parliament?

9. What effect did the war produce on American commerce? What was one of the great branches of New England industry? How was this affected? How did the Americans make English commerce suffer? Show the extent of this. Whom did privateering benefit? What is privateering?

10. In what other way did a few grow rich? In what condition did the war leave the mass of the people and the soldiers? To what did this lead?

11. What large tract was purchased in the beginning of the year 1775? What important emigration occurred in April of the same year? Where is Boonesboro'?

new territory was within the limits of the State of Virginia, the delegate was refused admission. In course of time, Virginia made arrangements with the Transylvania settlements, and they agreed to submit to her authority, and were organized as Kentucky County. West Tennessee was first settled at Nashville, by James Robinson, in the year 1779. East Tennessee had been previously settled in 1768 by the same man. These both remained under the government of North Carolina, to which the territory belonged.

13. New York had trouble with the "Green Mountain Boys." Previous to the expedition of Burgoyne in 1777, they organized a state government and named it Vermont; and the same year applied to Congress for admission. New York angrily resisted, because she said this was her territory; and the Vermonters were refused admission. They were far from being cast down by this, and immediately set about electing a governor and the other state officers. All through the war, and for years after, the quarrel was kept up between New York and Vermont. Not seldom blood flowed; but New York kept the latter out of the Union for a number of years.

14. **The Continental Congress.**—This great central authority during the war was composed of delegates as remarkable for ability and high character as any the world has ever seen. It began with few or no powers granted by the colonies, but soon found it necessary to assume and exercise power, and this it did very vigorously for some time. It called for troops; it appointed a commander-in-chief and generals; it issued paper money; it sent leading men to Europe to ask assistance. As the war went on, and the various states began to suffer, and gloomy periods of distress appeared, and the currency sank more and more in value, Congress found that it had no power to enforce its orders;

---

12. Under what name did the new settlements organize? What important step did the new government take? How was the petition received? What arrangement was in course of time made by Virginia? What settlement took place in 1779? When was East Tennessee first settled? Under what state did they remain?

13. With whom did New York have trouble about territory? What spirited movement did they make? What was their success before Congress? Did these greatly disturb the Vermonters? How did they show their independent spirit? How long did the quarrel continue? What is said of its bitterness?

yet, it never quailed, and in the darkest times it never despaired of the country.

15. It was a secret assembly, and sat with closed doors. A slight sketch of the proceedings was published once a month, and its sitting was continuous—that is, it adjourned from time to time, and had but one session from its beginning in 1774 until the year 1781, when, under the Articles of Confederation, annual sessions were adopted. Its full membership in its early years was less than sixty; but the number present seldom amounted to more than thirty, because the trying times of the long war drew many of its members home to attend to their affairs.

16. The president of Congress was the chief officer of the country, and this important position was filled by different leading men chosen from among its members. Philadelphia has the honor of being the city where Congress sat during the greater part of the war. It was compelled at times to change its place of sitting by the movements of the enemy, and finally, in 1785, removed to New York, where it went quietly out of existence in the year 1789 by the adoption of the Federal Constitution.

Presidents of the Continental Congress from 1774 to 1789.

Name.	Where from.	When chosen.
Peyton Randolph	Virginia	1774, September.
John Hancock	Massachusetts	1775, May.
Henry Laurens	South Carolina	1777, November.
John Jay	New York	1778, December.
Samuel Huntington	Connecticut	1779, September.
Thomas McKean	Delaware	1781, July.
John Hanson	Maryland	1781, November.
Edward Boudinot	New Jersey	1782, November.
Thomas Mifflin (General)	Pennsylvania	1783, November.
Richard Henry Lee	Virginia	1784, November.
John Hancock (sick at home)	Massachusetts	1785, November.
Nathaniel Gorham	Massachusetts	1786, June.
Arthur St. Clair (General)	Pennsylvania	1787, February.
Cyrus Griffin	Virginia	1788, January.

14. What was the great authority of the country? Of what kind of men was it composed? What powers were granted to it by the colonies? Can you give a reason for this? What did Congress do notwithstanding this? Mention a few of the measures by which Congress displayed its energy. In what condition did it find itself as the war went on? What is said of its courage?

15. In what respect did it differ from Congress in our own times? What is said of its session? How numerous was its attendance? Why was this so small?

16. How was the President of Congress regarded? Name from the table some of the men that filled it. What was the capital during the greater part of the war? Mention from the table other places where Congress held its sittings.

Different Places where the Congress met.

Philadelphia............ 1774–1776.	Philadelphia............ 1778–1783.
Baltimore............... 1776.	Princeton............... 1783.
Philadelphia............ 1777.	Annapolis............... 1783.
Lancaster and York..... 1777.	Trenton................. 1784.

New York.............. 1785–1789.

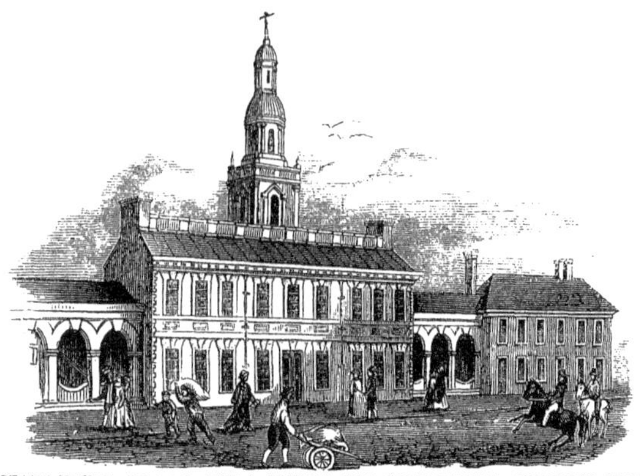

STATE-HOUSE, PHILADELPHIA, WHERE THE CONTINENTAL CONGRESS MET.

REVIEW QUESTIONS.—FROM THE YEAR 1779 TO THE CLOSE OF THE WAR.

1. Give the leading events of 1780.
2. What British general was in command in the South early in 1780?
3. Sketch his operations.
4. Why did he return North?
5. Who succeeded him? and state his movements.
6. Show how thoroughly South Carolina was overrun by the British.
7. Who were sent South to organize and command the American army?
8. Sketch the movements of both armies until the subjugation of the Carolinas.
9. What showed Cornwallis that this was not likely to be lasting?
10. What warlike movements occurred at the North in 1780?
11. What important event took place on the Hudson this year?
12. Sketch the career of Arnold from his first appearance in the history.
13. Where were the French this year, and what assistance did they give?
14. Where was Washington during the year 1780?
15. In what parts of the country was the fighting carried on during 1781?
16. What events show the alarming condition of affairs at the beginning of the year?
17. Give the leading events in the South previous to November, 1781.
18. Sketch the character of Greene as shown in his Carolina campaigns.
19. In what way did Washington show his skill in November?
20. How did Clinton try to counteract his movements?
21. What use did Washington make of the French fleet and army?
22. Describe the siege of Yorktown and the surrender of Cornwallis.

23. When was peace proclaimed?
24. Why was it so long delayed?
25. What were the terms of the treaty?
26. Where was the bulk of the army during the fall and winter of 1781?
27. What was the feeling of the army during the year 1782?
28. How much justice was there in these complaints?
29. What proposition was made to Washington, and how did he meet it?
30. How did he make his influence felt at a later time?
31. What pay did Washington himself receive?
32. What was the condition of the people at the close of the war?
33. How many nations were finally involved in it?
34. Of what advantage was this to the United-States?
35. Mention an important event in the European war.
36. Sketch the character of the tories.
37. Show the conduct of the Continental Congress during the war.
38. From what did its weakness, if any, originate?
39. Describe the meetings of Congress.
40. What kind of state governments existed during the war?
41. By what was the success of the American cause most endangered?
42. How did Congress try to remedy this in 1781?
43. Describe the benefits that sprang from Franklin's influence in France?
44. Give an account of the settlement of the country during the war.
45. Who was king in England during the Revolution?
46. Under what form of government were the United States for several years after the close of the war?
47. What was the form of government during the Revolutionary War?
48. When were the Articles of Confederation first framed, and when adopted?
49. Why were they found of little service? State this fully.
50. What unhappy rebellion showed this more plainly?
51. When and where did the Constitutional Convention meet?
52. What was its first object, and why changed?
53. Who were its president and secretary?
54. Name some of its leading members.
55. After how long a time were its labors concluded, and what was the proviso with regard to the Constitution?
56. Where was Congress during the meeting of the Convention?
57. What great act of Congress marked the year 1787?

MOUNT VERNON, THE HOME OF WASHINGTON.

CHAPTER IV.

FROM THE COMMENCEMENT OF WASHINGTON'S ADMINISTRATION, 1789, TO THE CLOSE OF JEFFERSON'S IN 1809.

SECTION I.

WASHINGTON'S ADMINISTRATION, 1789–1797.

1. THE 4th of March, 1789, the day on which the first Congress under the Constitution was to meet, was ushered in by the ringing of bells and the firing of cannon at New York, the temporary capital. A sufficient number of members to form a quorum for the transaction of business did not arrive until the 30th of March; and it was not until April 6th that the electoral votes were counted, and the unanimous election of George Washington as President, and John Adams as Vice-President, for a term of four years, was duly declared.

PRESIDENT WASHINGTON.

2. Washington, at his residence at Mount Vernon, was informed of his election by a messenger from Congress. He at once accepted the office, and in two days thereafter started for New York. In those days, when there were no railroads or steam-boats, travel was very slow. Washington's progress was still further delayed by the inhabitants on his route, who insisted on paying him the greatest honor. His journey was almost a constant ovation. The peo-

1. When was the first Congress to assemble? How was the day noticed at New York? What delay was there? When were the electoral votes counted?

ple erected triumphal arches; flowers were strewed in his way; mothers, with their daughters dressed in white, sang odes in his honor; and processions in every place of importance met and escorted him through the neighborhood. His progress was so slow that he did not arrive in New York until the close of the month of April.

3. On the 30th of April, on the balcony of Federal Hall, New York, Washington took the oath of office in presence of the Senate and Representatives in Congress, and a large concourse of spectators. He then retired to the Senate Chamber, and there delivered an address to both houses, which was listened to with the greatest respect. Congress

FEDERAL HALL.

first proceeded to arrange the executive department of the government. It created a Department of State, of the Treasury, and of War. Washington appointed Thomas Jefferson Secretary of State, Alexander Hamilton Secretary of the Treasury, and General Knox Secretary of the War Department. John Jay was made Chief Justice of the Supreme Court, and Edmund Randolph Attorney General.

2. How and where was Washington informed of his election? What answer did he give? How did he show his promptness? What hindered his progress? What is said of his journey, and of the honors that met him on his way? When did he reach New York?

3. Where and when did Washington take the oath of office? What immediately followed? What was the first public measure of Congress? How many and what departments were created? Who were placed at the head of these? To what positions were Jay and Randolph appointed?

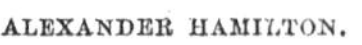
ALEXANDER HAMILTON.

4. The subject of the finances next received the earliest attention. In the month of January, 1790, Secretary Hamilton brought forward his plan in favor of paying the national debt in full, and also the debts of the states incurred in the war. This plan met with considerable opposition in Congress and throughout the country, but was finally approved.

5. During the same year, 1790, the seat of government was fixed at Philadelphia for ten years, to be removed in 1800 to a new city on the banks of the Potomac. During the following year, the Bank of the United States was chartered for twenty years; but this was accomplished only after very great opposition in Congress.

6. The Indians in the Northwest Territory had grown troublesome. The British agents were charged with stirring them up to claim the Ohio as their southern and eastern boundary. They lay around the banks of that river, and waylaid the boats of the immigrants, who were now crowding in great numbers into the fertile lands of the West. In the year 1790, General Harmar was sent against them, and was defeated with great loss. Next year, an expedition under St. Clair, governor of the Northwest Territory, met with the same disaster.

7. General Wayne, the hero of Stony Point, was then made commander, and brought the war to a conclusion at the battle of the Maumee, in the year 1794. Here the Indians were defeated with great slaughter. They made nothing, therefore, by their struggle with the white man, but were compelled to cede by treaty, in 1795, a great portion of their

---

4. What important measure next required the attention of Congress? What did Hamilton propose, and when? How was it regarded? Did it finally become a law?

5. To what place was the seat of government removed from New York? Was it to remain here always? When and where was it to go after that? When was the first United States Bank chartered? What is said of this?

6. In what direction had trouble arisen? Who were blamed as the cause of this? How did the Indians show their hostility? Who were sent against them in 1790 and 1791? With what success?

lands, amounting to more than 25,000 square miles, embracing the eastern and southern part of Ohio.

8. On the 4th of March, 1793, Washington entered on the second term of his presidency, to which he had been again unanimously elected. John Adams had also been rechosen Vice-President. The people of the United States, however, were far from being united in political sentiment. A large party were in favor of a strong national government, and were known as Federalists; their opponents were known as anti-Federalists. Washington, Adams, Hamilton, and Jay belonged to the party of Federalists. Jefferson, Madison, and Monroe were among the prominent leaders of the anti-Federalists.

9. The feeling had already grown very bitter between these two parties when the French Revolution broke out. In 1793, the French Directory sent out M. Genet (*zha-ná*) as embassador to America. On his arrival, he was so well received by the anti-Federalists in particular, and by many who had not forgotten the assistance of France during the Revolutionary War, that he presumed on this, and began to fit out privateers against English commerce.

10. France had declared war against England, and Genet's conduct was therefore very displeasing to Washington, who did not wish the United States to be involved in a war with England. Genet behaved so defiantly in the matter, that Washington requested the French government to recall him, which request was complied with in 1794. Genet's conduct and his recall increased the bitterness between the Federalists and their opponents, who now first began to call themselves Democratic Republicans.

11. Genet's public opposition to the government had oth-

---

7. Who brought the war to an end? When and where? What did the Indians gain by their struggle, and what is said of the treaty?

8. What occurred on the 4th of March, 1793? Who was elected Vice-President? What is said of the political feeling of the people? Who were the leading Federalists? Who were the leading anti-Federalists?

9. What is said of the feeling between these two parties? Whom did the French Revolutionists send out? How was he received in America? What did this encourage him to do?

10. How was Genet's conduct regarded by Washington? Why? What did Washington do? Did the French government accede to this? What was thought in the United States of Genet's recall? What name had the anti-Federalists taken?

er evil results; for it encouraged rebellion among the people of Western Pennsylvania. One of Hamilton's modes of raising revenue was by a duty on whisky. These Pennsylvanians formed secret societies, and determined not to pay this duty; and at length became so bold in 1794 that Washington was compelled to order a military force to put them down. On the appearance of this, the "Whisky Rebellion," as it was called, suddenly came to an end.

12. In spite of Washington's great care not to offend England, by showing too great a leaning toward France, the English government treated the United States in a way that seemed likely to end in war. Her agents were charged with inciting the Indians in the West, and she was unwilling to give up some of the Western posts, as she had agreed to do by treaty. John Jay was sent as special embassador to England, and was fortunate in being able to conclude a treaty with that government which settled the question of the Western posts and other points in dispute. But this treaty did not please the opponents of Washington. When news of it arrived in America, Jay was burned in effigy, and Washington was freely censured. The treaty was, however, approved by the Senate in 1795.

JOHN JAY.

13. At the end of the year 1793, Jefferson retired from the cabinet; but the agitation between the two great parties continued. Washington suffered much annoyance from the abuse of his opponents, but kept on his way, conscious of the purity and rectitude of his intentions. In the month of September, 1796, he issued his famous Farewell Address

---

11. What other bad result came from Genet's conduct? What was the cause of their grievance, and what did they resort to? How did Washington meet this? What was the consequence?

12. In regard to what had Washington shown great anxiety? How did England regard this? What complaints were made agsinst her? Who was sent to England to try to restore friendly feelings? What did he accomplish? How was the treaty regarded in America?

to the people of the United States, in which he announced his fixed determination to retire from office at the end of his second term.

14. The canvass for the election that followed was conducted with great rancor. Both parties put forward their chief men—the Federalists, John Adams; and the Republicans, Thomas Jefferson. After a bitter contest, the former was chosen President; and Jefferson, having received the next highest number of electoral votes, was chosen Vice-President.

15. Congress had already voted a reply to the Farewell Address, expressing the fullest confidence in Washington's wisdom and integrity. During the winter, nearly all the Legislatures sent resolutions expressive of the same feelings. Throughout the country, the voice of party clamor against Washington was almost hushed. On the 4th of March, 1797, he was present at the inauguration of President Adams, and there received the warmest manifestations of regard from assembled thousands. In a few days afterward he retired to his home at Mount Vernon.

SECTION II.

JOHN ADAMS'S ADMINISTRATION, 1797–1801.

1. John Adams, the new President, was one of the early and active Massachusetts patriots. As a member of Congress, he from the first took a prominent position, and was one of the celebrated committee that reported the Declaration of Independence. In 1778, he was sent as commissioner to Europe, and remained abroad ten years, actively engaged on important public business. During his residence

---

13. Who retired from the cabinet at the end of 1793? What is said of the state of party feeling, and of Washington's conduct in relation to it? What important event occurred in 1793?

14. Who were put forward as candidates for the presidency? How was the canvass conducted? Who were elected President and Vice-President? Is this the way in which the Vice-President is chosen at present?

15. How did Congress and the states treat Washington's Farewell Address? State what is said in connection with the inauguration of Adams. Where did Washington retire?

abroad, in the year 1785, he was appointed first minister to the court of England from the United States. Soon after his return from Europe he was elected Vice-President, in 1789.

PRESIDENT JOHN ADAMS.

2. The trouble with France did not come to a close with the recall of M. Genet. Jay's treaty with England displeased the French government to such an extent that the latter ordered Pinckney, the American minister, to leave the country; and a number of American vessels were taken at sea by French men-of-war. President Adams called an extra session of Congress to consider these matters; and three envoys, Pinckney, the late minister, Gerry, and Marshall, were sent to France to attempt the restoration of a friendly feeling between the two countries.

3. The French Directory, the name of the new revolutionary government, declined to receive them officially, and hinted that a present of money would pave the way for an arrangement. If this were not given, then there would be war. Pinckney's reply was very spirited: "War be it, then. Millions for defense, but not one cent for tribute!" Shortly after this, Pinckney and Marshall were ordered to leave France, because they were Federalists. Gerry, on the other hand, who was a Republican, and supposed to favor the interests of the French, was allowed to remain. This treatment of the envoys stirred the anger of the American

---

1. What is said of President Adams's earlier history? Of his later public offices?
2. What effect was produced by the recall of M. Genet? What new source of irritation disturbed the French court? In what way did they show their displeasure? How did Adams show his opinion of the seriousness of this? Who were sent to France?

people to such an extent that Congress at once prepared for war, and Washington was appointed commander-in-chief.

4. Fighting at sea followed. An American armed schooner was captured by the French, and a French frigate was taken by the United States ship Constellation. Before hostilities proceeded farther, the French Directory made proposals of peace, and, after some delay, Napoleon Bonaparte, First Consul of France, in the year 1800 signed a treaty at Paris. Washington did not live to see peace proclaimed. He died, after a short illness, at Mount Vernon, of a disease of the throat, on the 14th of December, 1799. All parties paid the greatest honor to his memory, and he was universally mourned as the Father of his Country. In Europe the sincerest tributes were awarded to the nobleness, purity, and grandeur of his character.

5. The seat of government was transferred to Washington in the year 1800, as originally provided for by Congress, Maryland and Virginia ceding a tract of land 10 miles square for the new city.

6. The difficulties with France led to measures that prevented the re-election of Adams to the presidency. While the excitement in regard to France was at its height, he recommended the passage of the Alien and Sedition Laws. The Alien Law gave power to expel all foreigners who were found plotting against the good of the country. The Sedition Law was aimed chiefly against the violent attacks on the government by the press. Adams thought these measures were for the good of the country. The majority of the people thought differently. At the election in 1800, the Republican party triumphed, and Thomas Jefferson was elected President, and Aaron Burr, of New York, Vice-President.

3. How were the envoys received? What was Pinckney's celebrated reply? What followed? How was the news received by the American people, and what measures were adopted?

4. Where did the first fighting take place? State what is mentioned of it. What put a stop to hostilities? When, where, and by whom, on the part of France, was the treaty signed? What memorable event took place in 1799? How was his memory regarded in America? And in Europe?

5. What change was made in the year 1800? In what year did Congress decide on the change? What states gave the land, and how much?

6. How many terms did Adams serve as President? What prevented his re-election? What were these measures? What was the Alien Law? What was the Sedition Law? Who was chosen President, and who Vice-President?

SECTION III.

JEFFERSON'S ADMINISTRATION, 1801–1809.

1. THE illustrious man who now became President of the United States had been deeply engaged in the long colonial struggles for freedom and independence. He took an active part in the early patriotic movements of Virginia, of which he was governor during the later part of the war. As a member of Congress and chairman of a committee, he, in 1776, drew up the Declaration of Independence, and again, in 1784, by his efforts, forever linked his name with the great Northwest Territory, principally ceded by Virginia to the United States. In Washington's first term, Jefferson was Secretary of State.

PRESIDENT JEFFERSON.

2. During the first year of Jefferson's administration, France received back from Spain, by a secret treaty made the year before, the Territory of Louisiana. The French, however, did not occupy the country, but allowed it to remain under Spanish rule. In the year 1803, the Spanish governor closed the port of New Orleans against American commerce. This conduct produced immense excitement west of the Alleghanies, and it was difficult to prevent the people there from rushing into war.

---

1. What is said of Jefferson's early career? What offices did he hold? With what two great affairs is his name connected?

2. What important change in American territory was made in 1801? Under what government did it remain? What occurred in 1803? How was this act regarded by the Western people?

3. It had long been Jefferson's great ambition to secure the territory on both banks of the Lower Mississippi for the United States, because he felt that whatever power held possession of the mouth of that river must also hold control of the valley above it. Livingston, the American minister at the court of France, was therefore urged to use every means to persuade Bonaparte to sell New Orleans to the United States. At this time, 1803, a great European war was about to break out, and Bonaparte, on that account not unwilling to be rid of these American possessions, to the surprise of Livingston, offered to sell the whole of Louisiana. The bargain was soon concluded, and the entire territory, embracing more than 1,000,000 square miles, passed into the possession of the United States for $12,000,000.

4. Congress divided this great tract into two territories—that which is now the State of Louisiana was named the Territory of Orleans; the other, of vast extent, was called the District of Louisiana. The purchase of French Louisiana was the great event of Jefferson's administration. It placed the Mississippi River in its entire length, and an immense district west of it, within the territory of the United States.

WAR WITH THE BARBARY POWERS.

5. For many years, the Barbary powers, Tunis, Tripoli, Algiers, and Morocco, on the southern shores of the Mediterranean, had seized the vessels of all nations that would not pay them annual tribute, and made slaves of their crews. The great powers of Europe had adopted the cheapest mode of saving their own trade, by making these pirates a yearly payment. The United States followed this custom, and, previous to 1801, expended nearly $2,000,000 in presents to them. But America was more than 3000 miles distant, and the Barbary pirates, regardless of a nation so far off, did

---

3. What value did Jefferson place on the control of the mouth of the Mississippi? What did he earnestly urge? Who was Bonaparte? What was the state of Europe in 1803? What offer did Bonaparte make? Why did he do this? Upon what terms was a bargain concluded? What was the extent of the territory?

4. How did Congress divide this territory? How was the purchase of Louisiana regarded? Why was it so important?

not hesitate to ill treat and attack American vessels that came in their way.

6. In 1801, the Bey of Tripoli declared war, and several American war vessels were soon on their way to the Mediterranean. A Tripolitan cruiser was captured after a hard fight. In 1803, Commodore Preble was sent with a fleet into Mediterranean waters. While he was endeavoring to punish the Emperor of Morocco by an attack on Tangiers, the frigate Philadelphia was blockading Tripoli. During this service she was chasing a vessel near shore, ran aground, and in this helpless state was captured by Tripolitan gun-boats. Bainbridge, her captain, and 300 of her crew, were made prisoners. The latter were reduced to slavery.

7. The Tripolitans did not keep their prize very long. About six months after, Lieutenant Decatur, in a small schooner, with a picked crew, ran alongside of the Philadelphia in the harbor of Tripoli, killed or drove the Tripolitan crew into the sea, and set fire to the vessel. All this was done under the fire of the enemy's batteries, yet Decatur escaped without the loss of a man. During the year 1804, Tripoli was repeatedly bombarded, and considerable damage was done to the forts and ships of the enemy.

8. The reigning Bey had an older brother, named Hamet, whom he had driven from the throne, and Eaton, the American consul at Tunis, undertook, with the assistance of Hamet, to capture Tripoli. Tunis was nearly 1000 miles from this point, and Eaton and Hamet commenced their long march with only 70 seamen and a small body of Egyptian soldiers. On their way they attacked and captured Derne. With the help of the fleet, they would probably have taken Tripoli when they arrived there; but the reigning Bey offered to make peace, and the American commissioner, Mr. Lear, accepted his terms. This put an end to the war in the

---

5. What were the Barbary powers? What had long been their custom? Did the powers of Europe submit to this? What had the United States done? Did these payments by the United States give American vessels security? Why was this?

6. What brought matters to a crisis in 1801? What capture was made? Who was sent with a fleet in 1803? What happened to one of the frigates? Why was she alone there? What happened to the captain and his crew? Where is Tripoli?

7. In what brilliant way did Decatur retrieve this disaster? Did he suffer much from the enemy? How was the American fleet kept busy during 1804?

Mediterranean, and the oppression of the Barbary powers on American commerce ceased for a time.

9. While these events were transpiring on the distant shores of Africa, the country was agitated by the death of General Alexander Hamilton, the friend and associate of Washington, who was shot in a duel at Weehawken, opposite New York, by Aaron Burr, the Vice-President. The

DUEL BETWEEN BURR AND HAMILTON AT WEEHAWKEN.

quarrel originated in political animosity. Burr had been nominated for governor of the State of New York, and Hamilton, feeling that he was a very unfit man to be governor, had opposed his election. After Burr was defeated he challenged and killed Hamilton, July 11th, 1804.

8. What is said of Hamet? What American was at Tunis? What plan did he arrange with Hamet? How far was Tunis from Tripoli? With what force did they commence their march? What place did they attack on their route? Where is Derne? What is said of their attempt on Tripoli? What prevented this? What effect did this treaty have on the war?

9. What unfortunate event occurred during 1804? How did the quarrel originate? What is said of Hamilton's opposition to Burr?

10. The same fall Jefferson was re-elected, with Clinton as Vice-President. In the year 1806, Burr was arrested by the government on an obscure charge of conspiring either to seize Mexico or to form an empire west of the Alleghanies. After a long trial, in which he defended himself with great ability, the jury brought in a verdict of "not guilty." But the killing of Hamilton, and his suspicious, intriguing conduct, notwithstanding his acquittal, ruined him forever in public estimation.

11. In the year 1807, a steam-boat constructed by Robert Fulton, a native of Pennsylvania, made a voyage from New York to Albany, a distance of about 150 miles, in 36 hours. This was the beginning of that great system of steam navigation which has extended over the inland waters of the United States, and which has exercised a powerful influence not only on the trade, but also on the settlement of the country.

FULTON'S STEAM-BOAT.

12. During these years, the great European war was raging between France on the one hand, led by Napoleon, and the other nations urged on by England. The latter power was mistress of the sea, and behaved in a very oppressive manner to American vessels, stopping them and taking from them what seamen she wanted for her ships of war. This she did on the plea that they were English citizens, and that she had a right to their services. The frigate Chesapeake was in this way fired into by the British man-of-war Leopard, and, after being boarded, four of her men were taken as deserters. Mr. Jefferson, compelled to take notice of high-handed outrages like this, issued a proclamation forbidding English ships from entering any American port until satis-

10. Who was elected President in the fall of 1804? Was Burr re-elected? What happened to him in 1806? What was the result of the trial? How was he regarded thereafter by the public?

11. What great improvement in navigation was made about this time? What was the first voyage made? What is said of the importance of this?

faction was made by the English government for its past offenses.

13. The United States merchant vessels were busily engaged, as neutrals, in conveying goods to all parts of Europe. England was determined to close French ports to trade, and she declared, in 1806, the French coast from Brest to the Elbe in a state of blockade. Then Napoleon, in retaliation, declared the British Islands in a state of blockade. As the European war went on, the British government, in November, 1807, passed the famous "Orders in Council," prohibiting all trade with France and her allies. Napoleon, not to be behind Great Britain, immediately proclaimed his decree at Milan, called the "Milan Decree," forbidding all trade with England and her colonies. In this way, American vessels were liable to be captured by French or British cruisers in attempting to trade with either country or its colonies.

14. In December, 1807, Congress passed an embargo that hindered American vessels from leaving United States ports, hoping in this way to punish France and England. It proved very objectionable to the New England and Middle States, on account of the injury it did to their commerce, and on March 1, 1809, it was repealed. In its place there was passed, in the same month, a non-intercourse act, prohibiting trade with France and England. In this state of political confusion Mr. Jefferson's administration ended. In the previous fall, Jefferson, imitating the example of Washington, declined a re-election at the close of his second term, and James Madison, of Virginia, was chosen President; George Clinton, of New York, was re-elected Vice-President.

---

12. What contest was going on in Europe at this time? What is said of the conduct of England? On what ground did she seize these men? What serious affair brought matters to a crisis? What did the President do in retaliation?

13. What lucrative branch of commerce were United States vessels engaged in? How did England attempt to stop this? In what way did Napoleon retaliate? By what more serious measure on the part of England was this followed? What then did Napoleon do? What now was the condition of the American shipping trade?

14. How did Congress endeavor to retaliate? What effect did it produce? After the embargo was taken off, what retaliatory act was passed? When did Jefferson's second term end? Who were elected President and Vice-President?

REVIEW QUESTIONS.—1789-1809.

1. When and where was Washington inaugurated?
2. Who was Vice-President?
3. How long was New York the capital under the Constitution?
4. Name the first secretaries of the different departments.
5. What was the first and greatest measure of Washington's administration, and who was the mover of it?
6. Why was this the greatest measure of his administration?
7. Give an account of the two great parties that sprang up.
8. By what was the feeling between these parties greatly increased?
9. How did Washington act in reference to Genet?
10. Why was it so necessary to act with prudence toward France?
11. How was the critical state of affairs with England brought to a settlement?
12. With what feelings was this regarded by a part of the country?
13. What determination did Washington announce in the fall of 1793?
14. Who were the rival candidates for the presidency in 1793, and which was chosen?
15. What can you state with regard to the close of Washington's administration?
16. State, without describing them, the principal events of Adams's administration.
17. Describe the conduct of the French government to our envoys.
18. How were these difficulties terminated?
19. What became the capital in 1800?
20. When and by what authority was this settled?
21. What prevented Adams's re-election to the presidency?
22. Who were elected President and Vice-President in 1804?
23. Who was named Secretary of State?
24. What were the leading events of Jefferson's administration?
25. Which of these was the most celebrated measure?
26. Give the history of the purchase of Louisiana.
27. Why was Jefferson so deeply interested in obtaining this?
28. What was the extent of the territory, and how was it organized after its purchase?
29. Give the origin of the war in the Mediterranean.
30. Name the principal events that marked its progress, with dates.
31. How and when was it brought to a termination?
32. What led to the death of Hamilton? Give the date.
33. What can you say of the future career of Burr?
34. What was the state of affairs in Europe about this time?
35. How did this affect the crews of American vessels; and what collision ensued?
36. In what way was American commerce affected by the European war?
37. What measures of retaliation did Congress pass, and when?
38. Describe what was the condition of affairs at the close of Jefferson's administration.
39. From 1789 to this time, how many and what states had been admitted into the Union?
40. From what territories or states were they formed?
41. Give the boundaries of the United States at the close of Jefferson's administration.
42. Give the boundaries of the United States at the beginning of it.

CHAPTER V.

MADISON'S ADMINISTRATION, 1809-1817.

SECTION I.

EVENTS PREVIOUS TO THE SECOND WAR WITH ENGLAND.

1. PRESIDENT MADISON was a member of the Continental Congress, and one of the most distinguished delegates in the Convention of 1787. He was also, for eight years, Secretary of State under Jefferson, and was thus, in some degree, prepared to encounter the formidable difficulties with France and England, which were increasing at the close of the last administration. French cruisers seized American merchant vessels; and, early in 1810, Bonaparte issued another and more offensive decree against American commerce. Toward the end of the year he revoked these decrees, and trade was resumed between France and the United States, although the former power still continued to capture American vessels.

PRESIDENT MADISON.

2. England, on the other hand, would listen to no terms. Her vessels cruised boldly off United States ports, and seized merchant ships as prizes. One of these cruisers, the Little

---

1. Mention some of the high offices that Madison had filled. With what difficulties did his administration begin? State what grievances the United States endured from the French. What occurred toward the end of the year 1810?

Belt, in the year 1811, on being hailed by the American frigate President, answered insolently with a cannon-shot. The President returned the fire with a broadside, and in a short time the guns of the Little Belt were silenced, but not until she had lost 33 men in killed and wounded.

3. To add to these difficulties, the Indians of the Northwest Territory were growing more and more uneasy as the white man pushed out into the wilderness, and had apparently forgotten the severe punishment that General Wayne gave them in 1794. Besides, it was believed that British emissaries were inciting them to war. Tecumtha, a Shawnee chief, became their leader, and was assisted by his brother, the Prophet, as he was called, a man of great influence among the Indians.

4. The American government determined to strike before Tecumtha could unite the Northwest tribes; and General Harrison was sent to destroy the town of the Prophet, at the junction of the Tippecanoe and Wabash Rivers. When he came near this point, November 6, 1811, the crafty Prophet sent forward some Indian chiefs, who met Harrison, and said that their leader would sign a treaty next day. This was only done to deceive the American general. In the morning, before daybreak, November 7, the Indians suddenly attacked him in his camp; but he was an old Indian fighter, and his men were on their guard. The battle was very severe, but when daylight broke Harrison ordered his men forward, and the enemy were defeated with great slaughter. This battle quieted the Indians for a time, but greatly helped to stir up the people of the Western country against the English.

5. There seemed to be nothing left for the United States but to go to war with England. She was determined to

---

2. What is said of the conduct of England? Describe the punishment given to one of the British ships.

3. What trouble was growing up on the Northwest frontiers? Who were believed to be exciting the Indians? Who were the Indian leaders?

4. What resolution was taken by the American government? Who was sent against them, and with what object? In what state are those two rivers? What happened on his march when near that point? What was the object of this embassy? How far did it deceive Harrison? What occurred? Describe the battle of Tippecanoe. What was the effect of the battle on the Indians and on the people of the West?

destroy American commerce. She had declared a blockade of the French ports without a sufficient force, and seized American seamen wherever she could find them. In addition, she was charged, as has been stated, with inciting the Indians on the frontiers. In April, 1812, Congress laid an embargo on British ships, and on June 19 President Madison proclaimed war against England. The President was thereupon authorized to enlist 25,000 men, to raise 50,000 volunteers, and to call out 100,000 militia for garrison duty in coast and frontier defenses. Henry Dearborn, of Massachusetts, was appointed commander-in-chief. In June, Louisiana became a state, and Missouri Territory was formed.

SECTION II.

Events of 1812.

1. **Invasion of Canada.**—The war opened on the Northwestern frontier in the month of July with the invasion of Canada by the American troops. In the early part of 1812, General Hull, governor of Michigan Territory, began his march against the Indians, who were again threatening the frontier settlements. After war was declared, he was ordered to invade Canada; and on the 12th of July he crossed the river from Detroit, then a small fortification, to attack the British post at Malden. Instead of moving with vigor, he waited in his camp at Sandwich, doing little for nearly four weeks; and a detachment, under Major Van Horne, sent by him to guard supplies, was surprised and defeated at Brownstown, August 5, by the British and Indians. In the mean time Malden had been strengthened by fresh troops and supplies, and Hull recrossed the river to Detroit.

---

5. Into what were the United States gradually forced? Enumerate the grievances against England. What retaliatory measure was passed by Congress? When was war declared? What preparations were made for the struggle? What changes were made west f the Mississippi? See Map, page 250.

1. How was the war opened? Who was General Hull? In what was he employed previous to the declaration of war? What change was ordered? What was his first movement? What is said of his conduct at Sandwich after his crossing into Canada? What occurred at Brownstown? Where is Brownstown? See Map, page 251. What was Hull forced to do, and why?

MAP OF THE UNITED STATES IN 1812.

2. While Hull was in camp at Sandwich, Fort Mackinaw surrendered without resistance to a British force, July 17. This fort was on the Straits of Mackinaw, then beyond the frontiers of civilized life, and was built as a protection for the fur traders. The garrison knew nothing of the declaration of war until they were called on to surrender.

3. General Brock came to Malden and took command of the British troops. Tecumtha was already there, with his Indians, to meet him; and the combined army then pushed across the river to Detroit, where Hull was fortified. While the Americans eagerly awaited the signal to fire on Brock's men, a white flag was raised on the fort, by Hull's order, as a sign of surrender. The American troops were overcome with rage and shame when they saw the signal. It was a most disastrous affair; for not only did Hull surrender the fort, with its garrison and stores, but he gave up the whole of Michigan Territory to the British, August 16th.

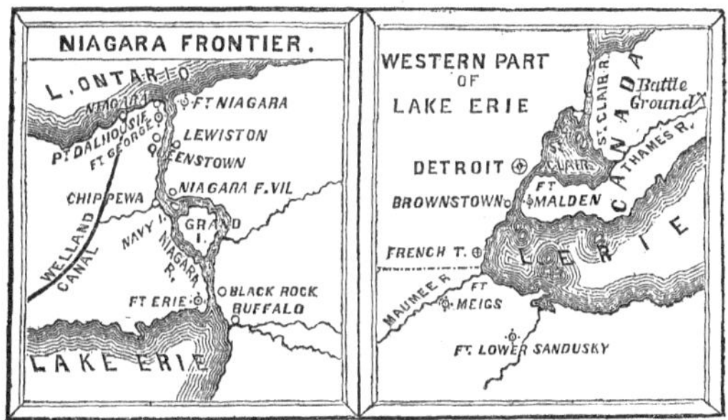

4. Later in the war, General Hull was exchanged for 30 British prisoners, and tried by court-martial for treason and cowardice. He was acquitted of treason, but convicted of cowardice, and sentenced to be shot. The President, however, pardoned him, because he had served his country faithfully as a soldier during the Revolutionary War.

---

2. What event occurred while Hull was at Sandwich? Where was Fort Mackinaw? For what purpose had it been built? What is said of the garrison?

3. Who took command of the British at Malden? Who also was there? Against what point did they move? What happened as the battle was about to begin? How did the American troops regard this? What were the terms of Hull's surrender?

4. How did Hull regain his liberty? What followed? What was the result of the trial?

5. A body of troops, principally New York State militia, commanded by General Van Rensselaer, was encamped at Lewiston, on the Niagara River. On the other side was Queenstown, held by a British force under General Brock. On the 13th of October, Colonel Van Rensselaer, a kinsman of the general, crossed with a portion of the militia, and drove the British from their batteries. In the battle that followed, General Brock was killed, and the British were again driven back. All day long General Van Rensselaer could not persuade more than 1000 men to cross the river to the help of their companions, the rest refusing because they were unwilling to go out of their own state to fight an enemy.

6. The result was that the British, who were heavily reenforced, attacked the Americans, and nearly all the latter were either killed, wounded, or taken prisoners. Among them was Lieutenant Colonel Winfield Scott, afterward a celebrated general, then a young man, who had crossed over as a volunteer. General Van Rensselaer resigned his command, in disgust with the troops, and General Smyth, of Virginia, was appointed to succeed him; but, after one or two fruitless attempts to move against different points, he also resigned.

7. The year's campaign on the land was unfortunate for the Americans. They retreated from Canada. They lost Detroit under circumstances disgraceful to their arms, and with it the whole of Michigan Territory. They failed at Queenstown, where all the troops that were engaged were destroyed or captured. A large portion of the country, particularly in the New England States, was opposed to the war, and these reverses on the land gave new strength to this opposition. Affairs would have borne a most discouraging aspect had not the American navy redeemed the national honor in a series of brilliant engagements at sea.

5. On what frontier was a body of troops stationed? What lay opposite? What movement was made by the Americans? When? What is said of the battle? What re-enforcements were sent across to the Americans? Why did the troops refuse to cross the river?

6. What was the result at the close of the day? Who was among the prisoners? How did General Van Rensselaer show his feelings? Who took the command, and what was his success?

7. What was the result of the campaign of 1812? Enumerate the disasters of 1812. What section of the people was opposed to the war? How did these reverses affect them? What saved the glory of the American arms?

8. **Events of 1812 at Sea.**—In August the British frigate Guerriere (*ger-e-are*) was met by the American frigate Constitution, under Captain Isaac Hull, near the Gulf of St. Lawrence. After a fierce fight of two hours, a portion of which was fought yard-arm to yard-arm, the Guerriere struck her flag. She was so completely riddled that Hull was forced to burn her, as he could not bring her into port.

DESTRUCTION OF THE GUERRIERE BY THE CONSTITUTION.

The Constitution was little injured. This contest gave immense satisfaction to the country, for it was the first victory gained over an English ship in fifty years. Captain Decatur, in the frigate United States, distinguished himself by the capture of the British frigate Macedonian, after a long and severe battle, and brought his prize safely into New York. The engagement occurred near the Azores, in the month of October.

8. What was the first naval engagement of the war? Where was it fought? What is said of the engagement? What did Captain Hull do with his prize? Why was this victory regarded with so much satisfaction? What battle occurred between two frigates in October? When and where did it occur?

9. The frigate President captured a packet ship, with two hundred thousand dollars in specie. The Wasp, an American sloop-of-war, commanded by Captain Jones, was not so fortunate. In October he fought and captured the war-brig Frolic, after a very bloody battle off the coast of North Carolina. While getting her in a condition to sail, a British ship of seventy-four guns came up and took both vessels into the Bermudas. In December the Constitution, under a new commander, Bainbridge, was cruising along the coast of Brazil, when she fell in with the British frigate Java. After a long engagement the Java struck her colors, but was too much injured to be taken to the United States, and was burned.

10. These victories over "the mistress of the seas," as Great Britain was haughtily styled, created immense rejoicing throughout the country, and equally surprised and mortified the people of England. The American privateers were also very successful in capturing British merchant ships. They swarmed in great numbers from our sea-ports, and took 300 vessels, many of them with valuable cargoes. In the fall of 1812, Madison was re-elected President.

SECTION III.

Events of 1813.

1. The year 1813 opened with vigorous war measures. Harrison, the hero of Tippecanoe, was already in command of the Army of the Northwest, General Dearborn was appointed to lead the Army of the Centre, and General Hampton was at the head of the Army of the North, near the shores of Lake Champlain.

2. **The Army of the Northwest.**—Harrison's head-quarters, during the winter of 1812–1813, were near Franklinton, Ohio.

---

9. What success did the frigate President meet with? What engagement took place off North Carolina? How did the Wasp lose the result of the action? On what coast, in December, did another engagement occur? Describe the battle, and what followed. Mention in order these four engagements.

10. How were these naval successes regarded by the Americans? In what other way were the Americans active and successful at sea? Give some idea of their success. What is said of Madison?

1. How did the year 1813 open? What was the arrangement of the troops?

General Winchester, with a portion of the troops, was at a fort on the Maumee. In January, the latter sent a part of his force to drive off the British, who were threatening Frenchtown, on the River Raisin. The enemy were dispersed, and soon after Winchester joined the detachment with the remainder of his troops, and encamped in the open fields. Altogether there were scarce 1000 men. General Proctor, marching from Fort Malden with 1500 British and Indians, attacked Winchester, and, after a bloody fight, forced him to surrender, January 22.

3. Harrison, while on his way to the assistance of Winchester, hearing of this disaster, took post at the Rapids of the Maumee, and threw up fortifications, which he called Fort Meigs (*megs*). On the 1st of May, Proctor opened the batteries against the fort, but General Clay, with 1200 Kentuckians, came to Harrison's relief. The British were attacked and defeated with some loss, and the siege was abandoned.

4. In July, Proctor came again, hoping for better success; but General Clay, now in command, was prepared for him, and the English general retired. He then moved against Fort Stevenson, at Lower Sandusky, commanded by Major Croghan (*crogan*), a youth of twenty-one. Proctor attacked the fort Aug. 2d, but was beaten back with great loss. The same night, being afraid of Harrison's approach, he returned to Malden.

5. A small squadron of British ships, under Captain Barclay, had command of the waters of Lake Erie. A young United States officer, named Perry, after great difficulties, built and equipped a fleet. A large part of the crews that manned these vessels was obtained from Harrison's army. On the 10th of September a severe battle was fought at the

2. Where were Harrison's head-quarters during the winter? Where, and under whom, were a portion of his troops stationed? What movement was made by Winchester in January? What is said of his carelessness, and the result? What is the battle called?

3. Where was Harrison at the time of the battle? Where did he go when he heard of it? By whom was he attacked here? What compelled Proctor to raise the siege?

4. When did Proctor make a second attempt? With what success? What was his next point of attack? Where is this? What was his success here? Why, when, and where did he retire?

western end of the lake, between Perry and Barclay, in which the Americans were completely victorious. During the battle his own vessel was rendered useless, and in the heat of the firing he went to another of his ships in an open boat, and continued the contest. Shortly after its close, Harrison

PERRY CHANGING HIS SHIP DURING THE BATTLE.

received Perry's laconic message: "We have met the enemy, and they are ours. Two ships, one brig, a schooner, and a sloop."

6. This important victory gave the Americans the command of the lake, and opened the way to Canada. Perry soon after conveyed Harrison's army across the lake; and Proctor at once abandoned Malden, and retreated with Tecumtha into Canada. Harrison pursued, and came up with him, October 5, on the banks of the River Thames. After a short but spirited battle, Tecumtha was killed, and Proctor

5. What ships had command of Lake Erie? Who managed to equip a fleet to contest the control of the lake? Where did he get his crews? When did the rival fleets meet? Which was victorious? What incident of this battle is given? What message shows the simplicity and directness of Perry's character?

saved himself only by the swiftness of his horse. Michigan Territory was once more in possession of the United States, and the northwestern frontier was, for the present, relieved from the fear of the British and Indians.

7. **The Army of the Centre.**—In April, General Dearborn, with 1700 picked men, sailed across Lake Ontario in Commodore Chauncey's vessels against York, now Toronto, the capital of Upper Canada. In the assault, April 27, General Pike, who led the advance, was killed, with one or two hundred of his troops, by the explosion of a magazine, and the British general and his troops retreated during the disorder. The Americans rallied, and captured the place, with a great amount of military stores.

8. As it was not a part of the plan to keep possession of York, the troops re-embarked on board the fleet, and, after landing at Sackett's Harbor, sailed against Fort George, on the Niagara. On the arrival of the Americans, the British general blew up his magazines, and fell back to Burlington Heights, near the western end of the lake. To this position he was followed by the Americans; but the British attacked them after midnight, June 6, and, though the enemy were driven back, they made prisoners of two American generals, Chandler and Winder. The Americans then retreated precipitately, and reached Fort George June 8.

9. As soon as the British learned that the Americans had left Sackett's Harbor, General Prevost, with 1000 men, landed, May 29, to attack the place. He was opposed so vigorously by General Brown, in command, that he fell back hastily to his ships, leaving behind him his wounded. General Dearborn, whom we left on the Niagara, soon after this allowed himself to be surrounded at Fort George, and was unfortunate in having a detachment of 600 men cut off by the

---

6. Why was Perry's victory so important? What immediately followed? Where did Harrison come up with the British and Indians? What is said of the battle that followed? What important consequences came from this battle?

7. What was the first movement of the Army of the Centre? What American naval officer commanded on Lake Ontario? What misfortune happened at York? How did the attack terminate?

8. How long did the Americans keep possession of York? Against what point did they next go? How did the British receive them? What misfortunes followed?

British. There was a great outcry raised against him for his ill success, and he was recalled.

10. General Wilkinson took Dearborn's place, and General Hampton was placed in command of the Army of the North, around Lake Champlain. An expedition, under Wilkinson in person, started against Montreal, to be joined on the St. Lawrence by General Hampton and a part of the Army of the North. When Wilkinson reached the Great Rapids, he sent General Brown forward with troops to cover the descent of the army. A confused battle followed, November 11, known as the battle of Chrysler's farm, in which the British were driven back, but with a loss of more than 300 men on the part of the Americans.

11. The plan was that Hampton should join Wilkinson at St. Regis; but Hampton was unable to do so, and the expedition was abandoned. Wilkinson went into winter quarters at French Mills, about nine miles east of St. Regis, and Hampton encamped at Plattsburg. Meanwhile Fort George had been abandoned in December, and the American forces, under General M'Clure, had been compelled to recross the river. The British in turn crossed over, took Niagara, and burned several small villages, among them Black Rock and Buffalo.

12. **Creek War.**—In the spring of 1813, Tecumtha visited the Southwest, and aroused the war spirit of the Indians. In the month of August, 700 Creeks attacked and took Fort Mims, on the west bank of the Alabama River, slaughtering nearly 400 settlers who had gone there for protection. Several divisions of militia were at once ordered into the Creek country. The principal villages of the Indians lay on and near the banks of the Coosa and Tallapoosa; their hunting-grounds extended much farther north. Generals Jackson

9. In what way were the British busy while the Americans were at Fort George? How was Prevost opposed, and with what success? What misfortune befell General Dearborn's force? How was this regarded by the American people and government?

10. Who succeeded him in the command of the Army of the Centre? Where was General Hampton? What expedition was planned? What movement was made at the Rapids? What was the result of the battle?

11. Where was Hampton to join Wilkinson? How was this carried out? Where did the troops go into winter quarters? What was taking place at Fort George? And on the Niagara?

and Coffee, at the head of volunteers from West Tennessee, were the first to move, and, after some minor encounters, inflicted severe blows on the Creeks at Tallasehatche, November 3, and at Talladega, November 8. General Floyd, with the Georgia Volunteers, attacked the Indian town of Autossee, November 29, and killed 200 warriors.

SEAT OF THE CREEK WAR.

13. The Indians, although poorly armed, assumed the offensive, and attacked Jackson at Emucfau, January 22, 1814, and, although they were repulsed, he fell back to Fort Strother. Three days after they again made an attack on him, and were repulsed. Jackson, at the head of a new force of 4000 Tennesseeans, advanced southward, and gave the Creeks a final and crushing blow at the great Horse-shoe Bend of the Tallapoosa, where 1000 warriors, with their women and children, occupied an intrenched camp. Here they were attacked March 27, 1814, and, after a desperate resistance, the battle was brought to a close by the slaughter of 600 warriors, and the capture of 250 women and children. This defeat entirely broke the spirit of the remaining Creeks, who, after their submission, were compelled to give up more than two thirds of their hunting-grounds.

14. **Events at Sea.**—Again the American navy raised the spirits of the country, cast down by the disasters of the army. On the 25th of February, the sloop of war Hornet,

12. Where have we already heard of Tecumtha? Where was he busy in 1813? How did the Creek War begin? Where were the settlements of the Creeks? How was the massacre at Fort Mims revenged in November?

13. State what is said of the energy of the Indians. Where had the Indians fortified themselves in March, 1814? What occurred here? What was the result of this battle? Notice on the map the places mentioned.

Captain Lawrence, at the mouth of the Demerara River, captured the British brig Peacock after an action of 15 minutes. So terrible was the fire of the Hornet, that the Peacock sank in a few minutes after she struck her flag.

15. When Captain Lawrence arrived in the United States in the spring, he was promoted to the command of the frigate Chesapeake, which lay at Boston, getting ready for sea. The British frigate Shannon, Captain Broke, with a highly disciplined crew, was cruising off Boston Harbor waiting for the Chesapeake, and Broke sent a challenge to Lawrence, offering to fight him in any latitude and longitude he might choose. This letter, however, did not reach Lawrence. Although the Chesapeake was badly manned with an untrained crew, and short of officers, Lawrence sailed out of Boston Harbor to meet him, June 1. The engagement took place some 30 miles from Boston Light, and ended, after a short but sanguinary battle of but 15 minutes, in the capture of the Chesapeake, and the killing or wounding of 146 of her crew; among the latter was Lawrence. His last words, when being carried below, mortally wounded, "Don't give up the ship," have become famous in American history.

16. This misfortune did not come singly. About the same time, the United States, Macedonian, and Hornet, in attempting to get to sea from New York through Long Island Sound, were driven into the harbor of New London, and there blockaded and rendered useless by a British squadron. In the month of August, the American sloop of war Argus was captured by the Pelican, while cruising in the British Channel. In September, the Enterprise, of 12 guns, Captain Burrows, captured the British brig Boxer, Captain Blythe, off the coast of Maine. Both commanders were slain in the action.

---

14. Where was the first naval battle of 1813? Describe the action.

15. How was Lawrence honored for his victory over the Peacock? Where was the Chesapeake? What British vessel was off the harbor? What challenge was sent by Captain Broke? What was the condition of the Chesapeake? Did this prevent Lawrence from meeting him? Where did the engagement take place? How did it end? What were his dying words?

16. What misfortune befell three American ships? What other disaster occurred at sea in August? What victory occurred in September?

SECTION IV.

EVENTS OF 1814-15, AND TO THE CLOSE OF THE ADMINISTRATION.

1. **Niagara Frontier.**—The campaign of the year 1814 was opened by the Americans on the Niagara frontier. In the beginning of May General Brown moved to that river from Sackett's Harbor with some 2000 men, and, after his arrival, his force was increased to more than 5000. He then crossed the Niagara, and Fort Erie surrendered to him without bloodshed, July 3. Next day, General Scott led the advance against the British under General Riall, at Chippewa, 15 miles distant. At midnight Scott was joined by General Brown with the main body, and a sharp engagement was fought on the following day, July 5th, in which the British were defeated with the loss of 500 men; the loss of the Americans was about 300.

2. Riall then fell back to Burlington Heights, and the Americans moved forward and occupied Queenstown, but soon after returned to Chippewa. The British marched to seek the Americans; and General Brown, although in less force than the British, at once ordered an advance, and General Scott, who was in front with 1000 men, unexpectedly found himself near the British army at Bridgewater on the 25th of July.

3. The enemy were strongly posted, but Scott immediately attacked them; and, on the arrival of the main body of the Americans, the fight became general. The most bloody part of the battle was fought for the possession of a slight elevation on which the British had planted a battery, whose guns commanded the field. The Americans captured this at the point of the bayonet, and thrice the British, re-enforced by troops under General Drummond, in the darkness of the night tried to retake it, but in vain. At mid-

---

1. When and where did the campaign of 1814 open? What was the first movement of the Americans? What occurred on the Niagara? What movement was next made? Describe the battle. Who commanded the British?

2. What were the next movements of both armies? What change was made in the English army? How did Brown act on learning the news? Who led the advance? Where and when did he come up with the British?

night, after the loss of more than 800 men on both sides, the ground was left in possession of the Americans. This midnight battle of Lundy's Lane, although glorious for the American army, proved a barren victory. The Americans were now so worn out that they could not drag off the captured cannon. Generals Brown and Scott were both wounded, and General Ripley next day withdrew the American army to Fort Erie. Here General Gaines soon after arrived and took command.

4. General Drummond, on the 4th of August, laid siege to Fort Erie. On the 15th he made a midnight assault, but was beaten back with the loss of 1000 men. Not discouraged, he still pushed forward his works; and, meanwhile, General Brown, who had recovered from his wounds, assumed command of the garrison. On the 17th of September the latter made a sortie from the fort, destroyed the enemy's works, and captured 400 prisoners; after which, Drummond soon raised the siege, and retired across Chippewa Creek. In October, General Izard arrived from Lake Champlain, by the way of Sackett's Harbor, with 4000 men, and took command of the Americans; but he did nothing but face the British at the Chippewa for several weeks. In November, fearing that Drummond would be re-enforced, he blew up Fort Erie, and recrossed to the American side. Fort Niagara was left in possession of the British.

5. **Events on and near Lake Champlain.**—When General Izard left Plattsburg, General Macomb took command of some 3000 men that remained. The English troops in Canada were meanwhile increased by the arrival of veteran soldiers, who, under Wellington, had been fighting Napoleon's armies in Spain. With 12,000 of these, General Prevost advanced by land against Macomb at Plattsburg on the

---

3. How did the battle begin? What was the centre of the contest? What is said of the struggle for this? When did the battle end, and with what result? Of what benefit was this victory to the Americans? Why was this? Why did General Ripley assume command? Who superseded General Ripley, and at what place?

4. Describe Drummond's movements and success. Who soon took command of Fort Erie? What spirited movement did he make? What effect did this produce on the British? Who arrived with re-enforcements? What did he accomplish? What did he do in November? What became of Fort Niagara? Where was Fort Niagara situated? See map, p. 200.

11th of September. Macomb, on his approach, fell behind the Saranac, a rapid stream which could not be forded, and the British spent four days in erecting batteries and preparing to cross.

6. The British plan of attack provided that Captain Downie, with his squadron, should force an entrance into the Harbor of Plattsburg, defended by an American squadron under Commodore MacDonough, at the same time that Prevost should attempt the crossing of the Saranac.

BRITISH ATTEMPTING TO CROSS THE SARANAC. From an old Print.

On the 11th of September Downie joined battle with Mac Donough, and, after a severe engagement of two hours and a quarter, the British commander surrendered. While the battle was going on in the harbor, Prevost was trying to cross the Sáranac, but was beaten back at every point. During the night the enemy retreated in disorder, leaving their sick and wounded behind, and a large part

5. What troops were left by Izard at Plattsburg, and under what command? What was the state of the English army in Canada? To what use were these troops put? What preparations did Macomb make to meet them?

of their military stores. Their whole loss was about 2500 men.

7. **Chesapeake Bay and Neighborhood.**—In the month of August, a British fleet, under Admiral Cochrane, appeared in Chesapeake Bay, and landed General Ross, with 4500 men, at Benedict, on the shores of the Patuxent River. He at once marched to attack Washington, the capital, fifty miles distant, but met with no resistance until he reached Bladensburg, six miles northeast from Washington, on the 24th of August. Here General Winder had stationed some militia to stop his advance, but these fled at the first fire. Commodore Barney, with his marines, and some pieces of artillery, stood firm, and checked the enemy for some time; but in the end Barney was wounded and captured, and his small force dispersed. The affair at Bladensburg was little more than a skirmish. Ross then marched to Washington, where, after burning the Capitol, the President's house, and other buildings, he retreated stealthily to his ships at Benedict.

VICINITY OF WASHINGTON, 1814.

8. A portion of the British fleet sailed up the Potomac as far as Alexandria, and captured 21 merchant vessels, 16,000 barrels of flour, and 1000 hhds. of tobacco. The rest of the fleet, with the troops on board, ascended to the head of Chesapeake Bay to attack Baltimore; and General Ross landed at North Point, on the Patapsco River, 14 miles below. While the troops were to move by land, the fleet was to attack Fort M'Henry, that defended the city, two miles distant; General Ross was killed at North Point September

6. What was the British plan of attack? When, and with what success, did Downie perform his part? What was Prevost's success on land? What were the British compelled to do?

7. What arrival took place in August? What was the chief point aimed at by the expedition? What resistance did Ross meet with? Where is Bladensburg? What preparations were made at Bladensburg to receive him? Where is the Patuxent River?

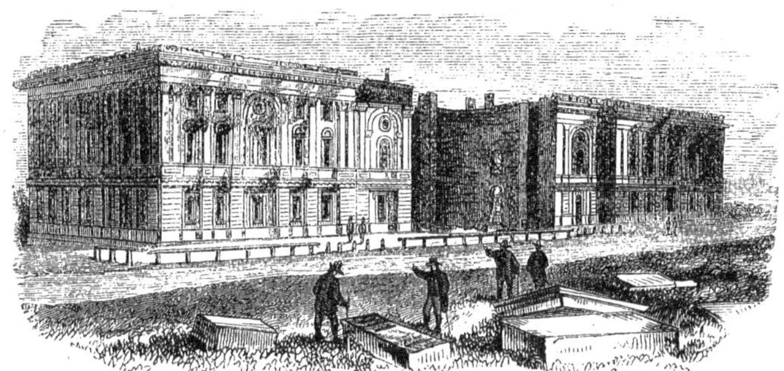

REMAINS OF THE CAPITOL AFTER THE FIRE.

12th, while riding in front to reconnoitre, and a sharp encounter followed, in which 200 or 300 fell on each side. Next day the British advanced to the city.

9. The same day, the 13th, the fleet bombarded Fort M'Henry, but without effect. In the night, the British force, without attempting an attack on the city, retired to their shipping, and sailed away. It was on board one of these British ships, during the bombardment, that the national song, "The Star Spangled Banner," was composed by an American gentleman, Francis S. Key, who had gone thither to ask the release of a prisoner, and was detained until the fleet was ready to sail.

VICINITY OF BALTIMORE, 1814.

10. **Operations of the British on the Coast.**—Baltimore and Washington were not the only points that suffered from the British fleet and armies. The coast of Maine was laid waste, Stonington was bombarded, the fisheries were suppressed,

8. In what was a portion of the British fleet meanwhile employed? Against what place did Ross next move? Where did he land? What was the plan of attack? How far was Fort M'Henry from Baltimore? What happened at North Point September 12th? What advance was made next day?

9. What was the fleet engaged in while the British were marching on Baltimore? What was the end of the expedition? What incident is mentioned in connection with the bombardment of Fort M'Henry?

and the salt-works on Cape Cod were only saved by heavy payments to the attacking force. Maritime commerce was so completely destroyed by the British blockade that the lights in the coast light-houses were ordered to be extinguished, because they were of use only to British ships. All the sea-ports on the coast were threatened, and were more or less fortified and defended by American militia.

11. **Operations in the South.** — Florida was at this time in possession of Spain, and regarded as neutral territory. Great Britain had done so much for the Spaniards in Europe during the great wars of Napoleon that she had no difficulty in entering Florida, and from that point annoying the United States. A British fleet arrived at Pensacola in August, took possession of the forts with consent of the Spaniards, and fitted out an expedition against Fort Bowyer, at the entrance to Mobile Bay, commanded by Major Lawrence. On the 15th of September they attacked this, and were repulsed with the loss of a vessel and a number of men. General Jackson, at the head of military operations in the South, acting with his usual energy, determined to expel the British from Pensacola. Marching rapidly, he entered the town with little resistance, November 7. The British commander shortly after blew up Fort Barancas, six miles below, and took to his ships.

12. Jackson then hastened to New Orleans, which was threatened by the British. Here he found the people in the greatest state of alarm, and it required a display of Jackson's iron will to bring things to order throughout Louisiana. He proclaimed martial law, collected and trained the militia, built fortifications, and prepared to make the best defense with the means at his disposal. While he was in the midst of his preparations, a British fleet entered Lake Borgne, the shortest passage by water to the vicinity of New Orleans. On board were 12,000 soldiers, and 4000 ma-

---

10. What other points on the coast suffered? What effect had the war on commerce? What is mentioned to show how utterly this was ruined?

11. In whose possession was the territory of Florida? How was it regarded? What is neutral territory? What use did Great Britain make of it? Why did Spain permit this? What preparations were made by the British in Florida? What success did they meet with? What celebrated man was in command of the American army in the South? What was his prompt determination? How did he succeed?

rines and sailors. The troops were many of them veterans, commanded by General Pakenham, and other able generals who had fought under Wellington in Spain.

13. To resist this formidable expedition, there was an American flotilla on Lake Borgne, and 5000 troops under Jackson, only 1000 of whom were regulars. The British barges, after a hard fight, captured the flotilla, and opened the way to the city, December 14. On the 22d, 2400 of the enemy, under General Keane, took post on the river bank, nine miles below New Orleans. Jackson fell on the advanced party on the following night, and, after inflicting a loss of 400 men on the British, retired, leaving 223 of his own force killed, wounded, and prisoners.

14. Four miles below the city, behind a deep and broad trench that extended from the Mississippi River to a swamp, Jackson threw up intrenchments. To defend these, he had now under his command a force of 6000 men. The solid land over which the enemy were compelled to move to the attack was less than a mile in width, and completely exposed to Jackson's fire.

15. The British twice tried the effect of a heavy cannonade, but this failed to produce any impression. On the 8th of January Pakenham ordered an assault, and pushed his troops forward across the open space against the American breastworks. The fire was so severe that the British were literally mowed down by the cannon-shot. Steadily these brave men closed their ranks and moved onward; but, as they neared the works, the Tennessee backwoodsmen opened upon them with their unerring rifles, and the British troops, broken and unable to face this, fled in confusion. General Pakenham was killed while trying to restore order. His next in command fell, and nearly 2000 were killed or wounded. General Lambert then collected the scattered troops,

12. To what point did Jackson next hasten? What state of things did he find here? To what measures did he resort to restore order? What occurred while he was busy at this? What was the size of the British force? What is said of the troops and their commanders?

13. What preparations were made to resist the British? What happened to the flotilla? What energetic movement was made by Jackson?

14. Describe the preparations made by Jackson for the defense of New Orleans. What force was behind these fortifications?

and withdrew to his shipping. The loss of the Americans was only seven killed and six wounded. Jackson's entire loss in the whole campaign was but 333.

BATTLE OF NEW ORLEANS. From an old Print.

16. Such was the remarkable battle of New Orleans, and the last land battle of the war. It is painful to think that the lives of so many brave men should have been sacrificed three weeks after a treaty of peace had been signed. But there was no ocean telegraph in those days, nor any swift steamers to bring the news. On the 14th of December, 1814, a treaty of peace was signed at Ghent by commissioners of Great Britain and the United States, and the news arrived on February 11. On the 18th peace was proclaimed by the President. The war began about the impressment of seamen and the rights of neutral nations; but the treaty said not a word about them, and the chief causes of the war were left to be settled at some other time. The people and the

15. What was made on these works? What was the great movement of the 8th of January? Describe the attack. What was the British loss? What was the loss of the Americans? What was done by Pakenham's successor? What was Jackson's entire loss in the campaign?

government were rejoiced at the news of peace, and manifested their joy in the most extravagant manner.

17. **Engagements at Sea, 1814–15.**—The United States frigate Essex, Commodore Porter, after a long and successful cruise, anchored in the harbor of Valparaiso, on the Pacific. Here, in March, 1814, she was attacked by a British frigate and a sloop of war, and was captured, but not until after a most bloody struggle. In January, 1815, Decatur, in the frigate President, soon after leaving the port of New York, was chased and captured, at the close of a long running fight, by a British squadron of five vessels, on the south shore of Long Island, but not until Decatur's ship was completely crippled.

18. In February, 1815, on a moonlight night, off Lisbon, Portugal, the frigate Constitution captured two British sloops of war, the Cyane, of 24 guns, and the Levant, of 18 guns, with a loss to herself of only 3 killed and 12 wounded. On March 23, the Hornet, Captain Biddle, captured, near the Cape of Good Hope, the British brig of war Penguin, of nearly equal force. The Penguin was so much cut up that Captain Biddle was compelled to destroy her. On the 30th of June, four months after the proclamation of peace, the American vessel Peacock, Captain Warrington, captured the Nautilus off the Straits of Sunda. He was informed before the capture that peace had been made, but he insisted that the Nautilus should strike her flag. Next day the vessel was restored to the British. This was the last event of naval warfare.

---

19. It has already been said that the American people were filled with joy at the news of peace. The country was indeed in a deplorable condition; trade was well-nigh ruin-

---

16. What is the sad reflection concerning the battle of New Orleans? Why would such a thing not be possible in our own times? When and where was a treaty of peace signed? About what had the war commenced? How were these points settled in the treaty? How was the news received in the United States?

17. State what is said of the frigate Essex. Who commanded her? What happened to the frigate President? Who commanded her? When were these two engagements fought?

18. How many naval engagements were fought in 1815 after the treaty of peace? Why was this? Describe the action in February; of March 23; of June 30. What is especially noticeable about the last? Where is Lisbon? Straits of Sunda?

ed; commerce was gone; little specie was to be seen, and the paper currency commanded no confidence. From its commencement the war had been very unpopular with the Federal party generally, and particularly with the New England States. It destroyed their trade, their fisheries, and their vessels at sea. The misfortunes of the American armies during the first year furnished them strong ground of complaint and anxiety.

20. **Hartford Convention.**—This dissatisfaction kept increasing as the war went on, and toward the end of the year 1814, when affairs looked very gloomy—for the Capitol had been burned, the American army had recrossed the Canadian frontier, and the British were threatening New Orleans—a New England Convention assembled at Hartford, Connecticut, December 14. It was composed of 26 delegates, all of whom, save three, were from Massachusetts, Rhode Island, Connecticut, and New Hampshire.

21. By the friends of the war it was charged against the Convention that it intended to make a separate peace with Great Britain, and leave the other states to continue the contest. This intention, carried out, would have been nothing more nor less than the withdrawal of New England from the Union. After a session of 20 days, the delegates prepared and sent out an address, moderate in its tone, and proposing nothing of the kind charged against them. The address was mainly a statement of wrongs, and recommended an alteration in the Constitution. But the war party spared no pains to expose the Convention to the hatred of the country, and for many years to be called a Hartford Convention Federalist was a name of deep reproach. By its opposition to the war, the Federal party was broken up.

22. **The Military Movements of the War.**—The grand plan

---

19. Where and with what party had the war been very unpopular? Why? What increased their discontent?

20. When did this discontent reach its highest point? State what was the condition of the struggle at that time. How did the dissatisfaction show itself in New England? Of whom was this Convention composed?

21. What was charged against this Convention by its enemies? What would this have been if carried out? What was the real character of its proceedings? What was the nature of the address? How far did this soften its enemies? What effect did the war have on the Federalist party?

of the American government, throughout the war, was to strike at Great Britain through Canada. The invasion of this employed nearly all the men and the energy of the government until the middle of the year 1814. It began with Hull's crossing the Detroit River in 1812, and it ended in October, 1814, by General Izard's blowing up Fort Erie and recrossing to the American side.

23. Throughout the war, the British troops generally outnumbered the Americans. The honor of the country was preserved by small armies, and by battles which, in the great wars of Europe, or in our own times, would have been little more than skirmishes. But a number of them were really very hard-fought battles—the Thames, Chippewa, Lundy's Lane, or Bridgewater, Fort Erie, Plattsburg. The generals who sustained the honor of the American army were General Brown, some years afterward commander-in-chief of the American army; General Scott the same; General Ripley, General Macomb, and Generals Harrison and Jackson, both of whom were afterward elected presidents.

24. **Naval Operations of the War.**—It is noticeable that the most brilliant victories of the war—those on the ocean and the lakes—were gained by that branch of the service which was very unpopular with Jefferson and his party. The nation had reason to be proud of the navy. The victories had been gained on an element where England had long claimed to reign supreme. The British people, on the other hand, were grievously annoyed, and tried in all ways to dull the edge of their defeat. They said that the American ships carried heavier guns and more men, and claimed that whenever these had been equal in the vessels of the two nations, the British had proved superior. But this did not prevent the Americans from rejoicing greatly over the humiliation of the English navy.

---

22. What was the great military plan of the American government? How is this seen? With what did it begin and end?

23. What is said of the battles of the war as compared with those of Europe? Which are instanced as hard-fought battles? Give the names of the most distinguished generals.

24. What point is worthy of notice in reviewing the war? Why did the victories of the navy give the Americans so much satisfaction? How did the British look on them? What excuses did they offer for the defeat of their vessels?

25. Privateering against British commerce was carried on with considerable success, and large fortunes were made in this business. The chief obstacle to their complete success was, that the American privateers could not bring their prizes into United States ports on account of the British blockading vessels. Hence an immense number of the captured ships were burned at sea. The whole number of British vessels captured on the lakes and ocean by privateers and national vessels was 1750. The British had not been far behind in activity; they captured 1683.

26. **Events after the Close of the War.**—When war broke out with England, the Dey of Algiers, under pretense that his presents were not what he had demanded, declared war. He captured an American vessel, and reduced her crew to slavery. The United States were too busy to attend to this until the end of the war; and on the 9th of May, 1815, Decatur was sent with a fleet of nine vessels to the Mediterranean. Near Gibraltar he captured an Algerine frigate, June 17th, and soon afterward appeared off Algiers. The Dey, terrified at the sight of the fleet, signed a treaty on the quarter-deck of Decatur's ship, surrendering the prisoners, and giving up in future all claims to tribute. Tunis and Tripoli were likewise compelled to pay for American vessels which they had allowed British ships to capture in their harbors.

27. In the fall of 1816, James Monroe, of Virginia, was elected President, and Daniel D. Tompkins, of New York, Vice-President. Both of these gentlemen represented the same political opinions as Madison's administration. In the month of December, Indiana, another state, formed out of the original Northwest Territory, was admitted into the Union.

---

25. What was pursued with great energy during the war? What interfered with the profits of privateering? What were the comparative losses of vessels on both sides?

26. What power took advantage of the war with England to harass our commerce? What instance is given? When and how did the United States notice this? How did Decatur punish the Dey? How were Tunis and Tripoli humbled?

27. Who were elected in 1816? To what party did the successful candidates belong? What important addition to the United States was made in December?

REVIEW QUESTIONS.—MADISON'S ADMINISTRATION.

1. Who succeeded Jefferson as President, and state what is said of him?
2. What was the conduct of France and England at the commencement of his administration?
3. What great contest was taking place in Europe at this time?
4. Where and in what way did Great Britain give the United States great annoyance?
5. What led to the Indian troubles in the Northwest?
6. Who were the Indian leaders, and what was their character?
7. Sketch the principal events in the Indian War.
8. State the grievances that led Congress to declare war against England.
9. Why did England need to impress American seamen?
10. When was war declared?
11. How long did actual hostilities in the War of 1812 continue, giving date of first and last battle?
12. To what extent was the war popular throughout the country?
13. Why was New England opposed to the war?
14. In what two parts of the country were military operations mainly conducted?
15. In which of them was the greatest amount of fighting done?
16. What was the great object of the United States government in its military movements in the North?
17. At what points on the frontier do we find the severest fighting during the war?
18. Which of these battles was fought within sound of Niagara Falls? Date?
19. How far was the invasion of Canada a military success?
20. Name the persons afterward distinguished who first appear in connection with events on the Northern frontier.
21. What were the British movements on the Chesapeake and that neighborhood in 1813?
22. What great disgrace was the American government compelled to endure in the year 1814?
23. Give the origin and principal events of the Creek War.
24. State, in a general way, the extent of the Creek country, as it was called. In what territory did it lie?
25. Give a brief account of British movements on and near Lake Champlain, and the result?
26. To what point was the seat of war changed at the close of 1814, and by whom?
27. How were the movements there repelled?
28. Who was the hero of events in that direction?
29. To what extent were the Americans successful on land during the war, stating this by successive years?
30. What successes redeemed the misfortunes on land?
31. Name a few of the most important naval engagements at sea and on the lakes, and the years in which they occurred.
32. Describe two or three of these that you consider most important.
33. Why were the naval successes considered of so much importance?
34. How many persons were afterward elevated to the presidency on account of their conduct in this war?
35. When did the war terminate?
36. Sketch the direction of the campaigns during each year.
37. Name the leading events of each year.
38. How did the treaty dispose of the questions that produced the war?
39. What occurred at Hartford in December, 1814?
40. What party did this Convention utterly break up?
41. What states were added to the Union during Madison's administration? Give months and years.
42. Out of what original territories were these states formed?
43. Who were elected President and Vice-President?

CHAPTER VI.

FROM THE YEAR 1817 TO THE BEGINNING OF THE MEXICAN WAR.

SECTION I.

MONROE'S ADMINISTRATION, 1817–1825.

1. JAMES MONROE had been an officer in the Revolutionary War, afterward a member of Congress, and latterly Secretary of War under Madison. He was a man of remarkably courteous manners and pleasing appearance. So popular was he, that both Republicans and those who were formerly Federalists united to elect him. His entire administration, in its peaceful relations with foreign powers, presented a striking contrast to the stormy times of Madison.

PRESIDENT MONROE.

2. In December, 1817, the western part of Mississippi Territory was admitted into the Union as the State of Mississippi, and the eastern portion was erected into Alabama Territory. This was presently the scene of an Indian war. Toward the end of the year 1817, the Seminole Indians, living in the Spanish Territory of Florida, assisted by the Creeks, committed depredations on the borders of Georgia and Alabama Territory. General Gaines, commanding the United States posts in that vicinity, attempted to reduce the Indians to obedience; but his force was not sufficient, and he was compelled to ask for aid.

---

1. What offices had Monroe held? What is said of his personal manners and popularity? What remark is made about his administration?

2. What state was admitted in 1817? What Territory was formed? What Indian war broke out in 1817? Who attempted to bring them to obedience? Where did General Gaines appear previously in this history?

3. General Jackson, in command of the Southern Department, was ordered to call out the militia and proceed to the scene of disturbance. At the head of about 1000 mounted Tennessee troops, in the month of March, 1818, he entered the Indian country, and in a short time laid waste their villages, and captured or destroyed their corn and cattle.

4. Thinking that the Spaniards had incited the Indians, Jackson entered Florida, and appeared before St. Marks, which he compelled to surrender. Soon after he seized two British subjects—Arbuthnot and Ambuster—and put them on trial before a court-martial, by which they were found guilty of inciting the Indians to war, and of supplying the means to carry it on. Both were sentenced to be hung, and were promptly executed.

5. Jackson, in the month of May, seized the town of Pensacola, and captured Fort Barrancas near it after a short resistance. The Spanish government was very indignant at Jackson's entering the territory of Florida in this warlike manner, but his conduct was fully approved by the government and people of the United States. It was now very evident that Spain could not long retain her hold on Florida. In the year 1819 it was ceded to the United States by treaty for 5,000,000 dollars, and, at the same time, the eastern boundary of Mexico was fixed at the Sabine River. In this year Alabama was admitted into the Union, making the twenty-second state. Maine, formerly a part of Massachusetts, was admitted in the year following.

6. The question of negro slavery was fast rising into one of national importance; and the states were beginning to be known as North and South, according as they favored the use of free or slave labor. In the Northern States the employment of the latter had nearly died out; on the other hand, it was steadily on the increase throughout the South-

---

3. What distinguished man was appointed to the duty? What force was placed at his disposal? What was his success?

4. What vigorous movement did he make, and why? Give an account of the affair of Arbuthnot and Ambuster.

5. What other energetic movement was made by Jackson in Florida? How was Jackson's conduct regarded by the American people and by Spain? What important change in territory took place in 1821? When was Alabama admitted? What other state was admitted in 1820?

ern States, where it received a powerful stimulus at the close of the previous century. In the year 1793, Eli Whitney, a native of Connecticut, invented a machine called a cotton gin, to separate the fibre from the seed, an operation which had previously been performed by hand. So slow and costly was the old process, that, but for Whitney's invention, the expense of cleaning upland cotton must have put a stop to its cultivation.

WHITNEY'S COTTON GIN, 1793.

7. From that year the cultivation of cotton spread with astonishing rapidity in all the states and territories south of Virginia, and year by year it employed more slave labor. The production of tobacco and rice depended also on the help of the negro, and the people of those states where these three great staples were produced considered slaves a necessity. It is to be remembered that in the great Northwest Territory negro slavery was prohibited by act of Con-

6. On what question had a division sprung up in the country? What is said of the two sections? What largely developed cotton culture in the South? What was this machine? What is said of the old process of cleaning cotton by hand?

gress; but in the territories formed south of that, slavery was sanctioned by law.

8. In New England, New York, New Jersey, Pennsylvania, and also in the Northwest States, where slave labor was not deemed a necessity, there was a growing feeling against slavery. In some of these states there had been, from the establishment of the government, a marked opposition to it, and this had expressed itself in Congress several times. This feeling showed itself powerfully in the session of 1818–19, when the bill authorizing the Territory of Missouri to form a state constitution was before the House. A motion was made to add a clause providing that there should be no slaves allowed in the new state. This was passed by a small majority, but failed in the Senate.

9. Next session the debate was renewed on the Missouri question. Again the House passed the bill restricting the introduction of slaves. The Senate returned it to the House with the clause prohibiting slavery struck out, and, as a concession to the anti-slavery sentiment, had inserted the provision that no slavery should exist in any states to be formed thereafter north of 36° 30′. After long debates, which were carried on so warmly as to threaten the stability of the Union, this clause was accepted as a compromise by a decided majority, and Missouri was allowed to come in as a slave state. This famous agreement is known as the Missouri Compromise, and was passed March 3d, 1820.

10. Next in importance to this was the question of the tariff, or a protective duty in favor of home manufactures. Soon after the close of the war, in the year 1816, a tariff bill was carried through Congress by the influence of the Southern States, against the wishes of the greater part of the North. It was particularly opposed by the Eastern States, which were largely engaged in commerce and navi-

---

7. How did Whitney's invention affect slavery? What other staples depended on slave labor? What celebrated provision was made in establishing the Northwest Territory? What was provided in territories south of this?

8. In what states was there a growing feeling against slavery? Why? Had this feeling shown itself in a public way? When and where did it show itself particularly? In what way? How did this motion succeed?

9. When was the debate in Congress renewed? How was the question settled? By what name is this great act known? When was it passed?

gation. In the year 1820, a revision of the tariff, increasing the duties, was proposed in Congress; and the Southern States, originally in favor of a protective duty, changed ground. During the same year Monroe was re-elected for a second term.

11. Another important measure of Monroe's administration was the recognition of the South American republics. Spain held in Mexico and South America an immense territory under her control. The people of this vast region revolted, and, having formed separate republics, gained their independence, and their nationality was acknowledged by the United States in the year 1822. Next year President Monroe announced in his message that "the American continents are not to be considered as subjects for future colonization by any European powers." This claim, that America belongs to republicanism, is called the "Monroe doctrine."

12. The year 1824 is memorable for the visit made by Lafayette, the friend of Washington, to the United States. Wherever he went he was received with the highest honor; and, on his departure to France, an American frigate was placed at his disposal by the government. Mr. Monroe's second term was drawing to a close, amid great political excitement as to his successor, and four candidates were put in nomination for the presidency—Andrew Jackson, John Quincy Adams, Wm. H. Crawford, and Henry Clay. None of these having received a majority of the popular vote, the election, as provided for in such cases by the Constitution, went into the House of Representatives in Congress, and John Quincy Adams, of Massachusetts, was chosen President for four years. John C. Calhoun, of South Carolina, had been elected Vice-President by the people.

---

10. What other great question was next discussed? When was a tariff first enacted by Congress? What position did the states at first occupy on this question? What change took place in 1820, and why? Who was elected in the fall?

11. What other important measure marked this administration? What great changes took place in Spanish territory? When were they recognized as nations? What is the "Monroe doctrine?"

12. For what is the year 1824 memorable? How was he received by the people and honored by the United States government? How was Mr. Monroe's second term closing? How many, and what candidates were put in nomination for the Presidency? In what way was the election decided? Why did it go to Congress? Who was chosen Vice-President by the people?

SECTION II.

ADAMS'S ADMINISTRATION, 1825–1829.

1. JOHN QUINCY ADAMS was the son of John Adams, the second President of the United States. From his early youth he received an excellent training in statesmanship, and was well fitted for the duties of his high office. He served as minister to the Netherlands, Portugal, Prussia, Russia, and England, was a member of the United States Senate, and Secretary of State under Monroe. During his administration the country was prosperous, but party spirit raged with great violence.

PRESIDENT JOHN Q. ADAMS.

2. Georgia had for some time been involved in trouble with the general government, and with the Creek Indians, about the lands of the latter, which the United States had agreed to purchase for the benefit of Georgia. These the government at length purchased in February, 1826, and the Creeks agreed to remove to lands provided for them west of the Mississippi. On the 4th of July, the same year, and the fiftieth anniversary of independence, the two ex-presidents—John Adams and Thomas Jefferson—died within a few hours of each other. The former had reached the age of 90, the latter was 82.

3. Toward the end of Adams's administration the debates on the tariff question in Congress were again revived. In the year 1828, a tariff with very high protective duties was passed. This bill was bitterly opposed by the greater part of the South, and defended with equal zeal by the Mid-

1. Sketch the career of John Q. Adams. What remark is made about his administration?

2. What trouble had arisen in Georgia? How was it settled, and when? What remarkable event occurred the same year?

DANIEL WEBSTER.

dle and New England States. Massachusetts, from being opposed to protection, now changed in its favor, Daniel Webster, of Massachusetts, being her eloquent and powerful representative.

4. In the midst of intense party feeling, growing out of these debates, the presidential election took place. General Jackson and President Adams were the rival candidates, and the former was elected by a great majority. John C. Calhoun, of South Carolina, was chosen Vice-President. This was regarded as a victory over the protective policy, and a triumph of the South over the North.

SECTION III.

JACKSON'S ADMINISTRATION, 1829–1837.

1. GENERAL JACKSON, whose military career has already been given, began his administration with the same fearless energy that marked his past life. The charter of the Bank of the United States was about to expire. In his first annual message, December, 1829, he took ground against renewing this charter, because he believed it was contrary to the Constitution of the United States. It was a bold step, because the bank was very powerful by means of its branches throughout the country, and had many warm friends. At first the bank gained the day, for Congress, in the year 1832, passed a bill to recharter it. Jackson refused to sign this

---

3. What debate was revived, and when? What was passed in 1828? What ground was taken by the North and South on this question? What is said of Massachusetts?

4. How was this measure received by the country? Who were the rival candidates for the presidency? Who were chosen President and Vice-President? How was this choice regarded?

bill, and, by doing so, conquered, because Congress was unable to pass it over his veto by a two thirds vote.

PRESIDENT JACKSON.

2. War with the Seminole Indians in Florida broke out in 1835. The government wished to remove them from their territory in Florida to land west of the Mississippi, but they were unwilling to go. Their great leader was Osceola, a brave, active, and crafty chief. General Clinch, stationed at Fort Drane, was threatened by the Seminoles, and Major Dade, with 117 men, was sent from Tampa Bay to his assistance. While Dade was on his march, he was suddenly attacked by the Indians, on the 28th of December, 1835, and all but four were killed. The same day, many miles distant from the scene of Dade's massacre, General Thomson and some of his friends were dining quietly outside of Fort King. Without warning, Osceola and a war party fell on them, and killed and scalped them all.

SCENE OF THE SEMINOLE WAR.

3. Three days after, on December 31, General Clinch had a battle with the Indians at Withlacoochee, 90 miles north of Tampa Bay. In February, 1836, General Gaines defeated them near the same place with severe loss. The Creeks joined the Seminoles in May,

1. Mention the principal events in Jackson's past career. How did he begin his administration? What did he at once attack, and why? Why was this a bold act? Who won the day at first, and how? What course did Jackson pursue? Who in turn triumphed, and why?

2. In what Territory were the Seminole Indians at this time? When did war commence with them? What was the cause of this? Who was their leader? State what is said of Dade's massacre. What other massacre showed that there was a well-concerted plan among the Indians?

1836, and this extended the war into Georgia and Alabama. Murders and devastation followed. Houses were burned, the fields were laid waste, and the settlers fled in terror from the vengeance of the red man.

4. The Creeks were in a short time severely punished by the United States troops, and submitted. Soon after, they allowed themselves to be transported west of the Mississippi. Still the Seminoles kept up the war. As fast as they were beaten by the troops they retired farther into the swamps and everglades, where it was difficult to follow them. In November, 1836, Governor Call, of Florida, with 550 men, found a large body of them in a swamp near the ground of Dade's massacre. Here he fought a severe battle, and finally repulsed them; but the war still went on.

5. Jackson's courage was again put to the test in 1832. During that year new duties were added to the tariff, and the people of South Carolina broke out into almost open rebellion. They resolved in Convention that the tariff acts were unconstitutional, and therefore "null and void;" and that if the government should attempt to collect the revenues in the harbor of Charleston, it would be prevented by force of arms. They also threatened to secede from the Union, and made preparations for war. The great leaders in these acts were John C. Calhoun, late Vice-President, and Colonel Hayne, both being at that time United States senators from South Carolina.

JOHN C. CALHOUN.

3. What check did the Seminoles receive a few days after? What battle was fought in February, 1836? What assistance did the Seminoles receive? How did this affect the war? State what followed.

4. What befell the Creeks? How did the Seminoles continue the war? What battle took place in November, 1856? Where was the scene of Dade's massacre? Did this end the war?

5. Where and on what did excitement break out in 1832? What resolutions did the South Carolinians pass? What did they threaten to do? Who were the leaders in this?

6. President Jackson acted with his usual energy and decision. He issued a proclamation denying the right of any state to set at defiance the laws of Congress, and warned the "nullifiers" of the danger of their course. He ordered a large body of troops to assemble at Charleston, under General Scott, and a ship of war was sent thither. Before blood was shed South Carolina fell back from her warlike position. In February, 1833, Mr. Clay, in Congress, brought forward a bill for the gradual reduction of the tariff, and for a time the discontent of the South was allayed.

7. While the excitement was at its height in Congress about the Bank of the United States, and the people of South Carolina were declaring nullification, the Sacs and Foxes, tribes of Indians living in what is now Wisconsin, commenced war on the whites in the spring of 1832. They were led by a chief named Black Hawk, and the short war that followed is known as the "Black Hawk War." The chief was, after some severe skirmishes, taken prisoner, and the Indians were removed beyond the Mississippi. The trouble lasted little more than six months, and was terminated in October, 1832.

8. In the fall of 1832, General Jackson was elected President for a second term, and Martin Van Buren, of New York, was chosen Vice-President. Jackson's contest with the power of the Bank of the United States did not end with his veto of the bill renewing its charter. In 1833 he ordered the removal of all the public money in its vaults to different state banks. This caused a great outcry from the friends of the bank and from the party opposed to the President. It also produced great distress among the mercantile community. Jackson, however, remained firm to his purpose, and, with the help of the House of Representatives in Congress, finally carried his point.

---

6. How did Jackson act? What was the spirit of his proclamation? What order did he issue? What fortunately prevented bloodshed?

7. What war broke out during these excitements? Who was their leader? How and when was it terminated? How long did the war last?

8. Who was chosen President in the fall of 1832? Who Vice-President? When and on what grounds was the quarrel between Jackson and the United States Bank renewed? What effect did this produce? How far did this turn Jackson from his course? How did the struggle end?

9. He was scarcely through with this struggle when, in 1834, he determined to call France to account. That government agreed, in 1831, to pay $5,000,000 for injuries done to American commerce during Napoleon's wars; but, for some years, the money was not forthcoming. President Jackson promptly ordered the American minister at Paris to demand his passports, and at the same time he urged Congress to make reprisals on French vessels. These active measures alarmed the French, and the money was paid.

10. In the fall of 1836, the election for President to succeed Andrew Jackson took place, when Martin Van Buren, of New York, was chosen President, and Colonel Richard M. Johnson, of Kentucky, Vice-President. During Jackson's administration two new states were added to the Union—Arkansas, admitted June, 1836, and Michigan in January, 1837. The whole number of states was now twenty-six.

11. On the 4th of March, 1837, Jackson left the White House and retired to his home, called the Hermitage, near Nashville, Tennessee. His fame as a President stands very high. In the administration of the government he proved himself to be a man of great honesty of purpose, of inflexible will, and of wonderful energy. He left the country free from debt, and respected throughout the world.

SECTION IV.

VAN BUREN'S ADMINISTRATION, 1837–1841.

1. MARTIN VAN BUREN, the next president, had filled the offices of United States senator, Governor of New York, Secretary of State, minister to England, and Vice-President under General Jackson. The last year of Jackson's administration had been one of great speculation and overtrading.

---

9. When, and with what nation, did trouble spring up? What was the origin of this? What energetic measures did the President adopt? What effect did they produce?

10. What was the result of the presidential election of 1836? What states were added to the Union toward the end of Jackson's administration?

11. To what place did Jackson go after the close of his term of office? Can you give the names of the residences of Washington and Jefferson? What is said of Jackson's administration? In what situation did he leave the country?

No sooner had Van Buren taken his seat as President than a financial panic overran the country. Merchants every where failed, and thousands in all walks of life were thrown out of employment. Government was implored to call an extra session of Congress, and adopt some measures to relieve the country. The President at first declined to do this, and the banks stopped specie payments.

PRESIDENT VAN BUREN.

2. Matters grew worse; and at length, in September, 1837, Congress met in extra session, but could do little to restore public confidence. It took years to bring trade back into its usual channels. At this session Van Buren proposed his plan of a sub-treasury. The public funds were to be kept in this, or its branches to be established in the chief cities. His idea was, that in them a large amount of money would be kept out of active circulation, and in that way speculation would be stopped. It failed to pass at this extra session, but was made a law in 1840.

3. In 1837 a portion of the Canadian people near the frontier rose in rebellion against Great Britain. They had many sympathizers on the American side, and for a time it seemed as though the lawless would involve England and the United States in a serious quarrel. The President acted with promptness, and sent General Wool to the border, with orders to prevent all expeditions from the United States.

---

1. What positions of prominence had Van Buren occupied? What took place soon after the inauguration of Van Buren? By what was this caused? To whom did the people look for help? What was the answer, and what followed?

2. What did the President do in September? How much good did this accomplish? Describe the plan proposed by the President at this session? What did he hope to effect by the sub-treasury scheme? How was it regarded by Congress?

The Canadian rebels, after some bloodshed, were put down by a British force.

4. The Seminole War was still going on. In October, 1837, Osceola, under a flag of truce, came to the American camp. General Jesup, who was in command, seized the chief, and he was sent to Charleston, and died in prison at Fort Moultrie. This, though a hard blow to the Seminoles, did not stop the war. Colonel Zachary Taylor, with 1000 men, attacked a large body of Indians at Lake Okeechobee, on Christmas day, 1838. Taylor lost 139 men, but the enemy were compelled to retreat. In 1839 a treaty was signed, although the fighting still continued at different points. The war was finally ended in 1842. It cost a great number of valuable lives, and the United States spent in its prosecution nearly $40,000,000.

5. The country had been unprosperous during Van Buren's term of office, and for this his administration was blamed. The result was, that in the election of President in 1840, Van Buren, nominated by the Democratic party, was defeated, and General William Henry Harrison, of Ohio, the nominee of the Whig party, was elected by a large majority. John Tyler, of Virginia, was chosen Vice-President.

SECTION V.

ADMINISTRATIONS OF HARRISON AND TYLER, 1841–1845.

1. GENERAL HARRISON had been member of Congress, Governor of Indiana Territory, and the conqueror in the battles of the Tippecanoe and the Thames. His first step, after his inauguration, March 4, was to call an extra session of Congress to remedy the finances of the country. Before Con-

3. What disturbance occurred on the frontier in 1837? How far was it feared that it would extend? What was done by the United States government?

4. What important event in the Seminole War took place in 1837? How did this affect the war? Describe Taylor's battle at Lake Okeechobee? To what did this battle lead? When was the war finally ended? What is said of its cost in men and money?

5. On whom was laid the blame of the financial misfortunes of the country? How did this influence the election for President in 1840?

gress assembled he died, April 4, just one month after he had entered the White House.

PRESIDENT HARRISON.

2. John Tyler, of Virginia, Vice-President, became, by the Constitution, President, April 6. He had been Governor of Virginia, a member of Congress, and United States senator. Congress met in extra session, and abolished the sub-treasury system. It passed a general Bankrupt Law to relieve merchants and others who had failed, and two bills to re-establish the national bank. President Tyler vetoed both bills. At this the Whig party, who had placed Mr. Tyler in power, were very indignant, and all of the President's cabinet, except Daniel Webster, Secretary of State, resigned. In 1842, Mr. Webster and Lord Ashburton agreed on a treaty fixing the northeastern boundary as it now exists. This question at one time threatened to produce war between the two countries.

PRESIDENT TYLER.

3. The year 1843 was marked by an insurrection in Rhode Island, known as the Dorr rebellion. The old charter of the colony, in existence for nearly 200 years, was still the constitution of the state. It no lon-

1. Who was General Harrison? What was his first act after his inauguration? What occurred on the 4th of April?

2. Who became President on the death of Harrison? What positions had he filled? What was done at the extra session of Congress? What produced angry feelings against Mr. Tyler among his own party? What resulted? What important matter was settled by Mr. Webster? Why was this so important?

ger pleased a large portion of the people, particularly because it required that all citizens should possess a certain amount of property before they could vote.

4. In attempting to alter the constitution very bitter feeling sprung up; two parties were formed, and each elected its governor. One of these, called the "suffrage party," chose Thomas W. Dorr governor, took up arms, and attacked the state arsenal, but they were driven off by the militia, assisted by United States troops. Dorr was finally arrested, tried for treason, and condemned to imprisonment for life, but in 1845 he was released. The "law and order party" yielded, however, to the wishes of the majority, and the Legislature passed a free constitution, November, 1842.

5. The disturbances in Rhode Island were scarcely ended, when a serious excitement broke out in Illinois between the people and a sect called Mormons. The latter professed to believe in a new revelation from God, received by their leader, Joseph Smith, on golden plates. Among the articles of the Mormon faith is one that teaches the doctrine of polygamy, or a plurality of wives. They settled at first in Missouri, but their conduct there was so offensive that it stirred up the anger of the citizens, and they were driven from the state.

6. They then settled in Illinois, where they founded a city called Nauvoo, and built a temple. Here they grew strong, and were increased by emigrants from nearly all parts of Europe. Conscious of their strength, they defied and broke the laws of the state. After one of these violations, Joseph Smith, the prophet, and his brother, were put in jail; and, while lying there, were shot by a mob, July, 1844. Next year, 1845, their followers were compelled to leave the city after it had been cannonaded three days, and in the year 1846 some of them began their march across the wilderness

---

3. What event marked the year 1843? How long had the Constitution been in force? Why was it now deemed objectionable?

4. What occurred in attempting to remedy this? What is said of the "suffrage" party? What became of Dorr? What concession was made by the "law and order" party?

5. What excitement followed close on the Rhode Island rebellion? Give some account of their belief, and its origin? Where did they first settle, and what was their experience here?

to the Rocky Mountains. Here, in the valley of Salt Lake, hundreds of miles from their old residence in Illinois, all that remained of them were gathered in 1848, and then was laid the foundation of the Territory of Utah.

7. That portion of the republic of Mexico bordering on Louisiana, called Texas, threw off the yoke of Mexico, and declared itself independent in 1835. After several battles with the Mexicans, its independence was recognized by the United States and the chief powers of Europe, but not by Mexico. In April, 1844, it asked to be admitted as a state into the American Union. The petition produced great excitement throughout the country, and was strongly opposed at the North, because it was felt that the annexation of Texas would bring on a war with Mexico, and increase the area of slavery. A treaty for its admission was rejected by the Senate, July 8th.

8. The question came before the country for decision in the election of President in the fall of 1844. The political excitement of the canvass was increased by a dispute between England and the United States for the Territory of Oregon, which threatened to involve the two countries in war. James K. Polk, of Tennessee, was chosen President, being the representative of the party that favored the admission of Texas and the claim of the United States to Oregon. At the same time, George M. Dallas, of Pennsylvania, was chosen Vice-President.

9. The question of the admission of Texas, thus approved by the people in the election of Mr. Polk, came again before Congress for final settlement when it met in December. On the 1st of March, three days before Tyler's term expired, a resolution annexing Texas to the United States finally passed, and was immediately signed by the President. Two

---

6. To what place did they go? What was their fortune here? What happened to their leader? How did the Illinois people rid themselves of the Mormons? Where did they emigrate? Where and when did they all at last find a home?

7. What important event happened to the eastern part of Mexico as early as 1835? When did Texas ask admission into the American Union? What did this request produce? Why? How did the Senate act on the petition?

8. Where did the question of the admission of of Texas go for a decision? What other important question came before the people in this election? Who were chosen President and Vice-President?

days later, he signed the acts admitting Florida and Iowa into the Union.

10. An event of no less importance to the country than the annexation of Texas took place in 1844. This was the operation of the first electric telegraph line in the United States. The celebrated man to whom the country was indebted for its introduction was Samuel F. B. Morse, a native of Massachusetts. The telegraph, it is now settled, was invented by him as early as 1832. In the year 1838, and for successive years, he was before Congress soliciting assistance amid great discouragements. It was not till the year 1843, on the last day of the session, when he had given up hope of assistance, that, to his surprise, Congress appropriated the sum of $30,000 to operate a telegraph line between Balti-

MORSE EXPLAINING THE TELEGRAPH TO A COMMITTEE OF CONGRESS.

more and Washington. The experiment was a complete success. The telegraph system soon spread throughout the

9. When did the Texas question come up before Congress? State the closing events of the last days of Tyler's term.

United States and over the continent of Europe. Professor Morse received the highest honors from foreign nations.

REVIEW QUESTIONS.—1817-1845.

1. Who was James Monroe, and what offices had he filled?
2. What was the general character of his administration?
3. Give its leading events, and dates.
4. What was the only warlike trouble during his presidency?
5. Who was appointed to the chief command against the Indians?
6. Give some account of Jackson's energetic conduct during the war.
7. To what acquisition of territory did this Indian war lead?
8. What is said of the cession of this territory?
9. What political distinction had begun to be drawn between the states?
10. To what remarkable invention was this partly attributable?
11. Explain how this was produced.
12. What was the feeling in the North in reference to negro slavery?
13. How was this shown in Congress during Monroe's term?
14. Give a sketch of the contest and its settlement.
15. What is understood by the Monroe doctrine?
16. Who were elected President and Vice-President in 1824?
17. What peculiarity was there about Adams's election?
18. Name the chief events of his administration.
19. Who were the candidates for the presidency in 1828?
20. Who was chosen, and how was the election regarded?
21. State the principal events in Jackson's military career.
22. What were the leading events of his administration?
23. Give an account of his contests with the United States Bank?
24. Mention some of the events at the beginning of the Seminole War.
25. Sketch the history of the South Carolina troubles.
26. How did Jackson act in reference to France?
27. Who were elected President and Vice-President in 1836?
28. Who was Martin Van Buren?
29. In what condition was the country in 1837?
30. How far was the administration able to remedy this?
31. What measure was proposed by Van Buren? Describe it.
32. Give an account of the Canadian troubles.
33. State the events preceding the end of the Florida War. Give dates.
34. Who were elected President and Vice-President in 1840?
35. What were the principal events of Van Buren's administration?
36. Why was he defeated?
37. Who was General Harrison, and how long was he President?
38. What account is given of his successor?
39. Give the leading events of Tyler's administration.
40. What was the Ashburton Treaty?
41. Give the particulars of the Dorr Rebellion.
42. Who were the Mormons? Give their movements up to the year 1846.
43. Give an account of the introduction of the electric telegraph.
44. What is said of Texas and its efforts for admission into the Union?
45. Why was its admission so strongly opposed?
46. How and when was the question settled?
47. What states were admitted into the Union from 1817 to 1845?
48. State the length of the different administrations, and dates.

---

10. What great invention was first introduced into the United States in 1844? Sketch the history of Morse's labors to introduce his invention, and his final success.

CHAPTER VII.

POLK'S ADMINISTRATION, 1845-1849.—WAR WITH MEXICO.

SECTION I.

COMMENCEMENT OF HOSTILITIES WITH MEXICO.

1. PRESIDENT POLK had been fourteen years a member of Congress, of which he was chosen speaker several times, and also Governor of Tennessee. His administration began with two stirring questions—war with Mexico, and the settlement of the Oregon difficulty. In the latter the United States claimed 54° 40′ as the northern boundary of that Territory. The question was finally settled peaceably in 1846 by a treaty fixing the boundary at 49°.

PRESIDENT POLK.

2. General Taylor, who distinguished himself in Florida against the Seminoles, was ordered to Texas in July, 1845, and in September took post at Corpus Christi, near the mouth of the Nueces (*nwa'ces*) River. The Mexicans considered this the western boundary of Texas; the Texans claimed the Rio Grande (*re'-o grahn'-da*) as the boundary. In January, 1846, Taylor was ordered to the eastern bank of the Rio Grande, and, on his way, threw up some slight works at Point Isabel, which he made a dépôt for supplies. On the 28th of March he encamped opposite Matamoras, and began to build a fort, whereupon General Ampudia (*am-poo'-*

---

1. Who was James K. Polk? What were the two principal events at the commencement of his administration? How was the Oregon question settled?

de-ah), stationed on the other side of the river, notified him that this was an act of war on Mexican soil. Presently the Mexicans crossed the Rio Grande, and surprised a small body of dragoons under Captain Thornton, killing or capturing nearly the whole party, April 26.

3. They then began to push in between Taylor and his supplies at Point Isabel, threatening his communications. Leaving Major Brown to defend the fort, the American general on the 1st of May marched to Point Isabel, which was menaced by the enemy. Here he received re-enforcements, and, with 2300 men and a large supply train, commenced his return to the Rio Grande. Next day, May 8, he met the enemy, 6000 strong, under General Arista, drawn up to dispute his way at Palo Alto (*pah'-lo ahl'-to*). Taylor at once joined battle, which lasted five hours, and was mainly carried on with artillery. At night the Mexicans retreated, with a loss of about 600. The American loss was 53, among whom was the brave Major Ringgold, of the artillery.

4. Taylor continued his march, and late on the following day, May 9, found the Mexicans prepared to oppose him at a ravine called Resaca de la Palma (*res-ah'-ka da lah pahl-mah*). The battle which followed was short and severe, ending in the capture of General La Vega (*vā'-gah*) and 100 prisoners, and the defeat of the Mexicans, with the loss of nearly 1000 men. Next day Taylor arrived at the fort on the Rio Grande, which had been constantly bombarded by the Mexicans during his absence. Major Brown was mortally wounded, and the brave garrison were anxiously looking for assistance. In honor of its gallant defender, it was named Fort Brown.

5. When Congress heard what occurred on the Rio Grande

---

2. Who was ordered to Texas, and when? Where did he first encamp? What dispute was there about boundaries? How did the United States government indorse the Texan claim? What did he do on his march? Where did he make his permanent quarters? How did the Mexicans regard this? When and where was the first blood shed in the war with Mexico?

3. What threatening movements were made by the Mexicans? How did Taylor act when he learned this? When and in what condition did he commence his return? What occurred next day?

4. What further opposition did he meet with? What was the result of the second battle? When did he arrive at the Rio Grande, and in what situation did he find things at the fort?

in April, it at once declared war, May 11, voted $10,000,000 for expenses, and ordered that 50,000 volunteers should be raised. A campaign was planned at Washington, embracing two separate expeditions. One was to rendezvous in the Far West, and push across the northern provinces of Mexico, and over the Rocky Mountains to California: this was the "Army of the West." The second was to march to the capital of Mexico, and was called the "Army of the Centre." Taylor's army, which was called the "Army of Occupation," was ordered to co-operate with the "Army of the Centre." Notwithstanding the opposition that the annexation of Texas had met with, the war was now a matter of national pride with a large part of the American people, and the government had no difficulty in obtaining volunteers for its armies.

CAMPAIGNS IN MEXICO.

6. General Taylor meanwhile crossed the Rio Grande, entered Mexican territory, and occupied Matamoras May 18. Here he received re-enforcements that brought his army up to the number of 6000 men. At Monterey (*mon-ta-rā*), the capital of the province of New Leon (*la-on*), there were heavy fortifications, defended by more than 9000 Mexicans under

---

5. When was war declared, and why? What warlike measures were decided on by the United States government? Describe the plan of the campaign.

General Ampudia. The city lay in the path of Taylor's march into the interior, and he determined to attack it on the 21st of September. After a continued assault of nearly four days, Monterey was taken by severe fighting, street by street and house by house. General Ampudia and the

CAPTURE OF MONTEREY.

garrison surrendered, and were allowed to march out with the honors of war, September 24. At the same time, Taylor agreed to an armistice with the Mexican government for eight weeks.

7. General Wool, with a re-enforcement of 3000 troops, had already commenced his march from San Antonio into Mexico. He crossed the Rio Grande, and when he reached Monclova, 70 miles from Monterey, he learned of Taylor's success. Upon the advice of the latter, he marched to a fer-

6. What was Taylor's next movement? In what direction did he determine to march? What lay in his way? What is said of the assault on Monterey? What terms were given to the garrison? In what direction is Monterey from Matamoras? What important agreement was made with the Mexicans?

tile district convenient to Monterey, where he was able to supply his own command, and also that of General Taylor, with forage and provisions. The armistice terminated on November 13. On the 15th, General Worth, with 700 men, took possession of Saltillo (*sahl-teel'-yo*). General Taylor, leaving a garrison at Monterey, went as far as Victoria on his way to attack Tampico (*tam-peé-ko*). At Victoria he learned that Tampico had already surrendered to a United States squadron under Captain Conner, November 14th. Wool, with his troops, joined Worth at Saltillo.

8. **The Army of the West.**—General Kearny was appointed to command the Army of the West, with orders to conquer the Spanish provinces of New Mexico and California. In the month of June, 1846, he started from Fort Leavenworth, on the Missouri, and, after a journey of nearly 1000 miles, reached Santa Fé, which he occupied on August 18. Leaving a garrison here, he continued his march to California. On his way he received information that the province had been already conquered. He then sent back the main body of his troops to Santa Fé, and, with 100 picked men, marched to the Pacific coast.

9. The conquest of California was achieved by Lieutenant Colonel Fremont and Commodores Sloat and Stockton. Fremont, a United States officer, was sent, in 1845, to explore the Salt Lake Valley, California, and Oregon. While busy with his explorations, he heard that war had been declared against Mexico, and, with his small force of 60 men, hastened to California. Here, being joined by some American settlers, he defeated the Mexicans in several sharp skirmishes, and drove them from that part of the country. All this was done by the beginning of July, 1846.

10. On the 7th of July, Commodore Sloat, with some

---

7. Describe the first movement of the division under General Wool? Where is San Antonio? What were his next movements? When did the armistice end? What took place soon after? Where is Saltillo? To what point did Taylor march? What prevented him from going there?

8. Who commanded the Army of the West? What was the object of this expedition? What is said of Kearny's long march? What prevented him continuing it to California with his whole command? What did he then resolve to do?

9. By whom was California conquered? How did it happen that Fremont was connected with its conquest? Describe his movements.

war vessels, bombarded and took Monterey, on the Pacific coast. On the 15th Commodore Stockton arrived, and, with Fremont, took possession of Los Angélos, August 17th. When Kearny arrived at Los Angélos in December, Fremont claimed the governorship; but the former, being his superior officer, would not consent to this, and assumed the office February 8, 1847.

11. Kearny, on leaving Santa Fé, ordered Colonel Doniphan to march into the Indian country, and compel the natives to promise peace. This Doniphan did, and then marched his command of less than 1000 men to Chihuahua (*che-whah'-whah*), which he entered about the beginning of March. On his route he fought and defeated more than 4000 Mexicans, under General Ponce de Leon, at Bracito (*brah-thé-to*), December 25th, and again at Sacramento, February 28. Having rested his little army in Chihuahua nearly six weeks, he pressed on to Saltillo, and joined General Wool May 22. His march, for more than 1000 miles through an enemy's country, was one of constant hardship, and is one of the most brilliant of the many brave acts that marked the Mexican War.

EVENTS OF 1847–48.

1. In the fall of 1846, during Taylor's armistice, the American government offered the Mexicans terms of peace. These they refused, and General Winfield Scott, as commander-in-chief, was ordered to carry the war to the city of Mexico. The plan of the ensuing campaign was very simple; he was to land near Vera Cruz, capture it, and then, by the shortest route, march to the capital. In accordance with this arrangement, Scott ordered Taylor to send immediately the best of his troops, and with them Generals Worth and Quitman, already distinguished for their bravery. Taylor was deeply mortified at receiving such an order, particularly as he was about to commence active operations; but Scott was

---

10. What was Commodore Sloat's part in the conquest? and Stockton's? Where is Los Angelos? What difficulty arose when Kearny arrived at this place?

11. What orders had Kearny left at Santa Fé? What was Doniphan's next movement? Where is Chihuahua? What battles were fought before he reached Chihuahua? What is said of his future movements, and of his march?

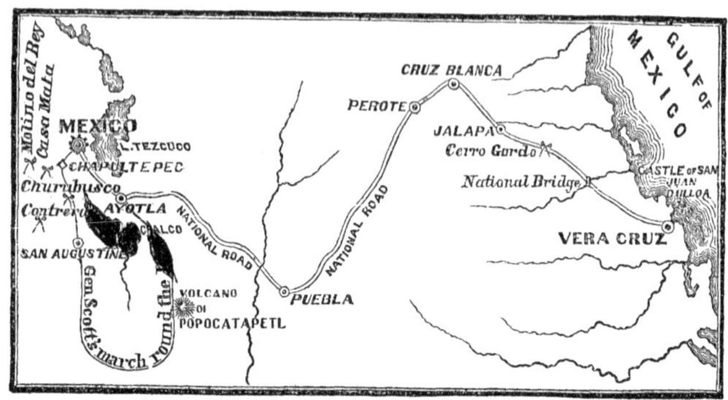

GENERAL SCOTT'S CAMPAIGN IN MEXICO.

his superior officer, and he shortly dispatched the required re-enforcements to the neighborhood of Vera Cruz.

2. **General Taylor's Operations.**—By the loss of these troops Taylor was left with little more than 5000 men, only 500 of whom were regulars. General Santa Anna, taking advantage of this weakness, moved against him from San Luis Potósi with nearly 20,000 Mexicans. Taylor determined to fall back and oppose the enemy in a narrow defile at Buena Vista (*bwa'-nah vees'-tah*), eleven miles from Saltillo. When Santa Anna came up, February 23, he was so confident in his overwhelming numbers that he sent word to Taylor he would give him one hour to surrender. The latter made use of the time in preparing for battle, which was continued from morning until sunset.

3. The Americans expected to renew the struggle next morning; but in the night Santa Anna retreated, leaving his dead and wounded, to the number of 2000, on the field. No other important operations followed in this part of the country. In the summer, General Taylor, leaving Wool in command, returned to the United States, where he was received with the most distinguished honor.

---

1. What attempt was made in the United States government in 1846, and the result? What was the plan of the campaign? What order did he send to General Taylor? Why was this felt severely by Taylor?

2. What was now the condition of Taylor's army? What advantage was taken of this? Where did Taylor propose to meet him? Describe the battle.

3. How was the battle decided? What operations followed? Where did General Taylor go?

4. **Campaign of General Scott.**—On the 9th of March, 1847, General Scott, with 13,000 men, landed near Vera Cruz. The city was defended by the strong castle of San Juan de Ulloa (*san-whahn-dā ool-lo'-ah*). On the 18th Scott opened fire on the city and castle from his batteries. In this bombardment he was assisted by a powerful fleet under Commodore Conner. On the 27th the castle surrendered, with 5000 prisoners and 500 pieces of artillery.

BOMBARDMENT OF VERA CRUZ.

5. On the 8th of April, the advanced force, led by General Twiggs, moved toward the capital by the Jalapa (*hal-lah'-pah*) road. Santa Anna, with 12,000 men, occupied the well-fortified mountain pass of Cerro Gordo, at the foot of the Cordílleras. General Scott, meanwhile, had joined Twiggs with the rest of the troops, making in all about 8500 men. Avoiding a direct attack in front, Scott fell suddenly on the

4. When, where, and with what force did Scott land? How was the city defended? Where is Vera Cruz? What is said of the siege, and the result?

enemy in a quarter he least expected. The heights were carried, and 3000 prisoners and 43 pieces of artillery were captured, April 18th.

6. The brilliant victory at Cerro Gordo opened the way for the American army to Jalapa. Continuing their march, they captured the strong Castle of Perote (*pa-ró-tă*), situated on a peak of the Eastern Cordilleras, which was abandoned on their approach, April 22d. The city of Puebla (*pweb'-lah*), with 80,000 inhabitants, and the second largest city of Mexico, was entered May 15th. Here General Scŏtt rested for several months, and waited for re-enforcements. This rest was greatly needed, for the climate had made sad havoc with the health of his men. At Puebla alone he was compelled to leave 1800 sick, and at Perote a great number died during the summer.

7. On the 7th of August General Scott left Puebla with a force increased to 10,000 men, and, on crossing the ridge of the Cordilleras, the army saw stretched out beneath them the beautiful valley of Mexico. In the midst of this lay the capital, defended by strong works, which guarded the approaches to the city, and behind these fortifications were 32,000 Mexicans. The direct approach by the Vera Cruz road seemed to General Scott beset with most danger; and he ordered General Twiggs to turn to the left and occupy San Augustine, eight miles south of the city, on the Acapulco (*ah-kah-pool'-co*) road. In front of this position were the fortified camp of Contreras (*con-tra'-ras*), the strong fortress of San Antonio, and the heights of Cherubusco (*choo-roo-boos'-ko*), crowned with cannon, and well garrisoned.

8. At sunrise, August 20, 1847, General Smith burst into the Mexican camp at Contreras, and captured it in little more than fifteen minutes. A large number of prisoners

5. What movement followed? Who opposed the march of Twiggs, and where? What was the amount of the American force when Scott came up? Describe the battle and its results.

6. What was the result of the battle of Cerro Gordo? What fortified place was next taken? What great city was entered the following month? How long did the army remain here? Why was rest necessary?

7. When and with what force did Scott leave Puebla? What lay between them and the capital? Describe the view the army had of the valley. What route did he take to advance to the city? Why did he choose this? What fortifications were to be taken before he could enter the capital?

THE ARMY COMING IN SIGHT OF THE VALLEY OF MEXICO.

and 33 pieces of cannon were taken. General Worth, on the same day, stormed and took possession of San Antonio. He then joined General Pillow, and, by assault, captured one of the defenses of Cherubusco; General Twiggs took another; and the heights fell into the possession of the Americans. Meanwhile Santa Anna, who lay with 12,000 men nearer the city, made the most vigorous efforts to assist his garrisons, but was driven back with heavy loss.

9. All these battles took place on the 20th of August. On that day more than 30,000 Mexicans, behind defenses of the strongest kind, had been utterly beaten by an army of Americans less than one third their number; 4000 Mexicans were killed and wounded, and 3000 prisoners were taken; the American loss was 1100. Next day, August 21, General Scott advanced within three miles of the city. Santa Anna asked for an armistice, which Scott granted, hoping to save

8. Describe the attack on the camp at Contreras. What was accomplished by Generals Worth, Pillow, and Twiggs? What was Santa Anna doing at this time?

further bloodshed; but the wily Mexican used the time to strengthen his works. As soon as Scott saw this he ordered an advance.

10. Two powerful works still defended the city—Molino del Rey (*mo-lē-no del rā*) and Chapultepec (*chah-pool-tā-pek'*). The first of these was stormed by General Worth, September 8, and taken, after severe fighting on both sides. Fourteen thousand Mexicans were driven out of these defenses by 4000 Americans. Four days after, September 12, the American batteries opened on the Castle of Chapultepec. Next day an assault was ordered, and, amid a scene of blood and carnage, the Americans entered the works. General Quitman pursued the fleeing enemy, and at nightfall rested at the gates of the capital.

11. During the night, Santa Anna, with what remained of his army, escaped, and left the city authorities to manage matters as they could. They came humbly to General Scott begging for peace; but the American general turned a deaf ear to their entreaties, and ordered his troops to enter the capital. On September 14, 1847, the American army occupied the grand square of the city, and the American flag floated over the public buildings.

12. When Santa Anna fled from the capital he made his way to the neighborhood of the city of Puebla, which was besieged by a Mexican force. Eighteen hundred sick Americans had been left there, under Major Childs, and he suffered great hardships in trying to defend the place. Fortunately, General Lane arrived with re-enforcements for General Scott, and instantly attacked Santa Anna, defeated him, and relieved the garrison.

13. The war was now at an end. Santa Anna was a fugi-

---

9. State the result of the day's work, August 20. What occurred next day? What agreement was entered into by the two opposing generals? To what use did Santa Anna put the time? Why was the armistice ended?

10. What powerful works defended the city itself? State how the first was taken. How was Chapultepec taken? What progress was made by another part of the army?

11. How did the Mexican army defend the city? By whom was General Scott met, and what was his answer to them? What important event occurred on September 14?

12. In what direction did Santa Anna march after he left the capital? What was the condition of things at Puebla? How were Santa Anna's plans overturned?

THE AMERICAN ARMY IN THE CITY OF MEXICO.

tive; his army was scattered. On the 2d of February, 1848, the Mexican Congress concluded a treaty of peace with the American commissioners at Guadalupe Hidalgo (*gwah-dah-loo-pä he-dahl'-go*). By the terms of the treaty Mexico agreed to consider the Rio Grande as the western boundary of Texas, and gave up to the United States the provinces of New Mexico and California. For this vast territory the American government was to pay $15,000,000, and to assume debts due to certain citizens of the United States amounting to $3,500,000. The treaty was confirmed by the United States, and peace was proclaimed by President Polk on the 4th of July, 1848.

14. The province of Upper California, stretching more than 650 miles along the Pacific coast, and nearly as many miles inland, contained at the close of the war scarce 15,000

---

13. What was the state of the war after the siege of Puebla? What took place in the beginning of the following year? Give the terms of the treaty. When was peace proclaimed?

persons. It was not long before a thronging population found its way into the new territory. In February, 1848, gold was first discovered at Captain Sutter's mill, on a branch of the Sacramento River, in Colóma County, and soon in abundance in that neighborhood. The news spread with great rapidity, and crowds, not only from the United States, but from all parts of the world, flocked to the land of gold. By the year 1850 the population was estimated at nearly 100,000; in 1852 it numbered 264,000.

15. In the year 1848 Wisconsin was admitted into the Union. The election for president was now approaching, and three parties appeared, each of which placed a candidate in nomination. The two great parties were the Whig and the Democratic. The former nominated General Zachary Taylor, one of the heroes of the war; the latter, General Cass, of Michigan. The third party put in nomination ex-President Van Buren, and laid down the principle that it is the duty of Congress to prohibit the introduction of slavery into any territory now possessed, or which may hereafter be acquired by the United States; hence it was called the Free Soil party. In the election that followed, General Taylor, of Louisiana, was chosen President, and Millard Fillmore, of New York, Vice-President.

REVIEW QUESTIONS.—1845-1849.

1. What was the Oregon difficulty, and how was it settled?
2. What were the causes of the Mexican War?
3. Who was President during its continuance?
4. What were the first hostile movements?
5. Where was Taylor prominent before this time?
6. What led to the battles of the 8th and 9th of May, 1846?
7. Describe them.
8. When and why did the United States declare war?
9. What different lines of operation were determined on?
10. What was the result of Taylor's expedition into New Leon?
11. Where is Tampico? What happened here?
12. What overtures of peace were made, and when?

---

14. What was the extent and population of Upper California at the close of the Mexican War? What event suddenly increased its population? What was the estimated population in 1850 and in 1852?

15. When was Wisconsin admitted into the Union? What is said of the canvass for the presidency? Which were the two leading parties, and who were their nominees? Give the principles and nominee of the third party. Who were chosen President and Vice-President?

13. Who commanded the Army of the Centre?
14. State some particulars of his previous history.
15. When and in what way did he interfere with Taylor's plans?
16. Describe the battle of Buena Vista.
17. In how many battles was Taylor engaged after this?
18. Describe the operations of the Army of the West. Give dates.
19. Sketch briefly the conquest of California.
20. What difficulties occurred there between rival officers?
21. Describe the movements of Colonel Doniphan.
22. Give a sketch of General Scott's first battle.
23. What route did his army take?
24. Name the battles that occurred between Vera Cruz and the city of Mexico. Give dates.
25. What mountains were crossed?
26. When and where did the army rest for some time?
27. Why was this rest so necessary?
28. What lay on the other side of the mountains?
29. How was the city of Mexico defended?
30. Describe the battles fought in the suburbs of the city.
31. How long a time intervened between the attack on Contreras and the entrance of Scott into the capital?
32. What Mexican general opposed Scott's advance?
33. Who was Santa Anna?
34. Where and when did he appear after the surrender of the capital?
35. When and where was a treaty of peace concluded?
36. Give the terms of the treaty.
37. What was gained by the war?
38. Name the principal American officers engaged.
39. What immediate advantage followed the close of the war?
40. How did this affect the population of the western coast?
41. Who were nominated in 1848 for President and Vice-President?
42. State the principles of the different parties.
43. Who were chosen President and Vice-President?
44. What state was admitted during Polk's term? Give date.

LIEUTENANT GENERAL SCOTT.

CHAPTER VIII.

FROM THE END OF POLK'S ADMINISTRATION TO THE BEGINNING OF LINCOLN'S, 1849-1861.

SECTION I.

TAYLOR'S ADMINISTRATION, 1849–1850.

1. PRESIDENT TAYLOR began his military career in the Northwest in the War of 1812. We have already seen him an active soldier in Florida, and one of the heroes of the Mexican War. In the month of September, 1849, the people of California met in convention, and adopted a constitution excluding slavery from the Territory. In the February following, California petitioned Congress for admission into the Union as a free state. Then arose a struggle in that body so bitter and so determined that many of the Southern members threatened to secede from the Union if California was admitted with a free constitution. Outside of Congress the excitement was equally great, and many were alarmed for the peace of the country.

PRESIDENT TAYLOR.

2. While the excitement was at its height, Henry Clay brought forward in the United States Senate a plan of compromise. Other statesmen did the same. Then a committee of thirteen was appointed, Clay being chairman, to consider the different plans. On the 9th of May, 1850, this com-

1. What is said of the new President? What movement took place in California in 1849? When did California seek admission into the Union as a state? What was the feeling in Congress on the subject of the petition? How far did the excitement spread?

mittee reported a bill admitting California with its free constitution, but proposing at the same time additional measures, on which account it was nicknamed the "Omnibus Bill."

HENRY CLAY.

3. The chief of these were that a tract of land east of California, on a part of which the Mormons lived, should be erected into the Territory of Utah, without slavery; also that New Mexico should be made a territory, and nothing said about slavery; further, that slavery in the District of Columbia should be abolished; and, last, a law was recommended providing for the arrest and return to their masters of all slaves that should escape into the Free States. While the discussion of this bill was going on in Congress, President Taylor was seized with a sudden illness, and died July 9, 1850. Vice-President Fillmore immediately assumed the office of President.

SECTION II.

FILLMORE'S ADMINISTRATION, 1850–1853.

1. The Compromise Act became a law September 9, 1850. President Fillmore, during his entire administration, enforced its provisions with all the powers of the government. It appeared for a time to quiet the excited feeling of the country; but the enforcement of that part called the Fugitive Slave Law gradually produced intense bitterness at the North. The law was there evaded, sometimes resisted; and this greatly increased the ill feeling in the Southern States.

2. Who came forward with a plan to harmonize these difficulties? What followed? On what did this committee determine? What name did the latter receive? Why?
3. Name the chief of these measures? What important event occurred while the debate was going on in Congress?
1. When did the Compromise Act become a law? How did Fillmore regard it? What effect did it produce on the country? How was it received in the North?

PRESIDENT FILLMORE.

2. In the year 1851, some wild and restless spirits in the South and Southwest banded themselves together for the invasion of the island of Cuba. Led by General Lopez, they landed on the coast of that island to the number of 480. Only a short time elapsed before nearly all of them were made prisoners; and Lopez, with a number of his followers, was shot by the Spaniards.

3. The United States, in the year 1852, came near being involved in a war with England about the deep-sea fisheries. A treaty had been made 34 years before, in which it was settled that the Americans should not fish within three miles of the shores of the British provinces. England claimed that this shut out the Americans from the large bays; the latter, on the other hand, said they had a right to fish in these, provided they kept three miles from the shores. The quarrel rose to such a height that England and the United States both sent war-ships to the disputed ground. Fortunately, bloodshed was prevented; and American fishermen finally, in 1854, secured equal rights to fish any where in the bays of the British possessions.

4. Mr. Fillmore's administration has the honor of sending out an expedition in the year 1852 to open the Japanese Empire to American trade. It consisted of a squadron under the command of Commodore Perry, the youngest brother of the famous Captain Perry of the War of 1812. The successful prosecution of the enterprise falls within the history of the next administration.

5. As the time approached for the election of President in

---

2. What expedition was started in 1851? What was its fate?

3. What dispute threatened danger in 1852? What treaty had been made with England in reference to the fisheries? What construction was placed on this by the English and American fishermen? To what point did the quarrel rise? How and when was the matter finally settled?

4. For what peaceful expedition is Mr. Fillmore's administration distinguished? Who commanded it?

1852, it was seen that the "Omnibus Bill" had not produced permanent peace throughout the country. The people were divided on the slavery question. The extreme party in the South talked earnestly of Southern rights; at the North a small but increasing minority urged that the government should separate itself from all connection with slavery. Both of these parties advocated a dissolution of the Union; but these were the extreme views. An influential body in the South, and a very large majority of the people in the North, adhered to the act of 1850.

6. The nominations for President were made in the fall of 1852. The Democrats presented the name of Franklin Pierce, of New Hampshire, and at the same time declared that they stood by the Compromise Act. The Whigs nominated General Scott, and they also affirmed the justice of the "Omnibus Bill." There were, however, leading Whigs and Democrats who thought the Compromise Act to be wrong; that the Territories ought to be free from slavery; that the general government infringed on the rights of the states by capturing fugitive slaves within their borders; and that the government should throw its influence against slavery. These persons met as the Free Soil party, and nominated John P. Hale, of New Hampshire. At the election Franklin Pierce received a large majority of all the votes cast; and William R. King, of Alabama, was chosen Vice-President.

SECTION III

PIERCE'S ADMINISTRATION, 1853–1857.

1. FRANKLIN PIERCE, a man of note in his own state, had been a member of Congress, and a United States senator. He had also distinguished himself as a brave and able officer in the Mexican War.

5. What was the state of political feeling in the fall of 1852? Give the extreme views North and South. What was the opinion of the great body of the people?

6. How many parties presented presidential candidates? What position was assumed by the Whigs and the Democrats on the Compromise Act? What were the views of the Free Soil party? What was the result of the election?

1. What official positions had President Pierce occupied?

PRESIDENT PIERCE.

2. A dispute had arisen with Mexico in 1852 about boundaries between New Mexico and the province of Chihuahua. This was settled in the early part of Mr. Pierce's term by the purchase of a large tract of land which was erected into the Territory of Arizona. Another early and most important measure was the sending out of expeditions in the year 1853 to explore the best routes for a Pacific railroad. This was the first movement in that great enterprise which, in our own day, has brought into rapid communication the Atlantic and Pacific coasts.

3. The Japanese expedition has been already noticed. In the summer of 1853, Commodore Perry entered the Bay of Jeddo, Japan, with his squadron. On the 14th of July he obtained an audience of the emperor, by whom he was received with high honors. Some necessary delay then occurred; but in the month of March, 1854, the commodore obtained a treaty by which the United States were allowed to trade with Japan. America has the distinguished honor of being the first nation of the West to which that empire opened her ports.

4. In December, 1853, Mr. Douglas, in the United States Senate, brought forward a bill for the organization of two new territories north of latitude 36° 30′, under the names of Nebraska and Kansas. In this famous bill was inserted the provision that slavery should be allowed to enter the territories if the people there desired it. This was generally known as "Popular" or "Squatter Sovereignty," and was contrary to the Missouri Compromise of 1820, which ex-

2. What dispute had arisen with Mexico? How was this settled? What important expeditions were sent out in 1853? What is said regarding these?

3. Give the further history of the expedition to Japan. When was it dispatched from the United States? What honor belongs to America for this?

pressly prohibited slavery in all territories north of 36° 30′. The bill met with great opposition in Congress, and produced intense feeling throughout the North. It, however, passed both houses, and became a law in May, 1854.

5. The contest was now removed from Congress to Kansas. The question whether slavery should be admitted being left to the settlers, a struggle commenced between the Free State and pro-Slavery men so bitter as to produce civil war in the territory. The struggle, which was watched with extraordinary interest throughout the whole country, was still going on when the time for the presidential election arrived in 1856. The Democratic party put in nomination James Buchanan, of Pennsylvania, and declared the Kansas-Nebraska Act to be just and proper. The Whig party had broken up and disappeared. The Republican party sprang into existence, adopting the views of the Free Soil party, and nominated John C. Fremont for President. A small party, known as the "Americans," or "Know Nothings," nominated Millard Fillmore. The Democrats triumphed, and James Buchanan, of Pennsylvania, was elected President, and John C. Breckinridge, of Kentucky, Vice-President.

SECTION IV.

BUCHANAN'S ADMINISTRATION, 1857–1861.

1. JAMES BUCHANAN had been a member of the United States Senate, afterward Secretary of State under President Polk, and minister to England during the administration of President Pierce. The Mormons in Utah, at the instigation of Brigham Young, their leader, broke out into open rebellion against the United States authorities in 1857, and ordered the United States judge from the territory. An army

---

4. What proposition was brought forward in 1853? What celebrated provision was inserted in the bill? By what name is this generally known? With what did it conflict? How was the bill received? What was its success in Congress?

5. How far did this settle the contest? What is said of the struggle? What took place during the height of the excitement? Who was nominated by the Democrats, and on what platform? What became of the Whig party? What party now appeared under a new name? What were its views? Whom did it nominate? What is said of the third party? Who were chosen?

of 2500 men was sent out to reduce them to obedience; but in the spring of 1858 the Mormons quietly submitted to the authority of the United States officers.

PRESIDENT BUCHANAN.

2. The contest about slavery in Kansas went on. But the slavery agitation was not confined to that territory; it was very violent in Congress, and spread throughout the country. This agitation was increased by the action of some of the Free States, which passed "Personal Liberty Bills" to secure fugitive slaves the right of trial. These acts filled the people of the Slave States with bitter indignation. In Kansas, both the Free State and the pro-Slavery parties claimed the government of the territory. After a severe and long-continued contest, the anti-Slavery party triumphed, and Kansas was admitted under a Free State Constitution, but not till the year 1861, in the following administration. Minnesota was meanwhile admitted in 1858, and Oregon in 1859.

3. On the night of October 16, 1859, John Brown, an active Free State settler in Kansas, and 21 companions, seized the United States Arsenal at Harper's Ferry, Virginia. This small party held possession of the arsenal for nearly two days. A body of state and national troops attacked them, killed 13, and captured the rest, except two, who escaped. On Brown's trial by the State of Virginia, he avowed that it was his object to produce a rising among the slaves, and then conduct them to the Free States. He steadily denied that he was aided or encouraged by any persons in the

---

1. What is said of President Buchanan? What trouble broke out in the Far West? What measures were taken by the government? How was the difficulty settled?

2. What is said of the slavery agitation in Kansas and elsewhere? What was the conduct of some of the Free States? How did the South regard this? What did both parties in Kansas claim? Which party finally triumphed? When was Kansas admitted as a Free State?

North, although every effort was made by the counsel of the state to draw from him this confession. Prompt conviction followed the trial, and John Brown and six of his companions were hanged.

4. The feeling in the South against the North after John Brown's raid greatly increased in bitterness; and the year 1860 was marked by a more violent agitation of the slavery question, which was increased by the presidential election. A Democratic convention met to nominate candidates at Charleston in the month of April. Those delegates who were advocates of extreme Southern views were unable to control the convention, and left it in a body; and those who remained nominated Stephen A. Douglas, of Illinois, for President. The Southern delegates met in June, and nominated John C. Breckinridge, of Kentucky. Another small party nominated John Bell, of Tennessee. The Republican party brought before the people Abraham Lincoln, of Illinois, as its candidate. In the election that followed, Mr. Lincoln was chosen President, and Hannibal Hamlin, of Maine, Vice-President.

5. All through the canvass the Southern politicians had threatened to carry the South out of the Union if Mr. Lincoln were elected. In December they began to put their threats in execution. On the 17th of the month a convention assembled at Charleston, and on the 20th declared the State of South Carolina to be no longer in the Union. As a reason for this course, it was alleged that the Northern States had violated the Constitution by passing the personal liberty bills, thus nullifying the Fugitive Slave Act, and by the election of a President opposed to slavery. The leaders, however, freely declared that secession was neither produced by Mr. Lincoln's election nor by the non-execution of the above act; the movement had been gathering head for thirty years. The states of Mississippi, Florida, Alabama, Geor-

3. Who was John Brown? What did he and his party do in October? What happened to him and his companions? What was Brown's statement on his trial? What attempt was made on his trial? What was his fate?

4. How did all this operate on public feeling at the South? How was this feeling increased? What is said of the Democratic Convention and its nomination? Mention the other nominees, and the parties they represented. Who were chosen President and Vice-President?

gia, Louisiana, and Texas followed the lead of South Carolina in less than six weeks.

6. On the 4th of February, 1861, delegates from six of the seven seceding states met at Montgomery, Alabama, and formed a government, called the Confederate States of America. On the 8th of February, Jefferson Davis, late United States senator from Mississippi, was elected provisional President, and Alexander H. Stephens, of Georgia, Vice-President. Both were shortly after re-elected for six years.

JEFFERSON DAVIS.

7. Before the Confederate government was organized in February, the Southern leaders seized all the forts and arsenals belonging to the United States within their borders, with the exception of Forts Moultrie and Sumter in Charleston Harbor, Fort Pickens, near Pensacola, and a few posts in Florida. In the places seized was an immense quantity of guns and military stores, valued at nearly $20,000,000, all of which fell into the hands of the Confederates.

8. The condition of things at Washington, during these proceedings, was very deplorable. President Buchanan took no active measures to prevent the seizure of United States property. General Scott warned him and urged him to act with vigor, but he did nothing. General Cass, of Michigan, Secretary of State, resigned in disgust because Buchanan would not interfere. The President's cabinet was composed largely of Southern men, or those who sympathized with them. The little army was scattered at far dis-

---

5. What threats had been made during the canvass? What occurred after the election? What took place on the 17th and 20th of December? What reasons were assigned in the Convention for this step? What states followed in the wake of South Carolina?

6. What important step was taken in February, 1860? Who were chosen permanent President and Vice-President?

7. What prompt movements were made by the South before the Montgomery Convention met? How much United States property was obtained by these seizures?

tant points. The navy was in the same condition. To crown all, the President was only half-hearted, and hesitated to use promptly the means at his command. There were attempts, during the winter, both in and out of Congress, to arrange matters; but nothing came of these movements, and the country drifted rapidly into civil war.

9. Affairs were meanwhile drawing to a crisis in Charleston Harbor. Anderson, with some sixty men, abandoned Fort Moultrie, and occupied the more important post of Fort Sumter. At different points on the harbor shore, and

FORT SUMTER.

at Fort Moultrie, the Carolinians planted cannon commanding the harbor and Fort Sumter. Anderson being short of provisions, and needing re-enforcements, the steamship Star of the West was sent from New York with supplies, and a detachment of 250 men to his assistance. At the mouth of the harbor she was fired on by the Carolina batteries, and compelled to return. This was on the 9th of January, 1861. In this state of affairs, marked by vigor and decision at the

8. How did the President act during all this time? Who warned him, and with what result? What was Cass's conduct? What was the character of Buchanan's cabinet? What was the situation of the army and navy? What was the chief difficulty? What is said of the attempts to harmonize the North and South?

South, and irresolution at the North, Mr. Buchanan's term drew to a close.

SECTION V.

GENERAL REFLECTIONS ON THE CAUSES OF THE CIVIL WAR.

1. As we have now nearly reached the beginning of the Civil War, it becomes necessary to review, in a brief way, the most striking events in that long line which led to this great calamity. We have seen that negro slavery in the United States began in 1620 with the importation of slaves by a Dutch vessel into the colony at Jamestown. The use of slaves was not confined to Virginia, but was encouraged, in course of time, in all the thirteen colonies. It will be remembered that the Puritans of New England enslaved the Indians at the close of the Pequod and King Philip's Wars.

2. Negro slavery, during the colonial times, spread and increased more rapidly in the South, because the climate there was warmer, the soil in many places richer, and because tobacco, which, until the close of the Revolution, was the chief production, needed cheap labor for its cultivation. The distribution of slaves throughout the original thirteen states, together with Tennessee and Kentucky, will best be seen from the following table, drawn up in 1790, seven years after the close of the Revolutionary War.

New Hampshire	158	Maryland	103,036
Rhode Island	952	Virginia	293,427
Connecticut	2,759	North Carolina	100,572
Massachusetts	none.	South Carolina	107,094
New York	21,344	Georgia	29,264
New Jersey	11,423	Tennessee	3,417
Pennsylvania	3,737	Kentucky	11,830
Delaware	8,887	Total	697,897

---

9. Where were affairs drawing to a crisis? What was the situation of things there? What attempt was made to re-enforce Anderson and provision the fort? and with what success? When was this?

1. What review now becomes necessary? What has already been seen elsewhere? Was slavery in this way confined to Virginia? How do we know that the holding of slaves was not regarded with abhorrence in the Northern colonies?

2. Why did negro slavery spread more extensively in the South? What was the whole number of slaves in the year 1790? What state had none? What great Middle State in proportion to its size had the smallest number? Which four states had the greatest number? Give the comparisons regarding the increase of slaves.

From this it will be noticed that from 1620 till 1790, a period of 170 years, the number increased from 20 to 700,000. Of these it is supposed that 300,000 at least were imported directly from Africa. From 1790 to 1860, a period of 70 years, the number increased from 700,000 to 4,000,000; and we must remember that the importation of slaves was forbidden after the year 1808.

3. After the year 1793, the cultivation of cotton as a great staple became possible by the remarkable invention of Whitney's cotton gin. The exportation began almost immediately after this, and thus the two great exported staples of the Southern States came now to be tobacco and cotton. Through these the interests of the South in slave labor kept growing stronger and stronger. On the other hand, in the North, becoming populous by free immigration, the opposition to slavery steadily increased. The South, previous to this new era introduced by the cotton gin—that is, until the close of the decade following the Revolution—was far from being a unit on the question of slavery. No one spoke more strongly against it than the great Virginian, Thomas Jefferson. When, as late as 1784, Virginia ceded her rights to Western territory, it was Thomas Jefferson who, in Congress, brought forward the proposition that all this great domain should be sacred to free labor.

4. As the Northern States increased more rapidly in population, the efforts of Southern statesmen were, on this account, constantly directed toward keeping up the balance of power; that is, in trying to prevent the admission of more Free States than Slave States. By these efforts they were able for a long time to keep the Senate equally balanced, because there were only two senators from each state; but they could not prevent the Free States from gaining, through their population, a majority in the House of Representatives.

---

3. What remarkable invention was made in 1793? How did this affect the industry and productions of the South? What is said of the relation of the North to slave labor? What is said of the early opinions in the South with regard to slave labor?

4. In what way did Southern statesmen try to offset the increase in population of the North? What did they accomplish? Why were they not able to keep up this balance in the House of Representatives?

5. To illustrate how carefully this admission of Free and Slave States was watched and regulated, we will notice the condition of things at three different dates—1819–1845, and 1848. At the close of the year 1819 there were twenty-two states, equally divided—eleven to the North, eleven to the South. The Northern States were New Hampshire, Massachusetts, Rhode Island, Connecticut, Vermont, New York, Pennsylvania, New Jersey, Ohio, Indiana, Illinois. The Southern were Delaware, Maryland, Virginia, North Carolina, South Carolina, Georgia, Tennessee, Kentucky, Alabama, Mississippi, Louisiana.

6. In 1845 there were twenty-six states. Missouri and Florida, two slaveholding states, balanced the two non-slaveholding states, Maine and Michigan. Though the balance of states was thus preserved, the preponderance of population was with the North, for there was an immense territory there rapidly filling with settlers: on the other hand, the area of Southern territory was exhausted. To meet this want, and at the same time retain the equal number of Free and Slave States, Texas, in 1848, was admitted, with her vast territory secured by the war; Wisconsin, a Free State, was admitted shortly after. Now there were 30 states, 15 Northern, 15 Southern. Shortly after the close of the Mexican War, California, Oregon, and Minnesota admitted, gave a majority to the North of three states, and in Congress a majority of six senators and sixty representatives.

7. We are now able to understand the object of those long struggles for power in and out of Congress which ended at last in civil war.

These were principally—

1. The contest on the admission of Missouri as a slave state, ending in the Missouri Compromise Act—1820—Monroe's administration.

---

5. For what purpose are the three dates, 1819, 1845, 1848, chosen? How many states were there in 1819, and how divided? Which of these were admitted after the Revolution?

6. What was the number of states in 1845? What states had been admitted since 1819, and how divided? What is said of the real balance of power between the two sections of the Union. In what way was this remedied in 1848? What was now the number, and how divided? How did the admission of California, Oregon, and Minnesota affect the question of supremacy?

2. The opposition of the South to the TARIFF, which they said was making the North rich at their expense—1828—Adams's administration, and onward.

3. The doctrine of NULLIFICATION and STATE RIGHTS, almost ending in secession and war—1832—Jackson's administration.

4. The ANNEXATION OF TEXAS, and, as a result, WAR with MEXICO—1846—Tyler's administration; 1846-48—Polk's administration.

5. The COMPROMISE ACT OF 1850, called also the Omnibus Act—Fillmore's administration—involving

6. THE KANSAS NEBRASKA STRUGGLE, through the abolition of the Missouri Compromise, thus permitting the people of new territories to determine the question of slavery in them, under what was known as the doctrine of popular or squatter sovereignty—1853—Pierce's administration.

This was the crisis of the struggle; and when in this the North gained the victory, the contest in Congress for power was seen to be virtually at an end. The South felt that there was nothing left for them but secession from a Union that they no longer loved; and the North determined that the Union should not be broken up. What could come of this but war?

8. But the Southern leaders, while preparing for war, repeatedly expressed their firm belief that the North would not fight, and that the separation would be a peaceful one; that, moreover, the North was disunited; and that, last and best of all, England and France would be on their side, because the greater part of the cotton produce of the world was in the South, and Europe needed this for her factories. On the other hand, the North felt equally sure that the South did not mean war, because they thought the South would never take up arms with 4,000,000 of slaves in their midst. They therefore treated the threats of the South as mere idle menace, and regarded their bitterness of feeling as arising out of their loss of power, which bitterness time would soon

---

7. What do we learn from this review? Name those that are mentioned. Describe each in turn. What was the turning-point of the long struggle? What was felt when this came? State the feelings of the South and North when this occurred.

remove. Each section was grievously mistaken about the feelings of the other, and a single spark was all that was needed to fire the magazine.

REVIEW QUESTIONS.—1849-1861.

1. How was Harrison distinguished before he became President?
2. When, and in what way, did California become a source of contention?
3. What was the object, and what were the chief points of the Omnibus Bill?
4. What important event occurred during the discussion of the bill?
5. Who succeeded Harrison?
6. How did the Compromise operate when put in force?
7. Who was President Fillmore?
8. Give the principal events of his administration?
9. What misunderstanding occurred with England in 1852?
10. How was this settled?
11. What expedition was sent out in Fillmore's administration?
12. Describe Senator Douglas's remarkable bill of 1853.
13. How was it received in Congress and by the country?
14. What took place during the excitement of the discussion, as evincing the feelings of the people?
15. What was the state of public feeling during the election of 1854?
16. What party came into existence then? and state its principles.
17. Sketch the principles of the other political parties.
18. Which views triumphed, and how?
19. Who was Buchanan?
20. What were the chief events of his administration?
21. Give the history of the Kansas question?
22. How was this complicated by the action of some of the Free States?
23. What was the great contest during Buchanan's administration?
24. Give the particulars of John Brown's raid, and the effect it produced.
25. How did all this affect the Presidential canvass?
26. State the particulars of the Conventions at Charleston and elsewhere?
27. What followed the election of Lincoln, and how soon?
28. State the ground of secession as given by the South.
29. Name the first Confederate States, and give account of their organization.
30. What is said of the movements in the South?
31. What did Buchanan do?
32. What attempts were made to compromise the quarrel?
33. Sketch the movements in Charleston Harbor?

---

8. What arguments did the Southern leaders give why secession would not lead to war? What views prevailed at the North? What is said of the mutual mistake?

CHAPTER IX.

LINCOLN'S ADMINISTRATION.—CIVIL WAR.—1861-1865.

SECTION I.

EVENTS OF 1861.

1. THE history of Abraham Lincoln, the new president, furnishes a striking proof of the fact that, in the United States, poverty prevents no citizen from rising to the highest position in the gift of the people. In the year 1818 his father moved from Kentucky into Indiana, where, at the age of eight years, young Lincoln, axe in hand, assisted in clearing away the forest. His entire school education, until manhood, did not amount to more than one year. At the age of twenty-one he removed to Illinois, where, while keeping a store, he studied law, borrowing each evening the law-books, and returning them in the morning. He was chosen to the Legislature, became a lawyer, was sent as representative to Congress, and, in a canvass for the position of United States Senator, was defeated by Judge Douglas. It was this contest that brought him prominently before the country, and led the way to his nomination as President.

PRESIDENT LINCOLN.

2. **Attack on Fort Sumter.**—When Lincoln entered on his duties, March 4, Major Anderson was still in possession of Fort Sumter. The Confederates heard that the United

1. Of what does Lincoln's life form an illustration? What is said of his early life, and of his studies after he reached manhood? What positions did he fill? What led to his nomination to the presidency?

States government would re-enforce and provision the fort at all risks; they therefore determined to capture it before this could be done. On the morning of April 12, they opened fire from their batteries, and the bombardment was continued for 34 hours. At the end of that time many of the guns in the fort were dismantled, and the handful of men composing the garrison was so utterly worn out, that Anderson was compelled to surrender. No lives were lost on either side during the attack.

3. The telegraph published throughout the country the news of the bombardment, and its result. In the South, and particularly in South Carolina, the people were wild with joy. At the North the news was generally received with astonishment and profound indignation. It was plain now that war had begun. There was no longer any doubt as to what the South meant, and 75,000 volunteers for three months sprang to arms at the call of President Lincoln, April 14. The attack on Fort Sumter united the South as well as the North. States that had before hesitated soon joined the Confederacy—Virginia on the 17th of April; Arkansas, May 6; North Carolina, May 20; and on the 20th of June, Tennessee, making the number of Confederate States eleven. Missouri and Kentucky remained neutral.

4. Virginia had scarcely passed the act of secession when 250 of her militia were sent to seize the United States Arsenal at Harper's Ferry. The officer in command, on their approach, April 18, destroyed a portion of the muskets, set fire to the buildings, and retreated north into Pennsylvania. At the same time the Virginians were planning to surprise the great navy yard at Norfolk. Hearing this, the officer in command, without waiting to strike a blow for its defense, spiked the cannon, scuttled or burned the war-ships, and set fire to the buildings. Notwithstanding this destruction, April 20, the Confederates obtained nearly 2000

2. What was the state of affairs in Charleston Harbor in March? On what did the Confederates resolve, and why? When was the bombardment begun? What is said of its continuance, and the result?

3. How was the news received in the South? How at the North? What did the people of the North at last realize? How did they show their spirit and determination? What movements took place in the South? Name all the Confederate States in June, 1861. What two states remained neutral?

cannon, besides a vast amount of stores; and they afterward raised some of the vessels that had been sunk. The United States property destroyed and captured here was valued at ten millions of dollars.

DESTRUCTION OF THE NAVY YARD AT NORFOLK.

5. Washington was threatened by the Confederate troops, but help was approaching from the North. On the 17th of April, only two days after the President's proclamation, the Sixth Massachusetts Regiment left Boston for the capital. On the 19th, while passing through the streets of Baltimore, it was attacked by a secession mob, and three soldiers were killed and eight wounded. It made its way, however, to the capital, where it was soon joined by other regiments from the Northern States. For the present the capital was safe, and President Lincoln, May 3, made a call for 83,000 men

4. In what way did Virginia first show her zeal? Against what other important point did her troops move? What was the conduct of the United States officer at that place? How did the Confederacy profit by this capture? To what extent were the United States losers?

for the army and navy, to serve during the war. The troops were speedily raised.

6. **The War in Virginia.**—The United States government held possession of Fortress Monroe, at the entrance to the Chesapeake. General B. F. Butler, of Massachusetts, was stationed here in May, with a force increased presently to 12,000 men. A detachment from General Magruder's army of 8000 Confederates was encamped so near the fort that they became troublesome. In attempting to dislodge them at Big Bethel, a party of the Union troops was defeated June 10th.

VICINITY OF FORTRESS MONROE.

7. A force, composed principally of Ohio and Indiana men, was sent, under General M'Clellan, into Western Virginia. He pushed the Confederates so vigorously that they were beaten at Philippi on June 3d, and again at Rich Mountain on the 11th of July. A few days after, at Carrick's Ford, on Cheat River, General Garnett, the Confederate, made a stand, but was himself killed, and his troops were compelled to flee. In the latter of these battles M'Clellan was assisted by an able officer, Colonel Rosecrans. On August 10, Rosecrans, now made a general, assaulted General Floyd, the late Union Secretary of War, now at the head of a Confederate force, at Carnifex Ferry, on the Gauley River, and compelled him to retreat. At Cheat Mountain, the Confederates, under Robert E. Lee, were repulsed September 14th, and shortly the enemy retired from Western Virginia.

8. The Union forces at Washington crossed the Potomac

---

5. What city was threatened by the Confederates? What was the first assistance that came to it from the North? What occurred on its march? How was Washington saved? What call was made by the President, and how was it met?

6. What important place in Virginia remained in the hands of the government? What force was here in June? Describe the skirmish that took place not far from this?

7. What occurred in Western Virginia in May? Who commanded the Union troops? What other officer distinguished himself there? What took place at the Gauley River? What was the result of all these successes? Where is Philippi? Romney? Cheat Mountain?

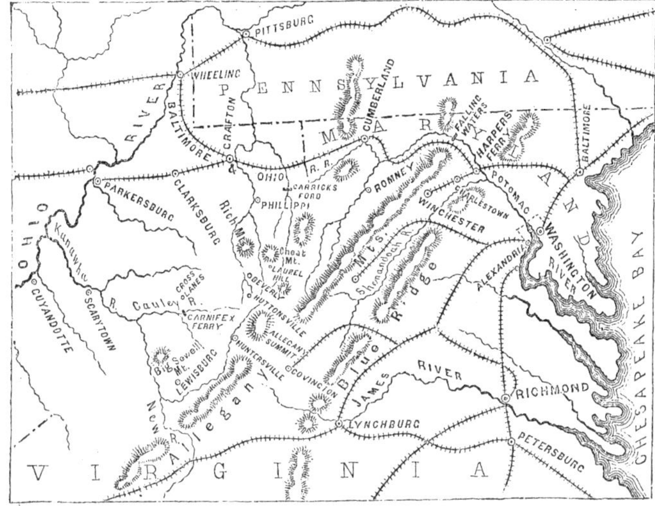

CAMPAIGN IN WESTERN VIRGINIA.

and occupied Alexandria, nine miles below Washington, May 23, General M'Dowell in command. The Confederate army, under General Beauregard (*bó-rā gard*), was encamped, toward the end of June, at Manassas Junction, 27 miles from Alexandria. As the Confederate government was about to assemble at Richmond, the new capital, on the 20th of July, it was deemed necessary by the United States government to make a forward movement. M'Dowell accordingly advanced, and, on the 21st of July, attacked Beauregard at Bull Run, a small stream in front of the enemy. The force on each side was between 20,000 and 30,000.

9. The fighting in the forenoon was favorable to the Unionists. As the day wore on, the enemy received reenforcements under General Joseph E. Johnston, and these turned the tide of battle. M'Dowell's troops were seized with panic, and fled in great disorder, leaving behind them nearly 1500 killed and wounded, and as many more prison-

8. What movement was made by the Union troops at Washington? Where was the Confederate army lying? Where, when, and by whom were they attacked? Where is Bull Run? Alexandria? Manassas Junction?

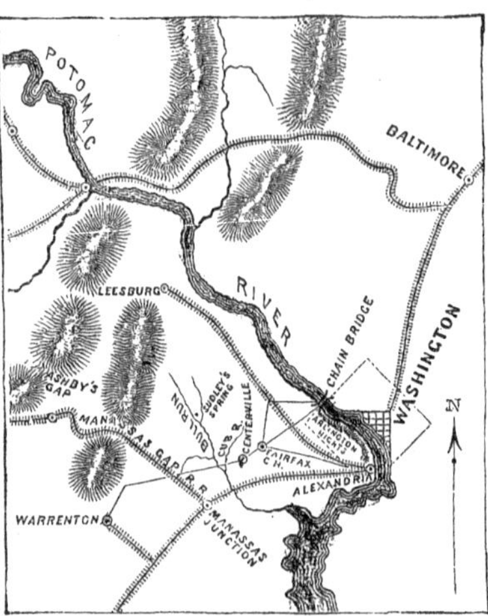

THE BATTLE OF BULL RUN.

ers. Beauregard did not pursue; had he done so, he might have entered Washington, so great was the confusion. As this was the first important battle between the two armies, the defeat at first greatly depressed the spirits of the North. The disgrace was all the harder to bear when it became known how the Confederates were re-enforced at so fortunate a moment. General Patterson, with 20,000 men, had been ordered to watch General Joseph E. Johnston, who had just been forced to evacuate Harper's Ferry, and prevent him from joining Beauregard at Manassas. Instead of this, he permitted Johnston to slip away from him to Bull Run.

10. After the battle, General M'Clellan was brought from Western Virginia to take command at Washington. Congress ordered a levy of 500,000 men, and the spirit of the people was such that this force was soon raised. M'Clellan was busy organizing and drilling these recruits during the fall and winter. The only noticeable event in the Potomac Army during the fall was the disaster at Ball's Bluff, on the Potomac, near Leesburg, Virginia, October 21st. Colonel Baker, United States senator from Oregon, at the head of nearly 2000 men, was sent by General Stone across the river at Edwards's Ferry, to attack General Evans at Leesburg. Here he was overpowered, himself killed, and his troops driven to the river side, where a great number were drown-

9. Describe the battle of Bull Run. What was the Union loss? What opportunity did Beauregard lose? What effect was produced at the North by the defeat? What made this felt more bitterly?

HARPER'S FERRY.

ed trying to cross to the Maryland side, sufficient boats not having been provided in view of disaster. The loss was very severe: only 1100 out of 1900 men returned.

11. **Events in Missouri.**—Although Missouri had not joined the Confederate States, the secessionists were making powerful efforts to carry her out of the Union. A secession camp, named Camp Jackson, was formed near St. Louis, in May, but was broken up by the activity of Captain Lyon, a United States officer. By this prompt movement the arsenal at St. Louis was saved. Large bodies of Confederates poured into Southwest Missouri, where there were important lead mines, very necessary to their armies. On the 17th of June, Lyon, now general, defeated Governor Jackson at Booneville. The governor was again beaten at

---

10. Who was appointed to the command of the army round Washington? How many men were called for? How was this call met? In what was M'Clellan occupied? What occurred on the Potomac during the fall? Describe the battle of Ball's Bluff. Why was the loss so heavy?

Carthage on the 5th of July by Colonel Sigel (*sē gel'*), after a severe engagement.

12. On the 10th of August a heavy battle was fought by General Lyon at Wilson's Creek, near Springfield, with a superior force of Confederates under Generals M'Cullough and Price. Lyon was killed, but the enemy were repulsed. After the battle the Union troops fell back to Rolla, near the centre of the state. General Price, in command of 20,000 Confederates, pushed westward toward Lexington, on the Missouri River, held by Colonel Mulligan with 2600 men. After a brave defense, Mulligan surrendered to Price on the 20th of September.

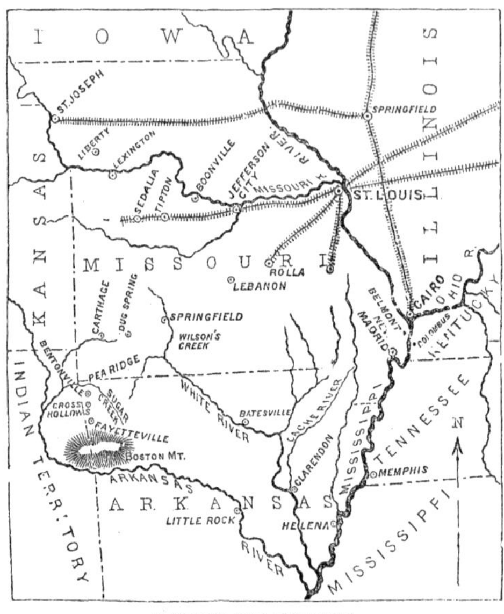

MISSOURI AND ARKANSAS.

13. General John C. Fremont, appointed to the command of the Western Army, now drove General Price before him south through the state. Fremont reached Springfield in October, and was preparing to attack the enemy, when he was removed from his command, November 2. General Hunter took his place; and the Union Army, instead of fighting, fell back to St. Louis, General Price following it. General Halleck superseded Hunter November 18, and push-

11. What was the state of things in Missouri in May? What part of the state was particularly important to the enemy, and why? Mention the battles in June and July. Where is Booneville? Carthage?

12. Describe the battle of Wilson's Creek. Where is this? What was the result? What was the next Confederate movement, and the result?

ed Price south toward Arkansas, the latter leaving his prisoners and military stores on the way.

14. Kentucky, like Missouri, had chosen to remain neutral. The Confederate government ordered General Polk to take military possession of the state, without regard to the wishes of its people. Polk at once occupied and fortified Columbus, thus blockading the Mississippi. Opposite this, at Belmont, Missouri, was stationed a body of Confederate troops. On the 7th of November, General U. S. Grant, having moved from Cairo, Illinois, with 3000 men, attacked the camp at Belmont, and at first drove the enemy with loss to the river. But delay occurred; Polk turned the guns of Columbus on the Union troops, and sent over re-enforcements. Grant was then compelled to retreat.

15. **Events on the Coast and at Sea.**—The Federal government, on the 27th of April, ordered a blockade of all the seaports on the Southern coast. The forts at the entrance to nearly all these ports had been seized by the Confederates before the war actually began, and it was necessary that they should be captured if the blockade was to be effectual. Accordingly, the first movement was made in August against Hatteras Inlet, where were two sand forts commanding the entrance to Albemarle and Pamlico Sounds. A combined force, under Commodore Stringham and General Butler, captured them on the 29th of August.

16. The extent of coast blockaded by the Union steamships was so great that it became necessary to have some harbor near the centre of the line where repairs could be made, and where military and naval supplies could be stored and obtained. Port Royal Harbor, South Carolina, was decided to be the most desirable. It was defended by Forts Walker and Beauregard, one on Hilton Head, the other on the opposite side of the channel. Commodore Dupont and

13. Who was made general of the Union troops? What was his success? Who succeeded him? State the movements of both armies. Who superseded Hunter? How did Halleck succeed?

14. What is said about Confederate movements in Kentucky? What occurred at Belmont? Why is the Belmont attack especially worthy of notice?

15. What important measure was adopted by the Federal government? What made the enforcement of the blockade difficult? What important capture was made in August?

General Thomas W. Sherman, at the head of a large naval and military expedition, captured these, after a brilliant engagement, November 7. Thenceforward Port Royal became a great dépôt for the Union fleets and armies.

17. As the blockade became more and more close, it was difficult for the Confederates to carry on trade with foreign nations. There were fast-sailing steamers, called blockade-runners, built in England specially for this business, and many of them were able, for a time, to elude the American cruisers. In a small steamer, two Confederate commissioners, Mason and Slidell, escaped from Charleston Harbor, October 12th, and reached Cuba, whence they took passage in the British merchant steamer Trent for England. Captain Wilkes, in the United States steamer San Jacinto, stopped the Trent at sea, boarded her, seized the two commissioners and their secretaries, and sailed with them to Boston Harbor, where they were imprisoned.

18. There was great indignation in England when the news of this seizure arrived. The English government promptly demanded satisfaction for the insult to her flag, and required the release of the Confederate commissioners. It was understood that France agreed with Great Britain in the propriety of these demands. In this critical situation, Mr. Seward, the American Secretary of State, hastened to send word to London that Captain Wilkes had acted without authority, and the commissioners were put on board a steamer at Boston and sent on their journey. Thus the danger of war with England, and possibly with France, which the Confederates greatly desired, was happily averted.

19. Fort Pickens was situated on Santa Rosa Island, opposite Pensacola Navy Yard. The latter was disgracefully surrendered to the Confederates when they were seizing forts and arsenals; but the fort was saved to the Union by the courage and patriotism of a Union officer, Lieutenant

16. What was necessary in order to make the blockade effectual? What was decided on? How, when, and by whom was Port Royal gained to the Union arms?

17. In what way did the Confederates break through the blockade? What memorable use was made of one of these blockade runners? State what is said of the stoppage of the Trent.

18. How did the English look on this conduct? What demands were made? How was the danger of war with England averted?

Slemmer. He was succeeded in the command by Colonel Brown, who arrived with re-enforcements. On a dark night, October 9, the Confederates came over in force from Pensacola, and, after surprising and severely handling a New York regiment, were driven off. Throughout the war, Fort Pickens firmly held guard over the approaches to Pensacola.

20. **Reflections at the Close of 1861.**—The Confederates had greatly the advantage at the commencement of the war. They were prepared to fight. The North did not think the South meant war, and was surprised. A large part of the army and naval officers was from the South, nearly all of which joined the Confederates. The enemy thus had trained generals to lead their armies from the very first.

21. By the seizure of the United States arsenals and navy yards the Confederates obtained, at the very beginning of the contest, a great quantity of cannon and small-arms. At Norfolk alone they captured 2000 guns. In population, and money, and industry, and machinery, however, the North had greatly the advantage; and it became tolerably plain, after the end of the first year, that it would be a war in which the North would win, if both sections were left to fight it out. Would they be left alone? That was the question. The Confederates hoped and believed that England and France would interfere, and this expectation very powerfully sustained them.

22. In 1861, the North suffered serious reverses in the loss of Norfolk, of Harper's Ferry, in the battle of Bull Run, and in the severe check at Ball's Bluff. Much, however, had been gained. Missouri was saved to the Union after hard fighting. Western Virginia had been preserved in the same way. The rapidly increasing navy had made the blockade effectual. The army, augmented by numerous levies to a million of men, was being drilled for future operations. The

---

19. Where was Fort Pickens situated? Was this in possession of the Confederates? Why not? Who was sent to command there? What happened there in October?

20. What remark is made regarding the North and South at the commencement of the war? State what advantage the South had in officers.

21. How and to what extent had the South been supplied with arms? In what had the North a superiority? What was plain at the end of 1861? What buoyed up the hopes of the Confederates?

South was also active, and was straining every nerve in preparation for the struggle of the next year.

REVIEW QUESTIONS.—1861.

1. What led to the attack on Fort Sumter?
2. What effect was produced on the North and South by the attack?
3. Name the Confederate States after June 20, 1861.
4. How did Virginia show her activity?
5. What results followed?
6. How was the capital saved from attack?
7. How was West Virginia preserved to the Union?
8. What officers first acquired celebrity here?
9. What led to the battle of Bull Run?
10. Describe the battle, and the results.
11. How was Missouri saved to the Union?
12. What distinguished men appear in the Missouri campaign?
13. State the plan of military movements in 1861.
14. Sketch the general condition of affairs, North and South, at the close of the year.

SECTION II.

EVENTS OF 1862.

1. At the beginning of the year 1862 the war had assumed immense proportions. It was no longer to be carried on by one or two small armies acting without concert, but through a wide, yet connected series of naval and military operations, some of them at points more than a thousand miles apart. The great objects to be accomplished by these fleets and armies were chiefly, in the West and extreme South, the opening of the Mississippi River to the Union armies; in the East, the capture of Richmond, now the Confederate capital; and the thorough blockade of the Southern coast.

2. In the West, General Buell was in command of an army, the headquarters of which were at Louisville; General Halleck, with another army, lay farther west, with his headquarters at St. Louis. In addition to these, a large fleet of river steamers and gun-boats, under Commodore Foote, was at Cairo, at the junction of the Ohio and Mississippi, waiting to assist in the impending military movements in that quar-

22. State the reverses endured by the North in 1861. Show, on the other hand, how much had been gained. How were the North busy at the close of the war? What is said of the South in the same connection?

1. How did the preparations for the year 1862 compare with those of 1861? What did the government aim to accomplish by these preparations?

ter. There were also operations in progress against the extreme South. A combined naval and military expedition, under Captain Farragut and General B. F. Butler, was preparing to enter the Lower Mississippi from its mouth and capture the city of New Orleans. The expedition was thus to form a part in the great plan for the opening of that river.

3. In the East, General M'Clellan lay along the Potomac with more than 150,000 men, getting ready to move against Richmond; and an expedition, under General Burnside and Commodore Goldsborough, was already on its way to attack the forts on Roanoke Island, on the coast of North Carolina. The plan of military operations for the year, although on a great scale, was very simple. By order of President Lincoln, all the armies were required to move forward on the 22d of February, and crush the Confederacy by their combined movements. Those in the West began a little in advance of this time, and will be noticed under

4. **Operations in Kentucky, West Tennessee, and Mississippi.**—On the 9th of January, Colonel Garfield, after a brilliant engagement, routed Humphrey Marshall, at the head of a Confederate force, on the Big Sandy River, in Eastern Kentucky. On the 19th, General Thomas, with severe fighting, defeated and drove the Confederates from Mill Spring, a strong place in the same part of the state. This was in the department of General Buell.

5. In Western Kentucky, in the department of General Halleck, the enemy had forts at Columbus on the Mississippi, and at Bowling Green on the Big Barren River. South of these, in West Tennessee, there were Fort Henry on the Tennessee, and Fort Donelson on the Cumberland. If we examine the map, we shall see how these opposed the march of the Union troops. General Halleck determined to pierce this line by capturing Forts Henry and Donelson, which he could easily reach by water, on account of the peculiar

2. What two great armies lay west of the Cumberland Mountains? In what way were the movements of these to be assisted? What expedition was preparing to enter the South from the Gulf? Of what general plan did this form a part?

3. What great army was in the East? State its object. What preparations were already made for the more perfect blockade of the coast? How were the first movements of their armies regulated? What operations anticipated this date?

4. What were the Union successes in Kentucky in the beginning of the year?

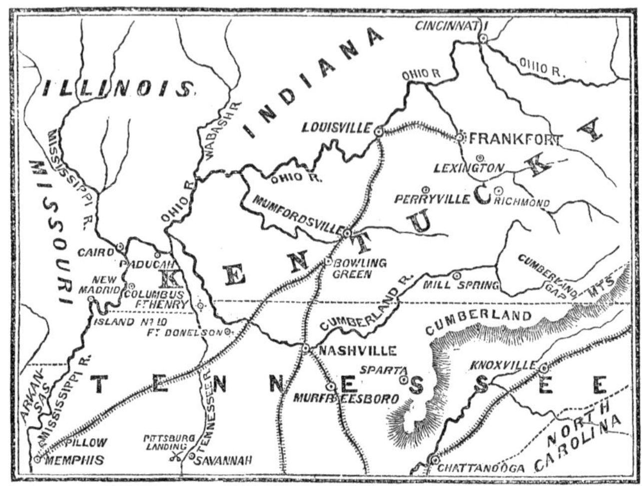

KENTUCKY AND WEST TENNESSEE.

course of the Tennessee and Cumberland Rivers. If he proved successful in this, he clearly saw that Nashville, the capital of the state, would fall into his hands, and the Confederates would be forced to evacuate Bowling Green and Columbus. The first point of attack was Fort Henry.

6. Commodore Foote, with his gun-boats, was sent up the Tennessee, and General Grant, with the troops, was ordered to proceed by land. Before the latter could get his men near enough to surround the works, the commander of the fort surrendered to Commodore Foote, after a heavy bombardment by the gun-boats, February 6. Nearly all the garrison, to the number of three thousand, escaped to Fort Donelson.

7. Although the latter was only twelve miles across the country from Fort Henry, it was six days before General Grant could march his army to that post. Of this delay the enemy made good use in re-enforcing the garrison and

---

5. What fortified places opposed the advance of the Union troops? Where were these posts? On what did General Halleck determine? Why did he make this choice? What was the first point of attack?

6. What arrangements were made for the capture of Fort Henry? How was it taken? Why did so many of the garrison escape?

strengthening their works. Grant was compelled to wait the movements of the gun-boats, which had to steam down the Tennessee, then up the Cumberland, stopping on the way at Cairo for supplies and re-enforcements for the army. The gun-boats did not reach the neighborhood of Fort Donelson until the 14th.

8. It was a much stronger place than Fort Henry, and had a garrison of fourteen or fifteen thousand men. In the attack on the 14th the gun-boats were severely injured and driven back by the Confederate batteries, Commodore Foote being seriously wounded. Grant's army, increased to the number of 30,000, had, in the mean time, gradually surrounded the fort. Through his lines the Confederates attempted to cut their way on the 15th; but after a bloody battle they were repulsed, and a portion of their intrenchments captured by the Union troops. Next day, the 16th, General Buckner surrendered Fort Donelson, and not less than 12,000 men. This was by far the most brilliant victory yet gained by the Union arms.

9. The line of Confederate defense through Tennessee and Kentucky was now shattered. Bowling Green was evacuated, and shortly after Columbus. The way was now open to Nashville, which was immediately occupied by the Union troops. The national army, re-enforced, moved up the Tennessee as far as Pittsburg Landing, where Grant again took the command, and General Buell marched from Nashville to join him there.

10. On Sunday morning, April 6th, before the arrival of Buell, the Confederate army, under General A. S. Johnston, Beauregard being second in command, suddenly fell on Grant's troops, encamped at Shiloh Church, near Pittsburg Landing, with the river in their rear. During a day's dreadful slaughter, in which Johnston was killed, the Union troops were driven back step by step to a small plateau near the

---

7. What was Grant's next movement? What delay occurred, and with what result? What was the cause of the delay?

8. Who began the attack, and when? What was the result? What is said of Grant's operations? How did the siege terminate?

9. What was the first result of the capture of these two forts? What followed? What was the next forward movement of the Union troops?

edge of the Tennessee, protected by the fire of the gun-boats. The Union army was saved that day by the extraordinary efforts of Brigadier General W. T. Sherman, who commanded a division. During the night Buell's troops arrived, and, on the morning of April 7th, Grant moved to the attack. Beauregard was compelled to fall back, and he slowly retreated to Corinth, Mississippi, some fifteen miles distant, commanding an important system of railroads.

11. General Halleck, made commander of the different Union armies in the West, brought them together, and, at the head of more than 100,000 men, moved against Corinth. Beauregard, seeing that he was greatly outnumbered, evacuated the place on the approach of Halleck, and on the 30th of May it was entered by the Union troops.

12. While Grant was fighting the battle of Shiloh, events of great importance took place on the Mississippi River. When the Confederates left Columbus they fortified Island No. 10, ten miles below. The position was so strong by nature, and they had so strengthened it by art, that they thought it could not be taken. But all these preparations could not stop General Pope with his Western men, nor Commodore Foote and his gun-boats. After a bombardment of twenty-three days, it was captured on the 7th of April, with 5000 prisoners, the same morning that Grant repulsed Beauregard at Shiloh.

13. Fort Pillow was the next strong point on the river, but before it could be invested Pope's army was withdrawn to join Halleck in his movement against Corinth. Commodore Foote, disabled by the wound he had received at Fort Donelson, was succeeded by Captain Davis, who, after a severe battle, destroyed a part of the Confederate iron-clads near Fort Pillow, May 10. The fort itself was abandoned on June 4, in consequence of the evacuation of Corinth by

---

10. State what befell Grant's army on the morning of the 6th of April? What was the result of the day's contest? How was the disaster changed into a victory? To what point did the Confederates retreat?

11. Who assumed the entire command of the Western armies? With what force did he move against the Confederates? How did they resist him?

12. What was meanwhile taking place on the Mississippi River? What is said of the preparations at Island No. 10? How was the Confederate confidence overthrown?

Beauregard. On the 6th of June Davis pushed down to Memphis, where he destroyed the Confederate fleet, and that city was immediately surrendered. The Union troops now held a line from Memphis, on the Mississippi, through Corinth, nearly to Chattanooga. All of Western Kentucky and West Tennessee were under their control.

14. The Confederates still held East Tennessee, and determined to make one powerful effort to restore their power in Kentucky. An army in two divisions, under Bragg and Kirby Smith, was sent there to make the attempt. Bragg, leaving Chattanooga, was to march northwestward, and Smith, starting from Knoxville, was to join him in the centre of the state. Smith moved in the month of August, and, after defeating the Union troops at Richmond, Kentucky, August 30, entered Lexington and Frankfort. He then moved toward the Ohio, threatening Cincinnati; but the active measures taken there by General Lewis Wallace compelled him to fall back, and he joined Bragg at Frankfort October 4.

15. Bragg's objective point was Louisville. On his march he captured, after two slight engagements, 4500 Union troops at Mumfordsville, September 17. General Buell, who lay at Nashville, on discovering Bragg's purpose, moved by forced marches to the relief of Louisville, and reached it only one day before the Confederates. Here he was shortly re-enforced to the number of 100,000 men. Bragg then fell back, ravaging the country, followed very slowly by Buell, who came up with him at Perryville October 8. Here a battle was fought, which, after severe loss on both sides, ended doubtfully. Bragg continued his retreat so leisurely that he was able to take out of Kentucky a wagon train of plunder forty miles in length.

---

13. What was the next strong point on the river? What is said of the operations against this fort? When and how was Fort Pillow occupied by the Union troops? Who succeeded Foote? Describe Davis's movements on the river. How can you show the progress made by the Union troops?

14. What part of Tennessee was still held by the Confederates? What expedition was arranged by the enemy? Describe Kirby Smith's movement in full. How is East Tennessee bounded?

15. What was Bragg's object? What success did he meet with on his march? How was he prevented from gaining his object? Why was the battle of Perryville fought, and with what result? What is said of Bragg's retreat? See Map, page 334.

16. While Bragg was in Kentucky, a Confederate army, under Generals Price and Van Dorn, threatened Grant at Corinth. General Halleck had been called to Washington to act as general-in-chief, and Grant was appointed to the command of the army west of the Tennessee. The latter, joined by General Rosecrans, moved against Price, and defeated him at Iuka, September 19. Grant then proceeded northward to Jackson, Tennessee, leaving General Rosecrans to defend Corinth with 30,000 men.

17. Here the latter was attacked on the 4th of October by Generals Van Dorn and Price, at the head of 40,000 Confederates. After a bloody battle they were driven back, with a loss of over 6000 in killed and wounded, and were afterward pursued for 40 miles. The Union loss was only 315 killed. For this brilliant victory Rosecrans was promoted to the command of the Army of the Cumberland in place of General Buell.

18. Rosecrans soon gathered the bulk of this army round Nashville, and marched to attack the Confederate army under Bragg, which lay at Murfreesboro', 30 miles distant. At Stone River, near that place, he himself was attacked and driven back, December 31. On the 2d of January the battle was renewed, and Bragg in turn was repulsed, but retreated in good order. This was one of the bloodiest battles of the war. The loss on each side was estimated at from 10,000 to 12,000.

19. Grant meanwhile arranged an expedition against Vicksburg, a strongly fortified position on the Mississippi, 400 miles above New Orleans. General Sherman was to move down the river from Memphis with 40,000 men, and the gun-boats under Porter; while Grant pushed forward by land from Jackson. At first the combined movements promised complete success; but, unfortunately, Van Dorn was able to get into the rear of Grant, cutting off his

16. What was meanwhile going on in Mississippi? Why was Grant in command in that region? Where is Iuka? What occurred here? What is said of Grant's movements?

17. Where, when, and by whom was Rosecrans attacked? How did the battle terminate? What reward did Rosecrans receive for this?

18. How did Rosecrans employ his new command? Describe the battle of Stone River. What is said of the losses on both sides?

supplies at Holly Springs, December 20, and the latter was compelled to abandon his purpose. Sherman, unaware of what had happened to Grant, started from Memphis on the day of this misfortune. Assisted by the gun-boats, he landed on the Yazoo River, and attacked the works on the bluff north of Vicksburg, but was repulsed with considerable loss. This battle of Chickasaw Bayou, December 29th, ended active operations in the Department of Mississippi for the year 1862.

THE WAR IN THE SOUTH AND SOUTHWEST.

20. **The War in the Southwest.**—In the spring, an important battle was fought in the department of General Halleck, on the northwest edge of Arkansas, at Pea Ridge, among

19. Where and what was now the strong Confederate post on the Mississippi? Where is Vicksburg? What expedition was arranged against it? How was the plan interfered with? Describe the attack and the result. What is the name of this battle?

the mountains. General Curtis pushed Price and M'Culloch out of Missouri in the early part of the year. General Van Dorn, at the head of 20,000 fresh men, on the 7th of March attacked Curtis, who, with not more than 11,000, had taken post on the heights around Sugar Creek. The battle lasted two days, and ended in the repulse of Van Dorn. Curtis was greatly indebted to the skill and gallantry of General Sigel for the victory at Pea Ridge.

21. **Opening of the Lower Mississippi. Capture of New Orleans.**—In the expedition against New Orleans, Captain Farragut was chosen to command the powerful fleet of 45 vessels, including mortar-boats, and General Butler the land troops, amounting to 15,000. By the beginning of March, the entire expedition was assembled at Ship Island, near the mouth of the Mississippi. About 30 miles from the Gulf, and 70 miles below New Orleans, the river channel was guarded by strong forts, St. Philip and Jackson, and by a chain which, resting on hulks, stretched across the river. During a terrible bombardment of six days, from the 18th to the 24th of April, Farragut came to the conclusion that the fire of the mortar-boats could not reduce the forts, and he determined to run past them.

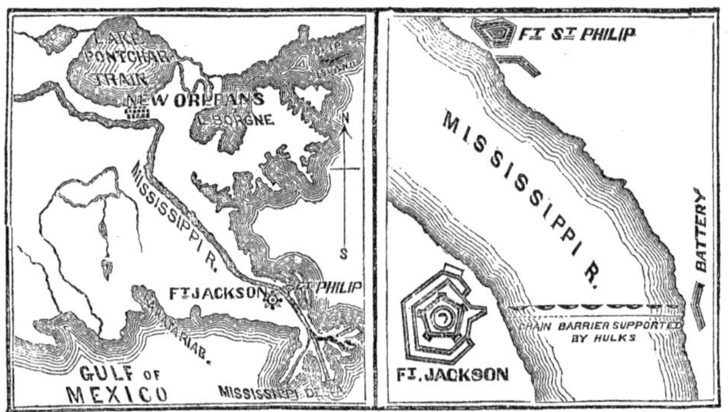

FROM NEW ORLEANS TO THE GULF. FORTS JACKSON AND ST. PHILIP.

20. What severe battle occurred in Arkansas in March, 1862? Where is Pea Ridge? Why was the battle considered so praiseworthy to Curtis and Sigel? See the numbers engaged.

21. State the preparations for the expedition against New Orleans. How was it defended on the river? What attempts were made against the forts?

22. On the 20th of April, the chain and barricades were, with great bravery, cut through, so as to permit a free passage for his ships. At three o'clock on the morning of the 24th he sailed up the river in the darkness, at the head of 17 vessels, carrying 294 guns. A dreadful battle ensued, but Farragut slowly passed Fort Jackson, and immediately attacked the Confederate fleet of 16 armed steamers, the steam battery Louisiana, and the iron-plated ram Manassas. When the morning sun had risen through the fog, Fort St. Philip had been passed, and the greater part of the Confederate fleet, including the Louisiana and the Manassas, had either been destroyed or captured.

PASSAGE OF FORTS JACKSON AND ST. PHILIP.

23. Next day, the 25th, Farragut appeared in front of New Orleans, which lay helpless under his guns. On the 28th, Forts St. Philip and Jackson surrendered to Captain Porter, who remained down the river in command of the mortar fleet. On the 1st of May, General Butler entered the city, and took possession of it with his troops. A part of Farragut's fleet was sent up the river, and occupied Baton Rouge, the capital of the state. The expedition of Far-

22. How was success achieved? Describe Farragut's movements fully.

ragut and Butler proved a complete success. The Lower Mississippi was opened, New Orleans wrested from the Confederates, and their iron-clad fleet completely destroyed. Farragut pushed up the river, and, passing the batteries at Vicksburg without much injury, met the fleet of Davis at Memphis.

24. **Operations on the Atlantic Coast. 1. Burnside's Expedition.**—Two long inland seas, called Albemarle and Pamlico Sounds, stretch from the coast far into the State of North Carolina. The object of General Burnside's expedition was to obtain the control of these seas by the capture of Roanoke Island, which commanded the entrance to Albemarle Sound, and was the key to all the rear defenses of Norfolk. In addition, the cities and towns on the main land were to be occupied, and the Confederate vessels and iron-clads building in these waters to be destroyed.

25. On the 11th of January, 1862, the expedition left Hampton Roads, and, after encountering a severe storm, passed through Hatteras Inlet on the 28th. The fleet came to anchor off Roanoke Island on the 6th of February, and on the 8th the army, assisted by the guns of the fleet, attacked and captured the fort, with 2500 prisoners. Two days after, the Confederate fleet in the Sound was all either destroyed or captured. On the 14th of March, Newbern, with 46 heavy guns and military stores, fell into the hands of Burnside after a severely-fought battle. The final and complete success of the expedition was reached on the 25th of April in the capture of Fort Macon, which defended the harbor of Beaufort, in North Carolina.

27. **2. Expedition against the Coasts of Florida and Georgia.**—The withdrawal of troops from Florida for service in the Confederate army permitted a Union expedition from Port Royal, February 28, to obtain easy possession of Fernandina and Fort Clinch; of Jacksonville, on the St. John's

23. What followed on the 25th and 28th? When was the city occupied by the United States troops? State the result of the expedition. What were Farragut's further movements?

24. Where and what are Albemarle and Pamlico Sounds? See Map, page 371. What was to be gained by Burnside's expedition?

25. What were the first movements? Describe the attack on Roanoke Island. What occurred on the 10th and 14th? What was the last success of the expedition?

River; of St. Augustine, with Fort Marion; and in Georgia of the important town of Brunswick, and also Darien, at the mouth of the Altamaha. These were all captured in the month of March.

27. **3. The Engagement between the Monitor and the Merrimac.**—When Norfolk was surrendered to the Virginians in 1861, the steam frigate Merrimac was scuttled and sunk. The Confederates afterward raised her, lowered her deck, covered it with a slant roof which they plated with railroad iron, fitted her with a long iron prow to act as a ram, and named her the Virginia.

28. A fleet of Union war-ships and smaller vessels lay off Fortress Monroe, in Hampton Roads, on the 8th of March, 1862. At noon, the Virginia, accompanied by two small vessels, steamed down to attack the fleet, and, utterly regardless of the shot and shell that rained harmlessly on her sides, struck the sloop of war Cumberland with her iron prow so dreadful a blow that she sank in a few minutes. The captain of the frigate Congress, fearful of the same fate, ran his vessel ashore, and was compelled to surrender. At sunset the ram steamed back to Norfolk, having destroyed two frigates and 250 officers and men, with a loss to herself of only two killed and eight wounded.

29. During the night, the Monitor, an iron-plated vessel of a new construction, invented by Captain John Ericsson, and commanded by Lieutenant Worden, arrived from the North at Fortress Monroe. Soon after sunrise next morning, March 0, it met and attacked the Virginia after she came out from the Elizabeth River. Although one fifth of her antagonist's size, she compelled the Virginia, after an engagement of several hours, to return disabled to Norfolk. The latter did not again appear in the harbor. Never had any arrival proved more fortunate. The little iron-clad Monitor had saved the rest of the fleet. The battle opened

---

26. What expedition left Port Royal in February? What did it accomplish? What made this success comparatively easy? In what month were these places occupied?

27. Describe the construction of the Confederate iron-clad Virginia. What was its origin?

28. What was the state of things in Hampton Roads on the morning of March 8? What occurred during the afternoon? How much damage was done by sunset? See Map, page 324.

a new era in naval warfare, and was the first contest in the world between iron-clad ships.

THE MONITOR AND THE VIRGINIA, OR "MERRIMAC."

30. **4. Closing of Savannah as a Confederate Port.**—An expediton against Fort Pulaski, one of the chief defenses of the city of Savannah, resulted in the surrender of the fort, April 11, to General Hunter, after a severe bombardment of 15 hours. By the fall of Pulaski, Savannah was thoroughly closed against a class of ships known as Anglo-Confederate blockade-runners. The city itself was not captured until December, 1864.

31. **Military Operations in Virginia. 1. Shenandoah Valley.**—General Banks, in command of the Union troops in the Shenandoah Valley, in accordance with the general forward movement ordered by the President, had advanced as far south as Harrisonburg toward the end of March. Thereupon that vigorous Confederate general, popularly known as "Stonewall Jackson," from the saying at Bull Run that his brigade "would stand like a stone wall," was sent into

---

29. What arrival came, and when? Describe what took place next day. Why was its arrival of so much importance? For what is the battle itself remarkable?

30. Where is Fort Pulaski? What happened here in April? What advantage was gained by the surrender of Fort Pulaski? For mention of these ships, see page 330. When was the city captured?

the Valley with a heavy force, and Banks fell back 50 miles to Strasburg.

32. Jackson, moving rapidly, attacked a body of Union troops at Front Royal, May 23, capturing a large number of prisoners, guns, and military stores. General Banks, hearing of this disaster to a portion of his command, retreated rapidly from Strasburg pursued by Jackson, and, by tremendous exertions, was able to cross the Potomac in advance of the latter, and thus save the bulk of his exhausted troops. In the entire pursuit Jackson captured several guns, 9000 small-arms, and between 2000 and 3000 prisoners.

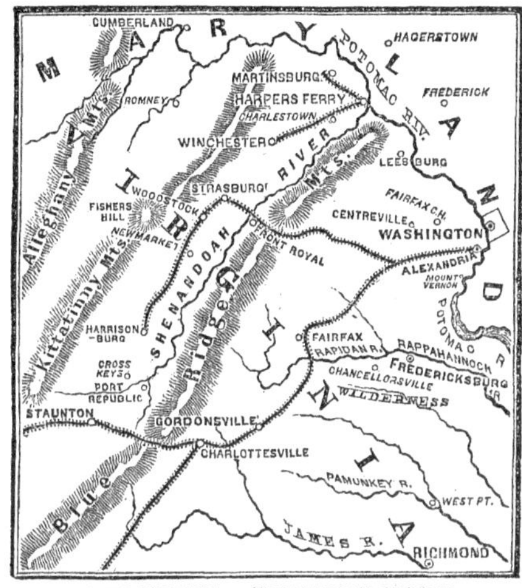

NORTH VIRGINIA.—SHENANDOAH VALLEY.

33. Generals Shields and Fremont were ordered into the Valley to intercept Jackson. The latter, learning this, moved south with the greatest celerity, but was brought to bay at Cross Keys, June 8, where a battle was fought which checked Fremont's advance. Next day Jackson struck Shields's division at Port Republic, and compelled it to fall back with considerable loss. Here the pursuit ended, and Jackson moved leisurely to join Lee's army in the battles for the defense of Richmond. He had performed a great service. With only 20,000 men, he had, by the rapidity of his movements, thoroughly alarmed the United States government for the safety of Washington, and had succeeded in occupying the attention of more than 60,000 Union troops, 40,000

31 Where is the Shenandoah Valley? What were the first movements of Banks here? Describe the first movements of the Confederates.

32. Describe the retreat and pursuit down the Valley. What were Jackson's trophies?

P 2

of whom, under the command of M'Dowell, were about to join M'Clellan in the Peninsula.

34. **2. Movements of the Army of the Potomac against Richmond.**—The great army of nearly 200,000 men, under General M'Clellan, which lay along the Potomac during the winter of 1861–62, began to move forward toward Manassas on the 10th of March, the enemy retiring as it advanced. The Union army presently returned to its camp near Washington, and it was determined in a council of war to move the bulk of the troops, amounting to 121,000 men, to Fortress Monroe, which was accomplished April 2.

35. From this point, April 4, M'Clellan commenced his march against the Confederate capital. Yorktown and its neighborhood, fortified and garrisoned by 10,000 Confederates under Magruder, lay in his way. M'Clellan, deeming the Confederate works too strong to be taken by an immediate assault, concluded to invest them. This occupied nearly a month, at the end of which Magruder evacuated the place, which was entered by M'Clellan May 4.

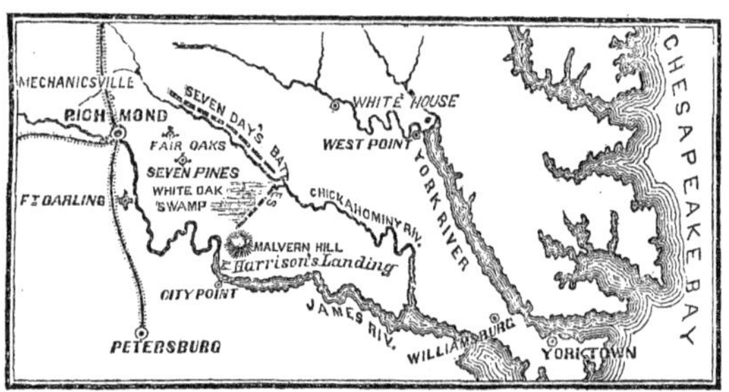

M'CLELLAN'S CAMPAIGN AGAINST RICHMOND.

36. His troops followed the enemy, and gained the battle of Williamsburg May 5, and that of West Point May 9. In

33. What prevented Jackson from remaining near the Potomac? When and where did his pursuers come up with him? What was the result? In what direction did Jackson then move? Why was the work that he had done so important? For places mentioned, see Map, page 345.

34. When and in what direction did the Potomac army move? What was the result? To what point was the army moved? What was the amount of force sent thither?

35. When did the advance commence? What was the first obstacle to be overcome? How did M'Clellan prepare to overcome it? What was the result?

less than three weeks from the time he left Yorktown his advance was within seven miles of Richmond. There was a great panic in the city; many persons left, and the Confederate Congress adjourned in haste. M'Clellan, however, did not advance, but employed the army in the swamps of the Chickahominy building bridges and constructing earthworks. His lines extended from Bottom's Bridge on the Chickahominy, to Mechanicsville on the north. The base of his supplies was at White House, on the Pamunkey River.

37. Norfolk, threatened by a division of the Union army, under General Wool, from Fortress Monroe, was abandoned by the enemy May 3, who were concentrating their troops for the defense of Richmond, and entered by the Unionists May 10. Before leaving Norfolk, the enemy destroyed the stores and burned the navy yard. On the 11th of May they blew up the famous ram Virginia, which it had been hoped would defend James River. This was now open to within eight miles of Richmond, and the gun-boats, with the little Monitor, went up on the 15th to force a passage, but were stopped by the heavy guns of Fort Darling, and driven back badly injured.

38. On the 31st of May, the Confederate troops, which had time to collect in great numbers around Richmond, attacked the south wing of the Union army, which had advanced to Seven Pines and Fair Oaks, south of the Chickahominy. The battle continued next day, June 1, and the enemy were finally repulsed after a severe battle, their general, Joseph E. Johnston, being seriously wounded. The Union army now lay within six miles of the city of Richmond, and a portion of General Hooker's command went within three and a half miles of it.

39. General Robert E. Lee was appointed to the command

---

36. What occurred May 5 and May 9? State what is said of his progress, and the effect it produced. How was his advance delayed? How far did the Union lines extend? Where was the base of his supplies?

37. What important movement near the peninsula was made by the Confederates in May? Why was this done? What did they do before leaving Norfolk? What occurrence happened on May 11? In connection with what attack does the Monitor make its appearance?

38. What did the slowness of the Union army permit the Confederates to do? Describe the battle of Seven Pines and Fair Oaks: see Map. Where was now the advance of the Union troops?

GENERAL ROBERT E. LEE.

of the Confederate army after Johnston was disabled at Fair Oaks. While M'Clellan was on the point of marching on the defenses of Richmond, Lee, on the 25th of June, fell suddenly on the Union right, and at Mechanicsville next day, the 26th, was repulsed with severe loss. On the following day, the 27th, the Union troops, who had fallen back, were attacked with great fury at Cold Harbor, or Gaines's Mill. With difficulty the army saved itself by crossing to the south side of the Chickahominy, and destroying the bridges.

40. Already M'Clellan, finding himself in danger of being cut off from his base of supplies at White House, had determined on a change of base to the James River; and the retreat began June 28, the wearied troops marching during the greater part of the night, and fighting all day. On the 29th, the rear of the retreating army was attacked at Savage's Station. On the 30th was fought the bloody but indecisive battle of Frazier's Farm.

41. Next morning, July 1st, the Union troops reached Malvern Hill, near the James. This had been hastily fortified with heavy guns, and was supported by gun-boats in the river. Late in the afternoon Lee hurled his troops against the Union batteries, but was driven back with dreadful slaughter. The battle had scarcely closed when the Union army was ordered to fall back to Harrison's Landing, farther down the river. The contest, generally known as the "seven days' battles," had ended. From Mechanicsville to Mal-

---

39. What officer was now appointed to the command of the Confederates? What was Lee's first movement? What occurred on the 26th and 27th? What was the condition of the Union army at the close of the 27th?

40. What decision had M'Clellan meanwhile reached? When did the retreat begin, and how was it continued? What occurred on the 29th and 30th?

vern Hill, M'Clellan had lost, in killed, wounded, and missing, more than 15,000 men; the Confederate loss was nearly 20,000. Richmond was saved, and the object for which the Army of the Potomac had been so long and so splendidly trained was entirely lost. The discouragement at the North, after this retreat, was nearly as great as after the battle of Bull Run. President Lincoln, on the very day of Malvern Hill, called for a fresh levy of 300,000 troops.

42. Lee had no longer any thing to fear from M'Clellan's crippled army. After waiting a month, in which he recruited and reorganized his troops, he marched north in the direction of Washington. In his way there was an army of 40,000 men, under the command of General Pope, who had been sent for from the West, and had united the various commands of Banks, Fremont, and M'Dowell. Lee pressed on rapidly, and his advanced corps attacked a portion of Pope's army, under General Banks, at Cedar Mountain, August 9th, and, after a severe struggle, the latter was defeated.

43. Pope fell back, contesting every mile of the way, and expecting help from M'Clellan's army, which had been ordered to join him; but re-enforcements came up slowly. At Manassas Junction, August 26th, the Confederates captured 8 guns, 10 locomotives, 7 trains, and immense quantities of stores. On the 28th Pope turned upon the enemy and drove them from Centreville. Next day, the 29th, he attacked them successfully at Gainesville, but on the following morning the battle was renewed, and Pope was compelled to fall back to Centreville. On Sept. 31st he was attacked at Chantilly, where, after a bloody battle, the enemy were repulsed.

44. Overpowered by superior numbers, he withdrew his wearied troops within the defenses of Washington. He had lost, in the campaign, not less than 30,000 men, and a large

41. What point did the Union army reach? How was it defended? What final blow did Lee hurl, and with what success? To what place did M'Clellan fall back? Why? How many days had this running battle lasted? What was the loss on both sides? How did all this affect the people of the North? In what way did the President and government show their determination?

42. What did these disasters to the Union army permit Lee to do? In what direction did he move? What was there to oppose him? Where had Pope already distinguished himself? Where and when was the first battle in the pursuit?

43. How did Pope act? What made his situation so critical? Mention the different engagements that occurred during the retreat, with the dates.

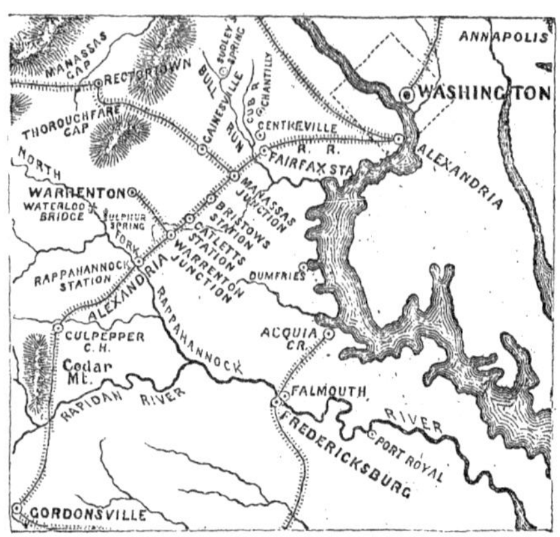

POPE'S RETREAT TO WASHINGTON.

number of cannon and small-arms, besides munitions and supplies. Pope was now relieved from the command at his own request, and M'Clellan was placed at the head of the Union army, which had been, meanwhile, heavily re-enforced.

45. Lee turned into Maryland, hoping that he would find volunteers and support there. In this he was greatly disappointed. He divided his army, and sent a large part of it, under Jackson, to capture Harper's Ferry, which was held by Colonel Miles and 13,000 raw troops, principally militia. Miles made a disgraceful surrender, after scarce any show of resistance, September 15th.

46. Jackson's expedition well-nigh proved the ruin of Lee. M'Clellan took the field September 7th, and pushed in between the two divisions of Lee's army at Turner's Gap. There he fought and gained the battle of South Mountain, September 14th. Lee, being in a perilous situation, retreated next day toward the Potomac, and took a position at Sharpsburg, with the Antietam River in front.

47. M'Clellan delayed his attack until the 17th, and by that time Jackson had come up rapidly from Harper's Ferry. On the 17th the battle of Sharpsburg, or Antietam, was fought between 70,000 men under Lee, and 80,000 under M'Clellan. At the close of the battle the position of the

---

44. Where did he retire? What had been his losses? What change was made in the command?

45. Where did Lee now move? What disappointment did he meet with? Where, and under whom, did he send a part of his army? What was its success?

46. How did M'Clellan take advantage of this movement? What battle was gained? To what point did Lee retire? Where is Sharpsburg? See Map, page 355.

two armies was nearly the same as at the beginning; yet the Confederates had lost 10,000 in killed and wounded, the Union troops about 11,500. M'Clellan did not renew the attack next day. On the night of the 18th Lee quietly crossed the Potomac, and continued his march slowly through Virginia without interruption. The Union army did not reach the south side of the Potomac until the 2d of November, more than six weeks after the battle.

48. President Lincoln and a great part of the North had become dissatisfied with General M'Clellan, and on the 7th of November General Burnside was appointed to the command. He moved the army toward the Rappahannock, intending to proceed against Richmond. Fredericksburg was chosen as the place of crossing. Lee had placed his men behind strong earth-works and a stone wall on the other side, some distance from the river. On the 11th and 12th of December Burnside crossed, and on the 13th attacked the Confederate works. At the close of that short winter's day he found himself repulsed, with the terrible loss of nearly 11,000 in killed and wounded. Of these there were left 6500 in front of the stone wall alone.

The Army of the Potomac was nearly demoralized by this dreadful defeat. It had become greatly dissatisfied with its leader, and the year closed in gloom on the trials of these brave but devoted troops.

49. **State of the War at the Close of 1862.** — The Union forces in the West had made decided progress during the year. Forts Henry and Donelson, and Island No. 10, were captured, and the Mississippi was opened as far as Vicksburg. From the mouth it had been entered, New Orleans captured, and the Confederate fleets of steamers and iron-clads destroyed. West Tennessee was brought thoroughly

---

47. How did Lee escape from his dangerous situation? What is said of the battle of Antietam? What was immediately gained by it? What was the loss on each side? What movement followed the battle of Antietam? When did M'Clellan move after him?

48. Who was appointed to the command of the Union army? Why was this done? What was his plan of the campaign? What is said of Lee's preparations on the south side of the river? Describe the battle of Fredericksburg, and the result. Where is Fredericksburg? (See Map, page 326.) What reflection is made on the state of the army?

under "Union rule," and the Southern limit of occupation in that region was marked by a line of posts from Memphis through Corinth, Mississippi, eastward toward Chattanooga.

50. On the coast the power of the national arms had been as strikingly shown. At the commencement of the year the enemy were in possession of Norfolk and every port on the Southern coast. At its close, Charleston, Mobile, and Wilmington alone remained to them on the Atlantic seaboard, and these were carefully blockaded.

51. East and north of Richmond there had been disaster. The defeats in the Shenandoah Valley, the seven days' battles on the Chickahominy, and the retreat of Pope, were far from being balanced by the battle of Antietam, followed as this was by the unharassed and deliberate retreat of Lee, and the Union slaughter at Fredericksburg. But, despite this, the national successes throughout the country warranted the profound satisfaction which was felt in the North, and particularly the West; and the government was cheerfully sustained in continued and still greater efforts to bring the struggle to a close.

REVIEW QUESTIONS.—1862.

1. Sketch the plan of operations for the year 1862.
2. How was the Mississippi opened from the South?
3. What progress was made in opening it from the North?
4. What skillful strategy was adopted in this?
5. What prevented the capture of Vicksburg in December?
6. State the principal events occurring on and near the Mississippi during the year.
7. Name the other principal battles west of the Alleghanies.
8. Describe the battle of Shiloh, or Pittsburg Landing.
9. How did Rosecrans rise to the command of the Army of the Cumberland?
10. To what position was Grant elevated this year, and why?
11. What were the principal events on the sea-board?
12. Give a short description of Burnside's expedition.
13. Sketch the important occurrences near Fortress Monroe in March.
14. Why was this so important?
15. What took place in the Shenandoah Valley early in the year?
16. Where is this valley, and why was it so important?
17. When, and with what object, did the Army of the Potomac advance?
18. Describe its movements until the month of June.

---

49. What was the progress of the national cause in the West during the year? State how much had been gained there.
50. What had been gained on the coast?
51. What is said of the state of affairs east and north of Richmond? How did the country regard the military movements of the year?

19. How near did this army seem to be to success?
20. Who commanded the Confederates until June 1, and who afterward?
21. What prevented M'Clellan from moving on Richmond in June?
22. Describe what followed.
23. What use did Lee make of M'Clellan's defeat?
24. By whom was he opposed, and with what success?
25. What great battle checked Lee's invasion?
26. What led to it, and what prevented its being a complete Union success?
27. What change in the Union army did the escape of Lee produce?
28. What was the result of Burnside's campaign?
29. Give a general review of the progress of the war at the end of 1862 in the West; on the sea-board; and in Virginia.

SECTION III.

EVENTS OF 1863.

1. In the fall of the year 1862, President Lincoln warned the Confederate States that, unless they returned to their allegiance, he would declare every slave within their borders free on the 1st of January, 1863. Punctual to his warning, on that day he issued his celebrated Emancipation Proclamation. In this he declared all slaves forever free in those states or parts of states then under the control of the Confederates.

2. The plan of military operations for the year 1863, adopted by the Federal government, did not vary much from that of the preceding year. Its great object in the West was the opening of the Mississippi by the capture of Vicksburg, thence to pass eastward into Mississippi, Alabama, and Georgia, and to occupy East Tennessee, the great centre of Union feeling in the heart of the Confederacy. In the East the plan was to push toward Richmond, through Virginia, with the Army of the Potomac. In addition to these military operations, a powerful expedition was to be sent against the defenses of Charleston.

3. **Operations in Virginia, and Invasion of the North.**—General Burnside had lost the confidence of the army by his failure at Fredericksburg, and, at his own request, was relieved from the command. Joseph Hooker was appointed in his

1. What proclamation did Lincoln issue in the fall of 1862? How did he carry out his warning?
2. How did the plan of operations for 1863 compare with that of 1862? What were the great objects on the West? on the East? What naval expedition was planned?

GENERAL JACKSON.

stead, January 25th. Toward the end of April he crossed the Rappahannock with 120,000 men, and took the road to Richmond by way of Chancellorsville. Here he was attacked by Lee, and, after a terrible battle, which lasted through the 2d and 3d of May, he was defeated, with the loss of 12,000 men. He then recrossed the Rappahannock. It was in this battle that the famous "Stonewall" Jackson was mortally wounded in the darkness, through mistake, by his own men.

4. Lee, as soon as he had driven off Hooker, tried the plan of 1862, and moved quickly to invade the North in the first week of June. Hooker's army, by rapid marches, threw itself between Lee's army and Washington, and in this way protected the capital. Lee turned northward by the Valley of the Shenandoah, and entered Pennsylvania, plundering and burning as he went. The people of the North made extraordinary efforts to resist him; troops poured into Pennsylvania, and George G. Meade was put in command of the army in place of Hooker.

5. Meade took up a strong position on some hilly ground near Gettysburg, Pennsylvania, where he was attacked by Lee. Each army had about 80,000 men. The battle began on the 1st of July, and lasted to the close of the 3d, when Lee was compelled to fall back, after terrible slaughter. On the 4th of July the Confederate army recrossed the Potomac, and retreated to the south bank of the Rapidan, where it prepared to dispute the passage of the river by the Union

---

3. Who was placed in command of the Union army in January? Why was this change made? What was Hooker's plan? What route did he take? Where is Chancellorsville? Where and what disaster did he meet with?

4. What was Lee's movement after the defeat of Hooker? What saved Washington? What route did Lee finally take? What is said of the efforts made to resist him, and the change in the command of the army?

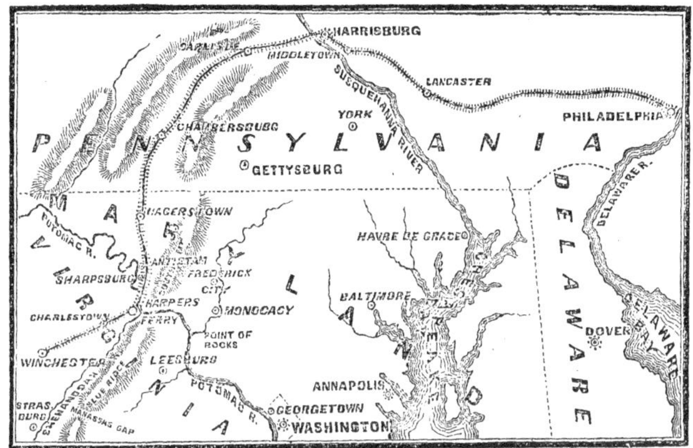

PART OF PENNSYLVANIA, MARYLAND, AND VIRGINIA.

army. The invasion of the North was, however, at an end. The battle of Gettysburg was decisive of this point. It cost Meade 24,000 men, and Lee nearly 40,000 in killed, wounded, and missing. The latter commenced the invasion with an army of 100,000; at its close it was reduced to 40,000.

6. **Operations in Arkansas and Mississippi.**—At Vicksburg the year 1862 ended, as has already been noticed, with the defeat of part of Grant's army, under Sherman, at Chickasaw Bayou. The latter kept his troops busy, and in January, 1863, accompanied by Admiral Porter and his fleet, moved up Arkansas River, and captured Arkansas Post, January 10, after a severe battle.

7. General Grant adhered to his great purpose, the capture of Vicksburg. For three months in the beginning of the year he made several attempts to take it from the Yazoo side, but failed. He then turned his attention to the south side, and moved his army along the west bank of the Mississippi, from Milliken's Bend to New Carthage, below Vicksburg, intending to cross the river and fight his way to the

5. Where did Meade come up with Lee? Where is Gettysburg? How long did the battle last? What was the result? State the loss on each side. What was Lee's loss during the sortie?

6. What was the closing movement of 1862 at Vicksburg? What was done by a part of that army in January? Where is this place?

rear of the city. To furnish the means of crossing, transports, accompanied by gun-boats, ran past the Vicksburg batteries on the 16th and 22d of April, not without severe loss from the terrible fire that was poured on them.

UNION VESSELS PASSING THE VICKSBURG BATTERIES.

8. While Grant was thus busy, he dispatched Colonel Grierson, at the head of 1700 cavalry, on a raid through Mississippi, to cut the enemy's communications east of Vicksburg by destroying the railroads. Leaving La Grange, Tennessee, about fifty miles east of Memphis, April 17, Grierson passed round Pemberton's Confederate army; and in 16 days, after traversing 800 miles of hostile country, and destroying railroad bridges, stores, and arms, reached Baton Rouge, Louisiana, May 2, with a loss of only 27 men.

9. From New Carthage Grant advanced south, nearly op-

7. How was Grant busy at the beginning of the year? What was his next movement? How and where did he move his army? How did he get the transports down the river?

8. What happened while Grant was engaged with these preparations? Describe this raid and its results.

posite Grand Gulf, which he attacked with the gun-boats, but was repulsed, April 29. Next day he crossed lower down at Bruinsburg, the landing for Port Gibson, and, advancing, defeated a part of Pemberton's army at the latter place, May 1. This compelled the evacuation of Grand Gulf. On the 14th of May he defeated General Johnston at Jackson after a severe battle; and, pushing in between him and Pemberton, defeated the latter in two battles on the 16th and 17th, driving him into Vicksburg.

10. In 17 days from the time Grant landed below Grand Gulf he was in the rear of the city with his army. Pemberton was there closely shut up, and Johnston lay to the east unable to assist him. Twice Grant tried to take the works by assault, but failed, with heavy loss. There remained nothing but to commence a regular siege. This was followed up so steadily that, on the 4th of July, Pemberton surrendered, with about 30,000 troops prisoners of war. Thus Lee's retreat from Gettysburg and the surrender of Vicksburg were telegraphed throughout the North the same day, July 4.

11. During the siege of Vicksburg General Banks was besieging Port Hudson, another strong place lower down the Mississippi. When the Confederate commander there heard that Vicksburg had been taken, he surrendered to Banks, July 8th. The Mississippi River was now open to the Union vessels throughout its whole length, never again to be closed during the war.

12. **Events in Tennessee and Georgia.**—After the battle of Murfreesboro', the army of Rosecrans lay quiet for several months. In the last week of June it was again in motion, and pressed Bragg out of Tennessee into Georgia. Bragg was then heavily re-enforced, and attacked Rosecrans at Chickamauga, near Chattanooga River, on the 19th of Sep-

---

9. What was Grant's first point of attack? Where did he next go, and with what result? What is said of the battles of the 14th, 16th, and 17th of May?

10. How long did it take him to reach the rear of Vicksburg? What was now the condition of both armies? What attempts were made to capture the city? What is said of the siege and surrender? What great event happened elsewhere at nearly the same time?

11. What was going on lower down the Mississippi? How did the surrender of Vicksburg affect operations here? What mighty result was at last achieved?

tember. The battle was continued next day. Rosecrans himself was driven off the field, but General Thomas, with his corps, kept up the fight, and retreated in good order. The whole army then fell back as far as Chattanooga, having lost 16,000 men and 51 guns. Bragg's loss was about 18,000. At Chattanooga Rosecrans was closely besieged by Bragg, and suffered greatly from want of supplies.

13. Soon after, Rosecrans was removed from the command of the Army of the Cumberland, and Grant was placed over all the Western armies. His arrival, and that of Generals Sherman and Hooker with re-enforcements, speedily changed the aspect of affairs round Chattanooga. Bragg's army was attacked. Lookout Mountain, opposite the town and near

CAPTURE OF LOOKOUT MOUNTAIN, NEAR CHATTANOOGA.

the river, was carried by storm, November 24, by General Hooker. Next day, 25th, Missionary Ridge, close by, was occupied. Bragg retreated into Georgia, and shortly after was deprived of his command.

---

12. When did the battle of Murfreesboro' take place? What generals were opposed there? How long was it before Rosecrans moved, and with what results? What is said of the battle of Chickamauga? Where is Chickamauga? Who distinguished himself in this battle? What is said of the final retreat?

13. Who superseded Rosecrans after this disaster, and with what powers? What effected a change at Chattanooga? What movements followed? Where is Chattanooga? Lookout Mountain? Missionary Ridge? Who disappears from the Confederate army?

14. After the battle of Missionary Ridge, Sherman was sent from Grant's army north into East Tennessee, to help General Burnside, who had gone with an army to protect the loyal people of that region. He was now closely besieged in Knoxville by General Longstreet, and in great straits for provisions. On the 29th of November the enemy made an assault on Burnside's works, which, for heroic daring, was unsurpassed during the war, but they were driven back with great slaughter. On the 3d of December Longstreet heard that Sherman was approaching, and at once raised the siege and retreated into Virginia.

15. **The War in the extreme Southwest.**—On the day that Vicksburg surrendered, General Holmes, who commanded the Confederates in Arkansas, attacked Helena, but was repulsed by General Prentiss with severe loss. In September, General Steele, at the head of the Union troops, moved from Helena, beat Marmaduke, who opposed him, and then drove Price out of Little Rock, the capital. In October the Confederates were chased as far south as Red River.

16. Away out in Indian Territory there was fighting. In Kansas, also, the guerrilla Quantrell, with 300 bandits, committed great excesses. He entered Lawrence, plundered the bank, burned the houses, and murdered 140 persons in cold blood. Before a sufficient cavalry force could be gathered in the neighborhood, he and his band escaped.

17. **Morgan's Cavalry Raid.**—Another Confederate raid, although on a larger scale, was that of General John Morgan, at the head of 3000 cavalry, through Kentucky, into Indiana and Ohio. Starting from Sparta, Tennessee, June 27, he pushed north through Kentucky, crossed the Ohio into Indiana, traversed the southern border into Ohio, and, passing north and around Cincinnati, endeavored at several places

---

14. What expedition was sent by Grant after these battles? What was the situation of General Burnside? What was he doing at Knoxville? Where is Knoxville? What is said of the assault on the 29th of November? How was Burnside finally relieved?

15. What disaster happened to the Confederates in Arkansas on the 4th of July? What other movements took place there in September? To what point were the Confederates driven? See Map, page 000.

16. To what extreme point in the Southwest did the war extend? What excesses were perpetrated in Kansas?

to recross the Ohio into Virginia. Gun-boats patroling the river prevented his crossing, and, forced eastward, he had a race for his life, followed by a Union force that had tracked him all the way from Kentucky. Different detachments of his troops were captured after sharp encounters. At last, July 27, Morgan himself, with what was left of his band, surrendered at discretion, near New Lisbon, Ohio, exactly one month from the time he started from Tennessee.

18. **Events on the Coast.**—On the 1st of January, Galveston, Texas, was captured by the Confederates under Magruder. A valuable United States steamer and a great quantity of stores fell into the hands of the enemy. It was a sad affair for the Union cause in Texas, because it furnished the enemy with one more port through which they could obtain supplies from abroad.

19. **Expedition against Charleston.**—A great naval expedition, under Admiral Farragut, sent against Charleston, met with signal defeat, April 7. In attempting to pass the forts and batteries in the harbor, nine iron-clads were badly injured. Another expedition, principally of land troops, was sent to that harbor three months after. On the 10th of July, General Gillmore, the commander, made a lodgment on the south end of Morris Island, and threw up batteries. From these he bombarded Fort Sumter in the harbor, and Fort Wag-

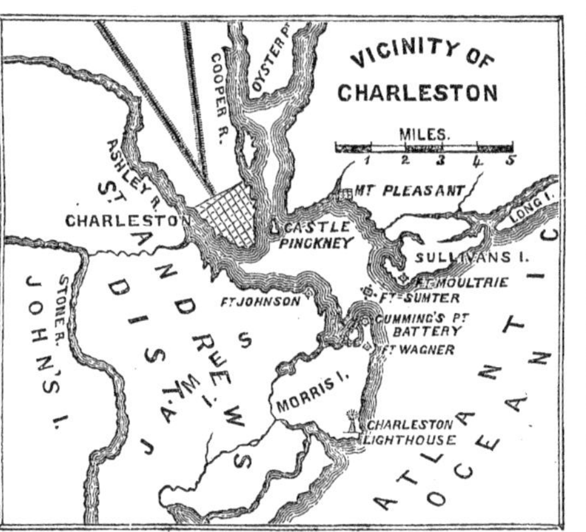

17. What other raid was started? Describe his route, and the measures that were taken to capture him. What was the result?

18. What important place on the coast was lost by the Unionists in January? What did they lose besides the place? Why was this disaster so unfortunate?

ner on Morris Island. On the night of September 6th Fort Wagner was evacuated. Fort Sumter was completely destroyed on its land side, and shells were thrown into the

FORT SUMTER.—LAND SIDE AFTER THE BOMBARDMENT.

city of Charleston. Although the harbor was still held by the enemy, the Federal ships were now enabled to watch it so thoroughly that no blockade-runner could get in or out. Thus the Confederates lost one more port.

20. **State of the War at the Close of 1863.**—The Union cause had again made great progress during the year. The Federal troops had been beaten, it is true, at Chickamauga and at Chancellorsville; the North suffered greatly by Lee's invasion of Pennsylvania; the Confederates seized and held Galveston; and the iron-clad fleet was driven back from Charleston Harbor.

21. On the other hand, there were marked successes. A great part of Arkansas was gained and held firmly, and Missouri was freed from the Confederates. By the capture of Vicksburg and Port Hudson the entire Mississippi was controlled by the Federal gun-boats. Thus the immense supplies from Texas and the Red River country sent formerly to the Confederate armies in the East across the Mississippi were stopped. Bragg had been driven out of Tennessee

---

19. What attempt was made against Charleston in April? With what success? What occurred in July? See Map for the situation of these points. What other expedition followed? What is said of General Gillmore's mode of attack, and its success? What did Gillmore's success enable the Federal ships to accomplish?

20. State the principal misfortunes experienced by the Federal cause in the year 1863.

into Georgia. East Tennessee was occupied. Lee had suffered a disastrous defeat at Gettysburg, and the attempt to transfer the war to Northern soil failed. Charleston Harbor, although held by the enemy, was now so sealed up after the capture of Fort Wagner as to be useless to them.

22. Then supplies from Europe were almost cut off by the blockade. The South was becoming weaker in men and in resources of every kind. In the North, each year seemed to be adding new determination. Fresh troops were demanded by the government and granted by the states. The city of New York seemed for a short time an exception. In the month of July, during Lee's invasion, while all the city regiments had gone to Pennsylvania, a riot broke out. The draft was resisted; public and private property was burned; the negroes were chased on the streets, abused, and killed by the rioters. At length the riot was put down, but not until it had lasted three days and after heavy loss of life. Afterward the draft went on.

23. The cost of the war was enormous. At the end of 1863 the debt reached $1,300,000,000, and the preparations for the next year were on such a scale as would necessarily increase this amount. Still the North was prosperous. The war created a demand for all kinds of labor; paper money was abundant; every thing went on as in peace, and a foreigner could scarcely have realized, from any evidence of distress at the North, that the United States were waging one of the most tremendous wars in history.

In the month of June, Western Virginia, which had remained constant to the Union cause, was separated by Congress from Virginia, and erected into a separate state.

---

21. What were the successes of the Unionists in Arkansas and Missouri? On the Mississippi? What immediate advantage was gained by the last? What was gained in Tennessee? What is said of Gettysburg? of the effect of the capture of Fort Wagner? What contrast is made between the resources of the North and South?

22. How was the war affecting the spirit of the North? What place seemed an exception? State what occurred there this year. How long did this last? Did this not stop the draft?

23. What is said of the cost of the war? How is this seen? What was the state of prosperity at the North? What evidence is given of this?

REVIEW QUESTIONS.—1863.

1. With what great event did the year 1863 open?
2. What was the plan of operations for the year?
3. Who was placed in command of the Army of the Potomac?
4. What was his success?
5. How did Lee profit by this?
6. How was he opposed, and by whom?
7. Why was the battle of Gettysburg so important?
8. What extent of time did Lee's invasion cover?
9. For what other event was July 4, 1863, celebrated?
10. What two renowned generals were engaged in the battles that preceded this siege?
11. Sketch Grants movements on the Mississippi and neighborhood.
12. Describe the famous cavalry raid during this campaign.
13. What place surrendered after the fall of Vicksburg?
14. How was Rosecrans busy in the year 1863?
15. Who saved the army at Chickamauga?
16. How was the Union army saved at Chattanooga?
17. Describe the battles in that neighborhood.
18. Why was East Tennessee considered so important?
19. Sketch the state of affairs at Knoxville in November.
20. What Confederate raids marked the year?
21. What disaster occurred in Texas?
22. Why was this particularly unfortunate?
23. What took place in Arkansas?
24. Mention the operations near Charleston, and what was gained there.
25. Give a general review of the results of the fighting in 1863.
26. What events were transpiring in New York during Lee's invasion?
27. What new state was admitted in 1863, and under what circumstances?
28. Name the principal Union generals and naval officers engaged during this year.
29. Name the Confederate generals.
30. Give the principal events of 1863.

SECTION IV.

EVENTS OF 1864.

1. BEFORE proceeding to trace the operations of the different armies during the year 1864, the efforts of the Confederates on the ocean, which were brought nearly to an end during this year, will first be noticed. The Confederate government determined, at the very beginning of the war, to strike where the United States were open to attack, by either destroying American merchant ships with armed vessels, or by driving them from the ocean.

2. The first step, as early as May, 1861, was the establish-

---

1. What is here first to be noticed? At what determination did the Confederates arrive at the beginning of the war?

ment of privateering. This had only moderate success, because the Confederates had no open ports into which the privateers could bring their prizes, and neutral powers would not permit the use of their ports for that purpose. The first privateer was the Savannah, fitted out at Charleston, carrying only one gun, and not much larger than an ordinary pilot boat. Her career was short; she was captured the same day after she ran the blockade by the United States brig Perry.

3. In the beginning of May, the Confederate cruiser Sumter, commanded by Captain Semmes, was prepared for sea at New Orleans, and in July escaped to sea, and captured some American vessels. She continued her cruise until February, 1862, seizing and burning merchant ships, and was then blockaded by the Tuscarora at Cadiz, where she was sold by Semmes, and the crew was discharged. The Nashville, another of these early Confederate cruisers, succeeded in escaping from Charleston to England in October, 1861, and returned to the United States in 1862, running the blockade, and bringing with her $3,000,000 worth of stores. One year afterward, March, 1863, she was destroyed by the ironclads, near Fort M'Allister, on the Savannah River.

4. The Confederates now turned to British ship-yards for the supply of armed cruisers. The Florida, originally named the Oreto, built near Liverpool, sailed into Mobile Bay under British colors, August, 1862. In January, 1863, she ran the blockade, and, after destroying in three months fifteen vessels, was finally seized in the harbor of Bahia, Brazil, and brought to Hampton Roads. Here she sank in an accidental collision with another vessel. The Georgia, built at Glasgow, Scotland, after a short cruise, was captured in 1863. The Chickamauga burnt ships to the value of half a million of dollars. The Tallahassee destroyed in ten days thirty-three vessels; and the Olustee was also busy in the same work.

---

2. When did they put this purpose in execution? Was this successful, and why not? What is said of the first privateer?

3. What is the history of the Sumter? Sketch the career of the Nashville.

4. Who now supplied these privateers? What is the history of the Florida? What three other Anglo-Confederate cruisers are mentioned? What is said of them?

5. The most active and notorious of all the Anglo-Confederate cruisers was the Alabama, built at Liverpool, and allowed to escape to sea against the earnest remonstrance of the American minister in England. She was commanded by Captain Semmes, formerly of the Sumter; but her crew was British, her guns were British, and under the British flag she approached unsuspecting merchant vessels, and captured or destroyed them. After a long career, during which she never entered a Confederate port, she sailed into the harbor of Cherbourg, France, where she was blockaded by the United States war steamer Kearsarge, Captain Winslow.

6. Ordered by the French government to leave the harbor, the Alabama was attacked, June 19, 1864, by the Kearsarge, five miles from shore, and sunk, after an engagement of one hour and a quarter. Her commander, Semmes, was

DESTRUCTION OF THE ALABAMA BY THE KEARSARGE.

5. What was the most active of them all? What is said of her building and her escape? What stamps her character? Who commanded her? Where was she in the beginning of 1864?

rescued from the water by an English yacht that hovered near during the battle. The Alabama captured 65 merchant vessels, and destroyed property worth 10 millions of dollars. Her cruise rises to first-rate importance as forming the ground of a claim by the United States against England for damages to American commerce—a claim still unsettled in 1870, and which has already threatened serious difficulty between the two nations.

7. The Union government, with immense armies and undiminished resources, proceeded steadily in its work of crushing out the Confederacy. The plan of operations for the year 1864, in the spring, resolved itself into the two simultaneous movements—one of Sherman eastward into Georgia with the armies of the West; the other of Grant, with the Potomac army, toward Richmond—and the capture of the remaining Confederate sea-ports. A movement of secondary importance was made in the beginning of the year from Port Royal, South Carolina, under General Seymour, to Florida. At Olustee he received a disastrous defeat, February 20, and was compelled to return.

8. **Operations in Mississippi.**—General W. T. Sherman left Vicksburg February 3, with the intention of destroying the railroads in northern Mississippi, and thus breaking the communications of that state with the rest of the Confederacy. His plans were somewhat disarranged by General Forrest, who defeated a large cavalry force from Memphis intended to join Sherman at Meridian, Mississippi. From this point, the intersection of two great railroads, Sherman returned to Vicksburg, after destroying 150

GENERAL W. T. SHERMAN.

6. State what happened to her in June. What was the extent of her depredations? Why is the cruise of the Alabama of so much importance?

7. What was the plan of operations for 1864? What movement was made to the coast of Florida, and with what success?

miles of railroad, 67 bridges, 20 locomotives, 28 cars, thousands of bales of cotton, and 20,000 bushels of corn.

9. The Confederate Forrest advanced north into Tennessee, laying waste the country, and captured Union City, Tennessee, March 24. Next day he appeared before Paducah, Kentucky, but was repulsed, with the loss of 1500 men. On the 12th of April he attacked Fort Pillow. The garrison, principally negro troops, made a brave resistance, but were forced to surrender. After they had thrown down their arms, a number were shot in cold blood, or otherwise brutally murdered. Forrest's raid accomplished nothing for the Confederate cause.

10. **The Red River Expedition.**—Early in March an expe-

WAR IN THE SOUTHWEST. RED RIVER EXPEDITION.

8. On what expedition did General Sherman start in February? What interfered with his plans? How far was Sherman successful?

9. State Forrest's movements in March. Describe what occurred in April.

dition was sent into the Red River country, Louisiana. The advance consisted of 10,000 troops from Vicksburg, under General Smith, and this was joined by a fleet of gun-boats under Admiral Porter. Sailing up Red River, the army landed and captured Fort de Russy with the help of the gun-boats, March 14. On the 21st Natchitoches was entered.

11. General Banks soon after joined with troops from New Orleans, took command, and pushed on toward Shreveport, at the head of navigation on Red River. Near Mansfield, at Sabine Cross Roads, he was attacked by the enemy on April 8, and met with a severe reverse. He then fell back to Pleasant Hill, where the enemy was repulsed, April 9. Banks continued his retreat, but on the way was opposed at Cane River, where he routed the enemy, April 23, and arrived at Alexandria on the 25th.

12. When Banks moved toward Shreveport, Porter and his gun-boats ascended the river. Hearing of the disaster to the troops, Porter dropped down to the rapids or falls of Alexandria, with the loss of one of his boats. The water in the river had fallen so low that he could not pass the falls; and it seemed for a time as though the boats must be destroyed or fall into the hands of the enemy. Fortunately, Lieutenant Colonel Bailey, formerly a Wisconsin lumberman, constructed an immense dam below the rapids, and when the water had risen, the boats were floated over in safety. The expedition then returned to the Mississippi. Banks was relieved of his command, and General Canby was appointed in his stead.

13. Steele, the Union general in Arkansas, moved from Little Rock, March 23, to co-operate with Banks, and had arrived near Shreveport when he heard of the defeat of the latter. Being severely pressed by a superior force of the enemy, Steele then fell back, fighting all the way, to Little Rock, which he reached May 2. The entire Red River expe-

---

10. What expedition was sent out in March? Where is the Red River country? Of what troops did the advance consist? What was their success at first?

11. By whom was the army joined? Describe his movements and the battles that followed? For these places, see Map, page 367. To what place did he retreat?

12. What happened to the gun-boats? How were they saved from destruction? To what point did the expedition return? What change was made?

dition proved both useless and disastrous, and was a source of great mortification to the North.

14. **The Changes at the Head of the Union Armies.**—In the beginning of March Grant was appointed lieutenant general and commander of all the armies of the Union. He immediately removed his head-quarters to the Army of the Potomac. At the same time Sherman was appointed to the command of the Military Division of the Mississippi, which embraced three great armies—that of the Ohio, the Cumberland, and the Tennessee.

15. This was a change of great importance, because the operations in the East and West could now be made to assist each other. The two large armies of the Confederacy were under Lee and Johnston. That under Lee guarded Richmond; the other, under Johnston, covered Atlanta, in Georgia. Grant's plan of the campaigns for 1864 required that Sherman should strike the army of Johnston, while, at the same time, he himself, with the Army of the Potomac, should crush Lee and capture Richmond.

16. **Sherman's Campaign to Atlanta.**—Sherman commenced to perform his part by leaving Chattanooga, on the Atlanta campaign, May 7, with nearly 100,000 men. Johnston, at the head of the Confederate army, numbering 70,000, disputed his advance. Outflanked by Sherman at Dalton, he fell back to Resaca, where a severe battle was fought May 14 and 15. Johnston, again outflanked, made a stand at Dallas, where he was defeated, and Allatoona Pass turned, May 25–28. At Lost Mountain there was heavy fighting June 15, 16, 17, and at Kenesaw Mountain June 22 to July 3. By the 10th of July Johnston had fallen back within the fortifications of Atlanta.

17. The Confederate government, dissatisfied with John-

---

13. Describe the movement intended to co-operate with Banks. What is said of the Red River expedition?

14. What distinguished honor did Grant now receive? and also Sherman? What armies were combined under the latter?

15. Why was this change so important? What and where were the chief Confederate armies? What was Grant's plan of the campaigns?

16. When and from what place did Sherman commence to move? What was his force? What army opposed him? What military movement did Sherman adopt? Mention the different battles that were fought. What was the result on the 10th of July?

ston's retreating policy, ordered General Hood to supersede him; and Hood attacked Sherman three times during the month of July, only to be defeated. The latter tightened his hold on Atlanta, and at last, by a masterly movement, got in between two parts of Hood's army. This compelled Hood to evacuate the city, and Sherman's advanced corps entered it September 2. His campaign from Chattanooga

BATTLE OF ATLANTA.

had cost him 30,000 men. The Confederate loss probably exceeded this. Atlanta had been a place of great importance to the Confederates. Here were extensive manufactories of cannon and munitions of war, and it was at the crossing of several railroads. Sherman rested here to recruit his army and to prepare for his famous march of 200 miles across Georgia to the sea.

17. What change was made in the command of the Confederate army, and why? What success followed this change? What was Hood forced to do, and why? What had the capture of Atlanta cost? What made it of so much importance? How was Sherman occupied after the capture?

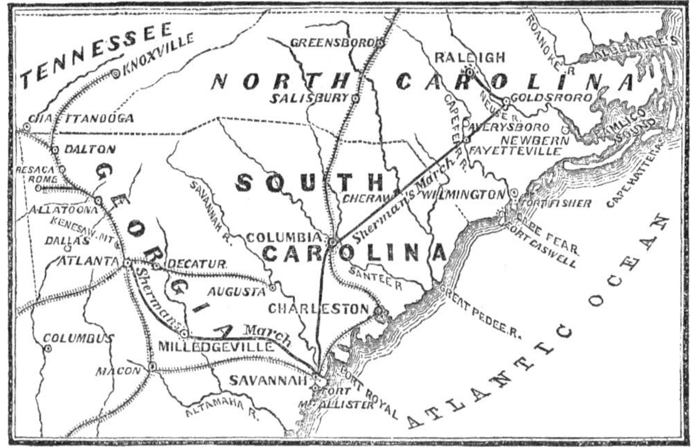

NORTH CAROLINA, SOUTH CAROLINA, AND GEORGIA. SHERMAN'S MARCH.

18. **Advance of Hood to Nashville.**—Hood, in order to draw the Union general out of Georgia, moved north into Tennessee. Sherman at first followed him with a part of his troops, but soon tired of pursuing an enemy that would not fight, and returned to Atlanta. He presently arranged with General Thomas, now at the head of the Army of the Tennessee, that the latter should watch Hood. Thomas's army was heavily re-enforced from the North, and he fell back toward Nashville, followed by the Confederates. A severe battle was fought at Franklin by General Schofield on the 30th of November, and Thomas retired within the fortifications of Nashville.

GENERAL THOMAS.

19. Hood followed him, and, while making preparations

18. What was Hood's plan? How did Sherman at first act? What arrangement did he make? What were Thomas's movements? What battle was fought in November?

to move on the Union works, was himself attacked suddenly by Thomas, December 15. On the second day of the battle of Nashville the Confederate army was completely routed. Next day, the 17th, the Union troops commenced the pursuit, and continued it for over 50 miles. The Confederate army of 40,000 men was nearly destroyed.

SIEGE OF NASHVILLE.

20. **Sherman's March to the Sea.**—While Hood was moving into Tennessee, Sherman cut his own railroad and telegraphic communications with Chattanooga, burned Atlanta, and on the 14th of November commenced his march across Georgia to Savannah with 60,000 men. He met with little resistance, and in four weeks reached the neighborhood of Savannah. On the 13th of December he stormed and took Fort M'Allister, which commanded the river. On the 21st, five weeks from the time he left Atlanta, he entered the city, which had been evacuated by the enemy, and sent the

19. What brought on the battle of Nashville? What is said of it and of the pursuit?

news of its capture, as "a Christmas present," to President Lincoln.

SHERMAN'S ARMY ON ITS MARCH TO THE SEA.

21. **The Campaign in Virginia.**—Grant's part of the great forward movement began by crossing the Rapidan River, with 140,000 men, on the morning of the 4th of May, General Meade being in immediate command. This was only four days before Sherman left Chattanooga. Grant, after crossing the river, entered a tract called the Wilderness. Here Lee's army, numbering about 100,000, attacked him on the 5th, near the old battle-ground of Chancellorsville. After three days' hard fighting, and terrible slaughter on both sides, Lee fell back to Spottsylvania Court-house, where the battle was renewed. It was on the morning of the 11th that Grant, after six days' very hard fighting, sent his famous dispatch to Washington, containing these now historic

20. What important movement was begun by Sherman in November? What was his success? What was taken on the 13th and 20th?

words, "*I propose to fight it out on this line, if it takes all summer.*"

22. The battle of the 12th of May was probably the most severe, the loss on each side being not less than 10,000. Finding that Lee could not be driven in front, Grant moved by the enemy's right flank, crossed the Pamunkey River at Hanover Town, and attacked Lee, strongly fortified, at Cold Harbor on the 1st of June, but was repulsed with a loss of 2000 men. On the 3d, a second attack, which lasted little more than half an hour, was made, in which Grant's loss was 7000. The entire Union loss in the Army of the Potomac from the 5th of May to the 13th of June was 54,551 men in killed, wounded, and missing. Lee's was about 32,000.

A BATTLE-SCENE IN THE WILDERNESS.

21. When did the Potomac army begin to move? What was its size, and who was in command? Where was the first battle fought? How many days' fighting followed? What was Grant's determination?

22. What is said of the battle of the 12th? What movement was Grant compelled to make, and with what success? Describe the terrible losses at Cold Harbor. What is said of the losses on each side in the campaign up to this time?

23. Before Grant reached Spottsylvania, he dispatched Sheridan, May 7, with 10,000 cavalry, to break the railroad connection between Richmond and the Shenandoah Valley and Lynchburg. In this he met with considerable success, and went within a few miles of the Confederate capital. On the 25th of June he rejoined Grant. As a part also of Grant's movement, General Butler moved in force from Fortress Monroe toward Richmond, and occupied City Point and Bermuda Hundred on the James, May 5. On the 16th he was attacked by the Confederates, and forced back between the James and Appomattox Rivers at Bermuda Hundred, where his force was hemmed in, and rendered useless for an immediate advance on Richmond.

24. A movement was also made up the Shenandoah, to assist operations on Lee's flank and rear. On the 1st of May Sigel moved up the Valley with 10,000 men, and was routed at Newmarket on the 15th by Breckinridge with considerable loss. Hunter succeeded Sigel, and defeated the enemy at Piedmont June 5th. He then approached the important point of Lynchburg. Lee, becoming alarmed for its safety, sent a strong force to its relief, and Hunter retreated into Western Virginia.

25. Grant began to move his army, re-enforced to 150,000 men, across the James on the 15th of June. On the 18th he assaulted Petersburg, which had been hastily fortified by a part of Lee's army. It was a place of great importance, because it was the centre of several railroads connecting Richmond with the South. In four days Grant's losses in the assault were 9000 men. With his repulse at Petersburg the siege of that place and of Richmond began. Grant's movements had thus far cost him 64,000 men. Lee had lost about 38,000. The struggle was now a simple question of the resources of the North against the exhausted energies of the South.

---

23. What movement was made by Sheridan, and for what purpose? What was his success? What other movement did Grant plan? What happened to Butler?

24. State the operations in the Shenandoah Valley in May? also in June? What was the result? What was the object of these movements?

25. Where did Grant move in June? What place did he assault, and with what success? What is said of the losses of each army from the commencement of the campaign?

26. An attempt was presently made to break Lee's lines by running a mine under one of the enemy's forts. On the morning of the 30th of July, four tons of powder were exploded in it, and over the chasm that was made the Federal soldiers charged. But the enemy turned their guns upon them, and drove them back with the loss of 5000 men. On August 18, 19, 20, Grant seized and destroyed a part of the Weldon Railroad south of Petersburg. This contest of three days cost Grant 4500 troops. There was more severe fighting, continuing as late as December; and throughout the winter the Union army was occupied in extending their intrenchments, and endeavoring to break the enemy's communications.

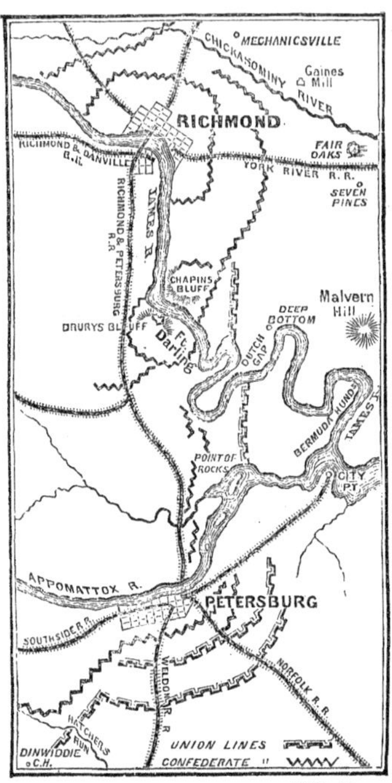

PETERSBURG AND RICHMOND, 1864–65.

27. **Early's Raid into Maryland and Pennsylvania.**—It has already been seen how the co-operating army failed in the Valley of the Shenandoah. Hunter's retreat into West Virginia left Washington exposed, and Lee, quickly perceiving this, ordered Early, with 20,000 men, to advance north, hoping, perhaps, that this would compel Grant to raise the siege of Petersburg. Early marched with great rapidity, crossed the Potomac, and entered Maryland July 5th.

28. At Monócacy River, July 9, he defeated General L.

26. To what mode of attack did Grant resort in July? Describe it, and state the result. What great success did he meet with in August? See map. What is said of later events around Petersburg?

27. What followed the misfortunes of the Union army in the Shenandoah Valley? What advantage was taken of this? In what direction did Early march?

Wallace with considerable loss. A portion of the Confederate troops went within gunshot of Baltimore and Washington. Laden with booty, Early retired up the Shenandoah Valley, pursued by General Wright as far as Winchester, where a portion of the Confederate army was defeated, July 20. Turning on the Union troops near Winchester, he drove them back with loss. Crossing the Potomac, he entered Pennsylvania, burned a great part of the town of Chambersburg July 30, and, with a considerable quantity of plunder, returned to the Shendandoah Valley.

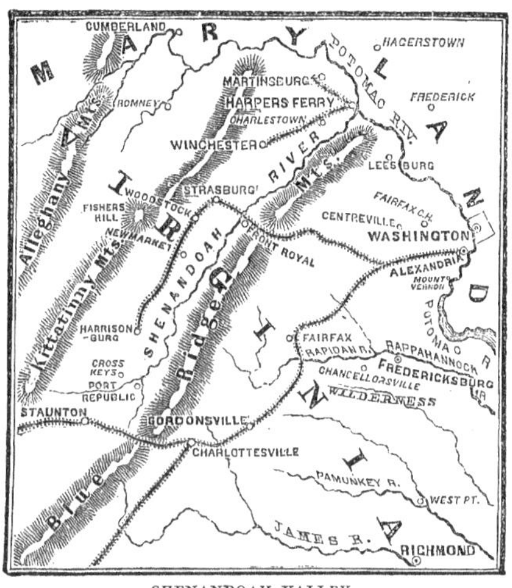

SHENANDOAH VALLEY.

29. Sheridan, who had been appointed general in that quarter, followed Early, and came up with him at Winchester. Here a battle was fought September 19, and Early was defeated. Three days after, Sheridan routed him at Fisher's Hill with heavy loss. The fertile Shenandoah Valley had year after year furnished a large part of the supplies for Lee's army. Grant determined that this should end, and Sheridan, by his orders, burned all the crops, mills, barns, and farming

GENERAL PHILIP SHERIDAN.

28. With what opposition did he meet? Describe his movements to July 20, inclusive. Sketch the movements that followed.

tools, and swept the cattle along with him as he moved back.

30. Early followed the Union army, and suddenly attacked it, October 19, at Cedar Creek, when Sheridan was absent. The Union troops were badly driven in the first part of the fight, and fell back to a new position. At this critical moment Sheridan arrived, and, by his courage and energy, restored his lines, ordered an advance, and changed the rout into a Union victory. Early's troops, broken up into small parties, fled in confusion for more than thirty miles. The Valley was cleared of Confederates, but this had been done at heavy cost. Sheridan's campaign of one month was at the expense of 17,000 men killed, wounded, and missing.

31. **Events on the Coast. Mobile Bay.**—Mobile was one of the most strongly fortified cities of the Confederacy. Two strong fortifications, Gaines and Morgan, besides a number of batteries, commanded the entrance to the bay. An expedition, consisting of a powerful fleet, under Admiral Farragut, and a land force commanded by General G. Granger, was sent against Mobile in July.

32. Farragut attacked the forts on the 5th of August. To enable him to see and direct the operations of the fleet, he had himself lashed to the main-top of his own vessel, the Hartford. The fleet fought its way past the forts with the loss of only one iron-clad. When it got above them, the iron-plated ram Tennessee attacked Farragut, but was disabled, and compelled to surrender after a short but desperate fight. The forts were soon after given up to General Granger. Mobile, as a port, was now effectually shut against blockade-running; but the city was not taken until next year.

33. **Expedition against Fort Fisher.**—There remained north of the Gulf only one port of entrance open to the Confeder-

---

29. Who took command in the Shenandoah Valley? What were his movements? What was done by Sheridan in the Valley by Grant's orders?

30. What attempt was made by Early to retrieve success? Describe the battle. At what cost was Sheridan's success accomplished?

31. What is said of Mobile? Where is it situated? What movement was made against it, and when?

32. Describe Farragut's arrangements. When was the attack made? What followed? What advantage was gained by the capture of the forts?

ates — Wilmington, North Carolina. This was commanded by Fort Fisher, a work of extraordinary strength. Admiral Porter, with a fleet, and a land force of 8000 men under General Butler, were sent against it in December. On the 24th the bombardment was begun with the heaviest fleet that had been employed during the war. The troops landed above the fort after the bombardment, but General Butler decided that it was too strong to be taken by assault. The expedition then returned to Fortress Monroe.

FARRAGUT ENTERING MOBILE BAY.

34. **Destruction of the Iron Ram Albemarle.**—One of the bravest and most dangerous acts of the war was the blowing up of the Albemarle, an iron ram, at Plymouth, North Carolina, which place had been recaptured by the Confederates with the help of this vessel. It had afterward done great damage to the Union vessels in Albemarle Sound. Lieutenant W. B. Cushing, on the night of the 27th of October, in a small steamer manned by a volunteer crew, sailed up the Roanoke River, and, with his own hands, fastened to

33. What was the only port remaining to the Confederates? Where was this? How was it defended? What expedition was sent against it, and when? Describe the attack, and state the result.

the Albemarle a torpedo, which was immediately exploded, and the ram sunk. All but Cushing and one other were either killed or captured. In consequence of the destruction of the Albemarle, Plymouth was surrendered on the 31st to the Union squadron.

35. **What had been achieved through the Year.**—The military events of 1864 opened with the Union repulse at Olustee, Florida, and Sherman's short campaign in northern Mississippi. These were followed, in March and April, by the misfortunes of Banks's expedition in the Red River country. The successes achieved by the Union armies during the remainder of the year were decided. Sherman pierced the southern part of the Confederacy by the capture of Atlanta, and followed this up by his march through Georgia and the capture of Savannah. Grant drove Lee within the defenses of Richmond, and held him there. Sheridan, in a series of brilliant engagements, swept the Confederate troops out of the Shenandoah Valley, and closed completely that avenue to the North, so often and so successfully used by the Confederates.

36. On the Atlantic coast Farragut entered Mobile Bay, and, by the capture of Forts Gaines and Morgan, closed the harbor against Confederate blockade-runners. Wilmington was, at the close of the year, the only port on the Atlantic open to the enemy, and this was destined soon to be in possession of the Union troops. East of the Mississippi, North and South Carolina and Georgia were all that remained to the Confederacy.

37. Still there was no relaxation of effort on the part of the North. Each fresh demand for men or money was met promptly, the more so because it was clearly seen that, by a few more vigorous movements, the war would be brought to a close. The South was exhausted.

38. During the summer the nominations for the presi-

---

34. What was the Albemarle, and where did it lie? Describe the circumstances attending its destruction. What important surrender followed this?

35. How did the year 1864 open? State Sherman's success; Grant's; Sheridan's.

36. What was the condition of things on the Atlantic coast? What territory remained in the possession of the Confederacy?

37. How far did the North relax its efforts? What is said of this? What is said of the South?

dency were made. The Democratic party nominated General George B. M'Clellan for President, and George H. Pendleton, of Ohio, for Vice-President. By the Republican party President Lincoln was renominated, with Andrew Johnson, of Tennessee, as Vice-President. In the election that followed, the latter were chosen by a large majority. In the month of October Nevada was admitted to the Union, making the thirty-sixth state.

REVIEW QUESTIONS.—1864.

1. How extensive was the Confederate navy during the war?
2. How did they make up for this want?
3. State in general terms what was their success.
4. Give the names of the different Confederate cruisers.
5. Sketch the career of the most celebrated one.
6. Where were the most of these vessels built?
7. How did the United States regard this conduct of England?
8. With what success did Sherman begin the year?
9. What Union defeat occurred the same month?
10. What change was made in the command of the Union armies?
11. Why was this advantageous?
12. What was the plan of the campaign for 1864?
13. Against what point did Sherman move?
14. When, and with what resistance, did he get into the neighborhood of Atlanta?
15. What change was made in the command of the Confederate army, and why?
16. What was the result of this?
17. What did the capture of Atlanta cost the Union army?
18. Why was this city so important?
19. State clearly how Hood was finally disposed of.
20. What was Sherman's next great movement, and its success?
21. When and where did Grant first move?
22. How did the time compare with that of Sherman's movements?
23. How was Grant's progress opposed, as shown by the battles and the losses?
24. To what line of defense did he force Lee?
25. What place now rose into immense importance as one of the defenses of Richmond, and why?
26. State briefly the result of Grant's efforts near Petersburg this year
27. What befell Grant's co-operating force in the Shenandoah Valley?
28. What advantage did Early take of this?
29. Who was chosen by Grant to take care of Early?
30. What battles were fought?
31. In what way did Sheridan punish the settlements in the Valley?
32. Describe the closing battle there during 1864.
33. What expedition was sent west of the Mississippi in the spring?
34. Sketch the principal events of the Red River expedition.
35. State the circumstances attending the Fort Pillow massacre.
36. What was the great naval event of the year, and describe it?
37. How many ports were now open to the Confederates on the Atlantic?
38. What attempt was made by a Union force on the coast of North Carolina?
39. State how much had been gained by the Union armies during the year.
49. Where were Grant and Sherman at the close of 1864?

---

38. What is said of the fall election for President and Vice-President? What state was admitted to the Union, and when?

SECTION V.

EVENTS OF 1865.

1. NOTWITHSTANDING the unfortunate issue of the attempt against Fort Fisher at the close of the previous year, Admiral Porter remained firm in the conviction that it could be taken. Another expedition was accordingly sent against it in January, 1865. Porter commanded the fleet, and General Terry the land force. The troops landed near the fort on the 12th, and the fleet bombarded it with terrific power for the three following days. On the 15th, Terry, after a bloody struggle, took the works by assault. On the 22d of February Wilmington was occupied by the Union troops.

2. The plan of the campaign had now become very simple. The Confederacy was in its last agony. Sherman's course lay northward through South and North Carolina into Virginia, and Grant's business was the capture of Petersburg and Richmond. Both these movements were carried through at a very early period in the year.

3. Sherman allowed his army to rest a month in Savannah. Toward the end of January he pushed through South Carolina to Columbia, the capital, and entered it February 17th. On his way he cut the railroad north of Charleston. Hardee, the Confederate general at that place, afraid of being hemmed in, evacuated the city February 17th, and moved north to join General Johnston in North Carolina. From Columbia Sherman pressed toward Fayetteville, North Carolina, which he entered March 12th. After sharp fighting, he reached Goldsboro' March 21st, where he was joined by Generals Schofield and Terry, who had come up from the coast with re-enforcements. General Johnston, with 40,000 men, lay at Raleigh, the capital of the state.

1. What opinion was entertained by Admiral Porter? How far did this influence General Grant? What was the result? What did the capture of Fort Fisher involve?

2. What is said of the plan of the campaign? What part was Sherman called on to execute? What did Grant keep immediately under his own control?

3. Where was Sherman at the beginning of the year? What were his first movements? What important result followed? In what direction did Sherman move from Columbia? What place did he reach at last? Who opposed him? By whom was Sherman joined?

4. **Operations in Virginia.**—All winter Grant's army was encamped in front of Petersburg, stretching away round to the southwest. On the 27th of February Sheridan was sent from Winchester, with a cavalry force 10,000 strong, up the Shenandoah Valley, to destroy Lee's communications by canal and railroad to the north and east of Richmond. Early was intrenched at Waynesboro, where he was attacked by Sheridan, and compelled to retreat, with the loss of 1600 prisoners. After an almost continued career of success, Sheridan joined the army near Petersburg March 26th.

5. Lee's situation began to grow desperate. He tried to break the Union lines at Fort Steadman, but was repulsed with loss March 25th. His only hope now was to be able to join Johnston's army in North Carolina, and prolong the contest. On the 1st of April, Sheridan, with 30,000 men, attacked Lee's position at Five Forks, and gained it. Then

GRANT AND LEE SIGNING THE TERMS OF SURRENDER.

---

4. Where was the Army of Virginia during the winter? What occurred in February? With what opposition did he meet? Describe Sheridan's movements.

followed Grant's attack along the whole front, and Lee's lines were pierced in several places. On the 3d of April, Petersburg was entered by the Union troops, and Richmond a few hours afterward. Lee fled westward, but was so closely followed that he was compelled to surrender his army to Grant at Appomattox Court-house, April 9th.

6. The joy that filled the hearts of the loyal people of the North at the news of Lee's surrender was turned to sorrow five days afterward. President Lincoln was shot in the private box of the theatre at Washington on the evening of April 14 by J. Wilkes Booth. On the morning of the 15th the President died. Almost at the same time he was shot, another assassin broke into the sick-chamber of Mr. Seward, Secretary of State, and, after wounding him and his son severely, escaped. Booth, tracked into Maryland, was captured in a tobacco-house near Port Royal, and killed by his pursuers. Four of his accomplices were tried and executed.

7. **Sherman's Operations.—Close of the War.**—At the beginning of April, the Confederate army under General Johnston was at Raleigh, closely watched by Sherman. On the 10th Sherman began to press him back, and on the 13th entered Raleigh. At this time news reached Johnston of Lee's surrender, and he at once made proposals to Sherman. On April 26th the terms of surrender were signed by both generals. Davis, the Confederate president, was captured on the 10th of May at Irwins-

GENERAL JOSEPH E. JOHNSTON.

5. What is said of Lee's situation, and his attempt to relieve it? What hope remained to him? How far did Grant permit him to attempt this? What followed Sheridan's attack? What great events occurred April 3 and April 9?

6. What sad occurrence took place a few days after the surrender of Lee? State the particulars. What other attempted assassination was made? What was the fate of the conspirators?

ville, Georgia, while trying to make his escape to the sea-coast. He was sent prisoner to Fortress Monroe. By the end of May all the Confederate armies in the Southwest had surrendered, and the CIVIL WAR was at an end.

REVIEW QUESTIONS.—1865.

1. Describe the movements in the month of January, 1865.
2. What important result was achieved by this?
3. What was the plan of operations during the year?
4. Describe Sherman's early movements and the result.
5. How did Grant open the campaign in Virginia?
6. What was the result of this?
7. To what point was Lee's mind directed?
8. How was this prevented?
9. When were Petersburg and Richmond occupied by the Union troops?
10. What became of Lee and his army?
11. Describe the lamentable event by which this was followed in a few days.
12. What were the military events in North Carolina immediately preceding Johnston's surrender?
13. What other events marked the close of the war?

SECTION VI.

JOHNSON'S ADMINISTRATION.

1. BY the death of Mr. Lincoln, Vice-President Johnson, formerly United States senator from Tennessee, became President, April 15th. Previous to this, on the 7th of April, the American minister, Mr. Adams, at the court of St. James, addressed a communication to the English government setting forth the depredations committed on American vessels by Confederate cruisers built, equipped, and manned in Great Britain. He claimed that the latter was responsible for the damage

PRESIDENT JOHNSON.

7. What were Sherman's movements in April? What occurred on the 26th of April? What led to this? What became of Jefferson Davis? When was the war every where at an end?

that had been done to American commerce. Correspondence on this subject was continued through the summer, but the English government refused to admit the validity of the claim, or to submit the question to the arbitration of any foreign government. This, known as the "Alabama" question, after the famous cruiser of that name, still remains unsettled (1870), and has been the cause of much bitterness of feeling between the two nations.

2. The war left a debt amounting, in June, 1865, to nearly $2,700,000,000. The interest on this, nearly all of which was payable in gold, amounted to $133,000,000. By means of duties on imported articles, and taxes on manufactures, incomes, etc., the amount necessary to meet this interest, and some $200,000,000 in addition to carry on the government, was raised without difficulty. To strengthen the confidence of the holders of government bonds in the good faith of the United States, the House of Representatives in Congress, on the 5th of December, 1865, with only one dissenting voice, passed a resolution declaring that the "public debt must and ought to be paid, principal and interest."

3. Another matter, not less important than the finances, which at an early day occupied the attention of President Johnson's administration, was the reconstruction of the Confederate States, and their readmission into the American Union. In a very short time after his inauguration, a serious difference of opinion on the best mode of accomplishing this began to manifest itself between the President and Congress. The latter appointed a reconstruction committee, to which was referred all the different propositions and resolutions presented on the subject.

4. On the 1st of February, 1865, Congress passed a resolution submitting to the Legislatures of the different states an amendment to the Constitution abolishing slavery. On

---

1. Who was now President, and when inaugurated? Describe the important demand made in April. How was this received by England? What farther is said about this?

2. What is said of the public debt and interest thereon? How was the interest on this met? What important measure was passed by Congress in December, 1865? What was the object of this?

3. What measure engaged the attention of Congress? What misunderstanding arose?

the 18th of December, William H. Seward, Secretary of State, formally announced that this, the 13th amendment, had been duly ratified by the Legislatures of twenty-seven states, and was therefore adopted as a part of the Constitution of the United States.

5. While civil war was raging between the North and South, France sent an army to Mexico to overrun that country, and to establish an empire there under an Austrian prince. After a series of severe battles, the Liberal or Republican party was defeated, and the French entered the capital in 1863. An election, which proved a mere mockery, was ordered on the question of the empire, and Maximilian, Archduke of Austria, was chosen emperor through the influence of French bayonets. The American government was not blind to what was transpiring in Mexico, and entered a respectful protest against the French interference in Mexican affairs. It limited its efforts to a protest, because it had enough to do in meeting the great demand made on its resources by the Civil War.

6. As that drew to a close, the feeling of the people of the United States in favor of Mexican liberty emboldened the United States government to demand of the French Emperor the withdrawal of his troops from Mexico. After some hesitation this was done. The Mexican Republicans thereupon attacked the forces of Maximilian, deprived of French assistance, with so much energy, that the emperor himself at last fell into their hands, and, with two of his generals, was shot, June 19, 1867. Thus ended the empire of Mexico.

7. An enterprise of the highest importance to Europe and America, the laying of the Atlantic cable, reached a triumphant success in the month of July, 1866. The first unsuccessful attempt to lay a telegraph cable between these two continents was made through the efforts of Cyrus W. Field, and others, of New York, in the year 1857. In June, 1858, there was another attempt and failure. In July, the same

4. What was the resolution of February? When and how was it declared to be adopted?

5. What was taking place in Mexico during the Civil War? How did the United States regard this? Why was it prevented from active interference?

6. What took place at the close of the Civil War? What was the result of this?

year, the laying of the cable was once more begun, and was completed from shore to shore in August; but, owing to some defect, it soon ceased to transmit messages. In 1865, the same company commenced to lay another cable. When the vessels had proceeded about 1400 miles from the Irish coast the cable parted, and the expedition returned to England.

8. These unsuccessful attempts had cost not less than $6,000,000. Undismayed by them, Mr. Field was able to persuade capitalists to make one more trial, and in July of the following year a new cable was laid with complete success. As if to make this the more marked, the fleet then proceeded to search for the lost cable of 1865, and in August grappled it, and brought it to the surface from a depth of more than two miles. It was then spliced, the relaying commenced, and a second cable was successfully laid. The entire distance from Trinity Bay, Newfoundland, to Valentia Bay, in Ireland, is a little less than 1700 miles.

9. The misunderstanding between the President and Congress continued, and in February, 1867, a bill was passed over the President's veto, placing a large part of the former Confederate States under military government. In the same month Nebraska was admitted into the Union over the veto of the President. With the same opposition, the reconstruction act, arranging for the reorganization of the former Confederate States except Tennessee, was passed in July, 1867. This was followed by other measures on the part of the President and of Congress, increasing the irritation between them, until at length, on the 24th of January, 1868, the impeachment of the President was ordered by the House of Representatives. After a tedious trial before the Senate of the United States, he was acquitted, on the 23d of May, of the charges brought against him. A two-thirds vote was necessary for his conviction, and one vote was wanting.

7. What wonderful enterprise ended successfully in 1866? How many unsuccessful attempts were made? Describe these.

8. How much had these attempts cost? Who was the moving spirit in these efforts? Describe the final success. How was this rendered more striking? What are the termini of the cable, and how long is it?

9. What occurred in Congress in April, 1867? What state was admitted this session? What measure was passed in July? To what important step did this lead?

10. Meanwhile affairs in the South were drawing nearer adjustment. Jefferson Davis, the Confederate President, who had been confined in Fortress Monroe ever since his capture, was released on bail in May, 1867. On the 8th of September, President Johnson proclaimed "amnesty to all engaged in the rebellion," with the exception of the leaders. Finally, on the 24th of June, 1868, Arkansas, Alabama, Georgia, Louisiana, North and South Carolina, were readmitted to the Union over the veto of the President, who took the ground that they never had been out of the Union.

11. On the 29th of March, 1867, a treaty was concluded between the United States and Russia, by which the latter sold to the United States all of her possessions in North America for the sum of seven millions of dollars. This treaty, ratified by the Senate on the 9th of April, added to the territory of the United States an area of 550,000 square miles, chiefly valuable, however, for the fisheries on its coasts. In the fall of 1868, both parties, the Republican and Democratic, prepared themselves for the presidential contest. Horatio Seymour, of New York, was nominated by the Democrats, and General U. S. Grant by the Republicans. In the election that followed the latter was chosen President, and Schuyler Colfax, of Indiana, Vice-President.

12. An Indian war began in the year 1864 in the Southwest, stretching through Southern Colorado and into Indian Territory. It reached such dimensions in the years 1865 and 1866 that it drew toward it the earnest attention of government, and General Sheridan was sent out to superintend operations. In the fall of 1868 General Custar's cavalry pressed the enemy so closely that Black Kettle and a large party of his warriors were surprised and killed in the battle of the Wacheta (*wah-chê-tah*). This was the deathblow to the Indian disturbances in that quarter.

13. In February, 1869, both houses of Congress agreed to

10. What measure of clemency was adopted in May, 1867, and what other in September? What occurred in June, 1868?

11. What purchase of territory was now made, and from whom? What is said of its extent and value? State what is said of the nominations and election for the presidency.

12. Where and when did an Indian war burst out? Who was finally sent to bring it to an end? How did he succeed?

recommend to the Legislatures of the different states the passage of the fifteenth amendment to the Constitution of the United States, in the following words: "The right of the citizens of the United States to vote shall not be denied or abridged by the United States or any state on account of race, color, or previous condition of servitude."

SECTION VII.

GRANT'S ADMINISTRATION.

1. THE distinguished military services of President Grant during the Civil War have been already narrated. Previous to its commencement his name was unknown to the country, although he had served with credit as a subordinate officer during the war with Mexico. Hitherto (June, 1870) there have been but few striking points in the history of his administration. The year 1869 was chiefly remarkable for the completion of the Pacific Railroad connecting California with the Mississippi Valley—a distance of 1776 miles, and bringing New York in communication with San Francisco in seven days.

PRESIDENT GRANT.

2. The country, during the year that has elapsed, has, as a whole, been prosperous. The price of gold, which during the Civil War rose as high as 280 in currency, fell, in the month of September, 1869, to 110, and has—June, 1870—ranged but little above this point. The national debt has been reduced more than $120,000,000. The Confederate States have been readmitted to the Union, and a general

13. What important recommendation was made by Congress? Give the language of this.

1. What is said of President Grant's earlier history? For what is the year 1869 chiefly remarkable?

amnesty, under certain conditions, for all political offenses during the Civil War, has tended to soften the asperity of feeling that it left behind. The South, devastated by the march of armies, has begun to recover her former beauty, and her people are once more planting their fields, rebuilding their railroads, opening new routes for trade, and endeavoring to accommodate themselves to the novel requirements of free labor.

3. The history of the United States is now brought down to that period when, with a wide extent of territory and rapidly-increasing population, it has entered on a fresh career of great development. This expansion is to be seen in the building of railroads, in the opening of mines, in the increase of manufactures and of general wealth, and in the continuous flow of foreign immigration into new states and territories. With lavish expenditure of blood and treasure, the American people have resolved that the union of the states shall continue. Every lover of his country may truly exclaim, in view of what has been accomplished, MAY HER GREATNESS, STRENGTHENED BY PUBLIC LIBERTY AND VIRTUE, ENDURE FOREVER!

CHAPTER X.

SETTLEMENT AND GROWTH OF THE PACIFIC STATES.

I. CALIFORNIA.

1. IN the year 1579, Sir Francis Drake, the English navigator already mentioned, explored the coast of California, and named it New Albion. About two centuries after this, in the year 1769, the Spaniards established a mission at St. Diego (*de-á-go*). From time to time they planted new stations, which by the year 1803 had increased to eighteen in number. Beyond this they did nothing to promote the settlement of the country, the population of which amounted in 1831 to scarce 5000 whites. At the time of the de-

---

2. What is said of the condition of the country, the gold market, and the public debt? What is said of the Confederate States? What is said of the condition of the South?

EARLY GOLD MINING IN CALIFORNIA.

struction of Spanish power in the New World, 1822, the republic of Mexico erected the country on the Pacific into the province of Alta, or Upper California.

2. Emigrants from the United States began to find their way into the territory between the years 1843 and 1846, and when war was declared in the latter year they at once raised the flag of their country, and rose against the Spanish ruler. We have already seen that Fremont, when he arrived there, found them prepared for the struggle, and placed himself at their head. The subjugation of California followed, and its provisional government fell into the hand of General Kearny, of the United States army.

3. By far the most valuable portion of the territory acquired by treaty at the close of the Mexican War was the province of Upper California. It extended from about 109°

---

1. Where and when was Upper California first settled? What was it afterward named, and by whom? What is said of its settlement by the Spaniards? What happened to the Territory in 1822?

2. From what source did additions come to the settlers? To what did this tend in 1846? State all of this.

W. long., through the present State of Colorado, to the Pacific, more than 1000 miles; and from 42° N. lat., the southern boundary of Oregon, to the River Gila (*geela*) on the south, a distance of about 600 miles. It embraced what is now known as the State of California, Nevada, the western part of Colorado, and a considerable part of the Territory of Arizona—an area of 450,000 square miles.

4. The treaty of peace was scarce concluded between Mexico and the United States when the discovery of gold was made, February, 1848. This at once gave an impetus to the development of the Territory, which otherwise might long have remained comparatively unknown. Thousands flocked to the gold diggings, across the plains, or by the tedious voyage around Cape Horn, or across the isthmus of Panama. By the year 1850, two years after the discovery of gold, there were 100,000 persons in the Territory, where, at the close of the war, there were only 23,000. In the year 1852 the population had increased to 254,000.

5. In September, 1849, delegates, chosen by the settlers, met in convention at Monterey, and formed a free-state Constitution. They then applied to Congress for admission, and California was received into the Union, September 9, 1850. At the time it sought to be admitted, there was, as we have already seen, great excitement throughout the country on the question of slavery, and the petition of California to be allowed to come in with a free Constitution was not calculated to calm the angry waters of slave agitation. Its admission formed one of the items of the celebrated compromise measure—the Omnibus Bill, passed in 1850. On the admission of California, the boundaries of the new state were definitely fixed. To the east of its present boundary was created Utah Territory, embracing within its limits what is now the State of Nevada. The balance south of Utah was united with New Mexico, and is now known as part of Arizona.

3. Describe the limits of Upper California as ceded to the United States. What did it embrace?

4. What occurred about the time the treaty of peace was made? What effect did this immediately produce? What is said of the population?

5. What occurred in 1849? When did it become a state? Under what circumstances did it apply for admission? What were its boundaries?

6. All the world has learned of the wealth of California —the "Eldorado," or "Land of gold." It is rich also in copper and the ores of quicksilver. But it has already become equally celebrated for its agricultural riches; for its valleys raise in abundance wheat, which has found its way to the shores of the Atlantic. Its remarkable climate and soil are suited to the growth of the vine and the various Northern fruits, which flourish with a luxuriance that has no counterpart in less favored regions east of the Mississippi. Its trees are the wonder of the world; and the famous Valley of the Yosemité combines beauty, grandeur, and sublimity in an astonishing degree.

7. Facing the distant shores of Asia, with which it is con-

THREE BROTHERS—YOSEMITÉ VALLEY.

---

6. What is said of the mineral and agricultural resources of the state, and of her natural scenery?

nected by swift steamers, it is the great link between China and Japan on the one hand, and the United States on the other. To all these unequaled natural advantages, improved by wonderful energy, art has added that triumph of modern enterprise, the Union Pacific Railroad. But the best assurance for her continued progress lies in her widely-established system of common schools, in the intelligence and energy of her people, and in that regard for law, which out of anarchy has brought forward the young state of the Pacific, purified and braced to enter on her present career.

II. OREGON.

1. THE country west of the Rocky Mountains, extending north of 42° as far as the British line, was bought by the United States as a part of Louisiana in 1803. Little was known of the western part of this vast territory at the time of the purchase. In the year 1792, Captain Gray, of Boston, in a trading voyage to the Northwest, entered the river, which he named the Columbia, after the ship in which he sailed. On this discovery the United States based their claim to the territory watered by the Columbia River.

2. While negotiations were still pending for the purchase of Louisiana, the far-reaching mind of President Jefferson had recommended to Congress that a party be dispatched to trace the Missouri River to its source, cross the Rocky Mountains, and proceed to the Pacific Ocean. The company, commanded by Captains Lewis and Clarke, left their encampment, 21 miles up the Missouri, in May, 1804, and, after surmounting great difficulties, at the end of 18 months reached the entrance of the Columbia in November, 1805. On the route Lewis discovered the sources of the river now known by his name. Their return journey was still more serious, though more rapid, and they at length reached St. Louis in September, 1806, having been absent two years and four months.

7. What is said of the situation of California? How have these advantages been lately increased? What concluding remarks are made?

1. In what way did Oregon come into the possession of the United States? What American first visited its shores, and with what results?

2. When and how was the inland exploration of the territory made? Give a sketch of this expedition.

3. This expedition, although it extended the knowledge with regard to the territory, did not greatly promote its settlement. It was too remote from the United States, which were yet mainly confined to the Atlantic coast. For a long time the country was chiefly occupied by trappers and fur traders in the employment of the British Fur Company. An American association, the Pacific Fur Company, in 1811 built Fort Astoria, which, in the War of 1812, was taken by the British, but restored at its close. In 1818 the United States and England agreed to a mutual occupancy of the whole territory until the year 1828. At this time the treaty of joint occupancy was renewed, to terminate on either party giving one year's notice.

4. The first emigration of Americans came overland in the year 1839. From the difficulties attending so long a journey, additions to their numbers were very slowly made. So many arrived, however, that the attention of the British and American governments was drawn to the territory, and the latter, in 1845, gave the year's notice required to terminate the treaty. For a time serious trouble was apprehended between the two nations in relation to the settlement of boundaries. Happily, war was averted by the treaty of 1846.

5. Lying close to California, its growth in population was for a time seriously interfered with by the gold excitement. Congress very wisely, in 1850, passed an act granting lands to immediate and actual settlers. Since that time the population of the country has steadily increased. In the year 1848 it was organized as a Territory, and in 1853 that part of it north of Columbia River was erected into Washington Territory. On the 12th of February, 1859, Oregon was admitted as a free state. Its development is yet in its infancy. With a remarkably equable climate, and with good sea-coast advantages, it bids fair to occupy a commanding influence on the shores of the Pacific.

---

3. How far was Oregon benefited by this exploration? Why was this? How was the country occupied? What occurred here during the War of 1812? What agreement was made between England and the United States?

4. When did the first active emigration take place? To what did these new arrivals lead? How did the trouble end?

5. What interfered with the growth of Oregon? What remedy was tried for this? State the changes made in territorial limits. When was it admitted to the Union?

PRESIDENTS AND VICE-PRESIDENTS OF THE UNITED STATES.

NO.	PRESIDENTS.	FROM WHAT STATE.	INAUGURATED.	VICE-PRESIDENTS.	FROM WHAT STATE.
1.	George Washington	Virginia	April 30, 1789	John Adams	Massachusetts.
2.	John Adams	Massachusetts	March 4, 1797	Thomas Jefferson	Virginia.
3.	Thomas Jefferson	Virginia	March 4, 1801	Aaron Burr	New York.
				George Clinton	New York.
4.	James Madison	Virginia	March 4, 1809	George Clinton	New York.
				Elbridge Gerry	Massachusetts.
5.	James Monroe	Virginia	March 4, 1817	Daniel D. Tompkins	New York.
6.	John Q. Adams	Massachusetts	March 4, 1825	John C. Calhoun	South Carolina.
7.	Andrew Jackson	Tennessee	March 4, 1829	John C. Calhoun	South Carolina.
				Martin Van Buren	New York.
8.	Martin Van Buren	New York	March 4, 1837	Richard M. Johnson	Kentucky.
9.	William H. Harrison	Ohio	March 4, 1841	John Tyler	Virginia.
10.	John Tyler	Virginia	April 6, 1841		
11.	James K. Polk	Tennessee	March 4, 1845	George M. Dallas	Pennsylvania.
12.	Zachary Taylor	Louisiana	March 5, 1849	Millard Fillmore	New York.
13.	Millard Fillmore	New York	July 10, 1850		
14.	Franklin Pierce	New Hampshire	March 4, 1853	William R. King	Alabama.
15.	James Buchanan	Pennsylvania	March 4, 1857	John C. Breckinridge	Kentucky.
16.	Abraham Lincoln	Illinois	March 4, 1861	Hannibal Hamlin	Maine.
				Andrew Johnson	Tennessee.
17.	Andrew Johnson	Tennessee	April 15, 1865		
18.	Ulysses S. Grant	Illinois	March 4, 1869	Schuyler Colfax	Indiana.

SETTLEMENT AND ADMISSION OF THE STATES.

STATES.	SETTLED.			ADMITTED.
	When.	Where.	By whom.	
Virginia	1607	Jamestown	English	1776
New York	1614	New York	Dutch	"
Massachusetts	1620	Plymouth	English	"
New Hampshire	1623	Little Harbor	English	"
Connecticut	1633	Windsor	English	"
Maryland	1634	St. Mary's	English	"
Rhode Island	1636	Providence	English	"
Delaware	1638	Wilmington	Swedes	"
North Carolina	1650	Chowan River	English	"
New Jersey	1664	Elizabeth	Dutch	"
South Carolina	1670	Ashley River	English	"
Pennsylvania	1682	Philadelphia	English	"
Georgia	1733	Savannah	English	"
Vermont	1724	Fort Dummer	English	1791
Kentucky	1775	Boonesboro	English	1792
Tennessee	1757	Fort Loudon	English	1796
Ohio	1788	Marietta	English	1802
Louisiana	1699	Iberville	French	1812
Indiana	1730	Vincennes	French	1816
Mississippi	1716	Natchez	French	1817
Illinois	1720	Kaskaskia	French	1818
Alabama	1711	Mobile	French	1819
Maine	1625	Bristol	French	1820
Missouri	1764	St. Louis	French	1821
Arkansas	1685	Arkansas Post	French	1836
Michigan	1670	Detroit	French	1837
Florida	1565	St. Augustine	Spaniards	1845
Texas	1692	S. A. De Bexar	Spaniards	"
Iowa	1833	Burlington	English	1846
Wisconsin	1669	Green Bay	French	1848
California	1769	San Diego	Spaniards	1850
Minnesota	1846	St. Paul	Americans	1858
Oregon	1811	Astoria	Americans	1859
Kansas			Americans	1861
West Virginia				1863
Nevada		Carson City	Americans	1864
Nebraska				1867
Colorado			Americans	"

DECLARATION OF INDEPENDENCE.

A DECLARATION BY THE REPRESENTATIVES OF THE UNITED STATES OF AMERICA, IN CONGRESS ASSEMBLED, JULY 4, 1776.

WHEN, in the course of human events, it becomes necessary for one people to dissolve the political bands which have connected them with another, and to assume, among the powers of the earth, the separate and equal station to which the laws of nature and of nature's God entitle them, a decent respect to the opinions of mankind requires that they should declare the causes which impel them to the separation.

We hold these truths to be self-evident—that all men are created equal; that they are endowed by their Creator with certain unalienable rights; that among these are life, liberty, and the pursuit of happiness; that, to secure these rights, governments are instituted among men, deriving their just powers from the consent of the governed; that, whenever any form of government becomes destructive of these ends, it is the right of the people to alter or to abolish it, and to institute a new government, laying its foundation on such principles, and organizing its powers in such form, as to them shall seem most likely to affect their safety and happiness. Prudence, indeed, will dictate that governments long established should not be changed for light and transient causes; and, accordingly, all experience hath shown that mankind are more disposed to suffer, while evils are sufferable, than to right themselves by abolishing the forms to which they are accustomed. But when a long train of abuses and usurpations, pursuing invariably the same object, evinces a design to reduce them under absolute despotism, it is their right, it is their duty to throw off such government, and to provide new guards for their future security. Such has been the patient sufferance of these colonies, and such is now the necessity which constrains them to alter their former systems of government. The history of the present king of Great Britain is a history of repeated injuries and usurpations, all having, in direct object, the establishment of an absolute tyranny over these states. To prove this, let facts be submitted to a candid world:

He has refused his assent to laws the most wholesome and necessary for the public good.

He has forbidden his governors to pass laws of immediate and pressing importance, unless suspended in their operation till his assent should be obtained; and, when so suspended, he has utterly neglected to attend to them.

He has refused to pass other laws for the accommodation of large districts of people, unless those people would relinquish the right of representation in the Legislature—a right inestimable to them, and formidable to tyrants only.

He has called together legislative bodies at places unusual, uncomfortable, and distant from the depository of their public records, for the sole purpose of fatiguing them into compliance with his measures.

He has dissolved representative houses repeatedly for opposing with manly firmness his invasions on the rights of the people.

He has refused, for a long time after such dissolutions, to cause others to be elected, whereby the legislative powers, incapable of annihilation, have returned to the people at large for their exercise; the state remaining, in the mean time, exposed to all the danger of invasion from without and convulsions within.

He has endeavored to prevent the population of these states; for that purpose obstructing the laws for naturalization of foreigners, refusing to pass others to encourage their migration hither, and raising the conditions of new appropriations of lands.

He has obstructed the administration of justice by refusing his assent to laws for establishing judiciary powers.

He has made judges dependent on his will alone for the tenure of their offices, and the amount and payment of their salaries.

He has erected a multitude of new offices, and sent hither swarms of officers to harass our people and eat out their substance.

He has kept among us, in times of peace, standing armies without the consent of our Legislature.

He has affected to render the military independent of and superior to the civil power.

He has combined with others to subject us to a jurisdiction foreign to our Constitution, and unacknowledged by our laws, giving his assent to their acts of pretended legislation:

For quartering large bodies of armed troops among us:

For protecting them, by a mock trial, from punishment for any murders which they should commit on the inhabitants of these states:

For cutting off our trade with all parts of the world:

For imposing taxes on us without our consent:

For depriving us, in many cases, of the benefits of trial by jury:

For transporting us beyond seas to be tried for pretended offenses:

For abolishing the free system of English laws in a neighboring province, establishing therein an arbitrary government, and enlarging its boundaries, so as to render it at once an example and fit instrument for introducing the same absolute rule into these colonies:

For taking away our charters, abolishing our most valuable laws, and altering fundamentally the powers of our governments:

For suspending our own Legislatures, and declaring themselves invested with power to legislate for us in all cases whatsoever.

He has abdicated government here by declaring us out of his protection, and waging war against us.

He has plundered our seas, ravaged our coasts, burnt our towns, and destroyed the lives of our people.

He is, at this time, transporting large armies of foreign mercenaries to complete the works of death, desolation, and tyranny, already begun, with circumstances of cruelty and perfidy scarcely paralleled in the most barbarous ages, and totally unworthy the head of a civilized nation.

He has constrained our fellow-citizens, taken captive on the high seas, to bear arms against their country, to become the executioners of their friends and brethren, or to fall themselves by their hands.

He has excited domestic insurrections amongst us, and has endeavored to bring on the inhabitants of our frontiers the merciless Indian savages, whose known rule of warfare is an undistinguished destruction of all ages, sexes, and conditions.

In every stage of these oppressions, we have petitioned for redress in the most humble terms; our repeated petitions have been answered only by repeated injury. A prince whose character is thus marked by every act which may define a tyrant is unfit to be the ruler of a free people.

Nor have we been wanting in attention to our British brethren. We have warned them, from time to time, of attempts made by their Legislature to extend an unwarrantable jurisdiction over us. We have reminded them of the circumstances of our emigration and settlement here. We have appealed to their native justice and magnanimity, and we have conjured them, by the ties of our common kindred, to disavow these usurpations, which would inevitably interrupt our connections and correspondence. They, too, have been deaf to the voice of justice and consanguinity. We must, therefore, acquiesce in the necessity which denounces our separation, and hold them, as we hold the rest of mankind—enemies in war, in peace friends.

We, therefore, the representatives of the United States of America, in General Congress assembled, appealing to the Supreme Judge of the world for the rectitude of our intentions, do, in the name and by the authority of the good people of these colonies, solemnly publish and declare that these United Colonies are, and of right ought to be, free and independent states; that they are absolved from all allegiance to the British crown, and that all political connection between them and the state of Great Britain is, and ought to be, totally dissolved; and that, as free and independent states, they have full power to levy war, conclude peace, contract alliances, establish commerce, and to do all other acts and things which independent states may of right do. And for the support of this declaration, with a firm reliance on the protection of Divine Providence, we mutually pledge to each other our lives, our fortunes, and our sacred honor.

The foregoing declaration was, by order of Congress, engrossed, and signed by the following members: JOHN HANCOCK.

New Hampshire.—Josiah Bartlett, William Whipple, Matthew Thornton.

Massachusetts Bay.—Samuel Adams, John Adams, Robert Treat Paine, Elbridge Gerry.

Rhode Island.—Stephen Hopkins, William Ellery.

Connecticut. — Roger Sherman, Samuel Huntington, William Williams, Oliver Wolcott.

New York.—William Floyd, Philip Livingston, Francis Lewis, Lewis Morris.

New Jersey.—Richard Stockton, John Witherspoon, Francis Hopkinson, John Hart, Abraham Clark.

Pennsylvania. — Robert Morris, Benjamin Rush, Benjamin Franklin, John Morton, George Clymer, James Smith, George Taylor, James Wilson, George Ross.

Delaware.—Cæsar Rodney, George Read, Thomas M'Kean.

Maryland. — Samuel Chase, William Paca, Thomas Stone, Charles Carroll, of Carrollton.

Virginia.—George Wythe, Richard Henry Lee, Thomas Jefferson, Benjamin Harrison, Thomas Nelson, Jr., Francis Lightfoot Lee, Carter Braxton.

North Carolina.—William Hooper, Joseph Hewes, John Penn.

South Carolina. — Edward Rutledge, Thomas Heyward, Jr., Thomas Lynch, Jr., Arthur Middleton.

Georgia. — Button Gwinnett, Lyman Hall, George Walton.

CONSTITUTION OF THE UNITED STATES.

PREAMBLE.

We, the people of the United States, in order to form a more perfect union, establish justice, insure domestic tranquility, provide for the common defense, promote the general welfare, and secure the blessings of liberty to ourselves and our posterity, do ordain and establish this Constitution for the United States of America.

ARTICLE I. LEGISLATIVE DEPARTMENT.

SECTION I. *Congress in General.*

All legislative powers herein granted shall be vested in a Congress of the United States, which shall consist of a Senate and House of Representatives.

SECTION II. *House of Representatives.*

Clause 1. The House of Representatives shall be composed of members chosen every second year by the people of the several states; and the electors in each state shall have the qualifications requisite for electors of the most numerous branch of the State Legislature.

Clause 2. No person shall be a representative who shall not have attained to the age of twenty-five years, and been seven years a citizen of the United States, and who shall not, when elected, be an inhabitant of that state in which he shall be chosen.

Clause 3. Representatives and direct taxes shall be apportioned among the several states which may be included within this Union, according to their respective numbers, which shall be determined by adding to the whole number of free persons, including those bound to service for a term of years, and excluding Indians not taxed, three fifths of all other persons. The actual enumeration shall be made within three years after the first meeting of the Congress of the United States, and within every subsequent term of ten years, in such manner as they shall by law direct. The number of representatives shall not exceed one for every thirty thousand, but each state shall have at least one representative; and until such enumeration shall be made, the state of New Hampshire shall be entitled to choose three, Massachusetts eight, Rhode Island and Providence Plantations one, Connecticut five, New York six, New Jersey four, Pennsylvania eight, Delaware one, Maryland six, Virginia ten, North Carolina five, South Carolina five, and Georgia three.

Clause 4. When vacancies happen in the representation from any state, the executive authority thereof shall issue writs of election to fill such vacancies.

Clause 5. The House of Representatives shall choose their speaker and other officers, and shall have the sole power of impeachment.

SECTION III. *Senate.*

Clause 1. The Senate of the United States shall be composed of two senators from each state, chosen by the Legislature thereof for six years, and each senator shall have one vote.

Clause 2. Immediately after they shall be assembled in consequence of the first election, they shall be divided, as equally as may be, into three classes. The seats of the senators of the first class shall be vacated at the expiration of the second year, of the second class at the expiration of the fourth year, and of the third class at the expiration of the sixth year, so that one third may be chosen every second year; and if vacancies happen, by resignation or otherwise, during the recess of the Legislature of any state, the executive thereof may make temporary appointments until the next meeting of the Legislature, which shall then fill such vacancies.

Clause 3. No person shall be a senator who shall not have attained to the age of thirty years, and been nine years a citizen of the United States, and who shall not, when elected, be an inhabitant of that state for which he shall be chosen.

Clause 4. The Vice-President of the United States shall be President of the Senate, but shall have no vote, unless they be equally divided.

Clause 5. The Senate shall choose their other officers, and also a president pro tempore, in the absence of the Vice-President, or when he shall exercise the office of President of the United States.

Clause 6. The Senate shall have the sole power to try all impeachments. When sitting for that purpose, they shall be on oath or affirmation. When the President of the United states is tried, the chief justice shall preside; and no person shall be convicted without the concurrence of two thirds of the members present.

Clause 7. Judgment in case of impeachment shall not extend farther than to removal from office, and disqualification to hold and enjoy any office of honor, trust, or profit under the United States; but the party convicted shall, nevertheless, be liable and subject to indictment, trial, judgment, and punishment according to law.

SECTION IV. *Both Houses.*

Clause 1. The times, places, and manner of holding elections for senators and representatives shall be prescribed in each state by the Legislature thereof; but the Congress may at any time, by law, make or alter such regulations, except as to the place of choosing senators.

Clause 2. The Congress shall assemble at least once in every year, and such meeting shall be on the first Monday in December, unless they shall by law appoint a different day

SECTION V. *The Houses separately.*

Clause 1. Each house shall be the judge of the elections, returns, and qualifications of its own members, and a majority of each shall constitute a quorum to do business; but a smaller number may adjourn from day to day, and may be authorized to compel the attendance of absent members, in such manner and under such penalties as each house may provide.

Clause 2. Each house may determine the rules of its proceedings, punish its members for disorderly behavior, and, with the concurrence of two thirds, expel a member.

Clause 3. Each house shall keep a journal of its proceedings, and from time to time publish the same, excepting such parts as may in their judgment require secrecy; and the yeas and nays of the members of either house, on any question, shall, at the desire of one fifth of those present, be entered on the journal.

Clause 4. Neither house during the session of Congress shall, without the consent of the other, adjourn for more than three days, nor to any other place than that in which the two houses shall be sitting.

SECTION VI. *Disabilities of Members.*

Clause 1. The senators and representatives shall receive a compensation for their services, to be ascertained by law, and paid out of the treasury of the United States. They shall in all cases, except treason, felony, and breach of the peace, be privileged from arrest during their attendance at the session of their respective houses, and in going to or returning from the same; and for any speech or debate in either house, they shall not be questioned in any other place.

Clause 2. No senator or representative shall, during the time for which he was elected, be appointed to any civil office under the authority of the United States, which shall have been created, or the emoluments whereof shall have been increased, during such time; and no person holding any office under the United States shall be a member of either house during his continuance in office.

SECTION VII. *Mode of passing Laws.*

Clause 1. All bills for raising revenue shall originate in the House of Representatives; but the Senate may propose or concur with amendments, as on other bills.

Clause 2. Every bill which shall have passed the House of Representatives and the Senate shall, before it become a law, be presented to the President of the United States; if he approve, he shall sign it; but if not, he shall return it, with his objections, to that house in which it shall have originated, who shall enter the objections at large on their journal, and proceed to reconsider it. If, after such reconsideration, two thirds of that house shall agree to pass the bill, it shall be sent, together with the objections, to the other house, by which it shall likewise be reconsidered, and if approved by two thirds of that house, it shall become a law. But in all such cases the votes of both houses shall be determined by yeas and nays, and the names of the persons voting for and against the bill shall be entered on the journal of each house respectively. If any bill shall not be returned by the President within ten days (Sundays excepted) after it shall have been presented to him, the same shall be a law in like manner as if he had signed it, unless the Congress by their adjournment prevent its return, in which case it shall not be a law.

Clause 3. Every order, resolution, or vote to which the concurrence of the Senate and House of Representatives may be necessary (except on a question of adjournment), shall be presented to the President of the United States; and before the same shall take effect, shall be approved by him, or, being disapproved by him, shall be repassed by two thirds of the Senate and House of Representatives, according to the rules and limitations prescribed in the case of a bill.

SECTION VIII. *Powers granted to Congress.*

The Congress shall have power—

Clause 1. To lay and collect taxes, duties, imposts, and excises, to pay the debts and provide for the common defense and general welfare of the United States; but all duties, imposts, and excises shall be uniform throughout the United States;

Clause 2. To borrow money on the credit of the United States;

Clause 3. To regulate commerce with foreign nations, and among the several states, and with the Indian tribes;

Clause 4. To establish a uniform rule of naturalization, and uniform laws on the subject of bankruptcies, throughout the United States;

Clause 5. To coin money, regulate the value thereof and of foreign coin, and fix the standard of weights and measures;

Clause 6. To provide for the punishment of counterfeiting the securities and current coin of the United States;

Clause 7. To establish post-offices and post-roads;

Clause 8. To promote the progress of science and useful arts, by securing for limited times to authors and inventors the exclusive right to their respective writings and discoveries;

Clause 9. To constitute tribunals inferior to the Supreme Court;

Clause 10. To define and punish felonies committed on the high seas, and offenses against the law of nations;

Clause 11. To declare war, grant letters of marque and reprisal, and make rules concerning captures on land and water;

Clause 12. To raise and support armies; but no appropriation of money to that use shall be for a longer term than two years;

Clause 13. To provide and maintain a navy;

Clause 14. To make rules for the government and regulation of the land and naval forces;

Clause 15. To provide for calling forth the militia to execute the laws of the Union, suppress insurrections, and repel invasions;

Clause 16. To provide for organizing, arming, and disciplining the militia, and for governing such part of them as may be employed in the service of the United States, reserving to the states respectively the appointment of the officers and the authority of training the militia according to the discipline prescribed by Congress;

Clause 17. To exercise exclusive legislation, in all cases whatsoever, over such district (not exceeding ten miles square) as may, by cession of particular states and the acceptance of Congress, become the seat of government of the United States, and to exercise like authority over all places purchased, by the consent of the Legislature of the state in which the same shall be, for the erection of forts, magazines, arsenals, dock-yards, and other needful buildings; and,

Clause 18. To make all laws which shall be necessary and proper for carrying into execution the foregoing powers, and all other powers vested by this Constitution in the government of the United States, or in any department or officer thereof.

SECTION IX. *Powers denied to the United States.*

Clause 1. The migration or importation of such persons as any of the states now existing shall think proper to admit, shall not be prohibited by the Congress prior to the year one thousand eight hundred and eight; but a tax or duty may be imposed on such importation, not exceeding ten dollars for each person.

Clause 2. The privilege of the writ of *habeas corpus* shall not be suspended unless when, in case of rebellion or invasion, the public safety may require it.

Clause 3. No bill of attainder, or ex-post-facto law, shall be passed.

Clause 4. No capitation or other direct tax shall be laid, unless in proportion to the census or enumeration herein before directed to be taken.

Clause 5. No tax or duty shall be laid on articles exported from any state.

Clause 6. No preference shall be given by any regulation of commerce or revenue to the ports of one state over those of another; nor shall vessels bound to or from one state be obliged to enter, clear, or pay duties in another.

Clause 7. No money shall be drawn from the treasury but in consequence of appropriations made by law; and a regular statement and account of the receipts and expenditures of all public money shall be published from time to time.

Clause 8. No title of nobility shall be granted by the United States; and no person holding any office of profit or trust under them shall, without the consent of the Congress, accept of any present, emolument, office, or title of any kind whatever, from any king, prince, or foreign state.

SECTION X. *Powers denied to the States.*

Clause 1. No state shall enter into any treaty, alliance, or confederation; grant letters of marque and reprisal; coin money; emit bills of credit; make any thing but gold and silver coin a tender in payment of debts; pass any bill of attainder, ex-post-facto law, or law impairing the obligation of contracts; or grant any title of nobility.

Clause 2. No state shall, without the consent of the Congress, lay any imposts or duties on imports or exports, except what may be absolutely necessary for executing its inspection laws: and the net produce of all duties and imposts laid by any state on imports or exports shall be for the use of the treasury of the United States; and all such laws shall be subject to the revision and control of the Congress.

Clause 3. No state shall, without the consent of Congress, lay any duty of tonnage, keep troops or ships of war in time of peace, enter into any agreement or compact with another state or with a foreign power, or engage in war, unless actually invaded, or in such imminent danger as will not admit of delay.

ARTICLE II. EXECUTIVE DEPARTMENT.

SECTION I. *President and Vice-President.*

Clause 1. The executive power shall be vested in a President of the United States of America. He shall hold his office during the term of four years, and, together with the Vice-President, chosen for the same term, be elected as follows:

Clause 2. Each state shall appoint, in such manner as the Legislature thereof may direct, a number of electors, equal to the whole number of senators and representatives to which the state may be entitled in the Congress; but no senator or representative, or person holding an office of trust or profit under the United States, shall be appointed an elector.

[*Clause* 3. The electors shall meet in their respective states, and vote by ballot for two persons, of whom one at least shall not be an inhabitant of the same state with themselves. And they shall make a list of all the persons voted for, and of the number of votes for each; which list they shall sign and certify, and transmit, sealed, to the seat of the government of the United States, directed to the President of the Senate. The President of the Senate shall, in the presence of the Senate and House of Representatives, open all the certificates, and the votes shall then be counted. The person having the greatest number of votes shall be the President, if such number be a majority of the whole number of electors appointed; and if there be more than one who have such majority, and have an equal number of votes, then the House of Representatives shall immediately choose by ballot one of them for President; and if no person have a majority, then, from the five highest on the list, the said House shall in like manner choose the President. But in choosing the President, the votes shall be taken by states, the representation from each state having one vote; a quorum for this purpose shall consist of a member or members from two thirds of the states, and a majority of all the states shall be necessary to a choice. In every case, after the choice of the President, the person having the greatest number of votes of the electors shall be the Vice-President. But if there should remain two or more who have equal votes, the Senate shall choose from them by ballot the Vice-President.*]

Clause 4. The Congress may determine the time of choosing the electors, and the day on which they shall give their votes, which day shall be the same throughout the United States.

Clause 5. No person except a natural-born citizen, or a citizen of the United States at the time of the adoption of this Constitution, shall be eligible to the office of President; neither shall any person be eligible to that office who shall not have attained to the age of thirty-five years, and been fourteen years a resident within the United States.

Clause 6. In case of the removal of the President from office, or of his death, resignation, or inability to discharge the powers and duties of the said office, the same shall devolve on the Vice-President; and the Congress may by law provide for the case of removal, death, resignation, or inability, both of the President and Vice-President, declaring what officer shall then act as President; and such officer shall act accordingly, until the disability be removed or a President shall be elected.

Clause 7. The President shall, at stated times, receive for his services a compensation, which shall neither be increased nor diminished during the period for which he shall have been elected, and he shall not receive within that period any other emolument from the United States, or any of them.

Clause 8. Before he enter on the execution of his office, he shall take the following oath or affirmation:

"I do solemnly swear (or affirm) that I will faithfully execute the office of President of the United States, and will, to the best of my ability, preserve, protect, and defend the Constitution of the United States."

Section II. *Powers of the President.*

Clause 1. The President shall be commander-in-chief of the army and navy of the United States and of the militia of the several states, when called into the actual service of the United States; he may require the opinion in writing of the principal officer in each of the executive departments, upon any subject relating to the duties of their respective offices; and he shall have power to grant reprieves and pardons for offenses against the United States, except in cases of impeachment.

Clause 2. He shall have power, by and with the advice and consent of the Senate, to make treaties, provided two thirds of the senators present concur; and he shall nominate, and by and with the advice and consent of the Senate, shall appoint embassadors, other public ministers and consuls, judges of the Supreme Court, and all other officers of the United States, whose appointments are not herein otherwise provided for, and which shall be established by law; but the Congress may by law vest the appointment of such inferior officers as they think proper in the President alone, in the courts of law, or in the heads of departments.

---

* Altered by the 12th Amendment. See page 412.

Clause 3. The President shall have power to fill up all vacancies that may happen during the recess of the Senate, by granting commissions, which shall expire at the end of their next session.

SECTION III. *Duties of the President.*

He shall, from time to time, give to the Congress information of the state of the Union, and recommend to their consideration such measures as he shall judge necessary and expedient; he may, on extraordinary occasions, convene both houses, or either of them; and in case of disagreement between them, with respect to the time of adjournment, he may adjourn them to such time as he shall think proper; he shall receive embassadors and other public ministers; he shall take care that the laws be faithfully executed, and shall commission all the officers of the United States.

SECTION IV. *Impeachment of the President.*

The President, Vice-President, and all civil officers of the United States, shall be removed from office on impeachment for and conviction of treason, bribery, or other high crimes and misdemeanors.

ARTICLE III. JUDICIAL DEPARTMENT.

SECTION I. *United States Courts.*

The judicial power of the United States shall be vested in one Supreme Court, and in such inferior courts as Congress may from time to time ordain and establish. The judges, both of the supreme and inferior courts, shall hold their offices during good behavior; and shall, at stated times, receive for their services a compensation, which shall not be diminished during their continuance in office.

SECTION II. *Jurisdiction of the United States Courts.*

Clause 1. The judicial power shall extend to all cases in law and equity arising under this Constitution, the laws of the United States, and treaties made, or which shall be made, under their authority; to all cases affecting embassadors, other public ministers, and consuls; to all cases of admiralty and maritime jurisdiction; to controversies to which the United States shall be a party; to controversies between two or more states; between a state and citizens of another state; between citizens of different states; between citizens of the same state claiming lands under grants of different states; and between a state, or the citizens thereof, and foreign states, citizens, or subjects.*

Clause 2. In all cases affecting embassadors, other public ministers and consuls, and those in which a state shall be party, the Supreme Court shall have original jurisdiction. In all the other cases before mentioned, the Supreme Court shall have appellate jurisdiction, both as to law and fact, with such exceptions, and under such regulations as the Congress shall make.

Clause 3. The trial of all crimes, except in cases of impeachment, shall be by jury; and such trial shall be held in the state where the said crimes shall have been committed; but when not committed within any state, the trial shall be at such place or places as the Congress may by law have directed.

SECTION III. *Treason.*

Clause 1. Treason against the United States shall consist only in levying war against them, or in adhering to their enemies, giving them aid and com-

---

* Altered by the 11th Amendment. See page 411.

fort. No person shall be convicted of treason unless on the testimony of two witnesses to the same overt act, or on confession in open court.

Clause 2. The Congress shall have power to declare the punishment of treason; but no attainder of treason shall work corruption of blood, or forfeiture, except during the life of the person attainted.

ARTICLE IV.

SECTION I. *State Records.*

Full faith and credit shall be given in each state to the public acts, records, and judicial proceedings of every other state. And the Congress may, by general laws, prescribe the manner in which such acts, records, and proceedings shall be proved, and the effect thereof.

SECTION II. *Privileges of Citizens, etc.*

Clause 1. The citizens of each state shall be entitled to all privileges and immunities of citizens in the several states.

Clause 2. A person charged in any state with treason, felony, or other crime, who shall flee from justice and be found in another state, shall, on demand of the executive authority of the state from which he fled, be delivered up, to be removed to the state having jurisdiction of the crime.

Clause 3. No person held to service or labor in one state, under the laws thereof, escaping into another, shall, in consequence of any law or regulation therein, be discharged from such service or labor, but shall be delivered up on claim of the party to whom such service or labor may be due.

SECTION III. *New States and Territories.*

Clause 1. New states may be admitted by the Congress into this Union; but no new state shall be formed or erected within the jurisdiction of any other state; nor any state be formed by the junction of two or more states, or parts of states, without the consent of the Legislatures of the states concerned, as well as of the Congress.

Clause 2. The Congress shall have power to dispose of, and make all needful rules and regulations respecting the territory or other property belonging to the United States; and nothing in this Constitution shall be so construed as to prejudice any claims of the United States or of any particular state.

SECTION IV. *Guarantee to the States.*

The United States shall guarantee to every state in this Union a republican form of government, and shall protect each of them against invasion; and, on application of the Legislature, or of the executive (when the Legislature can not be convened), against domestic violence.

ARTICLE V. POWER OF AMENDMENT.

The Congress, whenever two thirds of both houses shall deem it necessary, shall propose amendments to this Constitution, or, on the application of the Legislatures of two thirds of the several states, shall call a convention for proposing amendments, which, in either case, shall be valid to all intents and purposes, as part of this Constitution, when ratified by the Legislatures of three fourths of the several states, or by conventions in three fourths thereof, as the one or the other mode of ratification may be proposed by Congress; provided, that no amendment which may be made prior to the year one thousand eight hundred and eight shall in any manner affect the first and fourth clauses in the ninth section of the first Article; and that no state, without its consent, shall be deprived of its equal suffrage in the Senate.

ARTICLE VI. Public Debt, Supremacy of the Constitution, Oath of Office. Religious Test.

Clause 1. All debts contracted and engagements entered into before the adoption of this Constitution, shall be as valid against the United States under this Constitution as under the Confederation.

Clause 2. This Constitution, and the laws of the United States which shall be made in pursuance thereof, and all treaties made, or which shall be made, under the authority of the United States, shall be the supreme law of the land; and the judges in every state shall be bound thereby, any thing in the Constitution or laws of any state to the contrary notwithstanding.

Clause 3. The senators and representatives before mentioned, and the members of the several state Legislatures, and all executive and judicial officers, both of the United States and of the several states, shall be bound by oath or affirmation to support this Constitution; but no religious test shall ever be required as a qualification to any office or public trust under the United States.

ARTICLE VII. Ratification of the Constitution.

The ratification of the Conventions of nine states shall be sufficient for the establishment of this Constitution between the states so ratifying the same.

Done in Convention, by the unanimous consent of the states present, the seventeenth day of September, in the year of our Lord one thousand seven hundred and eighty-seven, and of the Independence of the United States of America the twelfth. In witness whereof, we have hereunto subscribed our names.

George Washington, *President and Deputy from Virginia.*

New Hampshire.—John Langdon, Nicholas Gilman.

Massachusetts. — Nathaniel Gorham, Rufus King.

Connecticut.—Wm. Samuel Johnson, Roger Sherman.

New York.—Alexander Hamilton.

New Jersey.—William Livingston, William Patterson, David Brearley, Jonathan Dayton.

Pennsylvania. — Benjamin Franklin, Robert Morris, Thomas Fitzsimons, James Wilson, Thomas Mifflin, George Clymer, Jared Ingersoll, Gouverneur Morris.

Delaware. — George Read, John Dickinson, Jacob Broom, Gunning Bedford, Jr., Richard Bassett.

Maryland.—James M'Henry, Daniel Carroll, Daniel of St. Tho. Jenifer.

Virginia.—John Blair, Jas. Madison, Jr.

North Carolina.—William Blount, Hugh Williamson, Richard Dobbs Spaight.

South Carolina.—John Rutledge, Charles Cotesworth Pinckney, Pierce Butler.

Georgia.—William Few, Abraham Baldwin.

Attest, William Jackson, *Secretary.*

AMENDMENTS TO THE CONSTITUTION.

Article I. *Freedom of Religion, etc.*

Congress shall make no law respecting an establishment of religion, or prohibiting the free exercise thereof; or abridging the freedom of speech, or of the press; or the right of the people peaceably to assemble, and to petition the government for a redress of grievances.

ARTICLE II. *Right to bear Arms.*

A well-regulated militia being necessary to the security of a free state, the right of the people to keep and bear arms shall not be infringed.

ARTICLE III. *Quartering Soldiers on Citizens.*

No soldier shall, in time of peace, be quartered in any house without the consent of the owner; nor in time of war, but in a manner to be prescribed by law.

ARTICLE IV. *Search Warrants.*

The right of the people to be secure in their persons, houses, papers, and effects, against unreasonable searches and seizures, shall not be violated; and no warrants shall issue but upon probable cause, supported by oath or affirmation, and particularly describing the place to be searched, and the persons or things to be seized.

ARTICLE V. *Trial for Crime, etc.*

No person shall be held to answer for a capital or otherwise infamous crime, unless on a presentment or indictment of a grand jury, except in cases arising in the land or naval forces, or in the militia when in active service in time of war or public danger; nor shall any person be subject for the same offense to be twice put in jeopardy of life or limb; nor shall be compelled, in any criminal case, to be a witness against himself; nor be deprived of life, liberty, or property, without due process of law; nor shall private property be taken for public use without just compensation.

ARTICLE VI. *Rights of accused Persons.*

In all criminal prosecutions, the accused shall enjoy the right to a speedy and public trial, by an impartial jury of the state and district wherein the crime shall have been committed, which district shall have been previously ascertained by law, and to be informed of the nature and cause of the accusation; to be confronted with the witnesses against him; to have compulsory process for obtaining witnesses in his favor; and to have the assistance of counsel for his defense.

ARTICLE VII. *Suits at Common Law.*

In suits at common law, where the value in controversy shall exceed twenty dollars, the right of trial by jury shall be preserved; and no fact tried by a jury shall be otherwise re-examined in any court of the United States than according to the rules of the common law.

ARTICLE VIII. *Excessive Bail.*

Excessive bail shall not be required, nor excessive fines imposed, nor cruel and unusual punishment inflicted.

ARTICLE IX.

The enumeration in the Constitution of certain rights shall not be construed to deny or disparage others retained by the people.

ARTICLE X.

The powers not granted to the United States by the Constitution, nor prohibited by it to the states, are reserved to the states respectively or to the people.

ARTICLE XI.

The judicial power of the United States shall not be construed to extend to any suit in law or equity commenced or prosecuted against one of the United States by citizens of another state, or by citizens or subjects of any foreign state.

ARTICLE XII. *Mode of choosing the President and Vice-President.*

Clause 1. The electors shall meet in their respective states, and vote by ballot for President and Vice-President, one of whom, at least, shall not be an inhabitant of the same state with themselves; they shall name in their ballots the person voted for as President, and in distinct ballots the person voted for as Vice-President; and they shall make distinct lists of all persons voted for as President, and of all persons voted for as Vice-President, and of the number of votes for each, which list they shall sign and certify, and transmit, sealed, to the seat of government of the United States, directed to the President of the Senate; the President of the Senate shall, in the presence of the Senate and House of Representatives, open all the certificates, and the votes shall then be counted; the person having the greatest number of votes for President shall be the President, if such number be a majority of the whole number of electors appointed; and if no person have such majority, then from the persons having the highest numbers, not exceeding three, on the list of those voted for as President, the House of Representatives shall choose immediately by ballot the President. But in choosing the President, the votes shall be taken by states, the representation from each state having one vote; a quorum for this purpose shall consist of a member or members from two thirds of the states, and a majority of all the states shall be necessary to a choice. And if the House of Representatives shall not choose a President, whenever the right of choice shall devolve upon them, before the fourth day of March next following, then the Vice-President shall act as President, as in the case of the death or other constitutional disability of the President.

Clause 2. The person having the greatest number of votes as Vice-President shall be the Vice-President, if such number be a majority of the whole number of electors appointed, and if no person have a majority, then from the two highest numbers on the list the Senate shall choose the Vice-President: a quorum for the purpose shall consist of two thirds of the whole number of senators, and a majority of the whole number shall be necessary to a choice.

Clause 3. But no person constitutionally ineligible to the office of President shall be eligible to that of Vice-President of the United States.

ARTICLE XIII.

SECTION 1. Neither slavery nor involuntary servitude, except as a punishment for crime whereof the party shall have been duly convicted, shall exist within the United States, or any place subject to their jurisdiction.

SECTION 2. Congress shall have power to enforce this article by appropriate legislation.

ARTICLE XIV.

SECTION 1. All persons born or naturalized in the United States, and subject to the jurisdiction thereof, are citizens of the United States and of the state wherein they reside. No state shall make or enforce any law which shall abridge the privileges or immunities of citizens of the United States; nor shall any state deprive any person of life, liberty, or property, without due process of law, nor deny to any person within its jurisdiction the equal protection of the laws.

SECTION 2. Representatives shall be apportioned among the several states according to their respective numbers, counting the whole number of persons in each state, excluding Indians not taxed. But when the right to vote at any election for the choice of electors for President and Vice-President of the United States, representatives in Congress, the executive and judicial officers of a state, or the members of the Legislature thereof, is denied to any of the male members of such state, being twenty-one years of age, and citizens of the United States, or in any way abridged, except for participation in rebellion or other crime, the basis of representation therein shall be reduced in the proportion which the number of such male citizens shall bear to the whole number of male citizens twenty-one years of age in such state.

SECTION 3. No person shall be a senator or representative in Congress, or elector of President and Vice-President, or hold any office, civil or military, under the United States, or under any state, who, having previously taken an oath, as a member of Congress, or as an officer of the United States, or as a member of any State Legislature, or as an executive or judicial officer of any state, to support the Constitution of the United States, shall have engaged in insurrection or rebellion against the same, or given aid or comfort to the enemies thereof. But Congress may, by a vote of two thirds of each house, remove such disability.

SECTION 4. The validity of the public debt of the United States, authorized by law, including debts incurred for payment of pensions and bounties for services in suppressing insurrection or rebellion, shall not be questioned. But neither the United States nor any state shall assume or pay any debt or obligation incurred in aid of insurrection or rebellion against the United States, or any claim for the loss or emancipation of any slave; but all such debts, obligations, and claims shall be held illegal and void.

SECTION 5. The Congress shall have power to enforce by appropriate legislation the provisions of this article.

ARTICLE XV.

SECTION 1. The right of the citizens of the United States to vote shall not be denied or abridged by the United States or any state on account of race, color, or previous condition of servitude.

SECTION 2. The Congress shall have power to enforce by appropriate legislation the provisions of this article.

CHRONOLOGICAL TABLE.

1484. Columbus applied to Genoa for assistance.
1486. " sought aid from Spain.
1492. " sailed from Palos, Spain.
" " discovered America.
1497. The Cabots discovered Newfoundland.
1498. Columbus discovered South America.
" The Cabots discovered the Atlantic coast.
" Vasco de Gama discovered the Cape of Good Hope.
1499. Amerigo Vespucci visited America.
1506. Columbus died.
1510. Ojeda settled Darien, on the Isthmus.
1512. Juan Ponce de Leon discovered Florida.
1513. Nuñez de Balboa discovered the Pacific.
1517. Cordova discovered Yucatan.
1518. Grijalva explored the coast of Mexico.
1521. Conquest of Mexico by Cortez.
1524. Verazzani explores the coast of North America.
1528. Pamphilo de Narvaez's expedition to Florida.
1534. Cartier discovers the Gulf and River St. Lawrence.
1541. De Soto's expedition—discovers the Mississippi River.
1562. Huguenot colony at Port Royal.
1564. Huguenots settle in Florida.
1565. Melendez founds St. Augustine.
1576. Frobisher enters Baffin's Bay.
1579. Sir Francis Drake enters the Bay of San Francisco.
1582. Don Antonio de Espego founds Santa Fé.
1584. Amidas and Barlow sent out by Raleigh.
1585.–1587. } Unsuccessful attempts to settle Roanoke Island.
1602. Gosnold discovers Cape Cod.
1605. Port Royal, Nova Scotia, settled by De Monts.
1606. Grants to the London and Plymouth Companies.
1607. Jamestown settled by the London Company.
1608. Quebec settled by Champlain.
1609. Henry Hudson discovers the Hudson River.
" Champlain discovers Lake Champlain.
" Second Charter granted to Virginia.
1610. Starving time in Virginia.
1612. Third Charter granted to Virginia.
1613. Captain Argall pulls down the Dutch flag on Manhattan Island.
1614. Actual settlement of New York begins by the Dutch.
" John Smith explores the coast of New England.
1615. Cultivation of tobacco commenced in Virginia.
1620. Slavery introduced by the Dutch at Jamestown.
" The "Great Patent" granted to the Virginia Company.
" The Puritans settled at Plymouth.

1621.	Cotton began to be cultivated.
1622.	Indian massacre at Jamestown.
"	New Hampshire granted to Georges and Mason.
1623.	" " settled at Dover and Little Harbor.
1626.	The French explore the north shore of Lake Ontario.
1629.	Charter granted to the Massachusetts Bay Colony.
1630.	Boston settled.
1632.	Maryland granted to Lord Baltimore.
1634.	Maryland settled at St. Mary's.
1635.	Connecticut settled at Hartford, Windsor, and Wethersfield.
"	Roger Williams banished from Massachusetts.
1636.	Providence settled.
1637.	Pequod War in Connecticut.
1638.	Harvard College founded.
"	New Haven colony founded.
1643.	Union of the New England colonies.
1644.	Second Indian massacre in Virginia.
"	Charter granted to Rhode Island.
1660.	Navigation Act passed.
1662.	Charter granted to Connecticut.
1664.	New Jersey settled at Elizabethtown.
"	New York captured by the English.
"	North Carolina settled on the Chowan River.
1668.	The French settle St. Mary, north of Lake Huron.
1670.	South Carolina settled on the Ashley River.
1673.	Charles II. grants Virginia to Culpepper and Arlington.
"	Marquette and Joliet discover the Mississippi at the mouth of the Arkansas River.
1675.	King Philip's War.
1676.	Bacon's rebellion in Virginia.
1680.	Hennepin explores the Mississippi to the Falls of St. Anthony.
"	Charleston founded.
1682.	Pennsylvania settled by William Penn.
"	Delaware granted to Penn by the Duke of York.
"	La Salle sails down the Mississippi to the Gulf, naming the country Louisiana.
1685.	La Salle plants a colony in Texas.
1689.	King William's War.
1690.	Schenectady burned.
1692.	Witchcraft delusion in Salem, Massachusetts.
1697.	King William's War ended by the Treaty of Ryswick.
1699.	D'Iberville's colony on the Bay of Biloxi.
1701.	Detroit founded by the French.
1702.	D'Iberville lays the foundation of Mobile.
"	Queen Anne's War begun.
1710.	Port Royal captured from the French, and named Annapolis.
1713.	The Treaty of Utrecht ends Queen Anne's War.
1732.	Washington born in Westmoreland County, Virginia.
1733.	Georgia settled at Savannah.
1741.	"Negro Plot" in New York.
1744.	King George's War begun.
1745.	Louisburg captured from the French.
1748.	Treaty of Aix-la-Chapelle—end of King George's War.
1753.	Fort at Presque Isle built by the French.

1753.	Washington starts on his mission to the French commander, St. Pierre	October 31.
1754.	Convention at Albany to form a plan of union	June.
"	Battle of Great Meadows	May 28.
"	Fort Necessity captured by the French	July 4.
"	Fort du Quesne built by the French	
1755.	Braddock arrives from England as commander-in-chief	February.
"	Conquest of Acadia by the English	June.
"	The French defeated near Lake George	Sept. 8.
"	Braddock's defeat	July 9.
1756.	Great Britain declares war against France	May 17.
"	Oswego captured by the French	August 14.
1757.	Fort William Henry captured by the French	August 9.
1758.	Abercrombie's defeat at Ticonderoga	July 8.
"	Louisburg captured by Amherst	July 27.
"	Fort Frontenac captured by the English	August 27.
"	Fort du Quesne captured by the English	Nov. 25.
1759.	Ticonderoga and Crown Point captured by the English.	July & Aug.
"	Battle of Montmorenci	July 31.
"	Battle of Quebec	Sept. 13.
"	Surrender of Quebec	Sept. 18.
1760.	Attempt to retake Quebec by the French	April 28.
"	Montreal surrendered to the English	Sept. 8.
1763.	Treaty at Paris ends the French and Indian War	February 10.
1765.	Stamp Act passed	March 8.
"	First Colonial Congress at New York	October 7.
1766.	Stamp Act repealed	March 18.
1767.	New tax bill passed	June 29.
1768.	British troops arrive at Boston	October 1.
1770.	Boston massacre	March 5.
"	Repeal of duties excepting tea	May.
1773.	Tea destroyed in Boston Harbor	Dec. 16.
1774.	"Boston Port Bill" passed	March 31.
"	The "Continental," or second Colonial Congress met at Philadelphia	Sept. 5.
1775.	Battle of Lexington	April 19.
"	Battle of Bunker Hill	June 17.
"	Ticonderoga captured by Ethan Allen	May 10.
"	Crown Point captured by Colonel Warner	May 12.
"	George Washington appointed commander-in-chief	June 15.
"	Montreal captured by Montgomery	Nov. 13.
"	Attack on Quebec—Montgomery killed	Dec. 31.
1776.	Norfolk, Virginia, burned by Lord Dunmore	January 1.
"	British evacuate Boston	March 17.
"	Attack on Fort Moultrie	June 28.
"	Declaration of Independence	July 4.
"	Battle of Long Island	August 27.
"	New York evacuated	Sept. 14.
"	Battle of White Plains	October 28.
"	Fort Washington captured	Nov. 16.
"	Fort Lee occupied by the British	Nov. 20.
"	Washington's retreat through New Jersey	Nov., Dec.
"	Battle of Trenton	Dec. 25.
"	Commissioners sent to France	Dec. 30.

1777.	Battle of Princeton	January 3.
"	Tryon's expedition to Connecticut	April.
"	Sag Harbor, Long Island, captured by Colonel Meigs	May 23.
"	Ticonderoga captured by the British	July 5.
"	Battle of Hubbardton, Vermont	July 7.
"	Fort Edward abandoned	July 29.
"	Battle of Oriskany	August 6.
"	Battle of Bennington	August 16.
"	A British fleet arrives in Chesapeake Bay	August 25.
"	Battle of Brandywine	Sept. 11.
"	Battle of Saratoga, "Bemis's Heights"	Sept. 19.
"	Philadelphia captured by the British	Sept. 26.
"	Battle of Germantown	October 4.
"	Forts Clinton and Montgomery captured	October 6.
"	Battle of Saratoga, "Stillwater"	October 7.
"	Surrender of Burgoyne	October 17.
"	The British repulsed at Fort Mercer	October 22.
"	Washington encamped at Valley Forge	December.
1778.	The British evacuate Philadelphia	June 18.
"	Battle of Monmouth	June 28.
"	Massacre of Wyoming	July 3.
"	A French fleet in Narragansett Bay	July 29.
"	Battle of Quaker Hill, Rhode Island	August 29.
"	The British capture Savannah, Georgia	Dec. 29.
1779.	Sunbury, Georgia, captured by the British	January 9.
"	Battle of Kettle Creek	Feb. 14.
"	Battle of Brier Creek	March 3.
"	Capture of Stony Point by General Wayne	July 15.
"	Battle of Chemung, "Newtown"—Sullivan's expedition	October 9.
"	Paul Jones's victory	August 29.
"	Attack on Savannah—the Americans repulsed	Sept. 23.
1780.	Siege of Charleston begun	April, May.
"	Battle of Monk's Corner	April 14.
"	Charleston surrendered to the English	May 12.
"	Battle of Waxhaw Creek	May 29.
"	Battle of Springfield, New Jersey	June 23.
"	Second French fleet arrives at Newport	July 10.
"	Battle of Hanging Rock	August 6.
"	Battle of Sanders's Creek—first battle of Camden	August 16.
"	Battle of Fishing Creek	August 18.
"	Arnold's treason	September.
"	André executed	October 2.
"	Battle of King's Mountain	October 7.
1781.	Mutiny of the Pennsylvania line	January 1.
"	Greene's famous retreat	Jan. & Feb.
"	Articles of Confederation ratified	——
"	Richmond burned by Arnold	January 5.
"	Battle of the Cowpens	January 17.
"	Mutiny of the New Jersey troops	January 20.
"	Battle of Guilford Court-house	March 15.
"	Battle of Hobkirk's Hill—second battle of Camden	April 25.
"	Greene repulsed at Fort Ninety-six	June 18.
"	New London burned by Arnold	Sept. 6.
"	Battle of Eutaw Springs	Sept. 8.

1781.	Surrender of Cornwallis at Yorktown	October 19.
1782.	Cessation of hostilities	April.
"	Preliminary treaty of peace at Paris	Nov. 30.
1783.	Definitive treaty of peace at Paris	Sept. 3.
"	Evacuation of New York by the British	Nov. 25.
"	Washington resigns his commission	Dec. 23.
1786.	Breaking out of Shay's rebellion	——
1787.	The Constitution adopted by the Convention	Sept. 17.
1788.	The Constitution adopted by eleven states	——
1789.	First Congress meets at New York	March 4.
"	Washington inaugurated President	April 30.
1790.	Secretary Hamilton proposes his plan for the payment of the national debt	January.
"	General Harmar defeated by the Indians	Oct. 17, 22.
1791.	Vermont admitted into the Union	Feb. 18.
"	St. Clair defeated by the Indians	November 4.
1792.	Kentucky admitted into the Union	June 1.
"	Discovery of the Columbia River by Captain Gray	May 11.
1793.	Invention of the cotton gin	——
"	Difficulties with the French embassador Genet	——
1794.	Battle of the Maumee	August 20.
"	Whisky insurrection in Pennsylvania	——
1795.	Jay's treaty ratified	June.
1796.	Tennessee admitted into the Union	June.
1797.	John Adams inaugurated	March 4.
1798.	War with France anticipated	——
"	Washington appointed commander-in-chief	July.
1799.	Washington died at Mount Vernon	Dec. 14.
1800.	The capital removed to Washington	——
"	Treaty of peace with France	Sept. 30.
1801.	Thomas Jefferson inaugurated	March 4.
"	War against Tripoli declared by the United States	June.
1802.	Ohio admitted into the Union	November.
1803.	Purchase of Louisiana from the French	April 30.
"	Commodore Preble sent against Tripoli	——
1804.	Lieutenant Decatur destroys the frigate Philadelphia	February 3.
"	Hamilton killed by Burr in a duel	July 11.
1805.	Derne captured by Eaton	April 27.
"	Treaty of peace with Tripoli	June.
1806.	Blockade of the French coast declared by the British	May.
"	Blockade of the British Islands declared by Napoleon	November.
1807.	The Chesapeake fired into by the Leopard	June 22.
"	British "Orders in Council" prohibiting trade with France and her allies	Nov. 11.
"	Napoleon's "Milan Decree" prohibiting trade with England and her colonies	Dec. 17.
"	Embargo on American ships	Dec. 22.
"	Fulton's first steam-boat, the Clermont, on the Hudson.	Sept. 14.
1809.	Embargo Act repealed	March 1.
"	Commerce with Great Britain and France prohibited by Congress	March 1.
"	James Madison inaugurated	March 4.
1811.	Engagement between the United States frigate President and the Little Belt	May 16.

1811.	Battle of Tippecanoe	Nov. 7.
1812.	President Madison declares war against England	June 19.
"	Louisiana admitted into the Union	April 14.
"	General Hull invades Canada	July 12.
"	Surrender of Mackinaw	July 17.
"	Battle of Brownstown	August 5.
"	Surrender of Detroit	August 16.
"	Battle of Queenstown	October 13.
	Naval Battles.	
"	The Constitution captures the Guerriere	August 19.
"	The sloop-of-war Wasp captures the brig Frolic	October 18.
"	The frigate United States captures the Macedonian	October 25.
"	The Constitution captures the Java	Dec. 29.
1813.	Battle of Frenchtown	January 22.
"	Capture of York (now Toronto), Canada	April 27.
"	Siege of Fort Meigs	May 1.
"	Attack on Sackett's Harbor	May 29.
"	Battle of Sandusky	August 2.
"	Perry's victory on Lake Erie	Sept. 10.
"	Battle of the Thames	October 5.
"	Battle of Chrysler's Farm	Nov. 11.
	Naval Battles.	
"	The Hornet captures the Peacock	Feb. 24.
"	The Chesapeake captured by the Shannon	June 1.
"	The Argus captured by the Pelican	August 14.
"	The Enterprise captures the Boxer	Sept. 5.
1814.	The Creek War ended by the battle of the Horse-shoe Bend	March 27.
"	Fort Erie captured by the Americans	July 3.
"	Battle of Lundy's Lane	July 25.
"	Battle of Fort Erie	August 15.
"	Battle of Bladensburg	August 24.
"	City of Washington captured by the British	August 24.
"	Battle of Plattsburg	Sept. 11.
"	Battle of Lake Champlain	Sept. 11.
"	Battle of North Point	Sept. 12.
"	Bombardment of Fort M'Henry	Sept. 13.
"	Battle of Lake Borgne	Dec. 14.
"	Hartford Convention	Dec. 14.
"	Battle near New Orleans	Dec. 23.
"	Treaty of peace	Dec. 24.
1815.	Battle of New Orleans	January 8.
"	The frigate President captured by a British squadron	January 15.
"	The Essex captured by a British frigate	March 28.
"	War with Algiers	March.
"	Treaty of peace with Algiers	June.
1816.	Indiana admitted into the Union	Dec. 11.
1817.	James Monroe inaugurated	March 4.
"	Mississippi admitted into the Union	Dec. 10.
1818.	Pensacola, Florida (Spanish), captured by General Jackson	May 24.
"	Illinois admitted into the Union	Dec. 3.

1819.	Alabama admitted into the Union	Dec. 14.
“	Treaty for the purchase of Florida negotiated at Washington	February.
1820.	Missouri Compromise Act passed, admitting Missouri into the Union	March 3.
“	Maine admitted into the Union	March 15.
“	Florida purchased of Spain	October.
1821.	Missouri accepts the terms of the Compromise Act, and becomes a state	August 10.
1824.	Visit of Lafayette to the United States	August 15.
1825.	John Quincy Adams inaugurated	March 4.
1826.	Ex-Presidents Adams and Jefferson died	July 4.
1829.	Andrew Jackson inaugurated	March 4.
1832.	Black Hawk War	—
1835.	Seminole War begun	—
“	Dade's massacre by Seminoles	Dec. 28.
1836.	Arkansas admitted into the Union	June 15.
1837.	Michigan admitted into the Union	Jan. 26.
“	Martin Van Buren inaugurated	March 4.
“	Battle of Okechobee	Dec. 25.
1841.	William H. Harrison inaugurated	March 4.
“	President Harrison died	April 4.
“	John Tyler inaugurated	April 6.
1843.	The “Dorr Rebellion” in Rhode Island	—
“	Morse's electric telegraph—grant by Congress	March 3.
1844.	First telegraph line completed between Baltimore and Washington	—
1845.	Resolution of Congress annexing Texas	March 1.
“	Acts of Congress admitting Florida and Iowa	March 3.
“	James K. Polk inaugurated	March 4.
1846.	The northwestern boundary fixed at 49°	—
“	General Taylor ordered to the Rio Grande	Jan. 13.
“	Captain Thornton's party captured by Mexicans	April 26.
“	Battle of Palo Alto	May 8.
“	Battle of Resaca de la Palma	May 9.
“	Congress declared war against Mexico	May 11.
“	Matamoras captured	May 18.
“	Monterey captured	Sept. 24.
“	Battle of Bracito	Dec. 25.
“	Iowa accepts the conditions imposed by Congress, and becomes a state	—
1847.	Battle of Buena Vista	Feb. 23.
“	Capture of Vera Cruz	March 27.
“	Battle of Cerro Gordo	April 18.
“	Battle of Contreras	August 20.
“	Capture of Molino del Rey	Sept. 8.
“	Capture of Chapultepec	Sept. 13.
“	Mexico surrendered	Sept. 14.
1848.	Treaty of peace with Mexico	Feb. 2.
“	Gold discovered in California	February.
“	Wisconsin admitted into the Union	May 29.
1849.	General Taylor inaugurated	March 4.
1850.	General Taylor died	July 9.
“	Millard Fillmore inaugurated	July 10.

1850.	California admitted into the Union	Sept. 9.
1853.	Franklin Pierce inaugurated	March 4.
1854.	Commodore Perry's treaty with Japan	March.
1857.	James Buchanan inaugurated	March 4.
1858.	Minnesota admitted into the Union	May 11.
1859.	Oregon admitted into the Union	February.
1860.	South Carolina seceded from the Union	Dec. 20.
"	Steamer Star of the West fired into by the Secessionists at Charleston	January 9.
1861.	Kansas admitted as a state	January 29.
"	A Southern Confederacy formed by South Carolina, Georgia, Alabama, Mississippi, Louisiana, and Florida, at Montgomery, Alabama	February 4.
"	Jefferson Davis elected provisional president of the Confederacy	February 8.
"	Abraham Lincoln inaugurated President of the United States	March 4.
"	Attack on Fort Sumter	April 12–13.
"	Virginia joins the Confederacy	April 17.
"	Harper's Ferry Arsenal captured by the Virginia militia	April 18.
"	Massachusetts troops attacked in Baltimore	April 19.
"	Norfolk Navy Yard abandoned	April 21.
"	Battle at Philippi, Virginia	June 3.
"	Union troops repulsed at Big Bethel, Virginia	June 10.
"	Battle of Booneville, Missouri	June 17.
"	Battle of Carthage, Missouri	July 5.
"	Battle of Rich Mountain, Virginia	July 11.
"	Battle at Carricksford, Virginia	July 14
"	Confederate capital changed to Richmond	July 20.
"	First battle of Bull Run, Virginia	July 21.
"	Battle of Wilson's Creek, Missouri	August 10.
"	Capture of the forts at Hatteras Inlet, North Carolina	August 29.
"	Battle at Carnifex Landing, Gauley River, Virginia	Sept. 10.
"	Capture of Lexington, Missouri	Sept. 20.
"	Union disaster at Ball's Bluff, Virginia	October 21.
"	Battle at Belmont, Missouri	November 7.
"	Capture of Port Royal, South Carolina	November 7.
"	Seizure of Mason and Slidell on board the Trent	November 8.
1862.	Engagement at the Big Sandy River, Kentucky	January 9.
"	Confederates beaten at Mill Spring, Kentucky	January 19.
"	Capture of Fort Henry, Tennessee	February 6.
"	Capture of Roanoke Island, North Carolina	February 8.
"	Fort Donelson, Tennessee, captured	February 16.
"	Union expedition against Florida and Georgia dispatched	February 28.
"	Battle of Pea Ridge, Arkansas	March 7, 8.
"	The Ram Virginia sinks the Cumberland and Congress.	March 8.
"	Engagement between the Monitor and Virginia	March 9.
"	Capture of Newbern, North Carolina	March 14.
"	Battle at Winchester, Virginia	March 23.
"	Battle of Shiloh, Pittsburg Landing, Tennessee	April 6, 7.
"	Capture of Island No. 10, Mississippi River	April 7.
"	Capture of Fort Pulaski, Georgia	April 11.
"	Farragut passes Forts Jackson and St. Philip, Mississippi River	April 24.

1862.	Capture of New Orleans	April 25.
"	Capture of Fort Macon, and Beaufort, South Carolina	April 25.
"	Surrender of Forts Jackson and St. Philip	April 28.
"	Yorktown, Virginia, taken	May 4.
"	Battle of Williamsburg, Virginia	May 5.
"	Battle of West Point, Virginia	May 9.
"	Norfolk, Virginia, occupied by Union troops	May 10.
"	Banks's retreat down the Shenandoah Valley	May.
"	Battle at Front Royal, Virginia	May 23.
"	Corinth, Mississippi, taken	May 30.
"	Battle of Fair Oaks, or Seven Pines	May 31, June 1.
"	Lee assumes command of the Confederates in Virginia	June 3.
"	Capture of Fort Pillow, Tennessee	June 4.
"	Naval battle, and surrender of Memphis, Tennessee	June 6.
"	Seven days' battles from the Chickahominy to the James	June 25 to July 1.
"	President Lincoln calls for 300,000 troops	July 1.
"	Battle of Cedar Mountain, Virginia	August 9.
"	Pope's battles in defense of Washington	August 26 to Sept. 1.
"	Battle of Richmond, Kentucky	August 30.
"	Invasion of Maryland by Lee	Sept. 5.
"	Battle of South Mountain, Maryland	Sept. 14.
"	Capture of Harper's Ferry by Jackson	Sept. 15.
"	Battle of Antietam, Maryland	Sept. 17.
"	Battle of Mumfordsville, Kentucky	Sept. 17.
"	Battle of Iuka, Mississippi	Sept. 19.
"	Battle of Corinth, Mississippi	October 4.
"	Battle of Perryville, Kentucky	October 8.
"	Battle of Fredericksburg, Virginia	Dec. 13.
"	Battle of Holly Springs, Mississippi	Dec. 29.
"	Battle of Chickasaw Bayou, Vicksburg, Mississippi	Dec. 29.
"	Battle of Murfreesboro', Tennessee—first day	Dec. 31.
1863.	Emancipation Proclamation by President Lincoln	January 1.
"	Galveston captured by the Confederates	January 1.
"	Battle of Murfreesboro'—second day	January 2.
"	Arkansas Post captured by Union troops	January 11.
"	Attack on Fort Sumter repulsed	April 7.
"	Grierson's Union cavalry raid	April, May.
"	Union repulse at Grand Gulf, Mississippi	April 29.
"	Battle of Port Gibson, Mississippi	May 1.
"	Battle of Chancellorsville, Virginia	May 2, 3.
"	Confederates defeated at Jackson, Mississippi	May 14.
"	Battle of Champion Hill, Mississippi	May 16.
"	Battle of Big Black River	May 17.
"	General Grant assaults Vicksburg, Mississippi	June.
"	Lee's second invasion of Maryland	June.
"	West Virginia admitted as a state	June 20.
"	The Confederate Morgan starts on his raid	June 27.
"	Battle of Gettysburg, Pennsylvania	July 1–3.
"	Surrender of Vicksburg, Mississippi	July 4.
"	Port Hudson surrendered	July 8.
"	Draft riots in New York City	July 13–16.

1863.	Morgan captured near New Lisbon, Ohio	July 27.
"	Lawrence, Kansas, burned by Quantrell	Aug. 21, 22.
"	Fort Wagner evacuated by the Confederates	Sept. 6.
"	Steele's operations in Arkansas	September.
"	Battle of Chickamauga, Georgia	Sept. 19, 20.
"	Battle of Lookout Mountain, Georgia	Nov. 25.
"	Battle of Missionary Ridge, Georgia	Nov. 26.
"	Longstreet repulsed at Knoxville, Kentucky	Nov. 29.
1864.	Battle of Olustee, Florida	Feb. 20.
"	Sherman's expedition to Meridian, Mississippi	February.
"	Grant appointed Lieutenant General	March 3.
"	Fort De Russy, Louisiana, captured	March 14.
"	Forrest's raid—captures Union City	March 24.
"	Battle of Mansfield, or Sabine Cross Roads, Louisiana	April 8.
"	Battle of Pleasant Hill, Louisiana	April 9.
"	Forrest's raid, Tennessee—Fort Pillow massacre	April 12.
"	Plymouth, North Carolina, surrendered to the Confederates	April 20.
"	Battle at Cane River, Louisiana	April 23.
"	The Army of the Potomac crosses the Rapidan	May 4.
"	Battles in the Wilderness, Virginia	May 5–7.
"	Sherman begins his march toward Atlanta, Georgia	May 7.
"	Butler defeated at Bermuda Hundred, Virginia	May 7.
"	Battles near Spottsylvania Court-house, Virginia	May 7–12.
"	Battle of Resaca, Georgia	May 14, 15.
"	Battle of Newmarket, Virginia	May 15.
"	Battles at Dallas, Georgia	May 25, 28.
"	Sheridan's expedition north of Richmond	May, June.
"	Battle of Cold Harbor, Virginia	June 1–3.
"	Battle of Piedmont, Virginia	June 5.
"	The Potomac Army crosses the James River	June 15.
"	Battle of Lost Mountain, Georgia	June 15–17.
"	Petersburg assaulted	June 18–21.
"	Destruction of the Alabama by the Kearsarge	June 19.
"	Early invades Maryland	July 5.
"	Battle of Monocacy, Maryland	July 9.
"	Battles before Atlanta	July 20, 22, 28.
"	Chambersburg, Pennsylvania, burned	July 30.
"	Union repulse at Petersburg, Virginia	July 30.
"	Farragut's fleet enters Mobile Bay	Aug. 5.
"	Fort Gaines and Fort Morgan taken	Aug. 8, 23.
"	Weldon Railroad seized by the Unionists	Aug. 18.
"	Atlanta, Georgia, captured by Sherman	Sept. 2.
"	Battle of Winchester, Virginia	Sept. 19.
"	Battle of Fisher's Hill, Virginia	Sept. 22.
"	Battle of Cedar Creek, Virginia	October 19.
"	The Ram Albemarle destroyed	October 27.
"	Plymouth, North Carolina, recaptured by Union troops.	October 31.
"	Nevada admitted into the Union	October 31.
"	Sherman's march from Atlanta to the sea begun	Nov. 14.
"	Battle of Franklin, Tennessee	Nov. 30.
"	Fort M'Allister, Georgia, captured	Dec. 13.
"	Battle of Nashville, Tennessee	Dec. 15, 16.

1864.	Savannah captured by Sherman	Dec. 21.
"	First bombardment of Fort Fisher, North Carolina	Dec. 24.
1865.	Capture of Fort Fisher	January 15.
"	Capture of Columbia, South Carolina	February 17.
"	Charleston, South Carolina, evacuated by the Confederates	February 17.
"	Wilmington, North Carolina, captured	February 22.
"	Sheridan's expedition up the Shenandoah Valley, Virginia	February 27.
"	Early defeated at Waynesborough, Va., by Sheridan	March 2.
"	Fayetteville, North Carolina, occupied	March 12.
"	Battle of Goldsborough, North Carolina	March 21.
"	Confederate repulse at Fort Steadman, Virginia	March 25.
"	Battle of Five Forks, Virginia	April 1.
"	Capture of Petersburg and Richmond	April 3.
"	Lee's surrender	April 9.
"	Raleigh, North Carolina, entered by Sherman	April 13.
"	Assassination of President Lincoln	April 14.
"	Andrew Johnson inaugurated	April 15.
"	Johnston's surrender	April 26.
"	Jefferson Davis captured	May 10.
"	Surrender of the last Confederate force in the Southwest	May 26.
1866.	Atlantic Telegraph cable laid	July.
1867.	Amnesty declared	September 8.
"	Treaty for the purchase of Alaska ratified	April 9.
1868.	Impeachment of President Johnson	January 24.
1869.	General Grant inaugurated	March 4.
"	Pacific Railroad completed	May 10.

THE END.

BOOKS

FOR

SCHOOLS AND COLLEGES

PUBLISHED BY

HARPER & BROTHERS, New York.

☞ Harper & Brothers will send any of the following Works by Mail, postage prepaid, to any part of the United States, on receipt of the Price. Liberal Terms for Introduction.

☞ For a full Descriptive List of Books suitable for Schools and Colleges, see Harper's Catalogue, which may be obtained gratuitously, on application to the Publishers personally, or by letter enclosing Five Cents.

Abercrombie on the Intellectual Powers. 18mo, 75 cents.

Abercrombie on the Moral Feelings. 18mo, 75 cents.

Alford's Greek Testament. For the Use of Theological Students and Ministers. Vol. I., containing the Four Gospels. 8vo, Cloth, $6 00.

Andrews's Latin-English Lexicon, founded on the larger German-Latin Lexicon of Dr. Wm. Freund. Royal 8vo, Sheep, $7 50.

Alison on Taste. Edited for Schools. By Abraham Mills. 12mo, Cloth, $1 50.

Anthon's Latin Lessons. Latin Grammar, Part I. 12mo, Sheep, $1 25.

Anthon's Latin Prose Composition. Latin Grammar, Part II. 12mo, Sheep, $1 25

A Key to Latin Composition may be obtained by Teachers. 12mo, Half Sheep, 75 cents.

Anthon's Zumpt's Latin Grammar. By Leonard Schmitz, Ph.D. 12mo, Sheep, $1 50.

Anthon's Zumpt's Latin Grammar Abridged. 12mo, Sheep, $1 00.

Anthon's Latin Versification. In a Series of Progressive Exercises, including Specimens of Translation from the English and German Poetry into Latin Verse. 12mo, Sheep, $1 25.

A Key to Latin Versification may be obtained by Teachers. 12mo, Half Sheep, 75 cents.

Anthon's Latin Prosody and Metre. 12mo, Sheep, $1 25.

Anthon's Cæsar. With English Notes, Plans of Battles, Sieges, &c., and Historical, Geographical, and Archæological Indexes. Maps, Plans, &c. 12mo, Sheep, $1 50.

Anthon's Æneid of Virgil. With English Notes, a Metrical Clavis, and a Historical, Geographical, and Mythological Index. Portrait and many Illustrations. 12mo, Sheep, $1 75

Anthon's Eclogues and Georgics of Virgil. With English Notes and a Metrical Index. 12mo, Sheep, $1 75.

Anthon's Sallust. Sallust's Jugurthine War and Conspiracy of Catiline. With an English Commentary, and Geographical and Historical Indexes. 12mo, Sheep, $1 50.

Anthon's Horace. With English Notes. A new Edition, corrected and enlarged, with Excursions relative to the Vines and Vineyards of the Ancients; a Life of Horace, a Biographical Sketch of Mæcenas, a Metrical Clavis, &c. 12mo, Sheep, $1 75.

Anthon's Cicero's Select Orations. With English Notes, and Historical, Geographical, and Legal Indexes. 12mo, Sheep, $1 50.

Anthon's Cicero's Tusculan Disputations. With English Notes. 12mo, Sheep extra, $1 50.

Anthon's Cicero de Senectute, &c. The De Senectute, De Amicitia, Paradoxa, and Somnium Scipionis of Cicero, and the Life of Atticus, by Cornelius Nepos. With English Notes. 12mo, Sheep, $1 50.

Anthon's Cicero De Officiis. With Marginal Analysis and an English Commentary. 12mo, Sheep, $1 50.

Anthon's Tacitus. The Germania and Agricola, and also Selections from the Annals of Tacitus. With English Notes. 12mo, Sheep, $1 50.

Anthon's Cornelius Nepos. Cornelii Nepotis Vitæ Imperatorum. With English Notes, &c. 12mo, Sheep, $1 50.

Anthon's Juvenal. The Satires of Juvenal and Persius. With English Notes. Portrait. 12mo, Sheep, $1 50.

Anthon's First Greek Lessons. 12mo, Sheep, $1 25.

Anthon's Greek Prose Composition. Greek Lessons, Part II. 12mo, Sheep, $1 25.

Anthon's Greek Grammar. For the Use of Schools and Colleges. 12mo, Sheep, $1 25.

Anthon's New Greek Grammar. From the German of Kühner, Matthiæ, Buttman, Rost, and Thiersch ; to which are appended Remarks on the Pronunciation of the Greek Language, and Chronological Tables explanatory of the same. 12mo, Sheep, $1 50.

Anthon's Greek Prosody and Metre. With the Choral Scanning of the Prometheus Vinctus of Æschylus, and Œdipus Tyrannus of Sophocles ; to which are appended Remarks on the Indo-Germanic Analogies. 12mo, Sheep, $1 25.

Anthon's Jacobs's Greek Reader. Principally from the German Work of Frederic Jacobs. With English Notes, a Metrical Index to Homer and Anacreon, and a copious Lexicon. 12mo, Sheep, $1 50.

Anthon's Xenophon's Anabasis. With English Notes, a Map, and a Plan of the Battle of Cunaxa. 12mo, Sheep, $1 50.

Anthon's Xenophon's Memorabilia of Socrates. With English Notes, the Prolegomena of Kühner, Wiggers's Life of Socrates, &c., &c. 12mo, Sheep extra, $1 50.

Anthon's Homer. The First Six Books of Homer's Iliad. English Notes, a Metrical Index, and Homeric Glossary. Sheep extra, $1 75.

Anthon's Manual of Greek Antiquities. Numerous Illustrations. 12mo, Sheep, $1 50.

Anthon's Manual of Roman Antiquities, &c. Numerous Illustrations. 12mo, Sheep extra, $1 50.

Anthon's Manual of Greek Literature. 12mo, Sheep extra, $1 50.

Anthon's Smith's Dictionary of Greek and Roman Antiquities, from the best Authorities, and embodying all the recent Discoveries of the most eminent German Philologists and Jurists. Royal 8vo, Sheep, $6 00.

Smith's Antiquities. Abridged by the Authors. 12mo, Half Sheep, $1 50.

Anthon's Classical Dictionary of the Geography, History, Biography, Mythology, and Fine Arts of the Greeks and Romans, together with an Account of the Coins, Weights, and Measures of the Ancients, with Tabular Values of the same. Royal 8vo, Sheep, $6 00.

Anthon's Smith's New Classical Dictionary of Greek and Roman Biography, Mythology, and Geography. Numerous Corrections and Additions. Royal 8vo, $5 00.

Anthon's Latin-English and English-Latin Dictionary. For the Use of Schools. Small 4to, Sheep, $3 50.

Anthon's Riddle and Arnold's English-Latin Lexicon. With a copious Dictionary of Proper Names from the best Sources. Royal 8vo, Sheep, $5 00.

Barton's Grammar. 16mo, Cloth, 60 cents.

Beecher's (Miss) Physiology and Calisthenics. Over 100 Engravings. Cloth, $1 00.

Boyd's Eclectic Moral Philosophy. 12mo, Cloth, $1 50.

Boyd's Elements of Rhetoric and Literary Criticism. 12mo, Half Roan, 75 cents.

Butler's Analogy, by Emory and Crooks. 12mo, Cloth, $1 50.

Butler's Analogy, by Hobart and West. 18mo, Cloth, $1 00.

Butler's Analogy, edited by Halifax. 18mo, Cloth, 75 cents.

Buttman's Greek Grammar. For High Schools and Universities. Translated by EDWARD ROBINSON, D.D., LL.D. 8vo, Sheep, $2 50.

Calkins's Object Lessons. Illustrations. 12mo, Cloth, $1 50.

Calkins's Phonic Charts, for Teaching the Principles of Sound. Mounted. $3 00.

Campbell's Philosophy of Rhetoric. 12mo, Cloth, $1 50.

Capron's School Lyrics. 32mo, Flexible Cloth, 40 cents.

Collord's Latin Accidence, and Primary Lesson Book. 12mo, $1 50.

Comfort's German Course. 12mo, $2 00. (*Just ready.*)

Comfort's Teacher's Companion. 12mo, Cloth, 75 cents.

Comte's Philosophy of Mathematics. Translated from the Cours de Philosophie Positive. 8vo, Cloth, $1 50.

Crabb's English Synonyms. 8vo, Sheep extra, $2 50.

Curtius and Smith's Series of Greek and Latin Elementary Works. Revised and Edited by HENRY DRISLER, LL.D., of Columbia College, New York:

1. Principia Latina, Part I. A First Latin Course, by W. SMITH, LL.D., &c. 12mo, Flexible Cloth, 75 cents.

2. Principia Latina, Part II. A First Latin Reading-Book, containing an Epitome of Cæsar's Gallic Wars, and L'Homond's Lives of Distinguished Romans. With a short Introduction to Roman Antiquities, Notes, and a Dictionary. By WILLIAM SMITH, LL.D. 12mo, Flexible Cloth, $1 25.

3. Principia Latina, Part III. Latin Prose Composition, Rules of Syntax, with copious Examples, Synonyms, &c., by Dr. W. SMITH. (In Press.)

4. A Grammar of the Latin Language, for the Use of Colleges and Schools, by Dr. W. SMITH. (In Press.)

5. A Smaller Latin Grammar, by Dr. W. SMITH. (In Press.)

6. A Grammar of the Greek Language, for the Use of Colleges and Schools, by Dr. G. CURTIUS. Translated and edited by Dr. W. SMITH. (In Press.)

7. A Smaller Greek Grammar, from the larger Work, by Dr. G. CURTIUS, Professor in the University of Leipzig. (In Press).

8. Curtius's First Greek Course, containing a Delectus, Exercise-Book, and Vocabularies. Adapted to Curtius's Greek Grammar. Edited by Dr. W. SMITH. (In Press.)

Dalton's Physiology and Hygiene. For Schools, Families, and Colleges. By J. C. DALTON, M.D., Professor of Physiology in the College of Physicians and Surgeons, New York. With Illustrations. 12mo, Cloth, $1 50.

Docharty's Arithmetic. 12mo, Sheep, $1 50.

Docharty's Institutes of Algebra. 12mo, Sheep, $1 50.

Docharty's Geometry. 12mo, Sheep extra, $1 75.

Docharty's Analytical Geometry and Calculus. 12mo, Sheep, $1 75.

Draper's Anatomy, Physiology, and Hygiene. For the Use of Schools and Families. With 170 Illustrations. By JOHN C. DRAPER, M.D. 8vo, Cloth, $3 75.

Draper's Human Physiology, Statical and Dynamical; or, The Conditions and Course of the Life of Man: being the Text of the Lectures delivered in the Medical Department of the University. By JOHN W. DRAPER, M.D., LL.D. Illustrated by nearly 300 fine Woodcuts from Photographs. 8vo, 650 pages, Cloth, $5 00.

Physiology. Abridged from the Author's Work on Human Physiology. For the Use of Schools and Colleges. With 150 Engravings. 12mo, Cloth, $1 50.

Draper's Chemistry. For Schools and Colleges. With nearly 300 Illustrations. By HENRY DRAPER, M.D. 12mo, Cloth, $1 50.

Draper's Natural Philosophy. For Schools and Colleges. Nearly 400 Illustrations. 12mo, Cloth, $1 50.

Duff's Book-Keeping. 8vo, New Edition, revised and enlarged, $3 75; School Edition, Half Sheep, $1 25.

Faraday on the Physical Forces. Illustrations. 16mo, Cloth, $1 00.

Faraday's Lectures on the Chemical History of a Candle. Illustrations. 16mo, Cloth, $1 00.

Foster's First Principles of Chemistry. Adapted especially for Classes. 12mo, Sheep extra, $1 25.

APPARATUS necessary to perform the experiments laid down in this work furnished by HARPER & BROTHERS, carefully packed for transportation, for $45 00, *net*.

Foster's Chart of the Organic Elements. Beautifully Colored, Mounted on Rollers, with Cloth Back, $5 00.

Fowler's English Language in its Elements and Forms. With a History of its Origin and Development, and a full Grammar. For Libraries, Colleges, and High Schools. New and Revised Edition. With Index of Words. 8vo, Cloth, $2 50.

Fowler's English Grammar for Schools. Abridged from the Octavo Edition, and containing March's Method of Philological Study. For General Use in Schools and Families. 12mo, Sheep extra, $1 75.

Fowler's Elementary English Grammar for Common Schools. Revised and Enlarged. 16mo, Sheep, 75 cents.

French's Mathematical Series:

I.—First Lessons in Numbers, in the Natural Order: *First*, Visible Objects; *Second*, Concrete Numbers; *Third*, Abstract Numbers. Illustrated. 16mo, 40 cents.

II.—Elementary Arithmetic for the Slate, in which Methods and Rules are based upon Principles established by Induction. Illustrated. 16mo, 50 cents.

III.—Mental Arithmetic. (In Press.)

IV.—Common School Arithmetic, combining the Elements of the Science with their Practical Applications to Business. Illustrated. 12mo, $1 00.

V.—Academic Arithmetic. (In Preparation.)

Gray and Adams's Geology. Engravings. 12mo, Sheep extra, $1 50.

Gray's Natural Philosophy. For Academies, High Schools and Colleges. 360 Woodcuts. 12mo, Sheep extra, $1 50.

Greek Concordance of the New Testament. 8vo, Cloth, $5 00.

Hamilton's (Sir William) Discussions on Philosophy and Literature, Education and University Reform. 8vo, Cloth, $3 00.

Harper's Greek and Latin Texts. Carefully reprinted from the best Editions. Elegantly printed. 18mo, Flexible Cloth Binding, Seventy-five Cents a Volume.

Cæsar.
Sallustius.
Vergilius.
Cicero de Senectute and De Amicitia.
Ciceronis Orationes Selectæ. (In Press.)
Horatius.
Lucretius.
Xenophon's Anabasis.
Æschylus.
Euripides. 3 vols.
Herodotus 2 vols.
Thucydides. 2 vols.
Sophocles. (In Press.)

Harper's Classical Library. Comprising the best Translations of the most eminent Greek and Latin Authors. 37 Volumes. 18mo, Cloth, Seventy-five Cents per Volume.

Demosthenes. 2 vols.
Cicero. 3 vols.
Æschylus.
Horace and Phædrus. 2 vols.
Homer. 3 vols.
Sallust.
Xenophon. 2 vols.
Sophocles.
Ovid. 2 vols.
Livy. 5 vols.
Juvenal and Persius.
Cicero on the Orator.
Cæsar. 2 vols.
Virgil. 2 vols.
Euripides. 3 vols.
Thucydides. 2 vols.
Herodotus. 3 vols.
Pindar and Anacreon.

Harper's New Classical Library. Literal Translations of the Greek and Latin Authors. Portraits. 12mo, Cloth, $1 50 per Volume. The following are now ready:

Cæsar.
Virgil.
Horace.
Sallust.
Cicero's Orations.
Cicero's Offices, &c.
Cicero on Oratory and Orators.
Tacitus. 2 vols.
Terence.
Juvenal.
Xenophon.
Homer's Iliad.
Homer's Odyssey.
Thucydides.
Herodotus.
Demosthenes. 2 vols.
Euripides. 2 vols.
Sophocles.
Æschylus.

Harper's Ancient History. For the Use of Schools. By Jacob Abbott. With Maps, Woodcuts, and Questions. Square 4to, Half Roan, $1 25.

Harper's English History. For the Use of Schools. By Jacob Abbott. With Maps, Woodcuts, and Questions. Square 4to, Half Roan, $1 25.

Harper's American History. For the Use of Schools. By Jacob Abbott. With Maps, Woodcuts, and Questions. Square 4to, Half Roan, $1 25.

The above three, complete in one volume, Price $3 00.

Harper's School and Family Slate, with accompanying Cards, for Exercises in Writing, Printing, Drawing, and Figures. Slates, with a full Set of Cards accompanying each, $12 00 per dozen.

Harper's Writing Books, combining Symmetrical Penmanship with Marginal Drawing Lessons. In Ten Numbers. The first Six Numbers now ready. Price per dozen, $2 00. Liberal Terms for Introduction.

Haven's Rhetoric. For Schools, Colleges, and Private Use. 12mo, Cloth, $1 50.

Harrison's Latin Grammar. 12mo, Sheep extra, $1 50.

Henry's History of Philosophy. For Colleges and High Schools. 2 vols., 18mo, Cloth, $1 50.

Hooker's Child's Book of Nature. Intended to aid Mothers and Teachers in Training Children in the Observation of Nature. In Three Parts. Part I. Plants.; Part II. Animals.; Part III. Air, Water, Heat, Light, &c. Illustrated. The Three Parts complete in one volume, small 4to, Cloth, $2 00; separately, Cloth, 90 cents each.

Hooker's Natural History. For the Use of Schools and Families. 300 Engravings. 12mo, Cloth, $1 50.

Hooker's First Book in Chemistry. Illustrations. Square 4to, Cloth, 90 cents.

Hooker's Natural Philosophy. Science for the School and Family. Part I. Natural Philosophy. Illustrated by nearly 300 Engravings. 12mo, Cloth, $1 50.

Hooker's Chemistry. Science for the School and Family. Part II. Chemistry. Illustrated. 12mo, Cloth, $1 50.

Hooker's Mineralogy and Geology. Science for the School and Family. Part III. Mineralogy and Geology. Illustrated. 12mo, Half Roan, $1 50.

Kane's Chemistry. With Additions and Corrections, by JOHN WILLIAM DRAPER, M.D. Woodcuts. 8vo, Cloth, $2 00.

Knapp's French Grammar. A Practical Grammar of the French Language: containing a Grammar, Exercises, Reading-Lessons, and a complete Pronouncing Vocabulary. By WILLIAM I. KNAPP, Ph.D., late Professor of Ancient and Modern Languages in Vassar Female College, N.Y., and Author of "A French Reading-Book." 12mo, Half Leather, $1 75.

Knapp's French Reading-Book. Chrestomathie Française: containing, I. Selections from the best French Writers, with Copious References to the Author's French Grammar. II. The Masterpieces of Moilère, Racine, Boileau, and Voltaire; with Explanatory Notes, a Glossary of Idiomatic Phrases, and a Vocabulary. By WILLIAM I. KNAPP, Ph.D. 12mo, Half Leather, $1 75.

Lewis's Platonic Theology. 12mo, $1 75.

Liddell and Scott's Greek-English Lexicon. From the Work of FRANCIS PASSOW. With Corrections and Additions, and the Insertion, in Alphabetical Order, of the Proper Names occurring in the principal Greek Authors. By HENRY DRISLER, LL.D., Columbia College, N.Y. Royal 8vo, Sheep extra, $7 50.

Loomis's Elements of Arithmetic. Designed for Children. 16mo, 166 pages, Half Sheep, 40 cents.

Loomis's Treatise on Arithmetic. Theoretical and Practical. 12mo, 345 pages, Sheep extra, $1 25.

Loomis's Elements of Algebra. Designed for the Use of Beginners. 12mo, 281 pages, Sheep extra, $1 25.

Loomis's Treatise on Algebra. New Edition, revised and greatly enlarged. 8vo, 384 pages, Sheep, $2 00; 12mo, Sheep, $1 50.

Loomis's Elements of Geometry and Conic Sections. 12mo, 234 pages, Sheep extra, $1 50.

Loomis's Trigonometry and Tables. 8vo, 360 pages, Sheep extra, $2 00.

The TRIGONOMETRY *and* TABLES *bound separately. The Trigonometry*, $1 50; *Tables*, $1 50.

Loomis's Geometry, Conic Sections, and Plane Trigonometry. In One Volume. 12mo, 292 pages, Sheep, $1 75.

Loomis's Elements of Analytical Geometry, and of the Differential and Integral Calculus. 8vo, 286 pages, Sheep extra, $2 00.

Loomis's Elements of Natural Philosophy. For Academies and High Schools. 12mo, 352 pages, Sheep extra, $1 50.

Loomis's Elements of Astronomy. For Academies and High Schools. 12mo, Sheep, $1 50.

Loomis's Treatise on Astronomy. With Illustrations. 8vo, Sheep, $2 00.

Loomis's Practical Astronomy. With a Collection of Astronomical Tables. 8vo, 497 pages, Sheep extra, $2 00.

Loomis's Recent Progress of Astronomy, especially in the United States. A thoroughly Revised Edition. Illustrations. 12mo, 396 pages, Cloth, $1 50.

Loomis's Meteorology and Astronomy. For Academies and High Schools. 12mo, Sheep extra, $2 00.

Lowry's Universal Atlas. From the most Recent Authorities. 4to, Half Roan, $6 00.

McClintock's First Book in Latin. 12mo, Sheep extra, $1 50.

McClintock's Second Book in Latin. Forming a sufficient Latin Reader. With Imitation Exercises and a Vocabulary. 12mo, Sheep extra, $1 50.

McClintock's First Book in Greek. 12mo, Sheep extra, $1 50.

McClintock's Second Book in Greek. Forming a sufficient Greek Reader. With Notes and a copious Vocabulary. 12mo, Sheep extra, $1 50.

McGregor's Logic. 12mo, Cloth, $1 50.

March's Parser and Analyzer. With Illustrations. 16mo, Cloth, 40 cents.

March's Philological Study of the English Language. 12mo, Paper, 60 cents; Cloth, 75 cents.

Markham's (Mrs.) History of France, from the Conquest of Gaul by Julius Cæsar to the Reign of Louis Philippe. With Conversations at the End of each Chapter. Map, Notes, and Questions, and a Supplement, bringing down the History to the Present Time. By JACOB ABBOTT. 12mo, Cloth, $1 75.

Maury's Principles of Eloquence. With an Introduction by Bishop POTTER. 18mo, Cloth, 75 cents.

Mill's Logic. 8vo, Cloth, $2 00.

Mills's Literature and Literary Men of Great Britain and Ireland. 2 vols., 8vo, Cloth, $5 00.

Noël and Chapsal's French Grammar. 12mo, Cloth, $1 25.

Paley's Evidences of Christianity. 18mo, Half Roan, 75 cents.

Paley's Moral and Political Philosophy. 12mo, Cloth, $1 50.

Paley's Theology. Engravings. 2 vols., 18mo, Cloth, $1 50. The same, copiously Illustrated, 2 vols., 12mo, Cloth, $3 00.

Parker's Outlines of General History. 12mo, Sheep extra, $1 50.

Parker's Aids to English Composition. For Students of all Grades, embracing Specimens and Examples of School and College Exercises, and most of the higher Departments of English Composition, both in Prose and Verse. 12mo, Cloth, $1 25 ; Sheep, $1 50.

Parker's Geographical Questions. Adapted for the Use of any respectable Collection of Maps : embracing, by way of Question and Answer, such Portions of the Elements of Geography as are necessary as an Introduction to the Study of the Maps. To which is added a concise Description of the Terrestrial Globe. 12mo, Cloth, 50 cents.

Potter's Political Economy. 18mo, Half Sheep, 75 cents.

Potter's Principles of Science. Illustrations. 12mo, Cloth, $1 50.

Potter's School and Schoolmaster. A Manual for the Use of Teachers, &c. 12mo, Cloth, $1 50.

Proudfit's Plautus's "Captives." With English Notes for the Use of Students. By Professor JOHN PROUDFIT, D.D. 12mo, Cloth, 75 cents.

Renwick's Chemistry. 18mo, Half Sheep, 90 cents.

Renwick's Mechanics. 18mo, Half Sheep, 90 cents.

Renwick's Natural Philosophy. 18mo, Half Sheep, 90 cents.

Robinson's Greek Lexicon of the New Testament. A New Edition, revised and in great part rewritten. Royal 8vo, Cloth, $6 00 ; Sheep extra, $6 50.

Russell's Juvenile Speaker. 12mo, Cloth, $1 25.

Salkeld's First Book in Spanish. 12mo, Sheep extra, $1 50.

Salkeld's Roman and Grecian Antiquities. With Maps, &c. 18mo, Cloth, 75 cents.

Student's (the) Historical Text-Books:

THE STUDENT'S HISTORIES.

THE STUDENT'S HISTORY OF GREECE. A History of Greece from the Earliest Times to the Roman Conquest. With Supplementary Chapters on the History of Literature and Art. By WILLIAM SMITH, LL.D., Editor of the "Classical Dictionary," "Dictionary of Greek and Roman Antiquities," &c. Revised, with an Appendix, by Prof. GEORGE W. GREENE, A.M. Engravings. Large 12mo, 724 pages, Cloth, $2 00.

☞ A SMALLER HISTORY OF GREECE : The above Work abridged for Younger Students and Common Schools. Engravings. 16mo, 272 pages, Cloth, $1 00.

THE STUDENT'S HISTORY OF ROME. A History of Rome from the Earliest Times to the Establishment of the Empire. With Chapters on the History of Literature and Art. By HENRY G. LIDDELL, D.D., Dean of Christ Church, Oxford. Engravings. Large 12mo, 778 pages, Cloth, $2 00.

☞ A SMALLER HISTORY OF ROME from the Earliest Times to the Establishment of the Empire. By WM. SMITH, LL.D. With a Continuation to A.D. 476. By EUGENE LAWRENCE, A.M. Engravings. 16mo, Cloth, $1 00.

THE STUDENT'S GIBBON. The History of the Decline and Fall of the Roman Empire. By EDWARD GIBBON. Abridged Incorporating the Researches of Recent Commentators. By WILLIAM SMITH, LL.D. Engravings. Large 12mo, 706 pages, Cloth, $2 00.

THE STUDENT'S HUME. A History of England from the Earliest Times to the Revolution in 1688. By DAVID HUME. Abridged. Incorporating the Corrections and Researches of Recent Historians, and continued down to the Year 1858. Engravings. Large 12mo, 806 pages, Cloth, $2 00.

☞ A SMALLER HISTORY OF ENGLAND from the Earliest Times to the Year 1862. Edited by WM. SMITH, LL.D. Engravings. 16mo, Cloth, $1 00.

THE STUDENT'S HISTORY OF FRANCE. A History of France from the Earliest Times to the Establishment of the Second Empire in 1852. Engravings. Large 12mo, 742 pages, Cloth, $2 00.

THE STUDENT'S QUEENS OF ENGLAND. Lives of the Queens of England. From the Norman Conquest. By AGNES STRICKLAND. Abridged by the Author. Revised and Edited by CAROLINE G. PARKER. Large 12mo, 675 pages, Cloth, $2 00.

THE STUDENT'S OLD TESTAMENT HISTORY. From the Creation to the Return of the Jews from Captivity. With an Appendix, containing an Introduction to the Books of the Old Testament. Edited by WILLIAM SMITH, LL.D. Engravings. Large 12mo, 715 pages, Cloth, $2 00.

THE STUDENT'S NEW TESTAMENT HISTORY. With an Introduction, connecting the Old and New Testaments. Edited by WILLIAM SMITH, LL.D. With Maps and Woodcuts. Large 12mo, 780 pages, $2 00.

www.ingramcontent.com/pod-product-compliance
Lightning Source LLC
LaVergne TN
LVHW021132110826
845150LV00005B/1010

* 9 7 8 1 4 2 5 5 4 9 2 8 2 *